Stephen F. Kel... ... ...
Oxford, and the ... ...
he was for many ... ...
Tribune. In 1978, ...ısıon, working
on programmes su... ...*rld in Action* and *What the Papers Say*. Now a freelance writer, he devotes most of his time to writing about football and labour history. He is a regular contributor to many newspapers and magazines, and is also a Fellow in Media at the University of Huddersfield.

The author of highly acclaimed biographies of Kenny Dalglish, Graeme Souness, Bill Shankly and Alex Ferguson, as well as *Back Page United* and *The Kop*, an oral history of Liverpool's famous terrace, he lives in Manchester with his wife and two children.

Also by Stephen F. Kelly

Idle Hands, Clenched Fists
Back Page Football
Back Page United
Victorian Lakeland Photographers
A Game of Two Halves
The Kop
Graeme Souness: A Soccer Revolutionary
Not Just a Game
The Pick of the Season
Bill Shankly: It's Much More Important Than That
Dalglish
Fergie

Red Voices

A Revealing Oral History of
Manchester United from the
Terraces, Players and Staff

Stephen F. Kelly

HEADLINE

First published in 1999
by HEADLINE BOOK PUBLISHING

First published in paperback in 2000
by HEADLINE BOOK PUBLISHING

10 9 8 7 6 5 4 3 2 1

ISBN 0 7472 6079 6

Typeset by Avon Dataset Ltd, Bidford-on-Avon, Warks

Printed and bound in Great Britain by
Mackays of Chatham plc, Chatham, Kent

HEADLINE BOOK PUBLISHING
A division of the Hodder Headline Group
338 Euston Road
London NW1 3BH

www.headline.co.uk
www.hodderheadline.com

CONTENTS

ACKNOWLEDGEMENTS

My initial thanks should go to Manchester United Football Club and to the many people at the club who so kindly assisted me in this enormous task. They included directors, staff, players, former players and, of course, the many dedicated fans. I am also grateful to Bob Greaves, not just for his vivid reminiscences but also for assistance in contacting others from his generation.

In particular I would like to thank all those who so kindly gave of their time in order to be interviewed about their favourite club, and to those who helped pave the way for such interviews. They include, though not in any particular order, the following.

Martin Edwards, Brian Kidd, Bob Greaves, Kevin McAleny, Warren Bradley, Wilf McGuinness, Les Olive, Bill Foulkes, David Meek, Robin Murray, Kenneth Hastings, Ian Moss, Alf Davies and Lindsay Harding of the Greater Manchester St John Ambulance Brigade, the Greater Manchester Police Force, Cliff Butler, Ivan Ponting, Judith Swift, Tim Bamford, David Pye, Wilf Sudlow, Leon Swerling, Janet Swerling, Maxine Dunham, David Menasche, Andrew Davies, Derek Wynne, Simon Jones, Hugh Jones, Jones Executive of Eccles, Don Jones, George Reynolds, Matthew Reynolds, Alan Durrans, Michael Dunham, Joe Dillon, the *Manchester Evening News*, the Manchester Institute for Popular Culture, Manchester Metropolitan University, Manchester Library Services, Richard

Kurt, Jim Thornton, Alisson Thornton, Roger Hennell, Teresa Hennell, Ian Williamson, Sara Radcliffe, Barry Moorhouse, Roland Coburn, Lord Stan Orme, Irene Orme, Graham Stringer MP, Granada Television, Pete Holland, Danny McGregor, Adam Brown, Albert Thorpe, Sally Orpin, Paul Windridge, Barney Chilton, Andy Mitten, Andy Walsh, the University of Huddersfield, Gary Rhodes, Sean Wilson, Christopher Eccleston, Eamon Holmes, Graham Hobbs, Simon Thorp, Diane Modahl, Johnny Morris, Sir Bobby Charlton, Jim White, Tony Rowe Jones, Marjorie Rowe Jones, Mary Kelly, Laurence Cassidy, Mary Cassidy, Pat McDonald, Wallen Matthie, Rudi Kidd, *United Review*, Denis Law, Shay Brennan and Norman Whiteside.

Thanks are also due to my colleagues in the Media Division at the University of Huddersfield and also to the School of Humanities for providing me with a small grant to enable me to purchase some professional-standard recording equipment, and for their encouragement during the writing and compiling of this book. Recognition should also go to the Oral History Unit at the University of Huddersfield.

Interviews were conducted in a variety of places, including Old Trafford itself – often in the restaurant overlooking the pitch – homes, offices, pubs, wine bars, hotels, over garden walls, in a darkened film editing room, a bus garage, over the Internet, a cricket pavilion and, most bizarre of all, an old air-raid shelter. But wherever it was United fans spoke eloquently and enthusiastically about their team, and sometimes tearfully as they recalled that grey wicked day in February 1958 when they first heard of the Munich disaster. My apologies for raising such sad memories.

I would also like to pay tribute to my editor, Ian Marshall of Headline, whose enthusiasm and continuing encouragement were, as ever, vital to the completion of this book. Others at Headline who deserve mention include Nuala Buffini. I would also like to acknowledge the continuing advice and work of my agent John Pawsey, who over the years has been a guiding light through the maze of the publishing world.

But finally, and as ever, my especial thanks go to my wife Judith Jones whose love and support over the years can never be repaid sufficiently. And to our children Nicholas and Emma, who have continued to amuse and cheer me through the sometimes painful months of compiling this book.

Stephen F. Kelly
Chorlton, Manchester

A NOTE ON THE RESEARCH AND
EDITING OF INTERVIEWS

The vast majority of interviews contained within this book were recorded on a Sony Minidisc player. Each interview was then transcribed and broken into sections to be included in the relevant chapters. As little editing as possible has taken place. Where editing has taken place it has been carried out in order to make the interview as coherent and readable as possible. Hopefully the meaning has not been destroyed. Slang and dialect words have been kept in so that the reader can feel the character of the interviewee. However, interviews have not been included in full. Some repetitions and irrelevancies have been dropped. The occasional correction has also been made (to dates, games, players, etc) in order to save any embarrassment to the interviewee and to avoid any confusion for the reader. People's memories are not always as accurate as they imagine!

A number of interviews have also been included after a request was put out over the Internet. These interviews were in the form of a written statement. A few extracts from newspapers and magazines have also been included.

A full list of interviewees and their biographies can be found at the end of the book.

INTRODUCTION

It's an odd business, this being a football fan. It's illogical. We spend hundreds – in some cases, thousands – of pounds a year to watch ninety minutes of football on a chilly Saturday afternoon. Or traipse straight from work on a dark, frosty Wednesday night to stand or sit in the cold for the rest of the evening. Just to see twenty-two men kicking a ball around. And who, in days gone by, would have stood on rainsoaked terraces, squashed and sweating, hardly able to see what was going on? Or queued up for hours, maybe even overnight, just to get a ticket for a game? All this is to say nothing of the scale of emotions that the average football supporter experiences, the highs and lows, the passions, the dramas. We all remember those moments, those vows of 'never again', and how quickly they are forgotten. Yes, it's totally illogical.

On a phone-in programme not so long ago, former Conservative MP Edwina Currie berated a fan for complaining about an increase in ticket prices at his home club. 'Why don't you go and find another club to support?' she suggested helpfully. End of conversation. Anyone who knows the slightest thing about football knows that you cannot go around switching allegiances. It's something you're usually stuck with. And as most testify in these pages, it generally stemmed from their dad who took them to their first match, and as often as not it has been that first club to which they have maintained their loyalty.

1

There is an inescapable emotion attached to supporting a football club. It used to be geographical, and still is to a large extent. You supported the club where you lived. That was especially true before the sixties when transport restricted travelling but has increasingly changed as improved transport has opened up access to any club in the country. In the case of Manchester United, the number of coaches parked in the Warwick Road or any of the adjoining streets around Old Trafford at each home game give ample evidence to the argument. Just look where they've come from – the Midlands, London, Ulster, the South-west, Scotland. United are no longer just a Manchester club; they have a national following, although there are plenty in these pages who wonder why people living in Bournemouth or wherever can't support their own local club. Cynics would call it jumping on the band-wagon. But equally the droves who travel up from the Midlands and further afield each week are entitled to wonder where the Manchester people were when United were not doing so well. It cuts both ways. But by and large it's still about where you were born, where you live, your dad's, or sometimes your mum's, team and which was the first team you saw.

Football, as has been said more than once, is the people's game. Be that as it may, the people all too rarely get their chance to have their say. It's the players, the managers and, these days, the directors who seem to get most column inches. This book attempts to rectify that imbalance. *Red Voices* is primarily a *fan's* history of United. It is a collection of fans' memories; mostly thrilling but sometimes sad, humorous or acrimonious; of Cup finals, Cup defeats, European exploits, glorious players, and even moments perhaps best forgotten.

This book is also peppered with memories from a few professionally associated with the club whose recollections go back many years, such as former secretary Les Olive and chairman Martin Edwards. Les Olive, for instance, can recall those days shortly after the war when United employed just two administrative people – himself and Walter Crickmer. Between them they did everything from counting the gate receipts to mowing the pitch and organising travel. Today the club employs more than 400. And there are memories too from a handful of players, mostly Manchester born and bred, like Brian Kidd and Wilf McGuinness whose allegiances to United stretch back far beyond their official association with the club to when they were childhood supporters. There is Brian Kidd, still catching the bus from his mum's to Old Trafford even when he was playing in the first team, and Warren Bradley, who put in a day's work at the school where he taught before going to Old Trafford to line up against Real Madrid. It's a far cry from today's footballers.

Football has changed, and nowhere has it changed more than at Old Trafford. A super new all-seater stadium, dining areas, executive boxes, megastores, a museum, its own magazines and even an exclusive television channel. A different world from the days when 60,000 crammed on to the terraces, swaying and pushing after having queued up for hours on end simply to gain entry. And then being forced to relieve themselves where they stood because it was impossible on that crammed Stretford End to negotiate your way to the toilets. Little wonder it was a man's world. Friendships blossomed, songs were sung, the unifying cry was support for the team.

Although there remains, with many, a nostalgia for the past with its heady atmosphere, camaraderie, and passion of the terraces, those days will never return. All has changed. Old Trafford today is about comfort and convenience, family viewing American style. But that's not such a bad thing, as many witnesses in this book testify, provided of course that you have a ticket.

Before the war it was common for fans to walk to Old Trafford from all corners of Manchester. One fan even recalls how he and his friend trekked the entire way to Bolton to see United, and getting into the ground free of charge by climbing over a fence. For many during the poverty-stricken thirties

3

the only way they could afford to see United was by standing outside the ground and waiting until they opened the gates at three-quarter time to let the crowd out. Then they would nip in for the last twenty minutes or so. For youngsters it was an affordable initiation into live football. Travelling to watch United play away from home was a rarity. Few could afford it, and when they did, as Lord Stan Orme recounts, it was an adventure into a world they knew little of. It wasn't until the 1950s when full employment returned that people could afford to take either a coach or a British Railways Football Special. And after the Second World War there was that oddity – United playing all their home games at Maine Road because of bomb damage to Old Trafford. Surprisingly, Maine Road turned out to be a lucky ground, with United runners-up three years in succession as well as FA Cup winners. Years later when they first played in Europe they were again obliged to borrow Maine Road with its floodlights, and once more found it a lucky home.

But of course the history of United is dominated by one event: Munich. The disaster of February 1958 will remain permanently etched in the memories of those who lived through the trauma. All who spoke in this collection could recall vividly the moment when they first heard the news; the disbelief and then the eventual realisation that their favourites had died in the snow and slush of Munich. The city of Manchester came sharply and silently to a halt. For days many of those fans wandered aimlessly, numbed by the news. When United did kick off again eight of their players were dead, and others would never play again. That first game after Munich would also never be forgotten, with its black-edged programme and eleven blank spaces on the team sheet. Poignant memories which should evoke for everyone those nightmarish days. But from adversity came strength as Matt Busby, returning to the helm, helped guide United towards his dream of European success. Ten years after the disaster, United lifted the European Cup as thousands followed them to Wembley, turning the old stadium into a sea of red, even though United did play in blue that night. They were the first English club to win that trophy, the most European of all English clubs.

But then, although United had lifted the European Cup, within six years they were relegated. Busby had stepped aside after the European Cup triumph but none of his successors could come anywhere near emulating even his *minor* achievements. Wilf McGuinness tried. So too did Frank O'Farrell. But there was always George Best lurking drunkenly in some pub ready to upset plans. Finally Best was shown the door and another new face was appointed. Tommy Docherty rolled into Old Trafford preaching open football and promising a new attitude but even he could not halt the slide into the Second Division. The following season they were back, the Doc's prescription finally showing signs of working. And those fans who hiked across the country to fill the normally half-deserted grounds of the Second Division still have fond memories of those days of cavalier football. But Docherty, alas, could not quite take United to their past peaks. In the end a love affair, not with United, but with the physio's wife was the undoing of him. That initiated a further roundabout of managers. The dour Dave Sexton came and went, as did the more ebullient Ron Atkinson. There was the occasional FA Cup to cheer everyone up but there was also violence and racism on the terraces. It was not altogether a happy period for any football club. There was also that ugly word 'Liverpool', whose unrivalled triumphs at home and in Europe left United fans gaping and angry.

In November 1986 Alex Ferguson arrived from Aberdeen and began a quiet revolution that was to reap huge dividends in the years ahead. A youth scheme similar to that which had ushered in the Busby Babes was instituted, new scouts were appointed and a new attitude was engendered among the players and staff. In the thirteen years that Ferguson has steered the good ship United he has brought more success than any manager including Matt Busby. Five League titles (including three Doubles), four FA Cups, the League Cup, the European Cup-Winners' Cup and of course the European Cup itself, coming in a unique Treble. Within a year or so he could well be the most successful manager in the history of British football. Not a bad haul, considering the catcalls and abuse heaped on Ferguson at the back end of the 1980s. Thankfully, many are now ready to admit their error of judgement.

This book, then, is a tribute to all those who have supported United over the years, whether from the terraces, the stands or even the directors' box. It is in part a history of United, and in another way a history of fandom. It is about the social changes in society and the shift of football from a leisure pursuit to that of a big business. It is about the advent of television as the principal driving force behind the game of today and the increasing globalisation of the sport. The viewers may count in their millions, but what will always be fundamental to the sport are the fans who pack the grounds each Saturday for their dose of live soccer. Without them United would not be the club it is today.

CHAPTER ONE

The Pre-War Years

Flat Hats and Overcoats

Where did it all begin, this going to football matches? In Manchester it started long before Manchester United had ever been dreamt of. By 1878, when Newton Heath were formed, there were already leagues in and around the Manchester area with small groups of supporters, mainly friends and family, going along to support their team, though usually to home matches rather than away.

The roots of football go back to churches, working men's associations, even public houses. Wherever there were groups of young men, it was inevitable that the 'new' game of football would be played. Churches, particularly those of the more liberal variety such as the Methodists, led the trend, looking for a recreation to satisfy and attract more young people into their congregations. Catch them while they were young was their motto, although they also equated healthy bodies with healthy minds. Initially their youngsters had played baseball, rounders, or even cricket, but these were essentially summer sports. Football could be played in any season. All you needed was a plot of land and a couple of makeshift goal posts. It was ideal.

Fortunately it just happened to coincide with municipalisation and the growth of parks in our towns and cities. Public land was suddenly available for sports. And with increased leisure time, particularly on a Sunday, the parks were filled with families at play. Young ones enjoyed games, others exercised on bicycles, while the elders organised a picnic. The park offered cheap family entertainment. Sport, popular religion and municipality were just some of the rewarding and lasting legacies of the Victorian era.

Manchester United's roots were in the team known as Newton Heath. They had been formed in 1878 by a group of railway workers employed at the carriage and wagon department of the Lancashire and Yorkshire Railways. They were based at Newton Heath and played on a small ground in North Road but had to change half a mile down the road at the Three Crowns public house. Success was rapid, and they were soon looking outside Manchester for opposition. In 1885 they turned professional and were admitted to the Football Alliance in 1889, having failed by one vote to join the Football League. A couple of years later they applied and failed again, but when the League was enlarged in 1892, Newton Heath were finally admitted to the First Division.

In those days, supporting a football team meant little. Gates were generally low, rarely more than a few thousand; although the occasional game, when for instance Newton Heath played Small Heath or Manchester City, could attract as many as 20,000. Conditions were poor: terraces were usually no more than a cinder banking open to the rain and wind, while any stand was made of wood and not particularly large. Women never went to football and the cost of entry was still relatively high. It would not be until after the First World War that football became an overwhelmingly working-class spectator sport.

United's entry into the Football League marked a new development for supporters. They could now watch the finest teams in the land, although it was still very much a game with a northern bias. Of the dozen teams who had formed the Football League in 1888 half a dozen were within thirty miles of Manchester. Fans also began to travel in support of their local team. Improvements in transport, with a network of railways and cheaper fares, opened up the opportunity of travelling in support of your club. Supporters would journey by train, bus or tram, particularly to venues near Manchester such as Bolton, Oldham, Stockport, or Glossop. Travelling further afield was still relatively expensive and it would not be until the railway companies introduced their Football Specials with cheap prices that travelling to the likes of London or Birmingham became possible.

The major boost to United's fortunes came in 1908 when they clinched their first League title. A year later they won the FA Cup at the Crystal Palace and must have taken more than a few thousand spectators south to bolster the 71,000 crowd; the London and North West Railway ran excursions to Euston at eleven shillings for a day return. When United returned home victorious, thousands more greeted them outside Central Station. Office workers hung from their windows and many more lined the streets as the United party, in horse-drawn coaches, spiralled their way to the Town Hall. It would be the first of many such triumphal returns to the city.

Football was now becoming a business with huge increases in the attendance at games. United could attract as many as 40,000 and had already moved ground to Bank Street in Clayton to accommodate the increasing interest in the game. In 1909 they upped and moved again, this time to a purpose-built stadium close to Lancashire County Cricket Club at Old Trafford. It was designed by noted architect Archibald Leitch. The stadium was described in the press as 'a classic ground' with 'accommodation for 100,000 people'. Alas, it did not take quite that many. The plans had been scaled down as costs soared, but it was still a magnificent new home that could accommodate 60,000. There was a stand extending the length of one side close to the railway line while the other three sides and all corners were open to the elements. It was to be some seasons, however, before United actually filled their ground.

A year after they had moved United were champions again

although astonishingly only 10,000 turned up at Old Trafford to see them defeat Sunderland and clinch the title. Perhaps the fans had little faith in their side as United's main rivals Aston Villa looked to have the easier task that day. As it was, Villa surprisingly lost and United won. Three years later war broke out and football was set to enter a new era.

The inter-war years were not good for United. Arguably, it was the lowest point in their entire history. They won no trophies whatsoever and flirted dangerously with relegation to the Third Division North. In 1922 they had their first taste of relegation when they finished bottom of the First Division. Three years later they were back only to finish bottom again in 1931. Then in 1934 came the most dispiriting footballing moment in their history, as they ended the season travelling to Millwall needing a win in order to remain in the Second Division. Defeat would have cast them into the ignominy of the Third Division North, alongside the likes of Gateshead, Hartlepools United and New Brighton. Fortunately they won 2–0 and survived. The moment still lives vividly for many supporters of that time. Two seasons later United were Second Division champions, only to be promptly relegated the following season. The next season they were back: it was little wonder the music hall comedians nicknamed them the yo-yo team.

Despite the dreary football United could still draw 20,000 and more to an attractive Old Trafford fixture. When Bury came 41,000 turned up whereas the visit of Port Vale drew only 7,000 spectators. There were wide, empty, echoing spaces around Old Trafford. It must, at times, have made a strange sight, for in those days you could walk freely around three sides of the ground and, as some supporters point out, at half time the entire crowd would move towards the goal United were kicking into, leaving the rest of the ground totally empty.

Times were hard as well. The Depression left millions out of work and in a major manufacturing city like Manchester industry suffered badly. Thousands joined the city's dole queues and for years there was little hope of finding any work. The Government operated a brutal Means Test, only paying out to a small minority of claimants. The scheme guaranteed poverty. Families went hungry; people were simply unable to afford to eat properly. And, as one member of the St John Ambulance Brigade reveals, many of those who did go to games suffered with the heat and the crushing which, combined with a lack of nourishment, led to many simply collapsing on the terraces.

Generally, people could not afford to go to football matches. Even though the cost was minimal you could hardly go to a game and leave your family short. But there were ways. With about twenty minutes of a match remaining officials would open the main gates ready to let the crowds out. That was the cue for thousands to pour in. They would have been waiting outside, listening to the game, judging the score by the cheers of the crowd. Often somebody at the highest point of the terracing would lean over to shout the name of the scorer to the crowd below. It was better than nothing, and as the testaments of many in this chapter show, this was indeed their first means of introduction to football. Throughout the inter-war years football remained a male pursuit. Musical hall comedian Fred Karno might have run a successful women's football team but at Old Trafford the clientele was male and working-class. Flat hats and overcoats were the order of the day.

Travelling to away games started to become a little more common. When Stan Orme followed United to Barnsley it was an adventure, his first trip outside Manchester, and an occasion when he saw a coal-mining community for the first time. The experience left an indelible mark on the youngster that perhaps had some bearing on his future. When fans did travel it was always by public transport. Cars were the prerogative of the wealthy. Money for the working classes was so scarce that it was not uncommon for Salford lads to walk the entire distance to Bolton, Oldham or Bury, and back

11

in support of their team. The vast majority would walk to Old Trafford anyhow. They would often go to Maine Road as well, happy to support either United or City. All that mattered was seeing a game of football, not having some fixed tribal support of one team or the other. On the terraces they would talk and joke with opposition fans. There was no segregation, no animosity, no violence. You were football fans together no matter which team you supported.

Just weeks into the 1939–40 season came war. Professional football was disbanded and the league system postponed until hostilities ceased. Most reckoned it might be for a season or two. In fact, it was for seven long years. The heroes of the terraces, like the fans, packed their bags and went off to war. In place of the old league system regional leagues were set up but most Saturdays United were scratching around to find eleven players. Sometimes they had guest players or a player from another club who happened to be stationed in or around Manchester. An odd assortment of players represented United in those dark war years. Attendances were low; most supporters were in the Forces or working long hours as part of the war effort. There wasn't much time or money for a frivolous pursuit such as football.

Then on the night of Tuesday 11 March 1941, a cluster of bombs fell on Old Trafford, wrecking the main stand, causing a fire and damaging the pitch. The ground was a disaster area. There was no money for repairs and anyhow there were other priorities like winning a war. Fortunately Manchester City came to their rescue, offering Maine Road as an alternative. United had little option but to accept graciously. It would be eight years before they returned to Old Trafford.

———◆———

I saw my first game in 1923, or so my mother told me. I was only one at the time. My father took me. It was just a year or two after the great Billy Meredith had left. I don't know what the game was or who they were playing. The first game I really remember was the 1936–37 season. United had just got back into the First Division and that's what prompted me to go. The game was the local Derby against Manchester City. City had Matt Busby playing for them while United had the great George Vose. He was a fine player. I think he was captain that day. They're the only two players I can remember. We walked all the way to Maine Road. We didn't have any money for a tram.

I remember it was a big crowd and we were all very squashed. Oh, it was terrible. They lifted us youngsters over the heads and they passed us all the way down to the front. I can still see it, being carried over the heads of this huge crowd. And when we got to the front they seated us on a whitewashed wall. I remember that whitewashed wall very vividly. It had rained all day, drizzle. We were soaking wet. But when we came out of the ground we were perfectly dry. The rain must have stopped and we hadn't noticed. Six months later I had rheumatic fever. I always reckon it was because I got so wet that day.

WILF SUDLOW

The thing that sticks in my mind was that we always sat in the end of the stand, not in the middle but right at the end. The centre of the stand were the best seats, the side where the players came out. Sitting at the end would be slightly cheaper than the centre but of course a bit more expensive than standing. This would be the early 1930s, I would be nine or so.

There was never any trouble in those days at the game. People were always friendly. We used to get the tram to the ground and then we'd walk. I seem to remember that people dressed decently for the game, they didn't go in their working clothes. I was always football daft. I went to St Patrick's primary school until I was eleven and then I went off to De La

Salle College in Pendleton, it was a grammar school. There was this Brother Frederick there and he used to run the school football teams. He came into the class one day and said, 'I want you to go down to a place near the racecourse, near where the Cliff is.' Salford Boys used to play their matches at this place. One of the lads who played there with me was John Anderson who later went on to play for United and appeared with them in the Cup final. I played there for Salford Boys. John was a year older than me.

United were not such a good team in those days although they had some reasonably good players, such as George Vose and Jack Rowley.

LAURENCE CASSIDY

In my early teens in the early thirties I became a fan of Manchester United primarily because I lived in Sale, three miles from the ground. The predominant team in Manchester at that time was Manchester City. United were in the Second Division and nearly went into the Third Division North. A local baker used to take me to see Lancashire playing cricket at 4 p.m., after he had finished baking. He was also a Manchester United fan. In those days it had a lot to do with where you were born. If I had been born in Moss Side I more than likely would have been a City fan.

I became quite adventurous. I was still at school and a friend of mine said that there was a cheap train excursion to Barnsley to see United. So we went over at lunchtime, paid 6d for our train ticket. We had never been to another football ground other than Manchester United. I used to stand under the old stand there, the shed as they called it. In those days, of course, you could walk around the ground at half time and stand at the other end. Anyhow, I arrived at Barnsley and it would be about 1 p.m. and there were not many people there. Then suddenly at 2 p.m. there was a great influx of people and to my astonishment they all had black faces. It was miners.

14

It was my first introduction to a mineworker. They had just come off the shift and there was no pit baths in those days. They came straight up and into the ground. It shook me, quite frankly, and left a very poignant memory. It was the first time I had ever seen a coal miner.

Then in the late 1930s there was the question of Manchester United at the end of the season, having two games to play to go up into the First Division. It was the day of the Preston North End Cup final [30 April 1938, FA Cup final: Preston v Huddersfield Town] and there was a special train going from here, you could actually pick it up at Sale station. Two of the chaps I used to go to United with said – it was 7s 1d [about 35p] return to London – let's go, not to see Preston but to see United who were playing at West Ham. I saved up, got a ticket, turned up at midnight to get this train and to my astonishment these two chaps never turned up. They had no intention of coming. It was a pretty shattering experience. Anyhow I got on the train, went to London. Never been there before. Got on the tube, got out to West Ham which United lost. At Wembley George Mutch hit a penalty and Preston won. Coming back to London, I'd never seen anything like it. In those days football supporters used to create havoc in London but it was never reported. They used to congregate at Piccadilly Circus. The Scots always created problems after the England–Scotland games which I used to go to. Anyhow I came back home and they had to play the following week and had to win. Which they did [United beat Bury two–nil and were duly promoted in second place].

We went to games by public transport – trams, trains – there was never any trouble. It was a cloth cap situation. There were no boxes in those days, it was very much a working-class thing – meat pies at half time and so forth. And of course the players were much closer to the watching public, socially. My mother was a widow and she did cleaning for five shillings a day so I had to scrape money together to go to Old Trafford, it was only 3d on the tram. You may have had a rattle or a scarf but there was no fancy clothes or anything like that, not much spending, maybe 1d for a programme. Football was a very austere working-class game. I used to go with these two chaps who let me down over the Wembley thing. You always stood in similar places and got to know people. Later, having a season ticket was a luxury. In those days Manchester was a very poor city. Living here in Sale was looked at as snob end, but it wasn't.

There were virtually no women at the games then. It was all male, young and old men and boys, totally male-dominated. There were no fears either about going to the game. The record crowd at Old Trafford was seventy-six thousand. After the War, at Maine Road United played Arsenal and had eighty-one thousand. I never went to United one week and City the other. I couldn't have afforded it and any rate I never had the heart to do that. I was sold on United because I had such a close association with the club. But I never went out of my way to cultivate the players. I learnt early on in life not to get too close to your gods.

LORD STAN ORME

I adopted the same team as my father. He was born in 1895 and saw United play prior to the First World War. I was born in Gainsborough in Lincolnshire and we lived just four minutes from Gainsborough Trinity's ground. At the turn of the century they had been a Second Division side and were in the same division as Manchester United [United and Gainsborough Trinity were in the Second Division together for ten seasons between 1896 and 1906], so my father saw United play at Gainsborough on a number of occasions. For some reason he became a fan of United. Maybe they played particularly well when they were down here. But United became his club. My father loved football although I have to say that I never actually saw him kick a ball. He also had a brother, Ben, who lived in Manchester. But I think that

16

even in those days people from all over the country liked Manchester United; they were a popular club.

KEN HASTINGS

'Manchester United' stands for something more than any person, any player, any supporter. It is the 'soul' of a sporting organisation which goes on season after season, making history all the time.

UNITED REVIEW, 1937

The first game I went to, it must have been about 1937. And the first time I went the brother took me on the crossbar of his bicycle. We lived in Moss Side. He was a United fan even though we lived in Moss Side. I can't remember the team we played but the reason he took me was because two of his pals who used to go had stopped going because United were such a bad side at the time. In fact they got relegated that year. Now that didn't mean much to me at the age but I remember them saying, 'Oh we're going to go down,' and true enough, that season they did go down. My brother was very, very sad.

Now I didn't understand but I felt sad because he was sad, nothing to do with Man United. And then of course I started going a little more regular and then the War came and later I went off into the Army. I think in 1941 Old Trafford was bombed. In a way it was lucky for me because I lived near Maine Road and United played there during the war years. I therefore could go to Maine Road every week to see City one week, Man United the next.

Some of the players I remember before the War were Georgie Vose, George Roughton, Bill McKay. There was also Tommy Breen in goal, an Irish international. I remember my brother said to me, even before I'd seen a game, he said we'd be OK because we'd just bought Jack Rowley, from Bournemouth. 'He'll save us,' he said. But of course that

17

wasn't to be. There was also Stan Pearson who came from Salford and Johnny Carey from, I think, Home Farm. Of course when the War came these guys were all off into the Army. Now when we went to Maine Road they'd have guest players. We had a big RAF camp at Handforth so you'd never know what the team was going to be.

I saw United in the Second Division but of course they came up the next year and City went down. From being champions in 1937 City are still the only team to have been relegated the next year.

Everybody wore a raincoat with a belt around. A lot wore flat caps. The crowd would always let you in. There's times I been to Maine Road and never seen the pitch. You'd pay your money and you couldn't get up the terraces. All you could do was get into the tunnel and look up above the heads and now and again you might see a ball go into the air. But you couldn't see the pitch, the goals or anything.

When United were in the Second Division they didn't get big crowds; the fans stood outside handing out leaflets wanting a boycott.* Louis Rocca† – he was an old man to me in those days – he'd always walk around with an Alsatian dog. He'd walk around the pitch and he'd talk to the crowd. But they'd stand outside leafletting. Now Louis Rocca was one of the guys who put money into United when they were struggling. And I think that's when they got these new players like Rowley, Chilton. And then during the War of course they got a lot of players from Goslings, which was a greengrocers, fruiterers, down north Manchester. There was John Walton, Jack Crompton. They all played for this amateur club but

* In October 1930 fans organised a boycott of Old Trafford after a miserable start to the season. Instead of an anticipated 50,000, fewer than 25,000 turned up for the match against Arsenal. A heavy police presence stopped the protesters from persuading others to join the boycott: the low attendance was due more to the atrocious weather.
† Louis Rocca was an influential figure in the history of the club. Not only did he dream up the name Manchester United but saved them from bankruptcy on more than one occasion.

they were a very good side. And then the War, or near the end of the War, we got Ted Buckle who'd come out of the Navy, Allenby Chilton who was wounded on D-Day. He came back, recovered, and they all started coming back and we had less and less of the guest players.

One guest player I always remember was Pongo Waring, bald head. There was another guy from Aston Villa – the only man I know in those days who could throw a ball like they do now into the middle, like the Neville brothers. I think his name was Gardner. He was the only one who could throw a ball into the penalty area. Nobody ever did it then.

A lot of time, because you didn't have the money to go to a game, you'd go in at three-quarter time. It was all the kids. We were very poor though you didn't know it. At Christmas you'd get half a dozen lead soldiers and an orange. Times have changed. But we didn't worry. We'd be saying, 'Oh, three-quarters time soon,' and all the kids, the gates would open and we'd pour in; 'What's the score?' we'd ask and take it from there.

You could buy Oxo and the programme was a single sheet, costing one penny. I'd buy one sometimes or we might buy one between us. There was certain parts of the ground where you'd get to know the people and they'd have a sweep. You would pick a player from the hat for sixpence or something, and you'd all put your tanner in and he'd keep a tanner for doing it and the first goal you got paid out. I also remember a guy at Maine Road who'd lost a leg in the War and what he used to do before the game, he'd encourage people who had disabilities. He'd hop round the ground on one leg a couple of times. Then he'd put his artificial leg on and do it again. He used to get a good ovation off the fans, you know, they'd love it.

JOE DILLON

I was there at Old Trafford the day of the record crowd. It was Grimsby against Wolves in the FA Cup semi-final of 1939 when just under seventy-seven thousand turned up. I'd be about seventeen at the time. It was packed. I squeezed myself to the front of this crowd and I was right behind a barrier, near to the front. I didn't realise how dangerous that was. I was getting so squashed I was screaming. Then some fellas pushed me under the barrier. I had suddenly escaped. But it was so dangerous, it was terrible.

WILF SUDLOW

As a young boy it was a case of going when you could get free from your parents because they always wanted to know where you were. It was great fun. They used to put the children and young kids down at the front so that you always had a good view. The elder people always used to try and make sure that the young people were safe and secure. In those days you never had any problems, no fighting. It didn't matter who was playing, you went to see a football match. You were always happy of course if your own team won but primarily you went to see the match. You cheered whenever anything good happened, no matter which team. It was a good afternoon out for children, well protected and never any problems. People were more placid.

When I first went was when I was seven years old at Manchester City. That would be 1923. My uncle used to take me. There used to be a boys' corner there and all the youngsters were in that corner and you would be safe. I'd be about twelve when I first came to Old Trafford as it was a bit further away from where I lived, something like 1928. There was plenty of room, no crowding, a big stadium with plenty of room in it. When I say very few I mean eight or ten thousand. A lot of people, but not for a ground like Old Trafford. United were not such a famous club then; no, they were very up and down. I think this was a great part of the enjoyment in those days. Nothing was taken for granted; they either won or they lost and we didn't worry too much about places in the division whether they were top or bottom. They were our team and we cheered them whatever. Players also used to move between City and United, this was the camaraderie between the clubs at that time.

In 1934, I think United almost went into the Third Division North. They were twenty-first in the Second Division then. I forget the team but they had to lose and United had to win, it was the last game of the season. There were only twenty-two teams in the division. This other team – it was Millwall, yes Millwall – and United won two–nil. I remember that now. That was the closest they ever came to going into the Third Division. Then I started doing something useful with my life and started with the St John Ambulance Brigade. It was much easier then because I could always persuade my mother that I was going on duty and again you didn't care who won or lost prior to the War. There was none of the antagonism.

There would be ten or twelve St John Ambulance members at Old Trafford in the mid-thirties depending on duties at the time. You used to sit in the corners. Two of you together, that's eight and then two or three by the main stand, along the wall and that was your position. You were always in the open air. You had no cover for treating casualties. Anybody who needed moving, you'd move them on a stretcher into the tunnel and put them in there and deal with them there. You had no sophisticated equipment. In those days you didn't get stone-throwing or bottles. They were usually incidents of an illness, people suddenly fainting or going into an epileptic fit, or people who were malnourished. These were hard times and people were poor, they would have come to the game without having eaten and they would faint in the crowd. Then you got one or two heart attacks but not as many as you get today. In those days if a player was injured we used to have to go and treat them. If it was a broken leg we would have to treat them on the pitch, make their leg secure and then carry them off. It was the responsibility of the St John to look after the player.

If you had a big crowd, especially over on the popular side, people got excited and fainted; if they went unconscious it was common for the crowd to pick them up and start rolling them over the top. The people round about would pick them up and shout, 'They're coming down,' and the victim would be passed over the heads all the way down to the front. Our people would be there waiting to collect them. It happened very often. I always said it was dangerous. As long as they got them out of the way so that they could carry on watching. It was impossible for us to go through that crowd. Sometimes you'd be nowhere near a set of steps or gangways and once the match had begun, the gangways were filled.

I was at Old Trafford for the record crowd between Grimsby and Wolves; it was the Cup semi-final in 1939 [25 March 1939, attendance 76,962. This remains the record attendance at Old Trafford]. I was on duty, the game was delayed slightly because we were using the pitch to put all the casualties on. We just didn't have room. We just put the casualties on the pitch and dealt with them there. It was also a warm day; people stood up and they would faint. It was that tight they sometimes would still be propped up. It was very dangerous.

We used to get deaths. That would put a damper on the whole staff. We might get three or four in a season. It happened at crucial moments: something exciting happened on the pitch, people would get over-excited and just go. It would be heart attacks. You'd try to put it out of your mind but it was difficult. I had one one Boxing Day. I was called out and this poor fellow had died. He was eighty-odd. I found out because the family had sent him out of the way because they were putting a big party on at home for him and his wife, it was their wedding anniversary. One of his sons was with him. I said, 'I'm terribly sorry, there's nothing we can do. The doctor's seen him and they've taken him to the hospital for verification; they'll see to you there.' Then I said, 'What was he doing here at his age?' and he told me. That upset me. It's not often I get upset but I did then. I got home and my wife

22

asked what was the matter and I told her. She said, 'Have you never thought, he died happy.' I said, 'No.' I hadn't actually but you know he probably did. He died happy. It put a different perspective on the whole thing. But for me I just had to get over it and get on with it.

ALF DAVIES

I've got this photograph somewhere; it's out of an old newspaper. It was taken in the 1920s of the crowd at United. There's fifty to sixty thousand of them stood shoulder to shoulder. You couldn't put a penny between them. But you know every one of them has a flat cap on and is wearing a white scarf. Most of them would have been unemployed. It cost a bob [5p] to get in and 6d [2.5p] if you were a youngster. And in that photograph there is just one banner. It's a piece of old card on a broomstick and it reads 'Give It To Joe'. That's Joe Spence. It's a lot different from today. I watched that United–Liverpool Cup final, and all those banners, all those Liverpool supporters singing and swaying. That picture sums it all up, the difference between football then and football now. Poverty then, affluence now. Times have changed.

WILF SUDLOW

I think I first started going when I was about between nine and twelve. I didn't go alone, I went with my elder brother. Once I got inside that ground and saw the players run out of the tunnel I knew that I'd be a Manchester United supporter for life. I'd not been to Manchester City otherwise things might have been different. Afterwards my brother said I could go as long as I went with some friends. In the 1930s there was a big unemployment slump and you had to be working to be able to go every week but we had a secondary consideration which we used to use. We used to walk from Salford – about three miles – to the ground before the kick-off and we would

23

wait outside. When they kicked off we might not be inside the ground but we were at the match. We could see the head and shoulders of the supporters inside the ground because there were not the stands in those days, it was all standing. Somebody would score and we could tell and we'd shout, 'Who scored?' and they would shout back to us who it was. Then at three-quarter time, that was what we had really gone for, because the gates were opened, not just to let us in but to let the crowd inside come out. So, we'd rush in and see the last twenty minutes for free. We were getting to the game for nothing. We didn't feel as though we were cheating: we just couldn't afford it.

The crowd didn't dress for a game like they do now. When I see these youngsters in their regalia I remember the only thing we had was a red and white scarf. I had one which was knitted for me by my sister. That was the dress code. Sometimes we managed a red and white paper hat but sometimes if it rained, and this did happen to me once, the colour would run down your face. But there were no red and white shirts or anything like that. In any case, there weren't those things on sale in those days.

There was more chatter leaving the ground than there is now. People now seem to come out of the ground and rush for their cars. There weren't a lot of cars in those days, not a lot had cars. You came out of the ground in hordes, everyone talking – 'he shouldn't have done this', 'was it offside', and so on. You played that match all the way home. Most people within two or three miles walked, certainly those from Salford. You could get a tram but walking was part of the day. Going down Trafford Road you'd see them all walking, past the canal and then into Trafford Park and there was the ground in front of you. But it was only on certain big matches that you got the crowds. They didn't get big crowds all the time as they do now. United were an average side although they still had a good name. Kids still wanted to play for Manchester United.

The visit of Manchester City was always an occasion and

of course Arsenal because of their manager Herbert Chapman; Chelsea were good in those days but not really Liverpool. They weren't such a great side then. But of course Everton and Dixie Dean were a big attraction.

Joe Spence was a favourite of mine. He was a centre forward, small and stocky but very, very fast. The phrase was coined: 'Give it to Joe'. When things weren't going right we'd shout 'Give it to Joe,' and he'd usually oblige with a goal or two to pull them out of the fire. A great character. He could play on the wing as well. We had a wonderful centre half called Clarrie Hilditch, a tall imposing figure, and the goalkeeper was Jackie Mew.

ALBERT THORPE

There was an element of Catholicism associated with the club, especially back in the 1930s. Remember, United had originated in Newton Heath which was a Catholic area and Old Trafford was in Salford, which again was a Catholic area with a large Irish population. It was the same with Collyhurst; that was an Irish Catholic area with big United support. United later had many Irish players like Johnny Carey and Jimmy Delaney. City, however, were not seen as a Protestant club. They were non-sectarian. But there was never any trouble between the clubs like there is in Glasgow, none whatsoever. I suppose the support in those days was simply geographical and it just happened that United were in Irish Catholic areas, so they got this reputation of being Catholic. Even today I suppose areas like Chorlton as well as Salford and Wythenshawe are considered United areas and they too have Irish populations. Of course Sir Matt then became associated with the club and that strengthened the Catholic image. You'd always see priests at the game; the word was that they got their tickets from Busby.

ALF DAVIES

I remember on one occasion with a pal, I'd be about fourteen, walking from Salford to Bolton to see United playing Bolton Wanderers. It was eight miles. We hadn't any money, so when we got there, there's a side-street by the ground where the back of the stand comes and we both climbed up and into the ground. I ripped my jersey on the barbed wire and the supporters inside helped us in. We saw the match and we lost. It was pouring with rain and we came out and I spotted our local Catholic priest and I said to John, 'There's the priest, don't let him see us.' Anyhow, he saw us before we could get away and he said, 'Now then boys, what are you doing here?' I said, 'Oh, we've been to the match,' but I didn't tell him we had climbed over because that would have meant confession on a Friday. He said, 'Well, how are you getting home?' We said we were walking and he said, 'You can't do that,' and he gave us the bus fare – but he walked us to the bus stop to make sure we got on the bus.

ALBERT THORPE

CHAPTER TWO

The Post-War Years

Crompton, Carey, Aston, Anderson . . .

On the morning of Monday 19 February 1945, Company Sergeant-Major Instructor Matt Busby agreed to become the new manager of Manchester United Football Club. It was unquestionably the most important signing the club has ever made in its entire history, although it passed with little comment at the time. Busby had played with Manchester City before the War, then with Liverpool and was still on Liverpool's books when he took the decision to join United. Indeed, in doing so, he turned down an offer from Liverpool to become their coach. United secretary Walter Crickmer knew a good man when he saw one. 'He will build up the team, and put it right where it belongs – at the top,' he commented as Busby, still in Army uniform, dipped a nibbed pen into the inkstand and signed on the dotted line. It ushered in a new era.

Busby was thirty-four years old. His task was considerable but he made one promise in his programme notes at the start of the new campaign. 'It is my policy,' he wrote, 'to play methodical and progressive football,' emphasising that 'This will always be my policy.' He would be true to his word.

Old Trafford had been badly bombed during the War. Grass grew from the terraces and a six-foot bush was sprouting on the pitch. It resembled a disused factory more than the famous football stadium that had once hosted an FA Cup final as well as internationals. As a consequence, United had been forced to up and move across the city to Maine Road. And yet, grand as United was, it still only employed two full-time people apart from the players and coaches. They were the club secretary Walter Crickmer and his assistant Les Olive.

Busby set about his task with gusto. Wholesale changes were needed. Most of the pre-war players were gone, either too old or now sporting other colours. Yet, despite the enormous changes, in his first match Busby fielded a side that was to be the nucleus of a highly successful team over the next five years. In that first match they defeated Grimsby Town 2–1 at Maine Road in front of 40,000. They quickly notched up five successive victories including a 5–0 hammering of eventual champions Liverpool. The title went to the wire with United, runners-up, a mere point behind champions Liverpool.

It was the same the following season, with United again runners-up, this time seven points behind champions Arsenal. But at least in that early summer of 1948 they won the FA Cup with a display that is vividly remembered to this day. The *News of the World*, oozing lyrically, called it 'Wembley's Finest Final'. Those who watched that Cup final still regard it as one of the most exciting and skilful in living memory. Television presenter Bob Greaves can still recite the entire team in less than six seconds. For the fans it was their first-ever trip to Wembley and their first major trophy since they had clinched the League title in 1911. The last time United had appeared in a Cup final had been 1909 at the Crystal Palace. Silverware had been a long time coming and now the city turned out to greet their returning heroes.

But it would not be long before more trophies followed. In 1949 they again finished as runners-up but at least had some compensation as they returned to Old Trafford after an absence of eight years, marking the occasion with a 3–0 win over Bolton Wanderers. Football was back on the west side of the city. The fans, too, were glad to be back home, particularly the Salford lads who no longer had to make that trek across the city to Moss Side. Swarming over the Trafford Bridge was far more fun.

The following year, 1950, they slipped to fourth in the table although they ended just three points behind champions Portsmouth. A year later they repeated their previous successes, once more runners-up. Four times in five years Busby's team had stood on the brink of League success, only to end as runners-up. Ever the bridesmaid, in 1952 they eventually cleared that final hurdle to take the title, partly thanks to a crop of new names which were appearing on the teamsheet. Roger Byrne had come into the side, initially as a winger but soon converted into a full-back, while Johnny Berry had been a record signing from Birmingham City. Ulsterman Jackie Blanchflower had also appeared but many of the old names remained. Pearson, Rowley, Carey, Crompton, Cockburn and Chilton were still there, though once the Championship had been pocketed, wholesale changes and a new philosophy would remove them from the teamsheet. One Championship, one FA Cup and four second spots, all in six years. It was an auspicious start for Busby. The fans loved it and many who saw that side still regard them as perhaps the finest of Busby's teams.

They were still austere years. The economy was gradually recovering from the war effort but consumer goods were few. By the early fifties televisions were beginning to appear but most information still came via the radio or the newspapers. Cars also were few and far between and anyone going to a match went either by bus, train or tram. At least it was an improvement on the pre-war years when most people walked to the ground. Football was cheap entertainment; a couple of pence to get in, maybe a penny for a programme and your bus fare. And there were big crowds. Old Trafford regularly attracted 50,000 and when they were playing at Maine Road, gates had been as high as 80,000. In those days you just turned up for a game, queued and paid your money at the turnstile. Once inside you stood on the terraces, swayed with the rest of them with no protection from the elements, and with the final whistle poured out on to the narrow streets of Moss Side and Rusholme or into the usual jam of people over Trafford Bridge. Amenities were scarce. There was little in the way of toilets and half the time it was impossible to reach them, so you just did it there and then. It was not a very pleasant place to be.

Needless to say, not many women went to football. It was a man's occupation although plenty of young lads went, often by themselves. As many witnesses recount here, the crowd looked after you. If you slipped they pulled you up, and if anybody did pass out their bodies were gently lowered over the heads of the crowd to the bottom of the terraces. The police had few problems.

Friendships blossomed on the terraces, as did betting syndicates. Bookmakers were illegal, so groups got together and betted on who might score the first goal – a shilling in the hat and draw out a name. It was that simple. Rival supporters also joined in, the banter always friendly, aggression a rarity. There was much to be said for Britain in the 1950s. People may not have had much money, but they had standards and discipline.

Everyone dressed much the same – flat caps and grey coats with maybe the odd increasingly popular trilby on show. There were no team shirts, no flags, no merchandising shops; just the occasional scarf, usually knitted by a granny or mum. Football was a working-class game and would remain so for another thirty years. Tribal instincts were few. You supported your team but were always appreciative of good football, whichever team played it. Fans of both sides mingled on the terraces, chatting, swapping banter, but always friendly. In Manchester it was common for fans to watch both clubs: City one week, United the next. With Old Trafford out of bounds due to wartime damage, Maine Road was the sole venue for Manchester football until United returned to Old Trafford in August 1949.

Few fans went to away games. The consequences of a long

and painful war dragged on for many years: money was scarce and travel costs still high. Privately owned cars were few and far between and anyone wanting to go to an away game had to travel by rail, although British Rail did offer reasonably priced Football Specials. But few could afford them.

As many testify in these pages, there were never any fears for youngsters going to games. Ten-year-old lads would go off on their own or with their pals to a game, often crossing the city on public transport, queuing for long periods and then standing in crowds of 60,000 and more. The older fans looked after the youngsters on the terraces, positioning them behind or in front of barriers or down by the running track, anywhere that was safe. Parents had few worries about the well-being of their children. Despite the huge, often uncontrolled crowds, accidents were rare. There were no stewards, just a handful of policemen and a few members of the St John Ambulance Brigade to look after crowds that often exceeded 60,000. For many children, entry into the ground at three-quarter time continued to be the means of initiation into this great game.

There were no floodlights. Maine Road did not switch on its lights until 1953. Any evening games could only be played in the summer months and then often required an early kick-off. Cup replays necessitated a mid-week afternoon kick-off with disturbing consequences for schools and the workplace as thousands furtively crept from their desks and lathes to make their way to the game. When United played Bradford Park Avenue in front of 70,000 in a Cup replay on a Monday afternoon in February 1949, the entire city ground to a halt with absenteeism. But that was the way it was, still remembered vividly and affectionately by those who supported United at the time, even though they did have to go to Maine Road.

I think it was 1948 when I first started going to Old Trafford. I think my dad allowed me to start going to reserve games. I was fourteen in 1948; it was possible I went to a couple of reserve games when I was twelve or thirteen and certainly after the 1948 Cup final which was probably one of the best on record. I can still recite the names of that team: Crompton, Carey, Aston, Anderson, Chilton, Cockburn, Delaney, Morris, Rowley, Pearson and Mitten. United beat Blackpool four–two at Wembley. There was no television of course; I'm not even sure there was radio commentary in those days. You saw it on newsreels at the cinema and you saw the usual truncated version, but everybody said it was one of the great Cup finals and of course it was. So the reserves started getting crowds of fifteen, eighteen, twenty, twenty-two thousand – it was like going to a major game just going to see the reserves at Old Trafford.

My other memories of those early days are of the first-team games being played at Maine Road of course, because Old Trafford had been blitzed. I do think that reserve games were sometimes held at Old Trafford but the first team played at Maine Road. Everybody went there by bus or bicycle; nobody had cars.

I remember vividly United beating Yeovil Town eight–nil, I think in probably the fifth round of the FA Cup and there were eighty-one thousand people packed into Maine Road and I was one of them. And in all honesty all I saw of that game, because I was on the main terracing opposite the main stand, the Kippax I think, would be the furthest third of the pitch because the crowd just ballooned in front of you. You couldn't see over their heads. You jumped up and down you *still* couldn't see because the terracing was very shallow, so all I saw was the far end, the far side; but it was a great occasion: eight–nil in an FA Cup tie. Wonderful to be there, but I didn't see much of it.

The other interesting thing about matches in those days was the composition of the crowd and the dress of the fans, because now even in the winter you see fellas in short-sleeved

T-shirts and United shirts in the freezing cold and very often bare chested walking into the ground. In those days people dressed sensibly and conformed to the weather. You wore overcoats, big shoes, hats, umbrellas even; you just dressed for the weather. I don't understand how fellas don't freeze and a lot of women go in skimpy little garments in the freezing cold. I don't follow that at all. And of course there were virtually no women in the crowds in the forties, fifties, sixties. If you saw a woman it was a novelty.

I first started going to the first-team games with a group of mates. It was a big day out but it didn't cost a lot. I used to go to virtually every game and it was going to watch United that helped to draw me into print journalism. At the age of sixteen I got a job on the local newspaper, the *Sale and Stretford Guardian*, and although I wasn't the sports reporter, I did the rugby union a lot for them. Before I got my job I used to go to the game, take notes at the game in a little notebook. I would then get home and get my exercise book out. I would write out my report of the game, as though for a newspaper and then at about seven o'clock in the evening I would trundle up the road on my bike and buy next morning's *Sunday Empire News* which actually came out on a Saturday night in the suburbs. It was slightly more updated in footballing terms than the footballing Pink so you got a proper precis. I used to compare my reports with those of whoever was writing in the *Empire News* and I used to think sometimes, 'Yeah I can do this,' and I suspect that probably led me when I joined the *Daily Mail* at the age of twenty-one, twenty-two in 1956. Even though I joined as a news reporter I fairly quickly inveigled myself into the Saturday sports reporting lark so I covered matches at you name the grounds in the north-west. I wasn't certainly covering United and Everton and Liverpool but I was covering Burnley and Oldham and Stockport and Crewe and Stoke and all those other clubs for many years on the *Daily Mail*.

BOB GREAVES

33

When I got back home in 1947 after the War I went straight to see United play. I remember Johnny Morris. Arsenal were well known for an iron defence, but Jack Rowley could break it down. What a player he was. He could turn on the ball and volley it, all in one move; a bit like Mark Hughes used to do in later years. What a forward line they had. I wouldn't like to say they were the best United side. There's been a few but they were as good as any of them.

When Old Trafford reopened I used to go where the Main Stand now is. I'd be somewhere on the half-way line. Opposite was what we called the cowshed; it was open at both ends. I tell you what I do remember – the toilets. Here was a club that was so rich, attracting crowds of fifty, sixty, even seventy thousand and yet the toilets were a disgrace. I can still smell them. Fat directors coining it while we had to suffer these smelly appalling toilets.

Sometimes when the crowd was so great you couldn't get to the toilet and you'd have to pee where you stood. You were shoulder to shoulder and couldn't budge. There'd be puddles everywhere. The Evertonians were bad. They had a reputation. I remember we played them once. One of them must have peed in this beer bottle. Suddenly the bottle's flying through the air, pee dropping down on everyone.

They used to have a band as well to entertain the crowd. The Beswick Prize Band. They'd be there most weeks, marching up and down, boom, boom, boom, a bit like the Salvation Army band. You couldn't afford to buy much at the ground. Sometimes I got a programme, although I never remember paying for one.

WILF SUDLOW

I left school in 1938 when I was fourteen and had a trial for United at the Cliff. They signed me up as an amateur and I went to play with the MUJACs, that's the Manchester United Junior Athletics Club. That was run by a Mr Williams. I was an amateur

34

with them. Then a year later when I was fifteen, war broke out. I wasn't really a United fan in those days. I used to support City and Bolton Wanderers. But United were the first team to ask me to join them, so I did. The man who had recommended me to United was the manager of Bury, Norman Bullock.

At the age of fifteen and a half I was playing in the Manchester League; this was wartime football and the reserve team and A-team had been combined. At one stage I was loaned out to Bolton Wanderers along with Bert Whalley but when I was seventeen United called me back. I think they were a bit worried that I was going to join Bolton, so they had me back at Old Trafford and immediately signed me as a professional. In fact, I signed the pro forms in the dressing room at Chesterfield where we had just been playing. I didn't earn very much; two shillings and sixpence as an amateur while the professionals were on a maximum of thirty shillings a week. But the War had started and I later joined the Army, serving in Germany.

Towards the end of the War I was sent to India and spent some time there. I played a lot of football in India. We played exhibition football. There was a Denis Compton side and a Tommy Walker team. Compton was the cricketer who also played for Arsenal while Tommy Walker was a Scottish international. I played in Tommy Walker's side and we travelled all over India playing matches between the two teams. Stan Pearson was there as well and he played in Denis Compton's side. I remember Stan saying to me, 'What are we going to do after the War, Johnny? There's ten inside forwards at United; we'll never get in the side.' So when I was demobbed I went to see Matt Busby, who was the new manager at United. I told him I wanted a transfer and he said, 'No, come down and train with the side and see how it goes.' Luckily, within three weeks I was in the side. Stan soon joined me in the team as well.

We had a great team, perhaps the best. That season we won the Cup we were fantastic. These guys here were all supporters in those days but they don't go now because the modern sides are nowhere near as good as we were. I'll tell you what, the football we played was brilliant and on muddy pitches as well. We won the Cup in 1948.

I didn't play in the game against Yeovil but I'll tell you a story about that. I was injured at the time but I went along to Maine Road. It was a Wednesday afternoon and there were seventy thousand there. We had a secretary at the time called Walter Crickmer. Well, a lot of local teams had come down for that game, players from Bury and Burnley and Bolton and they didn't have tickets. When they saw me outside, they all swarmed around me and asked if I could get them in. The gates at Maine Road had been closed as the ground was full. So I said, 'I'll go and see Mr Crickmer and see what I can do.' So I saw him and he said, 'I can't do anything at the moment, but if you go down there and tell the policeman to let them in, that should be OK.' So I told the policeman and he said, 'Fine, I'll open the gates here and let them in.' So he did, and about five thousand swarmed in. There was a huge crowd, including the local players, and they all just piled in through the gate. They all stood under the stands; I think thirty thousand would never have seen a thing. God knows how many people were inside the ground that afternoon. But we regularly played in front of crowds that size at Maine Road.

We were brilliant in the Cup final in 1948. I was so fortunate to play with so many great players. I left United in 1949 and went to Derby County and I tried to get Derby to play the same way as United. I used to think that all players were the same. But they're not. Derby were not good enough. They had one or two good players but they couldn't play the same football as United. That 1948 Cup final was just another game but we did have the satisfaction of playing on a good pitch. Wembley was renowned for being a fine pitch whereas most of the pitches up and down the country were just muddy and difficult to play on. A wonderful team, a wonderful game.

JOHNNY MORRIS

I was away in the Royal Navy for seven years and came back in 1946. United's ground had been bombed out, a blinking big hole in the middle of the pitch. United and City played at Maine Road on alternate Saturdays. Again there was camaraderie between the two clubs. These were the great days of football. They were there for about three years. After the War we had big crowds. You had all the people coming back from the Forces. The biggest crowd at Maine Road was eighty-four thousand for City against Stoke, I was there for that. [Manchester City v Stoke, FA Cup sixth round, 3 March 1934, attendance 84,569. This is a record for any game outside London or Glasgow.]

I remember once at Maine Road Jack Rowley was sent into the crowd by the referee. The ref had blown up for an infringement and he kicked the ball into the crowd so the referee sent him into the crowd to get the ball. 'You go and get it,' he told him. So he had to go into the crowd to retrieve the ball. This was the spirit in those days.

ALF DAVIES

About cub age I seemed to be good at soccer and I was encouraged to play. I played at centre forward in those days. I was the best out of the local clubs. That was my first recollection of playing in a team game. I played for the Boys' Brigade as an eleven-year-old. I can remember that being my first competitive season in junior football. I must have been quite good at school because they sent me for trials for the area. I always remember a lad called Charlie Tomlinson who was a year older than me getting in and I didn't. I was a couple of years younger than most of the players but I didn't think of that. I was in tears when I didn't get in and this Charlie Tomlinson, who was a better player than me at the time, got in. It was a bit of a blow to me. But the following year I got in and I became captain of Manchester Boys and then Lancashire and England Boys. In fact I captained England in 1952 as a fourteen-year-old at York City and we beat Northern Ireland five–nil and I was very proud. The following year I was captain again with Bobby Charlton in the England Schoolboys team.

My father took me to Maine Road every Saturday. He was a City fan but that didn't make any difference because United were playing there. He was really a Manchester fan. In those days you could support both teams and I supported both teams. The games that stick in my mind are not the City games but the United games. When United played Yeovil, there was a massive crowd. And we couldn't see because everybody was stood up. We were passed to the front and my father came down to the front at the end of the game when everybody had gone and collected us. That was the system. All the children were passed to the front.

I can also remember a Cup replay against Bradford and with a friend of mine, Harry Whittaker, we played truant from school. The queues for the buses to go to Maine Road were enormous, so we half ran and half walked and even then we couldn't get in because the crowds were incredible. There was a big double door by where the groundsman lived. These doors were pushed down literally, massive doors. There could have been deaths. So we went in and we still couldn't see. We walked right round the ground to the big flagpole end. I think United won five or six goals. I remember seeing a couple of them because I was on the other lad's shoulders – that was how we watched it. I was about twelve. [United won 5–0. The crowd figure is given as 70,434, 7 February 1949.] You didn't think about the dangers in those days or going at that age. My parents thought I was at school.

Other games I remember as a schoolboy must have been here at Old Trafford because they came back here in 1949. They used to take a photograph of the crowd and they used to circle you in. I was circled as a United supporter with my cap on and United scarf when they played Leeds in a Cup tie and they beat them [January 1951, United won 4–0]. John Charles played. I watched United with my scarf and coat on

38

and a rattle. I got a prize, I think it was five shillings and the photo as well. Now did I get the photo free or did I have to pay for it? Anyhow, we had to go and collect it. In fact, I've still got it.

WILF McGUINNESS

My first link with United is that as a schoolboy I was invited for a trial. And the way that they did a trial then was that they had a match that went on the whole of the afternoon, never stopped, and they just took boys on and off as they decided whether they would have another look at them. I had gone down with my father for this trial, it was about 1947, 1948. But at the end of the afternoon the match had stopped and I hadn't been invited on. So you can imagine, my dad just said, 'No way are you going to go to Old Trafford.' We didn't have any allegiance then. But Bolton were interested and I finished up there and I was there until I left university and went in the Air Force. But the funny thing was that my first game in the First Division was United against Bolton, so I knew all the lads in there.

I think going to a game was the highlight of the week for most fans. People worked five and a half days and the Saturday afternoon was the one break. On a Sunday one didn't do anything. As a young lad Sundays were hard work. So for fans it was the highlight of the week. There was limited entertainment and it was really very special. It would also be reasonably priced. On the other hand, the conditions that they tolerated on the terraces were pretty rough. But there would be a lot of friendship.

WARREN BRADLEY

In 1942 I went into the RAF and I was down in Brighton and I always remember the Preston North End centre forward and his brother used to play. He was the PT instructor. I was away until I was demobbed in 1947. And of course Busby arrived then. I didn't know anything about him except that he had played for Liverpool. I started going regularly and in 1948 I was able to get a Cup final ticket, I don't know how. Wembley was all standing in those days. United of course did not play at home then because Old Trafford had been bombed but they won every game by two clear goals and one of the greatest games I ever saw was United in the third round against Aston Villa. I went down to see that and United were winning five–one, then Villa brought it back to five–four and United scored a sixth to make it six–four. It was fantastic.

I'd come out of the Air Force and I used to go to the Lido in Sale and we formed an amateur football team, all ex-servicemen virtually, and we played these games though we weren't in a league. The German prisoners of war were based at Carrington and still hadn't gone home. There was a problem about them going back to East Germany and so – I was chairman of Lido Athletic – the Germans challenged us to a game. We said, 'OK, it'll be a bit of fun, the War's over.' One of the chaps who played against us had played for Austria as a centre forward and we got beat fifteen–nil.

I was at Maine Road when United were there. I had a season ticket there. Then I came back to Old Trafford when they cleared the stand but we sat outside in the rain. The season ticket holders, including the directors' box, were sat outside. You had to have raincoats on. There was no roof, so you were actually sat in the rain; not stood in the rain but sat in it. No roof at all, just the seats. At times you got pretty wet but you used to take a pac-a-mac.

But also arising out of being chairman of Lido Athletic, some of the United players used to come there, including Jack Rowley. Anyhow, United got to the Cup final in 1948 and I got a ticket – in fact we got tickets as a club – so I had the idea on the Friday after the Cup final, I said why don't we invite Manchester United to come to a function here and put a dinner on. To my astonishment the management agreed. All the arrangements were made and the following week the local police cancelled all leave to be at the Lido and arrangements were also made to have the Cup there. Jack Rowley then turns up at my house beforehand with the Cup. So we saw the police and they put the Cup in a police cell at the police station for safe-keeping. Well, all these people were filing in from the Town Hall to see the Cup. I even got a receipt for the Cup. We had the function and the whole team came – Matt Busby, Louis Edwards, the doctor even. It was very successful. It really consolidated my relationship with the club and I became close to them.

LORD STAN ORME

I suppose my earliest memories go back to my school days when I would be allowed by my parents to go off on my own to a football match. There was never any concern that I was in a sixty-thousand-odd crowd and I never had any concern. My schooling was through a school very near Maine Road. From the school playing fields when there was a match on at Maine Road, the crowd noise came across. I think that was an attraction to quite a few of the schoolboys and I was one of those but I soon moved on from Maine Road to Old Trafford where I felt more in love. But I've maintained an interest in City; in fact, I did have season tickets for both after being a schoolboy.

I can't remember the first game I would see but I guess that would be around 1947. I'd be about eleven or twelve. So that was obviously when United were playing at Maine Road, not at Old Trafford. I don't remember the precise game but I remember being overawed, walking into the ground and seeing a mass of people for the first time in my life. I actually think I was taken by a family friend who was an avid City fan. So probably the first game I saw was City. He always timed it. He had two seats, very upper crust he was, and he would take me on the odd occasion. And he would always time it for walking in as the teams were coming out and he used to say the cheer was for him, and not for the teams walking out. That always impressed me as a youngster. But of course he didn't take me to see the United games. But I must have gone to see my first United games in about 1948 with Jack Rowley, Charlie Mitten, those sort of days; Johnny Aston and his bandy legs, and that fantastic full-back Johnny Carey. He was a wonderful player, calm and collected. It was a good team.

I remember the 1948 Cup final because I was at school on a sports afternoon. We had entered the cricket season at school and the whole of the cricket pitches were full. Somebody somewhere had a radio and as you remember there were quite a few goals in that game and as each goal went in it was like a shockwave crossing the cricket ground where all these young teams were playing. It seemed to start at one end and take five minutes to get to the other. But it came over in waves and the excitement was terrific at the school.

But I did go to see them bringing the Cup home. My parents took me to see that. It was fabulous, the atmosphere and the camaraderie was wonderful; such good fun, no threatening aspect. I well remember the bus threading its way through. It came very late I do remember. It didn't arrive when it was expected. Great time.

I tended to be fairly low down mainly because not being a terrific size, I found that was the most comfortable for me. So I'd tended to be within ten yards of the front of all of the standing areas in those days and found that was least disturbance by the crowd. Surging by the crowd was extremely common in those days. So I tended, when I was at Old Trafford, to go further down so that the surging was going on mostly behind me, rather than where I was. It tended to be towards the corner flag of most of the games. I did have a period being half-way up the terracing. But again it was behind one of the goals at the Stretford End. I used to go quite a lot and stand in the same place because it meant you saw the

42

same people and I can remember doing that for a few years. But the majority of it was in the corners where the ground had a deep element to it behind the terracing.

I made many friendships. It was common to automatically be saying 'see you next week' and taking sandwiches with you. You automatically took some for your mate and he would bring an extra apple for you. And those were people who were acquaintances only on the terracing, you wouldn't see them any other time. I can't ever remember having experienced any particular violence. I suppose one always remembers the good things and less of the bad but I don't genuinely remember any really serious problem at all. I've never had any trouble at football matches.

MICHAEL DUNHAM

I was born in Salford and became interested in football and in this club because I was a local boy and it was the nearest club to home. The first game I can remember attending was with my father on a Boxing Day before the War. I can't remember which game, but I think it was a Second Division game against Nottingham Forest. I do remember being passed to the front of the terrace so that with other youngsters I could see over the fence. There was a wooden fence all the way around the pitch at the time and for many years after the War, just red railings and white behind the goal. I went to Maine Road once or twice during the War after the ground had been bombed, but only occasionally because we couldn't afford the fare and the entrance fee, but obviously I supported the club and read the newspapers with great interest.

I left school in 1942 and I had been playing football at school so I wrote to Walter Crickmer* who was the club secretary, asking for a trial. He wrote back and said that there was a vacancy in the club office and would I be interested, so

---

* Walter Crickmer was both club secretary and manager of United. He had spells as manager between 1931–32 and 1937–45, having been appointed as club secretary in 1926. He was killed in the Munich air disaster in 1958.

naturally I said I was very interested. I came along for an interview and he offered me the job, which of course I took. So that's how I started, doing general office jobs. I would send out the postcards to the players for the match on the Saturday, give travel instructions and the time of reporting and any correspondence, but there wasn't a great deal in those days.

I came into contact with the people who were running the two junior teams. We had an A-team who played in the Manchester League and a junior team who played in the South Manchester and Wythenshawe League. It was run first by Hamish Lockwood and later on for a long time by Jack Pauline. He acted as secretary for United juniors and attended Tuesday and Thursday evening for training, and met the players, paid expenses and looked after them on a Saturday together with Joe Travis who acted as the sponge man, the first-aid man.

There were a number of people at that time who gave their services free and worked quite hard and religiously for the club. The only full-time workers for the club were Walter Crickmer and myself. It was just the two of us running the entire club and if there were any tickets to be sold I'd sell them from here for the games at Maine Road. I also just dealt with general enquiries. When you think now . . . I think the last balance sheet showed four hundred and fifty full-time employees with the club and of course on a match day there's another thousand. So it's quite a change.

When I came the south stand was bombed and it was just left as it was after the fire with twisted steelwork around. On the other side, the end part of the north side by the corner had been hit. It was all terracing except the south side. There were incendiaries on the pitch itself but that was renovated, sowing grass and so on. But the bomb dropped in 1941 just before I started. The ground was just left. Walter Crickmer also did the mowing of the pitch. Before the War they called him Mr Manchester United; he kept the wheels turning before and during the War.

During the War we played in regional competitions and

played at Maine Road. It was Walter's job to find players to play each Saturday. There weren't many mid-week games. There were a number of players working at Trafford Park on munitions at Metro Vickers, so they were regulars. They came here training Tuesday and Thursday evenings after work. Then there were servicemen in the area, RAF and Army; then there were our own players in the services who might have been in reach, could travel and were able to play. And if there were other clubs' players in the area who didn't have a game we could invite them to play.

At the end of the War we were still at Maine Road and the Manchester City and United reserves played here at Old Trafford. It was my job to look after the visiting directors and pay the referee and linesmen and at that time we just had one adult turnstile and one junior, so I just paid the two gatemen for their services as well. That carried on until 1949 when we returned to Old Trafford. The staff that had been operating the match-day arrangements at Maine Road of course came here to do the same job, so that released me to play for the junior teams.

I went in the RAF in 1945 and came back in 1948, which was before the reserves started playing here. So I trained at the Cliff with the younger players and played on a Saturday. I was here when Matt Busby was appointed but being the junior office boy I wasn't aware of the board's decision. I knew Louis Rocca, who was chief scout at the club before the War and played a big part in attracting a lot of the young players to what was the MUJACs (Manchester United Junior Athletic Club). That was set up by Walter Crickmer and Louis Rocca before the War to attract young players, schoolboys, and they were assisted by three school teachers – Maurice Williams, his brother, and John Bill. If they saw any promising players at schoolboy level they encouraged them to come to Old Trafford. And that was carried on after the War by Sir Matt and emphasised with Bert Whalley and Jimmy Murphy [coach and assistant manager respectively]. During and before the War, Matt was with Liverpool. I think his appointment was in February '45 and he took up his duties in October '45 which was just before I went into the Air Force. It was Louis Rocca's recommendation. I think he knew him from his playing at City and Liverpool and knew his personality and strength of character. He obviously thought he was the right man for the job. The directors agreed with that and followed it up.

Louis Rocca had been at the club from a very early age doing all kinds of things. He was the chief scout and would go anywhere if he'd heard of a player or to check on a team. He was responsible for a lot of players coming to Old Trafford. He lived locally and was a real character. He wasn't tall – about five foot nine inches – stocky. I think the family were into ice-cream sales. We signed a player from Stockport County once for a bucket of ice-cream. But he was quite a character and would go to all the local grounds as well as league grounds looking for players. Sometimes he was recognised and once he was threatened with an umbrella by someone who thought he was going to steal all their best players. He had a lot of good contacts and for me as a young lad he was always a father-figure, looking after me. He had one office and I had the other office. He'd think nothing of offering me part of his lunch, or sharing his lunch even though it was special because he was a diabetic. He was around when Harry Stafford* and the dog were about and J. H. Davies put money into the club to save it. He was also about when James Gibson, Colin Gibson's father, also helped save the club, about 1931. Louis knew Harry Stafford and J. H. Davies.

We had no manager immediately before the War. Walter

* Harry Stafford, a former player and captain of United, helped save the club when it was on the verge of bankruptcy at the turn of the century. It was Stafford's dog, a St Bernard, who was helping collect money for the club which led to John Davies becoming involved with United. The dog had escaped from a fund-raising event and eventually found its way into Davies' hands. When Davies made contact with the owner, Harry Stafford, he was told the tale of United's financial crisis, whereupon Davies came to the rescue of the club.

Crickmer wasn't what you might call acting manager but he looked after the playing side with Bill Porter, the full-back; he was assistant manager. I'm not sure who picked the team. Tom Curry was the trainer and, as I say, Walter did a bit of everything. He was company secretary and he looked after the directors and board, travel arrangements, teams coming to and from, so that's how he got his nickname Mr Manchester United.

LES OLIVE

My earliest memory is of going to Old Trafford after the War with my father after it had been bombed. It was really only watching reserve team football because that's all there was at the time. One side of the ground wasn't in service at all so we only could watch on one side. You got just a few thousand going.

I also went to see United in a few games at Maine Road. I can't remember them all but I certainly remember going to the Yeovil game. I remember going to Maine Road with something like eighty-odd thousand there. All I could see of the ball was when it went up in the air, quite ridiculous really, but everybody seemed to be stood in lines, there was no pushing. Everybody was in caps, you know, typical pictures of football in the forties where everybody just stood and watched the game. You could walk through the lines as a small boy and no trouble.

My father used to take us and we always went to the Charlie Mitten corner, where Charlie Mitten used to cross the ball from, and as we got older we went further back in the stands and we watched virtually every week or every fortnight I should say, right up to my going in the Army in 1957.

HUGH JONES

You won't believe this but I started with Manchester United after I had finished with Manchester City. I had a couple of games with Manchester City. My father was on the council and he knew the City chairman and he got me a game with City. This was during the War. I think Les McDowall was the captain of City at the time. Then of course I went to finish off my air-crew training. But in the meantime I was able to get in a game or two with City. There was a fellow came to my dad's pub where I lived when I was on leave and he said, 'I want you to come down to Old Trafford for a trial.' So I went down, Johnny Carey was there, and they signed me up as a part-time professional. I was also a qualified teacher so I never played full-time.

Old Trafford had been bombed and it was in a bit of a state. I made my debut at Everton where we lost two–nil, I remember that quite distinctly. I also remember a game at Maine Road against Manchester City; Harry McShane was playing that day and he scored. I remember that because I opened my legs to let the ball go through, and Harry just put it into the net. We won two–one. We had such big crowds at games then.

Matt Busby was the manager. Whatever he told you to do, you did it. He was a great manager but the players were not frightened of him, he was never a bully or anything like that. Jimmy Murphy was there as well, he was a likely lad. I saw more of him because invariably I was playing in the reserve side and he was looking after them more. I used to go down and train in an evening. I'd go down straight after teaching at school, on a Tuesday and Thursday. On a Tuesday we trained at the Cliff and on a Thursday at Old Trafford itself.

When we went away with the reserves we rarely stayed overnight. But I do remember going to play Newcastle reserves at Newcastle and we'd stayed overnight. We'd gone up on the Friday. On the Saturday morning we went to have a look at Durham Cathedral. When we got back to the hotel, who should be in the hotel but Manchester City. I think they were playing Middlesbrough. We were having a bit of a giggle at them. They were asking us what we were doing in a hotel. 'You shouldn't be here,' they said.

I have never had that view that United was connected in any way to the Catholic church. The only thing I ever knew was that when we were having a team talk, Matt would tell anyone who was swearing to stop it immediately. He didn't like that. 'Oi, that's enough of that,' he'd say. He didn't stand for any swearing. But I don't think it was Catholic or non-Catholic. There was a mix of players. Harold Hardman was chairman then and I'm pretty sure he wasn't a Catholic.

When I was teaching at St Patrick's I was team manager of Manchester Boys and I had some good lads come through that team. Brian Kidd was one of them. He was at our school, St Patrick's. He was an intelligent lad. I still see him and he always makes me smile; he still calls me Mr Cassidy, never Laurie, or Laurence, always Mr Cassidy.

LAURENCE CASSIDY

I remember Wembley, 1948: there was a guy with a bell. Now all you had in them days was a bell and the old wartime gas rattles. And this bell came off the handle and hit a bloke on the head. He was in a real bad way. This was in Wembley itself. I got a ticket off a guy called Jimmy who had a lot of contacts. He got the tickets. I think I paid about five shillings.

We got a train and I borrowed some money. My mother was against my going. My father was dead by then but my mother didn't want me to go. 'Ooh London, no, you know what they're like down there,' she said. It was just a day trip, couldn't afford to stay overnight. It would have cost an arm and a leg in those days. It was a very exciting game. Even to this day they reckon it was a classic. At the time they were the only team to be behind twice and come back and win.

I remember going to Blackpool some ten years after and I went to buy a paper and who was there but Stan Mortensen [Blackpool and England centre forward who scored in the final against Manchester United]. I asked him, how did he manage that second goal and he said, 'I don't know, I just hit

49

it, that's all you can do and let the goalkeeper wonder where it's going to go.' All players in those days when they retired became either newsagents or publicans.

JOE DILLON

After the Army I went straight back to Old Trafford. By then we used to stand under the centre stand on the Popular side which is now the big modern stand. My two brothers and myself, my father and friends, we just used to meet at the same spot. You used to pay your money and come in. I was there the day under the centre stand when United were playing Arsenal and the fog came down. You couldn't see a thing. They never played the game. It was one murderous task to get out of the ground to get one of these vouchers to get us in for the replay. Never forget that one. It was just unbelievable. People were just giving up in the end and not bothering about the voucher.

We used to get the bus but we had to queue for hours. The queues to get back on the bus were enormous because then everybody went by bus. Very few people went by cars. Trams had gone by then.

We had gambling syndicates with the people around us on the terraces. We used to have a draw for the first goal. We used to put the ten forwards in from both teams because we didn't think anybody else would ever score, only the forward line, and then we'd have a draw. A shilling in or something like that and the first goal won the money. We'd put the names in a hat, in a cap. You'd put all the forwards in, draw them out.

But what was most interesting was that you could be stood next to, say it was Arsenal, you'd be stood next to an Arsenal supporter and he'd be there and he'd be telling you about his team. And he'd say, 'Who have you got next week and what are they like?' and you'd be chatting and discussing and you come out and you could say, 'We played bloody awful, we deserved to get beat.' There was never all this jumping up and down, 'Hit them, kill them'. This is why I never go any more: I can't stand this aggression. All they're looking at is one side, one colour. I've got the opportunity, we have season tickets. I just can't stand the aggression of this wanting to fight everybody if they've lost. They can't see that football's a game of two sides playing a skilful game and if one is better than the other you put your hands up and say that. And today we can't do that any more.

The worst thing was when the crowds, big crowds, the United supporters, they used to go to the end where United were kicking into and at half time they'd all move round and it was unbelievable. You had plenty of room and all of a sudden you couldn't breathe because you could walk from one side to the other round the Popular side, but you couldn't walk round the stands. You could walk round from Stretford End round United Road, inside the ground and choose anywhere you want; unbelievable. And everybody would go to the end United were kicking into and so you got to that end and you couldn't breathe. There was no such thing as away and home, everybody was together.

We used to get the one o'clock bus and be in the ground for about half-past one and stand until three o'clock kick-off. You didn't drink because it was difficult getting in and out. You hear tales of people urinating down terraces; I never saw any of that at Old Trafford. I used to come straight from work on a Saturday because I used to work Saturday mornings, because in them days you had to. Working in Manchester I used to get the bus in and go straight in and find them on the terraces, probably still in my working clothes.

In them days though they were fairly evenly split between City. In them days City weren't a bad side. There was also the Beswick Prize Band and everybody had to shout 'Throw it up'. The drum major, he used to have a stick going round like this; we wanted him to throw it up in the air like he used to do. The Beswick Prize Band, aye they were good. They'd walk round playing at half time. That was the whole of the entertainment. I can't really remember anything like snack bars or hot dogs, there was nothing like that.

HUGH JONES

It must have been late forties, early fifties, when I went to my first game. It was against Spurs. I remember Jack Rowley in particular, making a real fool of who was later to become Sir Alf Ramsey. Even in those days Ramsey was seen as someone who was perhaps middle-class, too posh to be a professional footballer. He always had his collar buttoned right up to the neck, never swore as far as I knew. Jack Rowley really enjoyed that game by taking the mickey out of him in a gentle way, by putting him in his place. He had his nose put out of joint that day. Ramsey was an England stalwart. I think Rowley must then have been mid to late career and he was later to move into management. But that was a good day. I don't remember the result. I was perhaps five or seven at the oldest.

I remember the elation, the slight apprehension, and real fear coming out of the ground. In those days the only way out of Old Trafford was over the bridge and when you consider there were sixty to sixty-five thousand people all trying to pour out at the same time, it was quite alarming for someone of my size to be in amongst so many people. But it was something which stayed with me forever. It was a good day.

People got to the ground on Football Specials. Virtually every bus going from Wythenshawe where I lived in those days from perhaps one onwards had *Match* on it. We all knew where it was going. As far as dress, we all wore grey, we all wore black. There were no club colours apart from scarves and rattles, which made a terrible noise. Flat caps, nearly everybody wore a hat of some sorts. If it wasn't a flat hat, it was a trilby. Even I wore my school cap. Bizarre.

The ground looked a grey-black. There was no colours. The only splash of colour really was the railings around the ground which were white, which you still see in a lot of old photos. The terraces, behind them, were painted red and the big scoreboard behind, which was there until the seventies. But very awe-inspiring. They call it the Theatre of Dreams now which sounds a bit grandiose but it is believable.

I couldn't go regularly because my father worked as a chemist, but when he got Saturdays off and United were at home we went. If City were at home sometimes we went there. In those days it was quite common to go to both clubs. People accepted that you were a United supporter. There'd be a little banter, a few minor insults but there was nothing violent and you went to enjoy the game of football, not to do City down or denigrate them in any way. Good days.

GEORGE REYNOLDS

United got huge crowds at Maine Road. In 1948 we had eighty-two thousand for the Arsenal game. Now that's a League record. And of course the FA Cup record was eighty-four thousand for Manchester City against Stoke. So that ground has both records. Now Yeovil in the FA Cup, that was the biggest crowd ever. A gate was pushed down, it just collapsed and there was thousands coming in without paying. It wasn't frightening. I was OK. It wasn't near me but I could see it. I would think there must have been ninety thousand at that match.

I remember an incident at Old Trafford after the War. They used to run out a minute before time, long ball into the middle and that was it, they'd kick off. One day at Old Trafford, five to three and United came out. Everybody's checking their watches, and United came out with three balls. We said, 'What's this?' It was a simple thing Mr Busby introduced to football. Get a bit warmed up before the game. Everybody was talking; 'What's this, why have they got three balls?' Simple, isn't it? Mr Busby brought it into football.

JOE DILLON

I was basically in what you might say was the enemy territory: I lived in Moss Side. The first game I saw at Manchester United was roughly 1947, can't think who it was, but I can tell you that it was Jimmy Delaney's debut and I went along with my dad. I think United won and Jimmy Delaney missed a penalty. He was probably noted for being a bit of a diver in the penalty area. Ever since that date I've always had a strong association with Manchester United. I saw the first game back here, I think 1949.* I wasn't in the Stretford Road End for that, I was in the Warwick Road End. Since then I've been strong Manchester United. I've been in the Warwick Road and before that in the Stretford Road. I got a season ticket in B-stand. But now I don't need a season ticket, I watch the game from somewhere else.

I've been to nearly all the Cup finals. I went to the '48 Cup final. I went to the '57 final but not the '58; I went to '63, the one with Tommy Doc and the ones since. I've basically gone with my father. I always went with my father. He saw the game here, I think it was against Bradford, which had they lost they would have gone into the Third Division.

Another game I saw here was when we played Arsenal in the Cup and I'll never forget it because in those days the police were great, they never bothered. They had the Beswick Street Prize Band marching around and an Arsenal supporter jumped on the pitch and marched along with the drum major with an umbrella and everything the drum major did, the Arsenal supporter did. When he threw the stick up, he threw the umbrella up, and when he marched, swinging it, he swung the umbrella and there was no problem, the police did nothing. We used to have a man running round with a wooden leg and he used to stand on the corner, whip his leg off and hop round, all the way around the pitch with a red and white scarf on. I don't know where he came

---

* After Old Trafford had been bombed in March 1941 United were forced to play at Maine Road. They returned to Old Trafford on 24 August 1949 when they beat Bolton Wanderers 3–0 in front of 41,748.

from or where he went, but he used to do it.

I found that in the forties and fifties people looked after you, especially the children. I went to see Manchester United play Yeovil Town. I went there on the Wednesday afternoon. I think there might have been eighty-four thousand at Maine Road. I also saw them play Arsenal at Maine Road and I think Arsenal won one–nil, but people then looked after people. The policemen treated people in a different manner as well; they gave people a bit of respect. They'd pick you up – I was picked up and passed over the heads and put on to the pitch; they lift you up and pass you along. They wouldn't do that now, they'd tell you to bugger off and stand somewhere else. That's a sad reflection on the times we're in. The aggression was not there then.

DANNY McGREGOR

Those players in the late forties, early fifties were, to a lad like me, just giant heroes. Jack Rowley, Johnny Carey, slippery Charlie Mitten. Let me tell you about Charlie Mitten.

Charlie Mitten, who's still alive I do believe, was probably one of the finest wingers I ever saw and there were a lot of good wingers in those days. Cheeky chappie Charlie Mitten he used to be known as, bit of a spiv, Charlie Mitten, he used to be. There were tales of him, when he eventually went to be manager of Newcastle United, of players being unable to get on the treatment table because Charlie's greyhounds, which he owned and operated and ran at race meetings, were being treated on the treatment table in preference to players. It wouldn't surprise me if it was true.

Charlie Mitten once scored a hat-trick of penalties. You tell me whether you have seen anybody in a major game score three penalties. Well, I did. Charlie Mitten against, I think, Aston Villa on a Wednesday afternoon. I'd wagged off school which was not my normal habit, but I'd wagged off school to go to this game and Mitten scored three penalties [March

1950; United won 7–0]. Not only did he score a hat-trick of penalties, which I think in itself is unusual, he pointed each time to the goalkeeper to the corner where he was going to slide rule his shot. They were always low and each one went precisely where he'd told the goalkeeper he was going to put them and the goalkeeper didn't get near any of them. Charlie Mitten was that good.

An interesting historical sideline about Charlie Mitten. Some people will remember, others won't, that United went to play some games, or possibly England did, in South America and Charlie Mitten decided to stay on in Bogotá and was signed up by a South American club and stayed there two or three years, a couple of seasons. He was banned almost indefinitely by the Football Association because he wasn't honouring his contract at Old Trafford. He just stayed on and made money, because Charlie was like that, and when he came back he was unable to play. Did Charlie ever play for United again? Pass. I'd have to look at boring old dusty record books for that, but that's the sort of character and personality that Charlie Mitten was. [Mitten never played for United again. On his return from Colombia he was immediately transfer-listed by United and in January 1952 moved to Fulham.]

Jack Rowley was my big hero and when I was working on the local paper, the *Sale Guardian*, I once managed to persuade my local editor that I should go and interview my hero. I didn't tell him that, I just said, 'Jack Rowley lives in Sale and he's going to Australia with the England party and I think we should do a feature about him.' So I went to his house, went quaking to meet my hero and I interviewed him and his wife. Jack was going off that week for I think three to four weeks and I deliberately left my winter gloves at his house so I could have an excuse to go back when he came back and meet him for a second time. I was that desperate. And in those days before I met him, on my way to work, I'd go deliberately early so that I could see Jack Rowley's car pass by at about half-past nine, just so that I could tell my mates that night that I'd seen Jack again, and his car in 1950-ish was a Standard Ensign, I think it was called, and the registration number was HGU 924. If you asked me if I could remember the registration number of my own car when I first got one many years later after that, no way, but I've never forgotten Jack's; HGU 924.

He's currently very ill in a nursing home in north Manchester which is very sad but he was a wonderful centre forward, a wonderful, wonderful centre forward. I once saw Alf Ramsey, playing for Spurs I suppose, tread all over Jack Rowley's chest. Jack Rowley fell down, Alf Ramsey walked over his chest with those huge heavy studs and I never liked Alf Ramsey from that moment because he trampled deliberately on my hero's chest. 'Bastard Ramsey' I thought at the time and nothing I've seen or heard of him since has altered that view one bit. 'Bastard Ramsey.'

BOB GREAVES

My all time favourite footballer was Stan Pearson. He was an inside forward, he was the creator. Jack Rowley, the centre forward, got most of the credit because he banged in the goals. He was daunting to watch. They had a move – I can remember it to this day – the goalkeeper would clear the ball and Stan Pearson would chest it down and Rowley would be running and he'd be on to it and through to goal. Stan was the creator along with Johnny Morris, the other inside forward. Those two made the 1948 side what they were. But we mustn't forget the captain, the full-back Johnny Carey, to this day one of the best full-backs ever. He was so unassuming. There were no raucous shouts like you used to get from Peter Schmeichel. Carey would just run across and have a quiet word. By his attitude he got the best out of his players. I saw United get three penalties and Charlie Mitten – he was the penalty taker – he took all three and put them all in the same place each time. On the third occasion he pointed to the goalkeeper and told him where he was going to put it. I had a chance to speak to him later and I asked him what was his method. He said if you aim for the stanchion inside the goal, either stanchion, and hit it reasonably hard, no goalkeeper in the world will save it. And that's what he did. He was the master of penalties, was Charlie.

ALBERT THORPE

CHAPTER THREE

The Fifties

The Busby Babes

United's post-war squad slipped gently into decline in the early fifties. Busby's side had enjoyed a phenomenal run: second, second, second, fourth and second in successive years from 1947 until they finally clinched the title in 1952. They had also won the FA Cup in style.

That side had served Busby and Manchester well but the years were catching up with them. Many of the players were now aged thirty and over; some like Johnny Carey and John Aston had been around since before the War. From champions in 1952, United dropped to eighth place the following season. Hardly a disaster, but enough for Busby to realise that a new team had to be constructed. It needed almost a total clear-out. New players had to be found and perhaps new styles adopted, although there were already one or two bright enough prospects plying their trade with the reserves and youth team.

One was full-back Roger Byrne, the obvious man around whom to shape the new formation. He'd come into the side during the 1951–52 Championship season and although he was still only in his early twenties, he showed a character and maturity way beyond his years; he was the ideal man to replace Carey as Busby's leader on the field. But even with Byrne in place, the changes were not going to happen overnight. The reconstruction would take a few years. Yet as United played out those early years in the fifties, a minor revolution was taking place elsewhere at Old Trafford.

Busby had been quietly grooming a youth side. During the 1952–53 season his youngsters had gone on to win the newly created FA Youth Cup for the first time in cavalier style, slamming in nine goals over two legs. In the first game at Old Trafford they had won 7–1 in front of a rapturous and remarkable crowd of almost 21,000.

Busby was so impressed by their maturity and god-kissed skill that they were quickly promoted and given their chance. Here, reckoned Busby, were a bunch of lads around whom he could possibly build a side for the future, and with so many of them so young they could easily be playing together for the next ten years or so. It was worth a try. And so, one by one the youngsters were gradually promoted. Ten of that Youth Cup-winning side – Colman, Edwards, Whelan, Pegg, Scanlon, Clayton, Kennedy, Cope, McFarlane and Lewis – would go on to play for United's first eleven. Not all were by any means successful but certainly half a dozen would become regulars, three of them eventually representing their country at senior level. During the 1952–53 season David Pegg, Dennis Viollet and Bill Foulkes were all thrown their chance. But the star of them all was a giant of a lad from Dudley in the West Midlands. Still only sixteen, he was already thirteen stone and standing six foot tall when Busby introduced him to first team football in April 1953. He would soon become England's youngest ever international. Naturally blessed with strength, speed and courage, he would roll the elastic of his shorts around his waist so that he could display his bulging thighs all the more. Duncan Edwards was to be the essential cog of the machine. If Byrne was the leader, Edwards was the fulcrum.

But as the 1953 Youth Cup side moved upwards to take their places among the seniors, others quickly slotted into their places. It seemed to make little difference; the youth side just went out and won the Cup again, this time with a crop of new faces, among them Bobby Charlton and Wilf McGuinness. So it went on until they had claimed it five years in succession. Busby had produced a conveyor belt of astonishing talent, and the more the youngsters excelled, the more the nation's youth wanted to join the ranks at United.

At the end of the 1953–54 season United had climbed into fourth spot. By then they had added a few signings to their ranks, including another young lad, Tommy Taylor, signed from Barnsley for almost £30,000. Taylor was the final piece in the jigsaw, a centre forward in the new style – not just a powerful goalscorer, but skilful as well. It was all beginning to come together. It was rock and roll football. They finished fifth the following season and then in 1956 clinched the first of their titles. A year later they were champions again and came within a whisker of lifting the Double. Only an appalling injury to goalkeeper Ray Wood in the final against Aston Villa prevented then from becoming the first team this century to achieve the Double. That season they netted a staggering 142 goals in all competitions. The romance of United had been born.

They had also become the first English team to enter the newly created European Cup. Champions Chelsea had been given the opportunity a year earlier but, under pressure from the FA, had politely declined. Nobody was going to tell Busby what he could do. It didn't take long for everyone to realise that here was a competition that combined all the romance of football with the finest of competition. In their first season United took Europe by storm, with a series of gloriously memorable victories before they finally succumbed to the mighty Real Madrid. Against the Belgian champions Anderlecht at Maine Road they slammed in ten goals, leaving the Anderlecht captain groping for words to describe United. Next in line were Borussia Dortmund, beaten 3–2 beneath the glare of the Maine Road floodlights. That set up a thriller with Spanish champions Bilbao. In a rare Spanish snowstorm United lost the first leg 5–3. Back home they faced the impossible, but roared on by a crowd of over 70,000 they trounced the Spanish club 3–0 to set up a semi-final against

European champions Real Madrid. Wilf McGuinness, a spectator at that game, still regards it as the most exciting and dramatic match he has ever seen.

United looked on course for the Treble but in the first leg at the Bernabeu stadium in Madrid, before a crowd of 125,000, they lost 3–1. They might have pulled back a two-goal deficit against Bilbao, but this was Real Madrid, the very best. And so, playing under the recently switched-on Old Trafford floodlights, they could only salvage a 2–2 draw and were out of the hunt. But it had been a memorable, often inspired foray into Europe, that not only gave United fans their first taste of European action but set in motion a dream that would one day become a reality.

Europe and the youngsters captured the imagination and a new generation of fans came on board, many of them inspired by the skills of teenagers only a few years older than themselves. For the first time English fans also followed their team across Europe. It was an adventure, discovering new countries, being ambassadors for their club. The future looked bright. Then came the tragedy of Munich.

It is of course, in the mists of time and given the dreadful circumstances, all too easy to romanticise the deeds of the Busby Babes. The living only recall the good that the dead did. Journalist Frank Taylor, who survived the Munich disaster, admits that captain Roger Byrne could sometimes be 'cocky' while that doyen of football reporters, Henry Rose, once argued that 'If Tommy Taylor is the best centre forward in England, I'll eat my hat.' And yet the Busby Babes overcame all reservations. Taylor undoubtedly had his critics but 128 goals in 189 appearances for United speaks for itself while 16 goals in 19 appearances for his country suggests that he could score at the highest level. Surprisingly, even those fans interviewed here recall that the Babes could often be as frustrating as they were inspirational. But about Duncan Edwards everyone agrees: he was simply the best.

By now the post-war years of austerity were giving way to

stability and increasing wealth. Luxury consumer goods were flooding on to the market. There were radios, televisions and even cars. Employment was at an all-time high. Everyone had a job as Britain worked its way out of the ruin of war and Europe was on everyone's lips. A European Common Market had been formed, and although Britain had declined membership, opportunities to travel in Europe were opening up for almost everybody. Fans not only travelled to Europe to watch United but were now buying televisions and cars. The televising of the 1953 Cup final was a landmark in television sport as a vast audience sat mesmerised in front of their newly acquired television sets. Manchester was lucky; City and United would feature in four Cup finals in the mid-fifties.

Travel to away games was becoming more frequent, although most still relied on public transport. Few walked to Old Trafford any more. They could afford the bus or train, and even a programme. Everyone was out to enjoy themselves, not least the Babes.

Because they were so young, and because so many of them hailed from Manchester itself, it was common to see the Babes about town. Unlike today, they did not hide away in expensive clubs or flash past in fast cars. They dressed in their drainpipe trousers, trilbies and velvet-collared jackets and frequented the same coffee bars, picture houses and dance halls as their fans. The Babes lived ordinary lives. They could be spotted on the bus, walking down the street or in the newsagents. Nobody bothered them. There might be the occasional nudge, or an autograph hunter, but the public were generally happy to let them get on with their lives. The only thing that ever worried the players was that somebody might tell the boss they had been spotted out late at night.

The Babes, as they were dubbed by Tom Jackson in the *Manchester Evening News* as early as 1951, brought a refreshing glow to post-war football. It was the beginning of a new era in English soccer. Matthews, Finney and Mortensen might play on a little longer but they would somehow always be associated with those grey, weary war years. Taylor, Edwards, Byrne and company represented something new. These were the beginnings of the years of youth, the rock and roll years. Who knows what the Babes might have achieved?

<hr />

I joined United in 1953. Both Bobby Charlton and I came here in the same week – Coronation week – we signed as amateurs. Bobby and I have been friends ever since. We used to go on holidays together when we were teenagers, Duncan, Gordon Clayton, so on. We were all friends. Coming to United was so different to school games. Jimmy Murphy* would say, 'You're not at school now, son.' He was the hard man, the man who polished us up, along with Bert Whalley.†

I didn't have a trial – didn't need one (*laughs*), sorry about that! I played with England Schoolboys and several clubs wanted to sign us. I still have newspaper cuttings saying these two boys will make it to the top and we were only fifteen then. We didn't really believe that. When we came here the first thing I thought was, so many good players, how am I going to get through this lot? The biggest influence was Jimmy Murphy who bullied you if you needed bullying or gave you sugar if you needed sugar. He got the best out of us. Mind you, there were some great players about and it rubs off. I was a full international by the age of twenty, which was pretty good. Whether I would have done that if the crash had not happened is a different story because I was the understudy to Duncan Edwards. At times they moved Duncan to let me in and I had a Championship medal by the age of nineteen. So I was a successful youth player. Then after the accident I didn't play right away because

---

* Jimmy Murphy was assistant manager of Manchester United under Matt Busby. Following the Munich disaster he took over as manager until Matt Busby could return.
† Bert Whalley, a former United player (1935–47), was appointed to the coaching staff where he remained until his death in the Munich disaster.

I had a cartilage operation which had stopped me going on the flight. I was fortunate not to go on that.

There was a terrific bond between us all. None of us had cars at the start, although we were teenagers when we got cars. Don't forget we were here from fifteen years of age. Bobby and I both had jobs – he went into engineering and I went into textiles in town, but only until we were seventeen and then we turned professional. When we were sixteen we went with the Manchester United youth team to Switzerland to play in a tournament, our first flight abroad, playing foreign teams. It was all new to us, staying in an hotel, learning new cultures. We were ordinary lads who didn't know the etiquette. But we learnt together, and winning together helped bond us, winning the FA Youth Cup five years on the row. We went on holidays together, Butlin's and places like that. Most footballers used to go there in our day. We'd bump into Jimmy Melia, the Liverpool player, and several Merseyside players. We had a bond with those lads as well. There was Jimmy Tarbuck as well. We didn't have cars so we'd meet in town and then rush for the all-night bus. If you missed the all-night bus then it was a walk home; nobody thought of taxis in those days.

Our big day out was a Monday after the game on Saturday. Behind here at the Stretford End was dirt and cinders and we used to play round there all Monday morning which was a perk, instead of running round the track. It was twenty-a-side, kicking the ball around, having fun. Then we used to go to Davyhulme Golf Club. We'd cadge a lift off some of the older players or we got the bus. We got a free lunch; they also paid for our fees to play golf in the afternoon or if it was bad weather we'd play snooker or cards. We had our evening meal there as well which was wonderful – two meals a day for free instead of having to go into Manchester and pay for them in a café. And then we used to go into Manchester and go into the pictures where if we showed our club pass we got in for nothing. Monday was the best day of the week without a shadow of a doubt.

In those days the players had £12, £14 or £16 depending on your age until you got to £20 which was the top wage. But you got £2 for a win and £1 for a draw and we won most games so we were doing OK. Tuesday was a good day because we could play a practice game on the main pitch instead of going to the Cliff. We used to use it that much that there was only grass on the corners by April. The last eight or ten games was played on dry dust. It was a big diamond shape of dust by the end of the season.

Then there was the Army, national service. I missed it through ill health. Nobody wanted to go in the Army. There wasn't a war on and it just seemed to interfere with your training. David Pegg and I didn't make it. Bobby Charlton, Eddie Colman, Duncan Edwards, Tommy and Gordon Clayton all went in. They got £1 a week wages from the club; it was ridiculous. You couldn't possibly manage on it. Because I didn't go in meant I trained here and I got in the first team before Bobby Charlton, Eddie Colman, even though they were older than me.

Tuesday was also a good night to go out if we didn't have a game on the Wednesday so we went to the dance halls, the Plaza. We all went together and stood in the corner like ordinary lads growing up, bit of a snogging session if we were lucky, maybe see them again, maybe not. That was it.

I can always remember going in the odd pub when we won the Youth Cup; I was seventeen, eighteen. It was lager and lime, no drinking really. We realised there was more to life than football. Matt Busby had to pull us up when we got older and said, 'Now lads, I'm hearing stories about you all going into town, drinking and things like this. If you have one drink, by the time the stories reach me, it's eight.' So he said, 'If you want a drink, get out of town. I don't mind you having a drink, go to somewhere like Glossop.' So we went to Glossop and we finished up having an all-night party which did us more harm than going down town. Somebody recognised us and that was it.

As we got older we got recognised but people didn't make a fuss of us. When we went training it was on the bus until I got a car. I'd pick my mate Eddie Colman up because he didn't have a car; I was a first-teamer, he was a reserve. I'd drive through Salford from Blackley, pick him up and there was a swing bridge and if we were late we always made the excuse the bridge was closed. All the lads in digs used to come to our house, it was open house; our parents were proud to have us there. Fish and chips on a Friday and then into town for the cinema, first house and back before ten. That was Friday night before the game. And Saturday night if we weren't courting we'd go into Manchester, either the cinema or the dance hall. Usually if we were courting it was the cinema because we didn't need to look for a girlfriend. Many's the time we'd be in there and all of a sudden you'd hear 'ahhh' and a big 'ughhh', and people suddenly standing up. It was footballers with cramp, in the thigh or the hamstring. You'd say, 'There's Colin Barlow of City', or 'There's Duncan, he's in here tonight.' You'd see players standing up with cramp because we didn't have any warm-downs as they do now, so we got cramp.

People used to say it's a Catholic club but I didn't notice this. We all palled out together and we didn't say, 'Oh, you're a Catholic, you're not'; we didn't see it that way at all. They might have done in the old days. Matt was a Catholic, Jimmy Murphy was a Catholic but Les Olive wasn't, nor was Walter Crickmer; the directors weren't either. Certainly we used to get a lot of priests at games and Davyhulme Golf Club on a Monday had Catholic priests there. We used to mix with them there. But we also used to pal out with the Jewish lads as well. We used to go to coffee places like Lyons or the Kardomha and drink coffee, or Lewis's for a few hours, chat up any gorgeous girls. We mixed in with everybody. Nobody thought of religion or race being different.

WILF McGUINNESS

When I played for the reserves the crowds weren't too big, just a couple of thousand. But just prior to the accident the reserve team would have six or seven internationals in it and they attracted big crowds. Also, earlier than that, the youth team had attracted big crowds. When the FA started the national youth competition we won it for the first five years with the Busby Babes coming through. The reputation was there locally. I think we played Blackburn Rovers and had thirty-three thousand at the semi-final in the FA Youth Cup. Our strong rivals then were Wolverhampton Wanderers with Stan Cullis [manager]. They had a particularly good youth team then so we had a couple of games with them which attracted big crowds and which we won. On one occasion we beat Nantwich twenty-two–nil at the Cliff. All the Busby Babes played in that – Edwards, Bobby Charlton. Of course at that time there were not many grounds with floodlights, but we had put floodlights on our training ground at the Cliff, so we had about five thousand spectators because the floodlights were also a novelty at that time. We didn't get them at Old Trafford until much later.

LES OLIVE

I used to see them regularly. I'd often see them on the bus. Duncan Edwards used to live in Gorse Avenue, he lived with Gordon Clayton. You'd see them around town, especially in the clubs on Saturday nights – Albert Scanlon, Dennis Viollet, see all of them. They were famous but they weren't superstars like today. Of course they weren't as good, not as fit, but any of those top players would have adapted to the fast game of today. They all lived nearby; a lot of them who were not married lived in digs at Chorlton, some lived near Busby in Kings Road. Of course it was very posh up there in Chorlton. Even later, you could go into the Bull in Salford and George Best was always in there. Then there was the Spare Wheel. You'd find Tommy Taylor, Duncan Edwards, Dennis Viollet in there. And also the Quadrant. They nearly all went in there, but not Charlton. I don't think he bothered. The word used to be that Tommy Taylor only drank tonic water but the tonic water was never put on the bar; it was always kept under the bar and he'd get his refill under the bar. The story was that there was always plenty of gin going in. You'd see them at the dance halls – the Ritz, the Plaza, Sale Locarno. Every Sunday night you'd see Duncan Edwards in there. Then there was the incident with the water pistol. Bobby Charlton was in on it. There was Charlton and a couple of others. They got these water pistols, got in a taxi and were squirting water at pedestrians. Then they got on a bus and did the same thing. They were hauled over the coals for that by Busby.

JOE DILLON

We used to run at the Stretford End behind the goal where the players come out. Above the corner it was wooden. How there was never an accident I'll never know. If the weather was bad or it was muddy we used to do runs all along the back. It was a good eighty to a hundred yards at the back. It was wooden and springy; it was nice to run on. We used to train up there. Then it used to drop down, there was only half the Stretford End, it didn't go right to the back as it does now. There was a little stand opposite the main stand which is now the North Stand with a little hut on it. The stand was about forty yards and the sides were empty. At the Manchester End all there was was a scoreboard; it was sometimes known as the scoreboard end. And then there was the stand we are in at the moment with pillars and girders and this didn't go back anything like it does today. Where the tunnel is here there were a couple of huts. All this was bombed of course and they left that for a while. When they first came back here they changed in huts outside and had to walk fifteen, twenty yards under the stand. So if the spectators were out they would see them. Then they built the dressing rooms here and this became a modern stand, but there were still the girders.

I played in the first game here under lights against Bolton Wanderers and we played in a shiny kit [25 March 1957 in front of a crowd of 60,862]. We didn't like the lights though. We didn't like anything like that: we lost two–nil. Lofthouse flattened me a couple of times. Twenty thousand were locked out, crowds going way back into Salford for the first game under lights. But it's a magnificent stadium now. Some people don't want change but you've got to have change – just look at this stadium now.

WILF McGUINNESS

I saw them grow up and related to them, in the sense that they were my similar age group. There were some super players. I can remember once being on a bus going along Chester Road at the top of Warwick Road, before it was Sir Matt Busby Way. I can't remember why I was on a bus, but it was mid morning and I saw Duncan Edwards and he'd obviously just been training. He was carrying his boots, he was in shorts, he had a top on and I can remember being staggered that I'd not noticed on the pitch, when I'd seen him play, the actual size of his thighs. This was walking along past a bus stop. This was an ordinary young fella and nobody took much notice of him. I recognised him instantly and was staggered by the size of this guy's legs and the obvious power and strength in such a young chap.

Generally I have to say everybody remembers how wonderful they were. They were terrific but they did lose games as well. I do recall more than once being dissatisfied with their performance, but they did seem to turn it on when it was the European scene and the bigger matches. They seemed to be more able to turn on a good performance. But I can recall Duncan Edwards, for example, playing centre forward and it was obviously experimental in some form or other, and he wasn't that good in that sort of position. But in the middle of

70

the field, I think he was terrific. He was a tower of strength.

I went to some of the Youth Cup games right at the very beginning when they were coming through. I used to enjoy those because there was so much space in the ground and obviously pretty good crowds were still going to those as that team was coming through. But it was far more spacious and it wasn't the struggle to get across the railway bridge as it was for a full first team. But yeah, I enjoyed the youngsters coming through because again I was a similar age so I could relate to that. I suppose it was that era that really cemented me with the club, and it's never gone away.

MICHAEL DUNHAM

I arrived at Manchester United in January 1953. Manchester was a big, dirty city in those days. It was forbidding in many ways coming to such a big city. But I didn't have any fear. It was a big adventure for me. I just wanted to play professional football and if that meant going to a big place like Manchester, then so be it. United had the best set-up, they had a terrific reputation with young players and that was principally why I came. I didn't have a trial or anything like that. United came in for me. I'd played for England Schoolboys and had been spotted by them. A number of clubs were after me but United were in first. But I was always going to be attracted by them. That's where I wanted to go. They'd won the first FA Youth Cup and went on to win it five years in a row with myself in that team. They had so many good young players on their books – Duncan Edwards, Eddie Colman, David Pegg and so on. I was just fifteen when I came, but as I say, I wasn't at all frightened; I just wanted to play football. I'd be a lot more frightened today if I was a fifteen-year-old coming to a big city like Manchester.

I lodged in a big house close to the ground. It was no more than a mile from Old Trafford. Of course in those days none of us had cars, we went everywhere by public transport, so our digs had to be near the ground. Most of the time we would walk to and from Old Trafford. There were twelve of us in this house. Remember that I was an amateur at first. I couldn't turn professional until I was seventeen, so I had to get myself a job. I worked as an electrical engineer in Altrincham for eighteen months, then I turned professional.

Old Trafford was very different then. There was only one end that was covered and that was the main stand. The Stretford End and the City End were both open and there was just a small covering on the north stand. I used to train at Old Trafford every day. We had a little hut outside the ground where we would go for treatment. That's how basic it was in those days. Then I would go to the Cliff to train on a Tuesday and Thursday evening.

Being a footballer then was not like it is now. The fans and the media were not as intrusive. We had to travel everywhere by bus but you didn't get hassled like players would now. We could go anywhere. I'd go to games at Maine Road, Bolton or Birmingham, get a ticket and stand on the terraces. No player could do that these days. We just mixed in with everybody. Of course we didn't have much spare time. I worked from 8 a.m. to 5.30 p.m. and then went to train. We didn't have much money either. But we would occasionally go to the pictures on a Monday or a Wednesday evening, down town, or to some coffee bar. But because we didn't have the money we didn't have a lot of choice, usually just the pictures.

My first game for the first team was against Charlton Athletic at Old Trafford [6 October 1956]. We won four–two and I scored twice. I'd been injured for about three weeks and Matt Busby came to me on the Friday before the game and asked me how the injury was. I'd been scoring quite a few goals in the reserves and, thinking he might be about to pick me, I said the ankle was OK. It wasn't really but in the end it didn't matter. After that I was in and out of the team for a while, depending on injuries to others. Then in 1958 I finally won my place. Old Trafford was an exciting place to be. We had the best team and we were playing in Europe and that was a fantastic adventure. Every game was a sell-out with huge crowds, especially for the European games. Even the youth team was drawing huge crowds to Old Trafford. It was a fabulous time.

SIR BOBBY CHARLTON

I was very young when I first came here and the only reason I know the date is because I kept the programme for my first game. It was in March 1952 when United played Wolves. It was the pre-Munich side. I don't remember a lot about the game but I went with my parents and went in the directors' box. I really started following United after the Munich crash because my father went on the board the day after the crash. The crash happened on the sixth of February and on the seventh of February he was co-opted on to the board. In those days I was at boarding school but obviously when I came home for holidays I started going to watch them, so I became a regular supporter in the spring of 1958 and I have followed them ever since.

In those days the games tended to be higher scoring and I can remember playing teams like Blackburn and Chelsea and very often we'd score six goals and the match could end up six–three or six–two and of course it was in the days of Dennis Viollet and Bobby Charlton and Albert Quixall. In those days there were crowds of over sixty thousand, and a tremendous atmosphere and predominantly standing as opposed to seating. So the noise levels were a lot greater than today.

The board then was in the east stand/south stand quadrant and I always remember that next door to the boardroom Les Olive had his office, the secretary's office, and it had a window that overlooked the pitch with bars on it so that nobody could break in. Then shortly afterwards they built a new extension. When they built the original shop they built an extension and put the boardroom above on the bit that jutted out of the south stand. So I can remember the very old boardroom. It was panelled, a bit dingy because it had no natural light. Sometimes my father would come to board meetings and he would bring me along; he would drive and I would wait outside for the board meeting to finish. In those days they had a club caterer who used to supply sandwiches and meat pies after the board meeting, so I would have a long wait while the board meeting finished so I would have started on the pies and the sandwiches waiting for the board to end.

MARTIN EDWARDS

I'll tell you about one of the Busby Babes – Duncan Edwards. I was chairman of my trade union branch, the AEU, in Broadheath and we used to meet every fortnight on a Friday night. I used to catch the all-night bus coming back at about twenty to twelve from Broadheath and I remember getting on one particular night and Duncan Edwards was sat there in the corner seat and the conductor was talking to him. Edwards was courting a girl in Timperley and he'd just taken her home. And you know Busby had them all in digs in Trafford with a landlady to look after them. I said to Edwards, 'Big game tomorrow.' And he said, 'Don't let anybody, especially the boss, know I'm on this bloody bus at quarter to midnight, he'll go mad!'

When I think back he was my all-time idol, he was the ultimate, the best footballer I've ever seen in British football. He had everything and he was a giant of a man. I remember also his partner on the other flank, Salford boy, Eddie Colman. He used to shake his hips. He was the exact opposite of Edwards but what a pair. I remember seeing Duncan Edwards play for England. When I went back to the factory there was a chap used to organise an annual trip to see England play Scotland, Wembley one year, Hampden the next, and you used to pay half-a-crown [12.5p] a week to save up for it. I remember seeing a game in Scotland. Edwards was only eighteen and he was playing, what a team that was. On the left wing was Tom Finney, on the right wing was Stanley Matthews and Duncan Edwards was spraying the ball out, one with his right foot to Matthews, then with the other foot to Finney.

LORD STAN ORME

We had only just bought a television, so viewing was essential whatever the programme. It was the first time I had been able to watch a United game and the first time I experienced anger in sport. It was 1957 – I was eight years old, very nearly nine. It was Cup final day in May – the Babes were unquestionably going to win the Double when some stupid Irishman in a claret and blue shirt decided to clatter into Ray Wood in a manner more reminiscent of a bull with a bee up its backside than a footballer.

I was brought up in a house devoted to rugby union. My father played rugby, my grandfather played rugby but I didn't. I preferred football. I was the blackest of black sheep! I hid my passion from my parents even on that day in May, but I seethed inside at the reckless challenge on Wood (and still do). I have watched the video of that moment a number of times since and what remains in the memory even more than Wood's prostrate body is the huge frame of Duncan Edwards ambling over towards McParland, standing over him, hands on hips. One can only imagine what he said – if he bothered to say anything at all. I only hope that the moment lives in McParland's memory even today. That was the moment, so soon after the start of my first game, that I unquestionably knew my fate, even if I hadn't realised it before. It was the moment that embodied the spirit of Manchester United and I was hooked.

PAUL WINDRIDGE

It was my first ever Division One game. I'd been to see a few matches at Tranmere but never to see a First Division game.

75

On the previous Saturday my dad had taken me to Goodison for the first time to see Everton play the Czech side Banik Ostrava. It was 1957 and an FA Cup Saturday but Everton had been knocked out and had a free day. They won comfortably that afternoon. Anyhow, I spotted in the programme that the following Wednesday Everton were at home to the League champions Manchester United, the famous Busby Babes. Lots of games were played in an afternoon in those days because they did not have floodlights. United were also looking odds-on to win the title again and had just beaten Bournemouth in the sixth round of the Cup. I spent the next few days broaching the subject of going to Goodison to see them. My father couldn't take me as he was working but on the Tuesday one of my pals up the road offered to take me. He was a bit older and promised to take care of me. I guess my parents must have been a bit worried as I was only nine at the time, but things were different then and kids were far more safe than they are today. The only proviso was that we went in the boys' pen and that I had to raise the money.

John came up with a cracking idea: getting some money back on the empties. In those days if you took the empty bottles of pop back to the shop you could get a penny or two. So, we trudged up and down the street knocking on doors to see if anyone would let us have their empties. It was a bit of a tradition then to let kids have the empties to make a bit of money. In the end we raised enough and off we went, by bus, ferryboat and then another bus. It was a bit of a journey.

I have to say at this point that I was not really going to see Everton. Peter Farrell, Tommy Eglington and the rest of the Irish lads might have had their good points but they hardly set the pulse going. No, I was going to see Edwards, Taylor and Byrne. But the sad thing was that when we got there we discovered that only Byrne was playing; the other two stars were injured, or maybe just rested. I was so disappointed. Even Viollet and Charlton were out. But there was Byrne, Berry, Bent, Whelan and Pegg. And in came a bunch of even younger players – Wilf McGuinness, Colin Webster and John Doherty. Ray Wood and Jackie Blanchflower made up the numbers. I don't remember much about the game, except being in the boys' pen which at the time was on the corner of the Gladwys Street End. Despite so many notable absentees United won two–one with Colin Webster scoring both United's goals in front of a surprisingly small crowd of thirty-four thousand. Six months later when United played at Goodison again seventy-two thousand turned up, a mid-week record for the club that still holds today.

But I always look back on that game, not because it was my first big footballing occasion but because it was the Busby Babes. A year later the disaster brought an end to that team and that era. But at least I can always say that I saw them and that they really were a side that captured the imagination.

STEPHEN F. KELLY

My first memories would be the 1957 Cup final when they played Aston Villa and McParland elbowed Ray Wood, broke his cheekbone, and Jackie Blanchflower went in goal. So, they were a man short after about five minutes and I suppose that was the start of it. I watched it on TV at home, I was about seven or eight years old. I certainly have vivid memories of McParland hitting Ray Wood. United ended up as under-dogs in that match and it was a kind of feeling that I wanted this team to win because they were the team who were a man short and they had this beautiful white strip with red patches on it. I think that helped as well because Aston Villa played in some awful strip. It sounds strange but it was United as the underdogs, backs to the wall, ten men against eleven.

I lived in Newcastle, Staffordshire which is near Stoke-on-Trent. My uncle, who was a brickie's labourer, used to work in Manchester and he would come back sometimes with the *Manchester Evening News* and I would read about United. I would read about this wonderful team and then ten months later there was Munich. I'm quite proud to say that I was a United fan pre-Munich but I had never seen the team play live.

I can't remember much about my first live game but I remember my uncle taking me on a rather tortuous journey to get to Manchester; I was about ten or eleven. I know they won but I couldn't tell you who they were playing. The ground was so big. I had been taken by my father to watch Stoke City, who at that time were in the old Second Division. They weren't the most exciting team to watch, especially when the newspapers were full of these exciting stories of the Busby Babes. That was the team I wanted to watch.

DEREK WYNNE

I suppose it was around about the 1956 sort of era. I was then about eight or nine, and was friendly with a friend of my father's who was called Charlie Davenport who was a very good Manchester United supporter at the time. He also went to the same church as we went to so I knew him very well and he introduced me to United.

And as it happens this particular chap is the father of Peter Davenport, whom I got to know very well when I was a teenager, taking him out in the pram, et cetera. But it was his father Charlie who got me interested in United and it was shortly after that that they played at Everton in 1958 and my father, who was an Evertonian, took me along on a Wednesday afternoon. This was shortly before the Munich air disaster. We went along and my father always used to take me to the stand next to the players' entrance on the pitch and we watched the game there with a huge crowd. Before the game started obviously the players were coming on the pitch and along trundled David Pegg and I was able to get his autograph, which with the events of later that particular year was very poignant. But that particular day United drew three–three, I think it was, and they were absolutely superb; so strong and powerful, their youth shining through and from that moment on I was definitely hooked.

KEVIN McALENY

I was born in Collyhurst which is a real hot-bed of United supporters. Different parts of Manchester have different supporters. When I was there, Nobby Stiles was at United as well. Mr Cassidy, who was my headmaster, played for United as well so there's always been tie-ups. St Patrick's had a name as a decent school producing footballers, not necessarily professionals, but amateurs. Collyhurst was an area of footballers and boxers. It was definitely a Red area.

My brother Bernard was a real big United fan. My father, funnily enough, was a Blue. He was born in Ancoats. It didn't cause any rifts, no. In the fifties City were having a real good period. No, it was never a problem. You'd go to games together in those days. There was none of this tribal warfare that goes on now. You'd get the Reds and Blues going to games together. You were confined to home games because you couldn't afford to travel to away games. In those days you went to watch great players; you'd see them doing things on the ball and you'd go out in the streets later and practise them yourself. You'd be kicking a ball against the wall, keeping it up and so on. You could do that in those days, nobody bothered. That's gone away from kids now. You'd also walk everywhere. You used to play for the school team on a Saturday morning and then go down to Old Trafford in the afternoon if they were playing at home. But even that's changed now.

I would go with Bernard to Old Trafford and then my school friends went as well. In them days you could be waiting at a bus stop and United supporters would pick you up in a car. They'd see you with a rattle and your rosette and they'd take you down to Old Trafford if you were stood on Rochdale Road. We used to get the 112 or 113 bus or we'd maybe get a lift. We went as a bunch, everybody congregated around the bus stop. They were all Red supporters.

I can remember my brother when they played Fulham going down to London in a removal van which they got from May Brown's, the pub at the corner of Rome Street. I can still see that removal van. That was the five–three game, the FA Cup semi-final during the 1957–58 season. All getting in the back of the van with my uncle Paddy. It was like an adventure, them going to London. It was something you didn't do in those days; London was a million miles away.

I can't remember the first game I saw at Old Trafford but I can remember the first away game. That was at Bolton with my dad. That was 1958. I always went in the Stretford End, queued up. I used to get directly behind the goal. I've still got a piece of coping stone from the Stretford End; I got it when they were pulling it down. It's out there in the garden. My first game? I was eight or nine. I vaguely remember the pre-Munich team but I don't recollect much, I was too young. It was just growing up in that environment that turned me into a United supporter, it wasn't that they were the Busby Babes or anything like that. It wasn't like it is now with all the publicity. They were just ordinary lads then. It was just young boys.

BRIAN KIDD

United was in my blood from the start. I didn't dare support anyone else. The first United thing I remember in the house was a glossy *Manchester Evening News* special. I think it came out around the time of the Munich crash. I remember flicking through it when I was four or five. There was things like Alex Dawson scoring a hat-trick against Fulham in the 1958 FA Cup semi-final. My dad used to tell me about Jack Rowley and Johnny Carey, but the thing I heard about most as a kid was the Busby Babes. Dad used to watch them from the terraces and Mam sold hot dogs inside the ground. This was before they met, so I grew up with two different views. My old fella would talk about Duncan, saying things like, 'He had legs like tree trunks,' and 'He was the best footballer I ever saw.' While my mam would add that he was really handsome as well. Dad also used to talk about Roger Byrne, claiming that he used to jockey full-backs into a position where he didn't have to tackle them, he just took the ball off them. And again my mam would say, 'Aye, but you could tell he was moody.'

CHRISTOPHER ECCLESTON

My dad was a big United supporter. It used to be a Christmas treat for me to go to Old Trafford with my Uncle Harry. He was a posh fellow from Handforth who had his own house. That was unusual in those days. I think the first game I saw was against Chelsea in the 1954–55 season. That was the season Chelsea won the title. I saw my first fight that day between grown men. This guy, he was a Chelsea supporter, got his face punched in. In those days the terraces were open and you could wander about them. I also remember seeing Jimmy Hill play for Fulham. I remember him hitting the bar. I also remember a game against Blackpool sometime around then. It had been snowing and the pitch was covered in snow. They had to mark the lines out with a red dye so that you could see the markings on the pitch. Stanley Matthews played that day which was unusual because Matthews rarely seemed to play against United. I distinctly remember that he fouled Duncan Edwards. I think United won two–one. I used to have a rattle, a massive thing it was. You couldn't take something like that into the ground these days.

I didn't go regularly as I was playing football myself. I used to play for Withington Boys and then I signed for North Withington so I was playing on a Saturday and then I played for Whitchurch Villa on a Sunday. I saw Manchester Boys play a couple of times. I remember Wilf McGuinness playing for Manchester Boys at Old Trafford and I think Dennis Viollet was playing that day as well. I was small then.

I also saw Real Madrid playing United in 1957 in the European Cup semi-final. There was a huge crowd there that night. There were young kids all around the pitch. I can't remember much else about that night except that United drew two–two. They'd lost the first game three–one in Spain.

ALAN DURRANS

I went to see the Babes when they played Bolton in the FA Youth Cup and there were thirty-odd thousand at Bolton. I went with me dad. You always saw them about here. If you came up here at the top of the road on a Sunday the players had to report after the game. Then they'd go down to the Quadrant for a drink. You'd see them a lot more. It was lower-key in those days. They're pop stars today. I remember seeing Sir Matt on the 62 bus at Chorlton Baths and I went up to him and asked him if he was Matt Busby.

The best player I've ever seen was Duncan Edwards. He could play anywhere, which he did. He could be tough, which he was, but he also had a lovely delicate touch. I remember seeing him at the Warwick Road End take a fellow and just beat him, not like George Best but more like Cruyff and I can see him going into people and just bowling them over. He was my favourite player.

We'd moved from Moss Side and got a house in Wythenshawe and I was at home when we heard the news of the disaster. I then watched them coming back on Princess Road near where the Post House Hotel is. That's where I stood and watched the coffins coming back from the airport. I didn't go to the ground. My mother told me; I was on the milk. I came home and usually went to bed in the afternoon. I would be about twenty-two, something like that. It was a painful experience. It's not only that, it was afterwards as well when you're looking back and asking how's Duncan Edwards going on, how's Matt going on; you understand what I mean.

I went to the Bilbao game. I was in the Kippax opposite the

main stand and I had a good position. I was not far from the wall. I think it was two–nil at half time and we needed another goal. Tremendous excitement. I also went to the Anderlecht game when we beat them ten–nil. A guy who was a Partick Thistle supporter came down who I knew from the Army. Great game.

Albert Scanlon, I knew him well; he was a personal friend of mine and I used to play football with him. I remember Albert breaking a window. He hit the window and the woman had pulled the window down so that it went through two windows and he came to our door and my dad whipped him inside and even to this day I don't suppose the woman knows who broke her window. But he was a great footballer, Albert. Me dad used to always say he hit the ball like a man. He had a tragic accident, Albert, I think when he was twelve-and-a-half or thirteen. They hit a bus going over the swing bridge in Salford. I think there were four in the car and one of them was killed. Albert never played football for over a year and that's why he used to always run with his hand sticking out because he had a plaster support that held his arm up. But it took twelve to eighteen months out of Albert's career and I think he'd have been a better footballer than what he was if that accident hadn't happened.

DANNY McGREGOR

I went on every trip to Europe. I played against Borussia Dortmund away and Shamrock Rovers here. In Dortmund we needed a draw. We drew nil–nil. I was also over in Bilbao for that game, in the snow. You know there was a lot of talk about us having been brushing snow off the runway but we did it as a joke, not to help anybody. We were brushing snow off the runway but we did it as a joke. We took off with snow and ice all over the place but we didn't think there was any danger. People talk about Munich – trying to take off three times was outrageous. It was that cold, we didn't expect it to be so cold in Spain. It was freezing on the plane going over there and the reason was that the skips with all our kit in wouldn't go in the hold so we had them on the plane and they were in front of the controls for the heating and being a chartered plane, nobody realised. So it was freezing going over there and the game was played in a blizzard at times. I didn't play, I was watching. And Billy Whelan got that late goal to make it five–three.

The best game I've ever seen for atmosphere was the return at Maine Road. That was a game. We needed three goals. I was part of the crowd. I've never, ever known atmosphere like it. It was jam-packed and from start to finish there was a roar, cheering the players on, oohs and ahhs, you could cut the atmosphere with a knife. They were sucking the ball towards the goal. Tommy Taylor was playing against a centre half called Jesus Garay. I've never known such passion; that was the game of my life, the biggest one ever for me. That was the game I most remember.

The greatest team ever I think was Real Madrid. The best club side I've ever seen – Gento, Kopa, Di Stefano, and later Rial Santamaria, Puskas. They were the best. But for the crash I think Manchester United would have become England's Real Madrid because we had players of that quality: the Edwards, the Colmans, the Byrnes, the Taylors, all of them, and they were so young. Mark Jones, he was twenty-three, he wore a trilby and smoked a pipe and he was the father. We were only twenty, twenty-one, twenty-two. And there was more to come with the likes of Bobby Charlton. But Real Madrid could also be tough. They had the cutting edge, the muscle. They kicked us out of the game in the Bernabeu. I remember Di Stefano sorting Jackie Blanchflower out, and Tommy Taylor also being sorted out and the referee . . . well. But it was a learning period for United. But for the crash, Manchester United would have taken over from them.

WILF McGUINNESS

My father and I always went to the football together. First we went to Maine Road. I was very little and I don't remember much about that, only that it was difficult to see and the huge crowds frightened me. Then when United moved back to Old Trafford we went to games there. But mainly, and best, I remember the Cliff. That was smaller, less crowded. Busby had built a great side: Carey, Rowley, Stan Pearson, Jimmy Delaney, et cetera. They won the Cup and later the League, but at the Cliff we could see an even greater team developing for the future. The Youth Cup had just started and it coincided with this great flowering of talent – United won it the first five years in a row. They played games to massive crowds at Old Trafford. There was a sense of history in the air.

I am always cautious of the retrospective creation of facts but at the time there *was* a real sense of history: Busby, the Babes, the enormous crowds and Europe. It felt special, we all knew that we were part of something important. Then the European Cup came along. The FA had, naturally, stopped all English clubs participating in this funny foreign distraction, and Chelsea, the first English club eligible, had complied. There was a sense of destiny about United. Busby saw over the horizon; it was assumed we would go in and it was assumed we were correct. The North doesn't like taking orders from the South. United entered the European Cup. It was further assumed we would win it.

We grew up with the players. My dad and I had seen them at the Cliff, then in the youth team, then the reserves, then the first team. It just seemed to happen naturally. They became the best team in England. There is an interesting similarity with the present side here; both teams are mainly English.

Europe has a sophistication that eludes us, though. The number of times the Babes got to the European Cup semi-finals and were beaten, usually it seemed by Real Madrid. At first it seemed we were unlucky, somehow we hadn't been beaten fairly. It is just that it had happened too often to be just luck: we had to learn to play in Europe.

PAT McDONALD

I went to all those games the first season in Europe. There was Anderlecht to begin with and they all scored except David Pegg; all the forwards scored. I remember Bilbao. Bilbao had won over there but were getting very tired towards the end. There was a ball going for a dead-ball kick near the old scoreboard end at Maine Road. Now one United player ran, got the ball, up the field, and of course we got a goal. But that was all because this one player ran and got the ball. I don't even remember who it was but it was because of him, he chased the ball when everybody else was flagging. It was a very wet night. It was a huge crowd and it was under lights at Maine Road. Remember, we didn't have lights at Old Trafford at the time, so we had to play at Maine Road. You used to get an awful lot of shadows from the lights then.

It was so exciting playing in Europe. You saw things you'd only heard of. Prior to that we'd had these Hungarians come over and we watched the match on television, against England. There was only one fellow had a TV set so we piled into his little house in Moss Side. We couldn't believe what we saw, when Puskas rolled the ball back and the defender goes one way, then he kicks it. Never seen anything like it. They beat England six–three, the first match we lost at Wembley to a foreign side. Now Bilbao had a player, Jesus Garay, played centre half. It was one of the most fantastic performances I've ever seen because they were under pressure throughout the game.

JOE DILLON

Going into Europe was a new adventure but you just got on with the job. We used travel agents to make all the arrangements. The first time after the accident when we went to Milan, nobody wanted to fly so we went by train. We went a bit earlier and I think Thomas Cook's had a courier travel with us. He was an ex-Army man and I think he was used to taking groups on holiday. When he said meet at ten, we are departing at ten, everybody would be there ready on the coach to go. But when you are dealing with football players they are not always there on time. I think he found it hard to understand why they were late.

LES OLIVE

When floodlights came in, it presented new problems for us in the St John Ambulance Brigade because we couldn't see the crowds. It was the mid-1950s and United played their first European games at Maine Road because they didn't have lights. The lights weren't very good you know, they were very poor. To be honest, at times you wondered how the goalkeeper saw the ball. When the ball came at a great speed to the goalkeeper, he had trouble.

The great problems for us was that it changed the colour of the patients' faces. Instead of being white they could look like they were jaundiced. It was very difficult to know what was wrong. We had to take them under the main stand where there was normal light. Nothing like the lights you have now. It was also difficult to see if there had been an incident on the terraces. It was the crowd who used to attract your attention, they'd shout to you to come over. I'd go to the spot where the noise was and they'd tell you then. When you got closer you could see the mêlée. People would then make room for you to get up to them, but it was difficult. They didn't pass the bodies over the top so much when the lights were on, they would just call us. That's why we used to spread people around the pitch perimeter more under the floodlights. We never had people on the terraces, it was too dangerous. Sometimes we might have people at the top of the terraces, but never on the terraces themselves.

ALF DAVIES

The last game at Maine Road was against Bilbao and they had to win. I don't know what the score was to get in the next round. I was at that game and then I went in the Army and I was in Hong Kong when I found out that the team had been killed. But I went straight from work to that game. I don't know how we met, all the family and friends that used to go to the game. We stood behind the goals. Just unbelievable. A magic night because nobody thought we had a chance of beating or progressing in the next round. It was just unbelievable.

I remember going to the first floodlit match at Old Trafford and I can see the headlines in the paper next morning: Busby's lights . . . *Burnden's whites dim Busby's lights*, because it was the first match and Bolton beat us.

They were a bunch of young fellas come through and played superb football. We're talking of people like Viollet and Duncan Edwards. Eddie Colman was very popular, a Salford boy of course. They were just a great team to watch. I think they really captured the imagination. I think that's the way to say it: they caught the imagination of the people in Manchester.

HUGH JONES

Duncan Edwards was the finest, most complete, player I've ever seen. I remember once we were playing Real Madrid. One of their players went down near the Stretford End and Edwards went over, bent down and picked this man up in his arms and took him off the pitch. Just bent down. Now that's strength.

JOE DILLON

You can see Duncan Edwards there on the wall. I actually met him twice at Lewis's. This must have been, probably, around about 1956. Nothing was printed in colour in those days but they brought out a fanzine type thing called the *Red Devils*. I've still got one now. The shirts and the tops of the socks on the photo were blotched in – that was the only colour on it. You queued which seemed like three days but was probably a couple of hours. At the top of Lewis's there used to be a theatre, probably still there. But the whole of the team was sat on the stage and we had to file past and you passed them this insert and you got them to sign it. Sometimes you could sneak a photograph in which you'd brought with you from the Charlie Buchan's *Football Monthly*. They were all very soberly dressed with collar and tie, all very well-mannered, all very quiet. I still get emotional now thinking of Duncan Edwards. When I actually met him I was about ten. I shook his hand. A great man.

Old Trafford had no floodlights. All European games which had to be played mid-week had to be played at Maine Road and I still think United hold the record for the crowd capacity at Maine Road. I went to the first game with a friend of mine when they beat Anderlecht ten–nil when it became apparent that Busby's dream of success in Europe was attainable. We came out at eight–nil to get a bus. Being out late on the streets of Manchester in those days wasn't as dangerous as now but parents still worried and wanted you home, so we came out at eight–nil. We were first on the bus and sat on the long seat at the end. The conductor said, 'What's the score, son?' I said, 'Eight–nil,' and he gave me a clip around the ear and told me not to tell bloody lies. I felt very put down. Nobody on the bus supported me. We sat there and a couple of minutes later someone else got on and he asked what was the score. 'Nine–nil,' they said. Then it became ten–nil. But no apology, nothing. That was the way it was.

After five, six–nil you were just so pleased you spent more time talking to your mates about a certain goal that happened or whatever, but the actual match itself I don't remember much. But I do remember Tommy Taylor's new haircut. He had, what was it called, a Nero cut with a fringe in front which was a bit bizarre for a miner's son from Barnsley. But he played well.

We also went to the Borussia Dortmund game. Not quite as exciting a game for a young lad. But now if I went I'd probably appreciate it more, a much closer result. We were getting old hands by then. Unfortunately I couldn't get tickets for the Bilbao game. Money was very tight in those days, not like now with credit cards. It had to be cash upfront then. We were never particularly well off. My mother just didn't see that it was that important. Again, for whatever reason, I couldn't afford the semi-final. I was probably on about two old shillings [10p] a week pocket money, and it might be four shillings [20p] to stand on the Stretford End. Money was tight.

GEORGE REYNOLDS

When the Babes were at their best there was no stopping them. I was at the Anderlecht match when they won ten–nil. Tommy Taylor got three. Dennis Viollet was playing and David Pegg. It was played at Maine Road. They overran them, and Anderlecht were considered to be a fine side. I went to all those European games. These foreign teams came with a reputation. They had different methods of playing. United's style didn't change; they had two men on the wing and they stayed there until they got possession. Today you don't see that because they have wing backs. In those days wingers were wingers and always speedy wingers, like Jimmy Delaney, and David Pegg later. The atmosphere was much better against the European teams than the ordinary League games because these teams came with such a reputation and to beat them was really something. And these games were also played under floodlights. The atmosphere under lights was much better than daylight. It was an outing, a social evening with the lights on. The Real Madrid game as well. Fantastic.

I went to see a lot of the Youth Cup games. I went when they beat Newcastle, I think it was twenty-five–nil. They were brilliant. And they all came through to become the Busby Babes. My wife lived in Stretford and she could tell me more about the Busby Babes than I could myself because most of the lads lived in the Stretford area. If they had a match on the Saturday, Busby would not let them out after Wednesday night to go socialising. Not only that, he would, on occasions, go around to Mrs Fullaway the landlady, to make sure they were in bed at certain times. When I moved to Stretford, Jackie Blanchflower was a neighbour. We had four or five who all lived in the Stretford area.

There's a public house called the Quadrant in Stretford. Bill Foulkes and half a dozen others would go there after the match. They used to give them a room of their own in the Quadrant and they used to buy pints but hardly drank them. When they had gone, the locals would come out of the Vault and dash into the room and finish off all the beer. You know footballers, they'd get a drink and put it down, then somebody else would order more and it would finish up being left on the table. The locals had a great time drinking it when they had gone.

ALBERT THORPE

There were some of us who were teachers and we'd go to watch the youth side at Old Trafford. I was standing there under the rickety old stand one day, near to the half-way line. I don't know who the kids were playing but Duncan Edwards was in the side. Now the ball in those days was made of leather and when it was wet it used to get very heavy. Well, this particular day it was raining and the ball must have weighed a ton. Edwards gets the ball just inside his own half, right in front of me, and he lets fly with a shot. It soared through the air. The goalkeeper got to it but the force of it took him straight into the back of the net. And that was the ball Edwards had hit from just inside his own half. Astonishing.

'Snake hips' Colman was another I vividly remember. He used to wriggle his hips when he came up against someone. Giggs tries it nowadays but he's not as good. And then there was Tommy Taylor. He was so good with his head. I get really upset now when I think of those lads. I don't know why, but I always end up crying.

WILF SUDLOW

Busby had the next office to me along there. I found him a lovely man, very much like someone you'd call your father. He'd always give you advice and he always had time for people. That's what I found very good: he always had time whether you were eighty or ten. Now don't forget I came here as an exec and I've seen both sides. If you got in the lift with Sir Matt he'd always let on, he'd never get in the lift and say nothing. If there was a child there he always rubbed the child's hair. He always had lunch in the Red Grill. He never ever sat on his own, there would always be someone from the club would sit with him. Lovely man. I went to his eightieth birthday party. When you opened out the menu it had the names of everyone who attended, famous names, and the man who spoke was Cliff Morgan and he gave the most magnificent speech I've ever heard. Everyone was in tears. He had the lovely Welsh lilt about him. He'd say, 'Sair Martt, he's like my farder, I'd be proud to call him me dad.' Bloody hell, everyone was in tears. Billy Liddell was there, Godfrey Evans, Denis Compton. There was no top table, everyone was spread out; an evening to remember.

DANNY McGREGOR

CHAPTER FOUR

6 February 1958

Munich

Like the assassination of President Kennedy or the death of
Princess Diana, the Munich air disaster is one of those
moments when all who were alive at the time can remember
precisely where they were when they first heard the tragic
news. The disaster of Thursday 6 February 1958 was to mark
a watershed not just in the history of Manchester United
Football Club but also in English football. The sadness was
not confined to Manchester alone but engulfed the entire
nation. The Busby Babes had captured the imagination of all
followers of football. They ranked alongside the other romantic
names of the era – Real Madrid, Honved, Moscow Dynamo –
as they swashbuckled their way across Europe.

We'll never know just how great a team they could have
become. But their youth and the fact that they had reached
the last four of Europe two years in succession must certainly
suggest that sooner or later they would have reached the
pinnacle in Europe. Eight players died in the disaster: Roger
Byrne, David Pegg, Tommy Taylor, Eddie Colman, Duncan
Edwards, Geoff Bent, Mark Jones and Liam Whelan, while
Jackie Blanchflower and Johnny Berry never recovered
sufficiently from their injuries ever to play again. There were
other club casualties too, with backroom boys Tom Curry and
Bert Whalley killed, along with secretary Walter Crickmer.
Eight journalists also died.

News of the disaster came late that afternoon. Most people first heard it on radio as a BBC announcer broke into the daily edition of *Mrs Dale's Diary* to report news of the air crash. In Manchester the stop press of the afternoon editions of the *Manchester Evening News* and the *Manchester Evening Chronicle* carried the first printed news. As many testify in these pages, at first nobody could quite believe that it had been serious. But as further news emerged, it spiralled like a whirlwind through the city. Crowds besieged the newspaper vendors outside the *Manchester Evening News*'s office on Deansgate, as further news poured on to the streets. Anxious groups then huddled around newspapers to read of the casualties. By teatime the entire nation knew of the disaster.

In Manchester, United fans wept openly in the streets as they read of the news. The writer H. E. Bates, in the most poignant of pieces, wrote at the time that he sat listening with 'a frozen brain to that cruel and shocking list of casualties that was now to give to that despised word Munich an even sadder meaning than it had acquired on a day before the War when a British Prime Minister had come home to London waving a pitiful piece of paper . . .'

Outside the ground on a desolately freezing night, the fans gathered in their hundreds. The weeping was public. It just seemed the obvious place to go. They clustered around taxis and outside the main office in the chill wind awaiting the latest news from Munich. It was a moment no United fan of that era would ever forget.

As the evening wore on the news grew grimmer. Captain Roger Byrne and record signing Tommy Taylor were both dead; Busby and Duncan Edwards were struggling for survival. Inside Old Trafford Busby's number two Jimmy Murphy wept in his office, as he and assistant secretary Les Olive attempted to sort out the consequential chaos. Families had to be contacted, permission had to be sought to postpone Saturday's fixture against Wolverhampton Wanderers and arrangements for officials, including Murphy himself, to travel to Germany the following day had to be hurriedly organised.

The bodies also had to be returned. They duly arrived days later with a dark, snaking procession of hearses carrying them from Ringway Airport, up Princess Road and towards Old Trafford. Thousands lined the route. And then the individual funerals. One at a time, day by day, the fans packed the streets as yet another silent cortege slipped by. They stood in the cold for hours to pay their final respects to a team that had once warmed the heart, awoken the passions and never knew the meaning of defeat. In cemeteries around Manchester they were buried alongside many old United favourites, heroes of previous generations.

Back in Munich, Busby and Edwards struggled on; the daily bulletins, at moments seeming optimistic, then taking a turn for the worse. Precisely three weeks after the disaster, twenty-one-year-old Duncan Edwards finally lost his battle for life in the Rechts der Isar hospital. It was scarcely believable. The young giant was dead. It broke a thousand hearts, and still does today.

United started to make the slow return to normality, if normality was ever again possible. On Wednesday 19 February they returned to the football field, playing their first match against Sheffield Wednesday in the fifth round of the FA Cup at Old Trafford. A vast crowd of just under sixty thousand turned up to pay their respects, with thousands more content to simply stand outside and cheer from a distance.

The message from chairman Harold Hardman on the black-edged programme cover read 'United Will Go On . . .' In the centre spread there were eleven blank spaces for the United team. It was a poignant team sheet that would forever live in the annals of football history. It was a night of mixed emotions, nobody quite sure whether to cheer or cry. Mostly they did both. Murphy, working almost alone, had pulled together a team of sorts. He'd been out and bought Aston Villa's rich prospect Stan Crowther and the experienced little man from Blackpool, Ernie Taylor. Others followed, including Warren

Bradley and two others from Bishop Auckland. Wednesday never had a chance. As many fans testify, the emotions simply swamped them. Roared on and playing almost in a daze, United romped home three–nil with debutant Shay Brennan, converted from full-back to winger for the occasion, scoring twice.

United would indeed go on, as clearly have the memories of the fans from that evening. They reached the final, disposing of West Brom and Fulham, before they came up against Lancashire neighbours Bolton Wanderers at Wembley. Up to then the adrenaline, sympathy and enthusiasm had kept them going, but on a warm May day at Wembley, with Busby back at the helm, they foundered. It was all too much for them. Nat Lofthouse shattered their dreams, bundling goalkeeper Harry Gregg and ball over the line. In truth United were always second-best to Bolton. But it had been a brave performance.

Nor should it be forgotten that the England side, already preparing for the 1958 World Cup, had been robbed of regulars Byrne, Taylor and Edwards, to say nothing of David Pegg and Eddie Colman, who might also have featured in the England line-up. With the Big Three in their starting eleven, England might well have proved more than a match for the eventual winners Brazil. Instead they were knocked out in the quarter-finals by the Soviet Union, having drawn with Brazil en route.

For the people of Manchester and the fans of United in particular, it was a cold time. There was a silence, likened by one supporter to the intake of breath that greeted the aftermath of the Luftwaffe attack on Manchester, as the light of the new day revealed the destruction of the city centre. In schools, children and teachers joined in prayers. At work not much was said, little needed to be added. Even now, forty years on, those fans who lived through the moment still weep openly as memories are recalled. The pain may never go away.

If any good did come out of Munich it was reflected in a

changing view of the club, turning the name of Manchester United into an international institution. Before, they were simply another English football club. After Munich, they were, rightly or wrongly, the nation's club.

I'd been out of the office and when I came back, Walter Crickmer's secretary, Alma George, had had a message from British European Airways saying that the plane had crashed at Munich. They didn't know any details initially but you can imagine that all at once everything happened. The phone was going mad, people trying to get information and over the evening the different snippets of information came through – somebody had died or been injured or taken to hospital. We needed to pass on the information to the families. Not everybody had a telephone in those days so it was a matter of getting the information through other people. For instance, my wife went round to two or three who lived near us to tell them what information we had.

So that was the first day. After that there was tremendous media interest. We had letters from all over the world expressing sympathy and they were delivered in van loads, sacks, it was incredible. But of course they all had to be opened, because among those were business letters from the Football League and so on and the FA, so we had the ground committee, stewards who come in on a match day, and still do, all volunteers. They would come along in the evening, get around the big boardroom table, open the mail, separate it so that I got what I needed. They did that for weeks afterwards. Another thing was the Lord Mayor's secretary came along and we tried to acknowledge everything. She came and sat at a typewriter and replied to all the letters of sympathy. So a lot of people rallied round.

I think initially I did not have a chance to stop and think. I'd be in at nine in the morning and if I got home at eleven at night, that was not a bad hour. We had a young daughter at the time and she went to stay with friends and my wife came in – she was a shorthand typist – so we were together. Somebody lent me a car because I didn't have transport at the time. It was a matter of ploughing through it. Of course there had to be board meetings. Jimmy Murphy went out with Jean Busby to Munich with the families, wives and girlfriends in some cases, to see those in hospital. I had to keep in touch with them. And then eventually the bodies were bought back to Old Trafford. We had a small gymnasium then; that was turned into a small chapel of rest overnight. And there was liaison with the local authorities and the police.

The bodies came to Ringway, Manchester Airport now, and the route back to Old Trafford was published in the newspapers, so you can imagine the crowds lining the route. Tremendous crowds, the pavements were packed all the way. I went out to the airport and came back with them and you'd see City fans with scarves on alongside United fans, just wanting to pay a tribute.

When the news broke fans came and thronged on the forecourt waiting for information. As snippets came through we were able to pass it on, though in some cases they would hear something on the radio and would come and tell us. That was traumatic in its way. That went on for some time until after the burials.

Manchester was a stunned city. A lot of people around at the time would be able to tell you where they were when they got the news. But for us, we had no time to think, we were battling away to keep on top of things. We had to play a match pretty quickly. We signed a couple of players – Ernie Taylor* and Stan Crowther. That was another part of the organisation that had to still carry on to make them eligible to play. Stan

---

* Ernie Taylor joined United from Blackpool for £8,000 immediately following the Munich disaster. Taylor, a full England international, had played in the famous 1953 FA Cup final. He made only thirty appearances for United.

Crowther* was signed at 6 p.m. before a 7.30 p.m. kick-off in a Manchester hotel and we had a police escort back to Old Trafford which got through in double-quick time, despite the amount of traffic coming to the game. The police were very helpful at that time. The Chief Superintendent in the local Stretford division actually went to Munich to identify the bodies which was a great help, because it was not a task anyone looked forward to.

We still had thirty thousand tickets unsold for the Cup tie against Sheffield Wednesday. They had to be made available and put on sale, so there was plenty going on. The other thing is that the directors were meeting quite often to keep abreast of things. Then when the bodies came back they had to be dispersed to the homes. We had to arrange for directors to represent the club at different funerals. I went to one or two as well. I went to Tommy Taylor, Roger Byrne, Geoff Bent. It was a matter of splitting up so that we had representation at them all, from directors' level to senior staff.

The first programme after the disaster was done by David Wicks, the editor. He did it, that was his job and he always did it. He liaised with Harold Hardman† for the message on the front. We didn't put a team in as we didn't know what it would be; that's what was to make it unique. David was another one who was there to help and relieve me a little bit. He just got on with it.

LES OLIVE

I'd twisted my knee on the Saturday when Manchester United played Arsenal. And we played the reserves here. I was down to go because the list went up on a Friday when they went to Arsenal, because not everyone had a phone and you couldn't

---

* Stan Crowther, signed from Aston Villa for £35,000, was allowed to play for United even though he had joined the club just hours before kick-off.
† Chairman of United 1951–65. A former player with United and Everton, he had not travelled to Belgrade for the match against Red Star.

contact players so easily. So we came down on the Sunday with our injuries and knocks and if anybody had to be replaced, they were. I came down and I had this twisted knee; it had locked, and it was diagnosed as a torn cartilage, so I couldn't go. I went to see a specialist early in the week and he said he'd need to operate, so I was supposed to go into hospital on the Friday. On the Thursday I was with a friend in Manchester who was connected with the newspapers and we were walking down Princess Street and I saw a placard which said 'United in crash on runway'.

My first reaction was that it was just a bump. I didn't think for one minute that there were serious injuries. We got the paper and it was a bit vague, the first edition. So we went right away to the *Evening Chronicle*'s offices which were on Shude Hill and I went in and that's when we found out. It would be around 4 p.m. They told us there were fatalities but didn't give any names. Then they started saying, 'So-and-so's injured but in hospital,' so we knew the ones mentioned were all right – Harry Gregg, Bill Foulkes. I remember praying, saying, 'Please God let them be safe, all my friends.' Then panic set in. This guy had a car so we drove home. My parents were distraught. There was a service every Thursday at Mount Carmel; the place was full, nobody sure who might have died. When we went to bed we knew there were deaths but weren't sure who. A lot of my friends had not been mentioned. It was only the next morning that we realised. We came here to Old Trafford and we came in the dressing room and we just sat looking at each other. There was Ronnie Cope, Ian Greaves, other reserves like Shay Brennan, Gordon Clayton, all looking at each other and not speaking. The reserve team coach came in and the word was 'go home, come back on Monday'. And that was it. We didn't go home; we went to Eddie Colman's parents' house because we knew by then about Eddie. We just sat with them, the parents, and Eddie's girlfriend. We were in a state of shock. After that it's all one mist.

I went to all the funerals. I can remember when the coffins

arrived; they weren't real coffins, they were big boxes, not like the coffins we knew. We went to Ringway and came back with them. There's a gymnasium which is now a room I worked in but it used to be a gym and all the coffins were placed in there.

It was tears, mist and shock and sadness. Every time we saw somebody the tears just flowed. I went in hospital a couple of weeks later after the funerals, then Jimmy Murphy took the team and all the fit ones to Blackpool and stayed at the Norbreck. They wanted to get them out of Manchester because Manchester was a dead place; it was just as though a bomb had hit the place. Everyone was in shock. I came out after the operation. I missed the Sheffield game, the first game, but was back for the West Brom game. By then they had bonded again, to play for their team-mates who were injured or who had died. They were playing not just for Manchester United but for the history of Manchester United, for those players and everything. The fans wanted them to do well. There was sadness but it was flying the flags for the lads. And when they did have such amazing results it did help to bond the team and the fans. There was so much sympathy from all over the world. It's remained ever since. I think that's why they have so much support all over.

WILF McGUINNESS

I was working in a factory. It's a world apart. You didn't get information then. Everybody now has transistors on the machine or on the desk, getting information minute by minute. But this rumour started in the factory that something had happened at Munich and it began slowly to seep through and people couldn't believe it. The whole factory went quiet. It still upsets me to talk about it. The shock went through the whole of that week. On the Saturday I couldn't rest at home; I got on the bus and went to Old Trafford and ten thousand others were stood by my side. I've never forgotten it. They

101

just stood there. Then of course we had post-Munich and getting to the Cup final purely on emotion. The team really wasn't good enough. I went to that first game afterwards but I can't remember anything, I was so emotionally upset. I was swept along purely on emotion. All the losses were tragic, but the most tragic of all was Duncan Edwards.

LORD STAN ORME

The day of the crash I was in the Ferranti machine shop. In football terms most of the people there looked toward Oldham Athletic. I was from Manchester, my thoughts lay with United. I was football mad and this led to much good-natured joking, so that, and I remember this distinctly, I was walking down a passageway that ran between the lathes, parallel to the railway lines. Outside it was dark and misty and one of the charge hands stopped me. Had I heard about the plane crash? The United plane had crashed. The thought, the first thought that flashed through my mind was that this was part of their joking with me. I immediately rejected it; this would have been an untypically cruel joke. I can't remember how the rest of the afternoon went. I was thinking about it all the way home. I then remember my dad coming home and us both listening to all the news we could find.

The other odd thing is how different it was then; there was no local radio, no Five Live, none of the news channels we have now. Certainly no Sky or CNN – how different it would be now. My dad and I just listened to all the scheduled news broadcasts, mainly on the radio. We began to list names, Edwards, Busby, Tommy Taylor, Liam Whelan, Eddie Colman, Geoff Bent, Mark Jones, Bobby Charlton, Harry Gregg, David Pegg, Jackie Blanchflower. So many.

One other memory is particularly vivid. It is the first game after Munich. In truth I don't really remember who we played, who scored or what the score was. The bare facts don't matter to me. The images of that night are vivid. We were outside the ground, there were thousands and thousands of people; it was a night match and the crowds are always worse for a night match. We were crammed in that narrow road (I think it is called United Road now, then it didn't have a name) that ran between the ground and Glovers factory. The crowds were pressed solid. There was a mood of hysteria in the air. My dad said that it was useless, we couldn't move. He said we should go home. My dad said this! Go home from a United game! So we started to move slowly, as best we could, back down the road to go home – then lo and behold, we found ourselves by an open turnstile. I still, to this day, don't know how we came to that turnstile, but we did. When we went in it was a haven of peace and quiet after the chaos outside. There was a policeman standing just inside the gate and my dad told him that he was needed outside, not in here.

We bought that famous programme, the one with no United team names printed in it. Before the kick-off it was announced that United had bought Ernie Taylor from Blackpool and Stan Crowther from Aston Villa. Ernie Taylor was a great but an ageing player; my dad thought Stan Crowther was the worst player to ever play in a United shirt. The impression given was one of building a team in a panic. In the event it was a united team of United players who played and won that match.

I hardly remember the details of the game; what I do remember was the night, the atmosphere, mainly the noise. When the whistle went for the kick-off there started a shriek. I have never heard a noise like it, before or since. It was like a shrill animal cry; it had a feminine sound to it. Remember this was 1958, there was hardly a woman in a football ground. There were a lot of women in the crowd that night. The sound went on solidly for forty-five minutes. Then for the whole of the next forty-five. It is the sound that I remember most from that night, with the sharp peaks when United scored their goals. A shriek, a scream, something like that.

PAT McDONALD

I can remember the disaster. I was in Rome Street. The first news we got of it was in the *Evening News*. They'd stopped to refuel, there were conflicting stories. It was such a strange feeling. It came over on the radio. There weren't many televisions then. When the news came through that they had actually crashed it was terrible. I was kicking a ball about when I first heard. It must have been about four o'clock. People were crying in the street, grown men; the devastation was unbelievable. It was such an eerie atmosphere. It was like people had lost their own. I was just coming up to nine. The school I went to was football mad, St Patrick's, it was a real football area. The atmosphere in school the next day was shocking. I know when you are young you don't fully grasp the seriousness, but you could sense it then even though you were so young. People were mortified.

BRIAN KIDD

As everybody says, they know where they were when they heard about Munich. I'd been to a meeting in Manchester and I happened to be in my father's car and we were coming out of the city. I suppose it would be five o'clock or thereabouts and my father wanted the evening paper, so we stopped at the news vendor at the corner of Princess Street and Portland Street. I got the paper and jumped back in the car again and there in the stop press, I can't remember what the precise words were, but it was sort of 'United in air crash at Munich', something of that nature and just having ten or twenty lines in the stop press. That was all that was in the paper at that early stage. Then getting home and of course turning on the radio, and then constant radio for what seemed like days. But the disbelief, I suspect, in reading the newspaper in the car between my father and myself was almost 'well, they won't have got that precisely right'; it would be far more low key than the first impression of the shocking headline. But as soon as we got home and the radio was on, it was very depressing indeed.

I remember being stunned and I suspect that feeling went on for weeks, really. The impression in the city was almost as I experienced as a very small lad after the Blitz in the city centre and knowing my parents were shocked that their place of work had been destroyed. It was described by my father as being similar to that. There was such a feeling that it was make-believe rather than it was the real thing. It took the heart out of the city, I'm sure. To some extent, even in my older age I don't feel a lot different about it.

I can still feel quite emotional and in fact when the celebrations – no, that's the wrong word – when the commemoration of the Munich disaster took place this year, I thought I would cope with that little ceremony before the match quite easily. But I have to say I got highly emotional at that and realised that there were a few other people of my age group who were the same. And I thought I probably could have coped with that without thinking about it. I had my daughter with me and she realised I was really living the moment again. I was very, very much affected by it – it took a while to get over that, I think.

There was a terrible silence everywhere. It was as though some louder noise would offend the situation in some way; almost as though we were all in church and you were expected to have a low level of voice and it was a whispering scene of dismay and astonishment, I suppose. But of course the fact that one or two of the well-known names did not die instantly was prolonging that feeling for a number of days. Going back to the main name again of Duncan Edwards. I know he survived for a few days and it was the feeling that you were almost on the ward where he was and therefore you didn't want to raise the noise level too high in order to give him the best opportunity to pull through. Of course, that was not to be. It was certainly a period when people didn't find it very easy to be happy over other events at that particular time. It's hard to describe. I suppose that it could have affected each individual. I think people felt related to it. I was one of many

105

thousands of fans who used to go regularly and felt part of it. Yeah, it was as though something had been taken away from us, part of our lives.

I didn't go to any of the funerals. I suspect you're going to ask me about the first game and yes, I was there. If I remember rightly it was an evening kick-off. I suspect about a Wednesday. I don't know what time we were allowed in the ground; but whatever time it was, I have a feeling it was about three or four hours before the actual game was due. I was there very soon after the gates were open and I was staggered by the number of people who were there at that point; and the feeling of uncertainty really about what was coming as well as the grief, I think is the right word, that everybody was feeling. I suppose it was quite amazing, the way in which the crowd could rise to the actual playing of the game at the end of the day. But I think that was almost a sense of relief that there was something to shout about, to make a noise about, when previously it had been the opposite. I suppose the grieving time was expected to be finished.

I think it was a couple of weeks, if not more, before the game was played after Munich. I remember they were allowed dispensation for a while. There were a few games that should have been played that weren't. I did feel at the time for the opposition at that particular game because that must have been highly difficult for them in those circumstances. I think there was a minute's silence, and nobody ever abused those sort of minute's silences, as occasionally has happened since. And I think that that commemorative day in 1998 was respected absolutely fantastically. I think that was part of one of the reasons why I got particularly emotional about it. I felt as though the people did understand how everybody felt in 1958 and that day and it was indescribable. It was certainly very moving, that's all I can say, really.

At that first game, it was almost as though the crowd realised they were making a noise but hadn't intended to, but did and felt relieved by the fact that they were able to do that.

That's the way it came over to me. But I think it would start off very uncertainly as to whether they should be making such a noise at the time. It did move on though, things did move on during the game. Everybody got animated, mainly I suppose because of the fact that they suddenly realised that this makeshift team was actually doing quite well, and almost the disbelief really at the end of the game of the result. I think it was almost a relief that everybody had got it off their chests, that they were able to make such noise and they had found their voices again at a football match.

MICHAEL DUNHAM

The Munich air disaster had such a terrible effect on myself. I was absolutely beside myself with grief. Being a young boy I was really affected by it. I think probably I was in school or I came home from school and heard it on the radio that there had been an aeroplane accident. So I think it was probably on the radio or I was told by my father that this had happened. It was totally mind-blowing, devastating that such young men should have been in this sort of accident. Of course the aftermath with Busby, et cetera, in hospital and on the brink of death was just so appalling.

KEVIN McALENY

In those days I had a scooter, a Lambretta. I was in insurance and I arranged to see a couple of girls to sort out their insurance. So when I go down to their house in Ardwick, it was about quarter to four. I was in one room sorting out the forms and they were in the other room. And one of the girls comes rushing in saying, 'United, United have crashed.' That was the first I knew.

I've still got the papers at home from the day after, the *Express*, the *Mail*. There wasn't much information at first but gradually it came through. It even gets to me now. It was unbelievable. These lads you'd seen, you felt as if it was part of you. You were part of that club, whereas today when I go they're all posing. People aren't there for the match. The players then were part of the community. I'm not for one moment saying I knew those players, they were just passing acquaintances, you'd see them around. Nobody ever bothered them.

When they brought the bodies back from Ringway Airport, I got my scooter on my own and I went on to Princess Road and I ended up near Princess Parkway, you knew the route. The crowds were that dense all the way. I stood there. Eventually as all the vehicles passed people had to get buses, weren't many cars in them days. Eventually they went to Old Trafford where they kept them overnight. It was a very sad time. I went to Old Trafford to pay my respects, everybody did. All day, for days on end, people were putting flowers down, not like it was when Busby died and people were putting all sorts down. It was just a few flowers down. In the streets lots of people pulled their curtains. Even the City fans, there was no animosity. You'd meet people and you wouldn't know what to say.

JOE DILLON

I was in Hong Kong when it happened. Of course communications weren't like they are today, you know. We found out on the camp and we got the information off another lad who was a very keen United supporter. He came from Manchester and was absolutely devastated, couldn't believe it. He thought it was just rumours going around.

HUGH JONES

I remember exactly how I heard about Munich. In fact, I remember more about how I heard about Munich than I do about my first two football matches. What I remember about

108

those two football matches after Munich was the crowd really. I think I have a memory of Shay Brennan playing but not a lot else.

I was walking along Barmouth Street which was a terraced street; the houses have gone but the street's still there in Beswick. It was just before my eighth birthday. We used to banter with each other as eight-year-olds do. A friend of mine was walking down the street the other way and he was a City supporter. This is not typical as I remember, and he probably didn't understand it; he was probably about ten or eleven. He shouted across the street, 'United's plane's crashed and they're all dead!' I didn't believe it.

Then when I got home and was told I was very upset. It was probably the first time that tragedy really touched my life. I didn't believe that things like that could happen. I remember being told, I remember going to the football matches, I remember the *Manchester Evening News* and the *Manchester Chronicle* at the time with the pictures of the funerals and looking at the pictures of the big crowds. Some of the players were buried not far away, but I don't have a single memory of what it was like in the classroom afterwards or that it was talked about. My guess is that people were less open about death in those days.

GRAHAM STRINGER

A terrible day. I was at school, I went to Poundswick Grammar and we'd heard nothing. I didn't cross the city and see the newspaper hoardings saying what had happened. I got home and my father was home and he broke the news. I didn't go to another game then until the late 1980s apart from the game when United had bought Albert Quixall from Sheffield Wednesday. It wasn't the same; I still followed them, I still am a big fan, but it wasn't the same.

GEORGE REYNOLDS

The one thing I remember about Munich was that my uncle, who was working in Manchester, came back with the *Manchester Evening News* special edition with a photograph of the team with black circles around the faces of the players who had lost their lives. I've still got it upstairs. I heard it at school and then later on the six o'clock news on the radio, then seeing what was in the papers the next day. I was only young but I knew that this was an awesome event. Then slowly the news filtered out.

The big thing I remember is that link between Matt Busby and Duncan Edwards; Edwards not dying immediately after the air crash and Busby struggling to stay alive and not being told about Duncan Edwards's death; I remember that being played out in the newspapers. I can still remember that now even though I was only nine or ten. Then there was that long period when they were still in the Cup but only had less than half a team to put out. Then losing to Bolton with Nat Lofthouse and that so-called shoulder charge. That was another one, if you weren't a United fan after 1957, then you certainly were after '58.

DEREK WYNNE

I remember the exact moment I heard about the Munich air disaster. My mum loved knitting. She'd knit for anyone; even to this day, if she hears someone's having a baby, she'll start knitting something for them. It was a pea-souper of a day, misty and cold. We were on the Ashton Old Road and we went into a wool shop. In those days you could order wool and my mum must have ordered some and we were going in to pick it up. Any rate, somebody came into the shop and said, 'Have you heard about United?' Some relative had come and told them. We thought they were joking at first but then realised it wasn't a joke. When we got home the radio was buzzing with the news. I remember my dad sitting there crying when they read out the names. You didn't see men crying in those days, especially someone like your dad. I was only eight or nine and to see your dad crying wasn't what you expect. It had a real effect on me to realise that it could mean so much to anyone. That moment, seeing my dad crying, probably had so much to do with shaping the kind of person I am. It made me into a much more sensitive person.

As the news came in it became more and more serious. It had an effect on the country as well. Although my sister was eight years older than me and a big United supporter I can't recall her being upset, but she must have been. Even the kids at school who were City supporters were upset. It was a bit more friendly in those days and everyone was upset. At school next day it was the talking point, it was on everybody's lips. We had prayers in assembly. By then more details had filtered through. It was worse than had at first been envisaged. I was already going to be a Red but the disaster sealed the deal.

CLIFF BUTLER

Everybody who was around at the time has their own memories of Munich and a lot of them are private, but in public terms I was working on the *Daily Mail*, based in Leeds as a Yorkshire-based reporter. I'd been there about a year and I'd quite enjoyed it, but it was a sub-office and I fancied coming back. So I arranged to come on a particular day.

I got on the train in Leeds mid-morning, arrived in Manchester I think lunchtime-ish, stepped out of the station at Victoria and saw an evening newspaper placard, the *Evening Chronicle* or the *Evening News*, I don't know which. It said something very simple like 'United in air crash drama'. And I thought, it'll be something small, never expecting it to be what it was. They'll have exaggerated it, I thought. So I got a paper and of course it was a very early edition and very little was known but it was obvious there had been a crash but there was little mention of deaths, injuries. I got a taxi to the office even though it was only down the road, walked in and I think

111

I and many other reporters and journalists and production staff probably walked out of that office the next time thirty-six hours later. I slept in the office certainly that night because as anybody can imagine, all hell was let loose.

The *Mail*, like all other national newspapers, had their own personnel on the plane, some of whom were killed. Peter Howard, chief photographer, and another photograph person, whose name I can't remember, but Peter Howard and someone else had survived it. Eric Thompson, that wonderful sports-writer, had died. He was a sportswriter and cartoonist unique in that his big match reports were accompanied by his own cartoons and drawings of the event, quite amazing. He was killed but because we had survivors from the *Daily Mail* who had access to telephones they were able to tell us details of people who were alive, people who were injured and, more to the point, people who hadn't survived and were dead, so that we in the Manchester *Daily Mail* office probably knew hours and hours beforehand – much more than the official news agencies, United as a club, and certainly the families.

A lot of the time that I and many others worked on that story on those first two awful days was spent talking to members of the families back here, players and supporters and officials, because from our own man, and men on the scene, we knew an awful lot more. I certainly knew that I was – if I say able to tell people it sounds not the right phrase, but I was able to tell people in some cases that their loved ones were OK, seriously injured, slightly injured and in one or two cases dead, because journalists in those days on big disasters, mining disasters, air disasters, very often were looked upon when you knocked on people's doors as the local priest, the local policeman. Very often you were breaking bad news to people.

I broke the news over the telephone to at least two families that their loved ones had died and one of those families was the family of Willie Satinoff who, from memory, was a textile merchant in Manchester who was one of the fans who were on the official plane. It was not an easy time and that's an understatement, but again when there's a job of work to do just like policemen and ambulancemen and paramedics, you get on with the work trying to do it as tastefully as you can but never forgetting of course that there's a product at the end of it, a newspaper. So it was half social worker, half journalist, and probably another half of being something else as well. Not an easy task but it helps you grow up; helps you grow up very quickly, that. You never wish it to happen but it is part of your growing-up process. I think you look upon it properly and sensibly and politely and you act as nicely as you can as a human being. Even though you've got a job of work to do, that other people argue you shouldn't be doing, because it involved death and distaste, well tough, but that's the way of the world.

The mood in the suburbs and the city, the mood every-where, everywhere around was just of quiet. I remember a lot of quiet. Nobody spoke, for days and days, in anything but hushed terms and tones. I remember going to the ground at one stage, basically to pay my own fan's little tribute, and everybody was either just standing and looking at the fabric of the ground, the stands, the walls or were walking around slowly in a semi-daze; hardly anybody spoke. I don't remember speaking to anybody and there were hundreds and hundreds of people coming and going but a lot were just standing and offering, I suppose, their own little prayers, their own un-spoken thoughts, paying their own tributes; but there was no conversation and the city itself was like that. As I say, whatever conversation there was, it was just very low, very quiet. It was like being at a funeral but before the funeral. I've never and I don't wish ever again to witness such mourning.

But then of course the world goes on; a makeshift team, players you've never heard of and, in the oldest of clichés, life goes on. But those first few days were dreadful, dreadful. And my memory of the weather was that it was sombre and grey. Everywhere was sombre and very, very grey. People looked

sombre and grey, grey-faced. It was awful. I've rarely sat back
and thought about it but I don't want to see it again.

BOB GREAVES

I remember it all quite clearly. There was all this consternation
over on the news side. Being a leader writer I was a little bit
removed and in a separate office. The news went around the
office like wildfire. It was about four o'clock and close to
going-home time when we became aware. At first you thought,
'Oh, the plane has just had a bump, a technical hitch.' Then it
became quickly apparent that this was not just one of those
exaggerated reports. It was deadly serious and of course the
entire office was then gathering around the tape machines.
The editor asked everybody to go home who was not part of a
selected group who would bring out a special edition, so we
were all politely moved on, including me. People were waiting
outside the front office for news and waited for that edition.
We just hurried home and listened to the radio.

The next day there was a strange dramatic atmosphere in
the office but in order to be professional the editor again
insisted everybody carry on with their normal tasks rather
than concentrate on this one story because there was still the
rest of the paper to produce. I wrote a leader on the tragedy
that was developing and how all of Manchester was waiting
with bated breath and anxiety to see the full extent of the
tragedy. It was that day that he asked me to cross over, as it
became apparent that he needed a specialist to write about
United, so he asked me to leave politics and join sport. News
reporters had been dispatched to Munich to cover that end
but he needed somebody to find out what was going to happen
at this end, to find out what was going to happen and how the
club was going to carry on as a football club. There were
reporters dealing with the coming home of the survivors and
arrangements that would have to be made for funerals. There
was also a sporting story to be told about whether they would

114

play the next game and there were stories to be written about the team that Jimmy Murphy would be trying to get out, and there was the postponed Cup tie against Sheffield Wednesday that should have been on the Saturday but was postponed for ten days or so.

It was my first game. I went by car from my home in Heaton Moor and I remember making my way there and wondering if I would ever reach Old Trafford because of the number of people on the road. There were as many coming away from Old Trafford as going because they had gone hoping to get in but had found it hopeless and had turned around and come away. It was a bizarre atmosphere at the ground. It wasn't so much a football match as a display of emotion. I remember Albert Quixall saying later after he joined Manchester United how difficult it was for Sheffield Wednesday facing this tidal wave of emotion willing Manchester United to win, how difficult it was to get themselves in the right frame of mind to play a game of football. And I think other teams subsequently in that Cup run must have also found it difficult. It was as if the whole nation was willing them along and they were swept along on this tidal wave of emotion as far as the Cup. But then of course, a Cup final is so different from an ordinary football match. It was in the new surroundings of Wembley and because Bolton had not enjoyed all that much success, it was so important to them and they wanted to win. United's emotional adrenaline had faded a little and the true strengths of the teams told and Bolton won, easily really.

Coming completely from outside was possibly slightly easier than if I had been reporting regularly in sport. I didn't have any great baggage with me. People forget that eight journalists were also killed, so suddenly there were eight deputies now working together so I suppose we supported one another. I remember the *Evening Chronicle* representative had not got a sporting background; Keith Dewhurst was his name, and he was new. It was the same with the nationals. It was deputies who took over, so we were all feeling our way.

I shall always associate those early days with the smell of swimming bath chlorine because Jimmy Murphy took what was left of the first team squad, plus the best junior players and the survivors as they came home, to Blackpool to take them away from the trauma that surrounded Old Trafford. As the bodies were flown home they were kept in an emergency morgue in the gymnasium, so you couldn't expect players to continue life normally with that kind of background and with funerals taking place. So he removed them to the Norbreck Hydro at Blackpool which was a big rambling hotel which had a swimming pool. He made that the temporary headquarters for the playing side. After training, the players would come back and change in the swimming pool area and Jimmy Murphy would give his update press conferences by the side of the pool. So I always associate that smell of chlorine with Jimmy Murphy's press conferences.

And of course there was a lot of speculation about what his first team would be. I suppose the biggest surprise was Shay Brennan who had been playing in the A-team, and who made his career later on as a full-back, but played in that first game as outside left. Murphy didn't have any natural wingers left, but Brennan scored twice in that game.

DAVID MEEK

It was great in those days. I used to know them all, the Viollets, the Charltons. I saw them on the pitch and got to know them. Munich was the great changing point for United. The players used to take it as an honour, not a duty to play for the team; they played their hearts out. In my opinion one of the great forces behind the Babes, apart from Busby, was Jim Murphy. He was great with the players, a fine fellow.

I was in Liverpool, I was working as a rep at the time. I was coming back and coming to Lime Street station, they're very friendly people. And as I was coming up the approach at Lime

Street one of the paper vendors said, 'United's had a smash,' and I said, 'Oh yes, which United?' and he says, 'Manchester United, your people.' He said, 'We don't know much, just that the plane's crashed.' When I got home of course I found out. That was the first I heard.

It was very, very mournful in Manchester. It was the topic of conversation on everybody's lips. The players were youngsters, they were all children really. What was Edwards, seventeen or eighteen? Dennis Viollet, I knew him as a boy, he lived in Moss Side, and big Frankie Swift, he had gone. He was a great United supporter too, regardless of the fact that he spent so long with the opposition. But that was the camaraderie in those days. It was a great tragedy because they were representing Manchester, they were us and it took years for the story to ever die down. I don't think it ever has. You get old codgers like me talking about the tragic day. They were just coming to their peak. It would have been fantastic had those lads lived, absolutely fantastic.

ALF DAVIES

I can remember the night of the Munich disaster very well because I was a paper boy at the time. I was working at Clark's on Mauldeth Road. I must have been about twelve. I went up there as usual at about a quarter to five. It was a snowy, sleety day. The papers were dropped off and that's when I first heard about it. It was all over the front pages of the Manchester papers although there wasn't much information. There used to be about sixteen of us worked on the paper round. We were all upset, all talking about it. The next day at school everyone was in tears. The headmaster, a Mr Organ, was a big United supporter. He said a prayer in the morning and everyone was crying. Every day at assembly he would mention Duncan Edwards. Then when Edwards died, he said another prayer. I remember that because I cried a lot then. Edwards was my hero, my favourite United player.

117

All my mates were United supporters; we were all so upset.

ALAN DURRANS

I found out when I came to the front door and heard a lot of people shouting. I thought there was a row going on. Then a neighbour said, 'They've all been killed.' I said, 'What are you talking about?' and he said, 'The football team, the plane's crashed and they've all been killed.' I stood there and thought, I wish somebody would come and talk to me about it. So, I went in and put the radio on. We didn't have a television. It said Duncan Edwards and Matt Busby were both very ill. Then it went on from there. It was a matter of watching the bulletins and wondering if Duncan would live or not, but he didn't. I went to one funeral, Eddie Colman, because I lived near the cemetery where he was buried. He was one of my favourites. I didn't have a car so I had to go to the nearest one. It was a sad time. Jimmy Murphy's first signing was an outstanding one – Ernie Taylor – and he never got the credit. For me he was the man who made Stanley Matthews. He did a great job for United.

The first game after Munich was against Sheffield Wednesday and they beat them. I went to that game. The atmosphere was terrific. I really felt sorry for Sheffield. They were losers as soon as they stepped on the pitch. I think we all felt sorry for them. There was tears before, during and then after the game 'cos they'd won. The disaster was talked about for months – everyone wanting to know how's Matt going on, how's Duncan? The others had made reasonable recoveries but Berry and Blanchflower never played again.

ALBERT THORPE

I can remember just before the Munich disaster my father had a cocktail party just before Christmas time and I remember Matt and Jean Busby were there. I can remember that quite clearly and that was only two months, less than two months, before the actual crash.

Now when the crash occurred I was actually up at boarding school but the matron knew of my father's connection with United, although he wasn't a director at that time; she knew that he was a friend of Matt Busby's and she came in the dormitory when we were getting ready for bed on the sixth of February and said that the plane had crashed. Obviously at the time I didn't know the severity of it. It was only in the papers the next day that the full severity of it came to light and how serious it was. But that was when I first heard the news; I was literally getting ready for bed at prep school.

I didn't come back to Manchester, I stayed at school. My father hadn't been on the plane although he was actually supposed to be, but he had cancelled for business reasons. There was no need for me to come home. But it was the next day my father came on to the board.

Harry Gregg and Bill Foulkes were clearly part of the rebuilding process because they had survived the crash and it took time for players to come back. Bobby was one of the first to come back, Dennis Viollet. There were one or two players who I don't think were ever the same after the crash; I'm thinking of players like Kenny Morgans, Albert Scanlon and even Dennis Viollet only stayed until 1960, two years after the crash, before he was sold to Stoke. But clearly it was a time of rebuilding with players like Ian Greaves, Ronnie Cope, Freddie Goodwin; they were all brought from the junior teams and into the first team. Shay Brennan was another one and we bought Ernie Taylor and Stan Crowther, so they had to be blooded into the side. Albert Quixall was also bought. I remember that very well, the night he made his debut; it was an evening game here at Old Trafford and it was a record British signing, £45,000, which was a fortune at the time, great excitement and Albert running out in front of a full house. It was quite an exciting period really; although it wasn't successful in terms of trophies it was an exciting team, an exciting forward line if you think of Charlton, Viollet and Quixall.

MARTIN EDWARDS

It changed my life. I was in the Air Force and I was playing football. The place where we were was the base for the air traffic control for the whole of Europe, military control. We'd trained in the morning and because I was an officer I went in the officers' mess after training and some of the chaps who'd been on duty on air traffic control came off duty and said there'd been this crash in Europe involving Manchester United. At that time, apart from playing in the Air Force, I was playing with Bishop Auckland as an amateur, and would have stayed as an amateur had it not been for the crash and gone and got a teaching job in the north-east and played at Bishops. So, ultimately, the crash led to me changing those ideas.

The crash was in February and the club found itself short of experienced players. Jimmy Murphy had known this friend of mine at Bishops, Derek Lewin, and it came about that Derek offered to find some players at Bishops. And also coincidentally Bishops had been knocked out of the amateur cup. They'd won it the previous three years and I'd been involved in the previous two, so Bishops weren't needing us. So Derek, Bob Hardisty and myself – it would be in March, fairly soon after the crash – came down and played in the Central League. There were ten thousand watching the 'stiffs', and we were the stiffs because sadly you'd had a whole team taken out, either through death or injury. Others had been made up into the first team so we just helped out in the reserves with a lot of young players. I would come down every Saturday and play, so I never really had a feel of Manchester because I was up in the north-east. It was more when I got in the first team and turned pro and came down to Manchester.

Playing away was a funny experience in that there was a definite atmosphere. The crowds were large, it was always their biggest crowd. I think there was a sort of expectancy. The crash had given Manchester United this aura and although they'd had this tremendous team, I think it was that crash that produced this aura. There was this expectation, anticipation. I suppose there was interest in the club because of the crash but it was different.

I would come down on a Friday and just play on a Saturday and on a Saturday night I'd just go and stay with my parents in Hyde if I was staying over. I was not training with them at that time. Lads who were injured who were getting better would come into the dressing room, so people would be welcoming them back, fellows I didn't know. Allied to the losses it did make for a strange atmosphere. People weren't sure how to deal with it. There were those like Bobby Charlton, Bill Foulkes, Dennis Viollet, Albert Scanlon who were quickly playing again. I played in a friendly match in Munich which was the first time they had flown since the crash. Previously they had played one or two matches in Europe but had gone by sea. But for this one we flew; it was the first time they had been back in an aircraft. That was definitely strange. Everyone was very quiet on the plane. It was quiet and people were naturally a bit apprehensive.

My first game was in November 1958. At the end of the season the crash occurred, I was looking for a teaching job. I was going to go back to the north-east but United asked me to stay on so I got a teaching job in Stretford and stayed as an amateur, still in the reserves. In early November I turned part-time professional on the Monday and I was on the team sheet on the Friday morning when it went up in the dressing room. It was against Bolton at Burnden Park. I'd been at Bolton a good seven years, knew all the staff. We lost. I was already twenty-five, but I didn't want to turn full-time because of the maximum wage. It was £20 a week. When the boss got better he wanted people committed to the future so he was always looking for a replacement. I was four years there altogether but had a cartilage operation after a couple of years. I left in 1962.

WARREN BRADLEY

It had been a terrible two weeks since the crash. It wasn't nice at all. We'd attended funerals of our friends and we were constantly getting reports of how the injured were. It was a very, very sad time. Old Trafford wasn't a nice place to be and Jimmy Murphy had taken all the professional playing staff away to Blackpool for a week before the Cup game.

At 10.30 on the morning of the game, I got a call at our hotel to go and see Jimmy Murphy. I thought he wanted to give me a telling off because I'd been out in Blackpool the previous night for a couple of pints. I was stunned when I was told I was playing. The day just flashed by after that. It was all a big rush to get tickets for my dad and brother and sisters. There was no time to think about making my debut. The team was just thrown together really. We never met up with Stan Crowther for instance, who signed from Aston Villa on his way to the game. We went to Davyhulme Golf Club for a pre-match steak and then to Old Trafford. Everyone was just lost in his own thoughts in the dressing room. There are always jokers in a football changing room but nobody was laughing or larking about that night.

The dressing room was a complete contrast to the wall of noise that hit the Reds when they appeared. The atmosphere was tremendous. Poor Sheffield Wednesday had no chance. From the moment we came out there was a continuous roar. United could have named any side that evening and they'd have won. The fans just lifted us and carried us along. It was incredible. I remember one of my goals was direct from a corner. It was the first time I had ever taken one. My only thought was to put in a decent cross. It was a bad corner and if it hadn't been for the wind it would have been the keeper's.

I scored another from close in and suddenly, from being plain old Brennan to most people, I was now 'Shay'.

Normally I would have gone for a drink after the match. But on that night I just wanted to go home. I'll never forget that so many friends and a great team died to enable that to happen.

SHAY BRENNAN

I well remember where I was when the news about the crash came through. I was in a café in Huddersfield. When I joined United I was aware of what we had to live up to and I knew that only Matt Busby could rebuild a team that was capable of being the best in Europe. All the sixties team did. I played with people who had been in the crash but they didn't talk about Munich. Busby certainly never did. It was an unwritten law that it was never mentioned.

I was still with Huddersfield Town at the time, but I remember travelling over the Pennines to Manchester on Wednesday 19 February to watch a makeshift United team take on Sheffield Wednesday in the fifth round tie that had been postponed because of Munich. It was just thirteen days after the crash and United's first match since the tragedy. I stood in the crowd at the scoreboard end and I'll never forget that fantastic atmosphere. It was something you had to witness to understand. Everyone in the ground seemed to be willing United to win, which they did three–nil, with a goal from Webster and two from Shay Brennan, who was playing outside left. Albert Quixall was still a member of the Sheffield Wednesday side, who didn't know what had hit them.

DENIS LAW

I was in the B-stand and well, you've seen the programme, nobody knew the team. The goals that were scored, Shay Brennan, were at the Warwick Road End. It was a left-hand corner kick, an in-swinger. Shay Brennan scored there and Albert Quixall played and Stan Crowther, that was his first game, and Ernie Taylor. The atmosphere? You know, you always had a mist about the place in those days, a fog. I think people smoked more and the smoke rose up and the trains were always knocking about at the back here so you always had some mist about the place. The atmosphere was quite quiet until the teams came on and then everybody got behind them and it was an emotional thing. I think, however, it was more emotional when the final whistle went. We were the underdogs; the team won purely on emotion, everybody got behind them. It was purely emotional. Everyone was an Eric Cantona that night. The crowd swept them along, the emotion was terrific. I can remember my dad crying, coming out afterwards.

DANNY McGREGOR

CHAPTER FIVE

The Sixties

Law, Best, Charlton and All That

There is an abiding memory. Matt Busby, blue suit, white shirt, red tie with matching red handkerchief tucked into his breast pocket, his face saying it all as he hugs each United player, the emotions welling inside him. Here is a man, tearful and scarred, who must, more than once during that evening at Wembley, have been swept back to that moment when his young team had been destroyed. His memory like an old black and white newsreel flickering disjointedly over the painful moments that shattered his life and brought an end to the lives of so many of his players and friends.

Bobby Charlton and Bill Foulkes, who suffered on that snowy afternoon in Munich, understood the joy; so did Brian Kidd, who admits in this chapter that they were all aware that they had to win this one for Matt. It was 1968 and United had just won the European Cup. They had realised Busby's dream.

Busby had been the first English League manager drawn by Europe. Chelsea had been the first club invited into the competition back in 1955 but the Football Association, fearful of a fixture pile-up and as regal as ever, ruled that they could not participate. But when United won the title the following season, there was no debate. Busby's dream now was to put United alongside the great names of European football – Real Madrid, Honved, Moscow Dynamo, Red Banner, Barcelona. He knew that his Busby Babes could match them all. Perhaps it was also his Scottishness, which kept him one step removed from the English establishment and their view that we had nothing to learn from others. Whatever it was, Busby was resolved to take United into Europe and even though the footballing authorities tried to stem his ambitions, the Old Trafford board backed him to the hilt. United were going into Europe and that was that.

Whether the Babes would have eventually conquered Europe will always be open to debate. But Munich had wrecked Busby's dreams. It took a further ten years to get back to where they had been. With so many of the Babes dead, it all had to be done with a sea of fresh faces. Denis Law, Maurice Setters, David Herd, Noel Cantwell, Paddy Crerand and John Connelly all joined up in the sixties, plus of course a fresh crop of youngsters. Only Charlton and Foulkes remained from the original Busby Babes. And here they were in 1968, first taking their revenge on the Spanish masters and then lifting the European Cup after a memorable performance against the Portuguese champions Benfica.

For the fans it was the crowning moment in United's history. Memories are still vivid. They poured south in their thousands, taking over Wembley stadium and turning it into Old Trafford for the night. To be able to boast that you were present for that match remains the ultimate medal of credibility for any United fan.

The fans were now supporting their side with even more fanaticism. There was chanting and singing from the terraces, sometimes abusive but often humorous. The Stretford End, packed with twenty thousand spectators, had become a focal point for support, every bit as vociferous and fanatical as the Spion Kop at Liverpool. The wearing of team colours had also become more common and pronounced. It was all about identification. Tribal boundaries appeared; no more one Saturday at Maine Road, the next at Old Trafford. Sadly, the 1960s also witnessed the first sparks of violence on the terraces. Like most clubs, Manchester United was not immune from the problem. There was a minority who set out to cause trouble, mainly at away games, terrorising local communities, ripping trains apart, and generally looking threatening. Winning the battle off the pitch seemed to have become every bit as important as winning it on the pitch. By the 1970s it would become an even more serious problem, with United's good name tarnished by the hooligan element. At the root of it all was an increase in tribal tensions. The days when fans could stand on the terraces alongside opposition fans were fast disappearing. By the 1970s, supporters would be segregated.

It was also partly a result of more and more fans travelling to away games. The 1960s witnessed a consumer boom, with cars flooding off the production lines and on to the roads. Whereas travelling to away games was once restricted to public transport, the car offered new opportunities. Groups of fans would club together to pay for petrol and travel by car to grounds all over the country. Television also added to tensions on the terraces. Each Saturday, *Match of the Day* presented and analysed the day's top games. Slow-motion replays would in time also question refereeing decisions, again adding fuel to the intensity of matches. It all heightened the competitiveness of football.

There was also now more money in the game. The maximum wage had been abolished in 1961 and suddenly footballers were among the new rich, paid handsomely while also able to realise high transfer fees. United themselves became the first club to smash the £100,000 barrier when they paid Italian club Torino £115,000 for Denis Law in 1962. The players upped and moved from the Old Trafford communities to the leafy suburbs, less likely to be spotted on the buses or in the coffee bars.

But then there was George Best; not just an outstanding player but also young, good-looking and with a mop of Beatle black hair. Best quickly became the idol of the terraces. And at times his off-the-field pop star antics attracted as much press attention as his footballing. George Best was undoubtedly football's first pop star.

With Law, Best and the effervescent Bobby Charlton lining up, United boasted as mesmerising a strike force as any side in the history of British football. Even today, their names conjure up images and memories of a rich bygone era. And so it all culminated in that warm May night at Wembley, sadly missed by Denis Law, who lay in a hospital bed.

The new Busby side had begun to display its abundant class by winning the FA Cup in 1963. Two years later they clinched the title and then repeated the exercise in 1967. Sandwiched in between all these trophies were some dazzling performances in Europe. The new United had arrived and all that was needed now was to win the ultimate prize: the European Cup.

———◆———

I arrived at Old Trafford when Matt Busby was still in hospital in Munich. Jimmy Murphy was manager when I got there. Then the boss came back and I didn't know him and he didn't know me. The first time I saw him was when he came in on crutches, whatever time that was. And then he slowly started to appear more and be able to walk reasonably, taking over from Jimmy more and more. I gather that before the crash he used to be a track suit manager but he didn't do that afterwards. His management style had to change as a result of the crash.

I always felt that he was extremely good at analysing other players. In his team talk he would go through player by player who you were playing against. His memory of who was a left-footed player, a right-footed player, quick or slow, was tremendous. He'd just go through the team. I felt that was his strong point, his analysis of the team, individual by individual. So for me, as a winger, he'd say, 'I want you to push him on the outside, just knock it and run,' or 'He'll try and force you on the outside, he's weak, play him on the inside.'

But in terms of his strategy, certainly when I played, I

never heard him talk about four–four–two. I know that since there's been quotes that the move to four across the back came at the club through him. When we played Real Madrid, all the English clubs were playing a pivoting centre half but Real Madrid of course were playing four across the back. So the left-back was wearing a number four and not a number three. In Europe they played four across the back. Now Sir Matt I felt never, I won't say *didn't* recognise it, but we never talked about different styles of play. When we played this friendly against Real Madrid at Old Trafford and lost six–something Harry Gregg's comment was, 'They only came over the half-way line six times and scored six times.' But why they did it was because they had Puskas and Di Stefano against the one centre half. We didn't change. To be fair, English clubs as a whole didn't talk much about a European style of play. I suppose you're looking into the sixties with Alf Ramsey when it was taken up. But not in the late fifties.

He could be hard. He had this nice easy exterior for the media and a very sociable fellow. Quietly spoken but ready to take hard decisions with his players. If he needed to drop somebody he dropped them. Most players will say he was quite firm about it. When you negotiated wages, he was quite firm. Wilf McGuinness went in to see him to negotiate a rise and came out having negotiated a cut. His public persona was of being a very amiable, quiet, friendly person. But you don't take that away. That was him. But in terms of managing the club he knew what he wanted. He was quite determined and firm.

Now Jimmy Murphy was quite different. When Jimmy Murphy gave a team talk he would be quite explicit what he wanted the full-back to do to the winger. The boss would speak in euphemisms – 'I want you to let him know you're there' – but Jimmy would tell him precisely what to do. Matt would never say, 'Kick him,' whereas Jimmy was explicit. Jimmy would get much more excited in the dressing room. He'd get excited with the juniors. I'd go down and watch the juniors play in an evening, then go in the dressing room and Jimmy would be talking to these fifteen-year-olds as if they were seasoned players with language to match. But his enthusiasm was tremendous. I didn't know Jimmy as a teenager, but the lads such as Brian and Wilf who'd been there from school had a tremendous admiration for Jimmy. They saw him as the architect of their success. He'd coached them, bullied them.

WARREN BRADLEY

Sir Matt had this wonderful way of making you feel you were a good player. He was charismatic, there was this presence. He was a lovely man. I never heard him swear. He had a lovely way of speaking to people. He knew everybody's name. When I was in the youth team and he came to watch you playing, the hairs would stand out on your neck. You wanted to impress. You felt he was aware of everything that was going on. He had a great assistant in Jimmy Murphy. He had a massive influence on the place. I think it's fitting when you see that statue. I was so pleased when we won the European Cup. I think most of the players will say the same: it was for Sir Matt, that was in the back of our minds.

If players did anything he didn't like, he'd say, 'Hey son, we don't do things like that here at Manchester United,' and that was the nice way of putting the responsibility on you. He didn't have to rant and rage. A look was enough off Sir Matt. It was the way he said it. And really, I suppose, when you look back, it's like the way you bring your children up. He was, without a doubt, a father-figure. For me it was the honesty as well. You might not like his decisions but he was always honest. Whatever decisions he took there's no doubt that it was for the good of Manchester United, that's for sure.

BRIAN KIDD

I'd do the normal teacher's routine but on Tuesday and

Thursday I would go down to the Cliff to train in an evening, but because it wasn't the first team I'd largely train with the young lads. It was interesting to see all these schoolboys they'd bring down for trials and training. They'd be the stars of their town's team but wouldn't even get a kick because there were better players. It was interesting to see the quality they could attract, so it was no surprise to see the quality come through in the years ahead.

If we were playing in London, the headmaster gave me the privilege of having a free period on a Friday afternoon so I could get off about three and travel down to London and take some books to mark on the train. The other lads of course had gone earlier on the Friday morning. I would meet them in London. There was a tradition to go to a show on a Friday night. I would meet them for the show and then go back to the hotel. From London we'd come back on the Saturday night but I wouldn't do any marking coming back. I suspect they thought I was a strange breed. Most lads hadn't had much education beyond fifteen, so people with degrees must have been viewed as a strange breed but I never felt there was any resentment. Young lads don't think about the future too much but maybe they thought, here I was being a part-time pro and doing other things, having another career. But if there was any envy it wasn't shown. It was a busy time, having two jobs.

As a player I never remember any real rancour. Being a winger I was fairly near the crowd but even at places such as West Ham which is a very tight ground, even more so then, I haven't any memories of bitterness or a sense of envy. They might have jeered if you missed a shot but nothing beyond that.

We'd get so much for a win and also a crowd bonus. I think we got £4 for a win, £3 for a draw. But most of the weeks there were sixty, fifty thousand, never less than forty thousand at Old Trafford, so we got £4 if there were sixty thousand or more. Now this is something the fans probably wouldn't realise. When we were shooting in with the single ball – you took only the one ball – we knew that when certain parts of the ground were full there were sixty thousand. If there were gaps at the corners you knew it wasn't sixty thousand and we weren't on as much crowd bonus. I'm sure the fans didn't realise that when we were talking and kicking the ball about before the match what we were doing was weighing up whether we were going to get any crowd bonus or not.

I'd go full-time in the summer during the school holidays so that was ideal. And because none of the League matches were played under floodlights, as soon as winter closed we played every Saturday. That suited me because I could go full-time in the summer, play those two mid-week matches in September when the light was OK. I'd also go full-time in the Christmas holiday and at Easter. Also we played Boxing Day, New Year's Day. When we played Real Madrid in a friendly at Old Trafford I did a day's teaching before I played against Real Madrid at night. A friend picked me up and took me home. I'd change into my professional footballer's suit as opposed to my teacher's tweeds and go to Old Trafford. So, I played against Real after teaching all day. Puskas, Gento, Di Stefano, Santamaria were all in the Madrid side. But we lost. And the next morning I was back in school for nine o'clock.

Travelling on the bus could be awkward even then although I was not that well-known. The fans would be keen to say hello. Most just wanted to do that but others wanted to say a few other things. It wasn't easy, especially for the superstars. Even though at that time it was still friendly it could still be awkward. It certainly removed any privacy. The press would ignore privacy, ring you up in the middle of the night, knock on the door. And that was for me. I have a lot of sympathy with the stars of today. The lads of that generation were very conscious that the boss had links all over the city, that it would be fed back to Old Trafford. The boss socialised a lot, the Cromford Club was home from home for some of them. Although it was known that they were there, at least they got the privacy; because that close friend of the boss owned the

Cromford, they got some privacy. The boss would be aware but at least he knew where they were.

WARREN BRADLEY

I had a dramatic introduction to Manchester United. I'd been to Old Trafford from the age of about six to watch reserve matches. My dad used to take me along on a Saturday afternoon, this would be 1956, maybe 1957. I don't remember much about it except that we went in the Old Trafford paddock. I'd be lifted up on to the bench on the cinder track around Old Trafford. I'd be mesmerised by it. But the first first-team match I went to was the game immediately after Munich. My dad took me along to that and all I really remember about that game is the queues getting in. I was quite worried about being pushed against the wall. We went into the Old Trafford paddock in that game. We just got in when the gates shut. I don't remember anything else about that game.

The first game I do remember better is the next one. That was one–nil in the Cup and I just remember the goal in the last minute. It left me with an abiding optimism that United will score at the end of the game. I also remember the sheer noise when that goal went in. After that I became an addict. I used to go with my dad on Saturday afternoons regularly and I suppose I became even more addicted when I started going on my own in the 1962–63 season. I abandoned my dad and started going with my mates from school. I went to every home game between then and 1968 with, I think, one exception when United lost three–two at home to Arsenal. I went to most away games in Lancashire, the Midlands and the odd London game. My dad worked for British Railways and I could get free passes and cheap tickets. Having abandoned him at Old Trafford, he got a season ticket in the Stretford End stand and then he'd take us to away games, either on the train or drive us to the Burnleys and Blackburns of this world with my mates from school.

My dad had a Ford Popular so initially we went to Old

Trafford in his car, sometimes with a mate of his from work and parked in streets towards the Manchester side of Old Trafford that don't exist now with old terraced houses. I used to have a rattle and scarf then. There was no uniformity about the scarves then. Most of them were knitted and my grandmother knitted mine as well as a red and white bobble hat. It was very much a flat hat society going to football matches. You'd go there; because I was a kid people would make way for you and let you stand in front of the barrier or behind the barrier, depending on what was the most convenient position. There was a certain camaraderie; people would share flasks around with you at half time, tea and coffee or whatever. When I stopped going to Old Trafford with my dad I used to catch the 53 bus and then walk from Trafford Bar.

Afterwards when I went on my own I used to drive my mates to get to Old Trafford at 1 p.m. so we wouldn't get locked out, particularly after the '63 season when there were a lot of full houses. It was all turn up and pay. I used to meet my mates outside Belle Vue greyhound track, we could all get buses to there, then we'd get on a 53 and we'd be in the ground for 1 p.m., often desperate for the rest of the crowd to get in in winter to warm us up. It was a pretty cold place to be, on the terraces at Old Trafford at 1 p.m. Or even worse, I used to get to railway stations – such as Victoria station to go to Lancashire grounds – early to make sure we got there. And we'd end up being absolutely frozen through by the time we actually got on the train. These Football Specials would arrive with absolutely frozen windows, more like cattle trucks in the early sixties.

GRAHAM STRINGER

I went to Gornic in Poland and then we went for a trip to Auschwitz. It would be in the early sixties, because I came out of the Army in '59. We went by British Eagle Airlines to

United striker Jack Rowley turns away after opening the scoring in the 1948 FA Cup final against Blackpool. United went on to win 4–2 in what was viewed as one of the all-time great finals. *(Popperfoto)*

United captain John Carey holds the FA Cup trophy aloft. *(Popperfoto)*

The new generation of Busby Babes celebrate winning the 1955 FA Youth Cup. Standing at the back on the left is Duncan Edwards, while Eddie Colman, Wilf McGuinness and Bobby Charlton are the three on the right at the front. *(Colorsport)*

The police battle to hold the crowds back from rushing to mob the players after United's victory over Portsmouth secured them the Championship in April 1956. Now Busby wanted to prove that United were the best club in Europe. *(Popperfoto)*

United's 10–0 hammering of Anderlecht in September 1956 is still their record victory in all competitions. Dennis Viollet scores the eighth goal, soon after which United fan George Reynolds remembers having to leave the stadium to get a bus home.
Popperfoto)

United's famous 3–1 victory over Athletic Bilbao in February 1957 took them through to the semi-final of the European Cup where they fell to the eventual winners Real Madrid.
Popperfoto)

Roger Byrne and Duncan Edwards look on as Ray Wood saves from Di Stefano during United's semi-final defeat against Real Madrid in April 1957. (*Popperfoto*)

An early 1950s floodlit game at United's training ground, the Cliff. (*Popperfoto*)

Newspaper headlines announce the tragedy of the Munich air disaster. (Both *Popperfoto*)

The whole city mourned the loss of the eight United players and, even now, more than forty years on, memories remain clear and painful. (*PA*)

A tearful crowd stood silently by the roadside as the coffins of those who died were brought home to Manchester. (*Popperfoto*)

The coffin of captain Roger Byrne is taken from Flixton parish church in Manchester for the short journey to the crematorium. (*PA*)

United captain Bill Foulkes leads the new team out for their first game after the Munich crash, on 19 February 1958. It was an emotional occasion for all concerned, and the team sheet in the match programme was famously left blank. (*Popperfoto*)

Shay Brennan scores direct from a corner to set United on their way to a 3–0 Cup victory over Sheffield Wednesday in that game. (*Popperfoto*)

Warren Bradley, who joined United in the immediate aftermath of the Munich disaster. (*Colorsport*)

Politician Stan Orme, a United fan since the 1930s. He recalls that on a trip to see United against Barnsley he encountered coal miners for the very first time. (*PA*)

Louis Edwards, Matt Busby and Les Olive, key figures in the post-war renaissance of the club. Les Olive was appointed assistant secretary in 1942 and is still a director of the club nearly sixty years on. (*PA*)

Krakow and we landed and we had problems and they had to find money. They didn't want Polish money and they had to find English money, the pilots did, to bribe people to unload and things like that. Going round the market place and people begging you to sell them your English currency; they'd give you ten times the value that they'd give you in the hotel just to get the pounds.

At the game I'd never seen so many people going mad. Our seats were gone when we got there – we were stood on a wall at the back of the ground in a snowstorm. You could hardly see the pitch. Looking through this blizzard with everybody going crazy. You've never seen so many empty bottles of vodka in your life and this guy, a Polish guy from Polish radio, says it's the only place in Poland where you can express yourself and people come to football matches to do this. We could see these police chasing into them with their batons. They weren't United supporters, there were only a few of us there. It was their own people. Absolutely plonkered on the vodka. After the game we stood there – it was a great game – and they were going around with sacks collecting the empty bottles of vodka. It was quite frightening what was going on on the terraces. Course, we won.

HUGH JONES

It was, I think, the '64–'65 season. I'd been to West Brom once before where I watched United get beat three–nil or something. It was a cold January, February day. I think it might have been the season United won the Championship. It was cold, the pitch was frozen and it must have been one of Don Howe's last games. He was playing right-back and Best was on the left wing. He scored one of the best goals I've ever seen him score. I've never seen it on video but he went up to Howe – he'd already put him on his backside a couple of times – he flicked the ball over his head and scored a goal at the near post. Very simple. He taunted Howe that day. It was great. It was only years afterwards that I realised the significance. I'd seen Best make his debut, he did a body swerve past Howe at Old Trafford. He didn't do anything else in that game but I read years afterwards that apparently Howe had said to him, 'You do that again to me, son, and I'll break your leg.' As I saw this match years later I realised that Best was paying him back. Howe retired afterwards.

GRAHAM STRINGER

My favourite players over the years? I've always liked Denis Law. He always was great to watch. All right, he was a bit volatile at times, but that's what made him. And the same with Best. Yes, they could get sent off. But the game could be as boring as hell on a real winter's day and you're getting drenched, then the next thing Best has picked the ball up from nowhere and just run at the defence and it's in the back of the net. Now the rest of that ninety minutes may have been dreadful, but that thirty-second burst made up for the whole game. I don't think you see that so much now. Giggs can do it occasionally.

Law epitomises the style of United. Even now people compare – whether it be Andy Cole or Stuart Pearson – whoever, they will always have to live in the shadow of Law. They called him the King and he still is. The flamboyance of him, for somebody who was not particularly big, yet he could get up to the ball. And at the same time having a slightly mischievous streak about him. It was always a standing joke: Christmas is coming, Denis'll get sent off, so he can go home for the New Year. You always knew he'd get banned. Cantona had it as well. As soon as Cantona lost the ball and started chasing back to win it, we'd all go 'aghhh' because he couldn't tackle to save his life and every fan would wait. Then he'd miss him and we'd say thank goodness for that. Beckham's the same when he's got his crazy head on him and Keane. I think people will say all right, he's going to miss so many games a

136

season but his work rate and what he gives the rest of the team is probably equal to it.

ROLAND COBURN

I went to Wembley. It passed almost over me in a flash because I was very much on the terraces. I think it was one of the very first times I'd ever been to Wembley and found myself fairly near the front. And how disappointed I was that the visibility was certainly lacking compared with the majority of other football grounds I'd been on where the terraces at least moved up at a reasonable angle from the ground, whereas in this case I was almost in the pit. I was behind one goal, the goal where Charlton headed his goal, and felt that the visibility only allowed me to realise that the players were attacking the other end. I could see the ball moving across but it was difficult to relate to the foreshortened ball passing when it was going along in the same direction as the pitch. I never forgave Wembley somehow ever again for not giving me better vision of that and I still think that's the case today. The sooner they knock it down, the better. But it was a terrific atmosphere. The noise I do recall was wonderful.

It was spoilt for a second reason to me because there was a young so-called United fan – that's not to denigrate the United fans in London – but this particular lad, I'm afraid, had had far too much to drink and I experienced my first dose of urination on the terraces and found that some penny-throwing was going on as well, which absolutely scared me at the time. To some extent the match became more of an event to me afterwards rather than on the actual occasion. I was obviously highly delighted that we won the Cup but I think the stadium was a big disappointment to me and it wasn't helped by my young friend, either.

MICHAEL DUNHAM

137

Watching the 1963 Cup final on TV was one of the most joyous occasions I can ever remember. There were red shirts everywhere – Denis and Paddy reigned supreme. I screamed and somersaulted to every goal and rejoiced that United were back. It had been a lifetime since the dark days of '58 when those young men had died.

My father's work moved him to Preston and we were off up north. The thought of leaving friends was distressing, but I was going to be nearer to Old Trafford, which made up for everything. I might now be able to get to a game. My time was to arrive that winter on an afternoon in December 1965. United were at home to West Ham and a friend and I stood at the side of the road hitching our way to destiny. Unfortunately, destiny had to wait a little longer than we expected as we ended up in Blackburn in a snowstorm. Having eventually made it to Manchester we caught a bus from Piccadilly and came face to face with Old Trafford for the first time. There are no words to adequately describe the feeling of that moment. My immediate thoughts were to get into the ground as quickly as possible because the game was long underway, but I found myself rooted to the spot, just standing there staring at the place as though hypnotised. I was there at last.

My friend grabbed me and dragged me from my reverie. It was already the second half and the score was still nil–nil as we ran past gate after gate desperate to find one open. We ran around the main stand and on towards the Stretford End, through the open gate and into Old Trafford itself. The moment I entered the stadium I will remember all my life. Up the concrete steps of the old Stretford End we ran. I could feel the atmosphere getting closer and closer until we could touch it at the top.

I remember looking down at the mass of people on the Stretford End and thinking I had reached my spiritual home at last. I felt a kinship which has lasted to this day. It didn't matter that the score remained nil–nil throughout, I was in awe of the red shirts. Actually seeing Denis, Paddy and Bobby playing under the floodlights was a superb moment. I relished the atmosphere, the singing and chanting, the camaraderie. The Stretford End became my second home. I stood there until they pulled it down at the end of the 1992 season. My spirit is still there and always will be.

The following season my now son-in-law and I bought season tickets and took seats next to each other in K-stand. That season was to herald a new dawn in the history of our club. The day the twenty-six-year wait ended on that sunny bank holiday Monday in 1993 I forsook my seat in K-stand and went back to the Stretford. I met my daughter under the Munich Clock where we clung on to each other with tears falling down our faces. I gave her my season ticket and made the pilgrimage to the other end of the ground. It was like 1965 all over again: they say you never forget your first time, and they're right.

PAUL WINDRIDGE

It would have been mid to late sixties, that sort of period. United were playing Villa away in an evening game and I asked could I leave school early to go to the match, because a lot of the teachers were strong United supporters. And they said no. The school I went to – Oppenshaw Tech – was next to a railway station and you could climb over the wall on to the railway station which is exactly what I did and I went. I caught the train into Piccadilly and got the Football Special. When I got back the next day, the head suspended me for a day or two. I was called into his office – he was very angry – and was told that this was not the way I was going to get into university. It seemed a big thing at the time, defying him and being sent home. I don't think I ever told my parents that I had been suspended from school.

GRAHAM STRINGER

I became a Manchester United supporter simply because of a friend, Paul Crimes, who at the age of eleven spoke non-stop about Man United and how great they were. Also because of the plane crash in '58 and because of the emotional ties, sympathies for the people who died and for Man United. I just became imbued with the Manchester United ethos and that was the team I began to support. It dipped a little in the early seventies and when they dropped into the Second Division, I lost a little bit of interest. But it was rekindled. Around about that time I was playing an awful lot of football myself, so I never had much chance to go and see United or any games.

My first game was in 1967, I can't remember exactly who it was they played – maybe it was Stoke City. My friend Paul Crimes took me to see this game. We got there and we worked our way down to the front of what is now the north stand and he told me that we should go over to the Stretford End. Now the only way to get there was to run across the pitch. We waited until the police officer turned his back. We were by the half-way line, so he said, 'Come on, let's run.' So we ran right across the corner towards the goal. Unfortunately Paul didn't make it. He got hit by some missile. I made it and got into the Stretford End and watched the game from there.

My concern was that I had lost my friend on my first time at Old Trafford, miles away from my home in Rusholme. It was the first time I had gone that far without parents to take me and I wondered how I would get back home; I was eleven and a half. But I made it home. I went round to Paul's house that evening to find out what had happened to him. He had a black eye and the St John Ambulance people had patched him up. Fortunately he had watched the game from a bench, the St John people had let him sit there. Anyhow, I was hooked. It was the first time I had seen a professional game so close up. Most people tell you the first game you go to you stay with. I remember listening recently to a phone-in programme and it was Edwina Currie who just didn't understand the emotions involved in supporting a football club. Some fans ringing in were complaining that they were being charged too much and she turned round and said, 'Why don't you go to another club?' Just totally illogical. Once you start supporting a team, it's there for life, irrespective of what happens.

I didn't go to City principally because of my introduction to United. Had I not been introduced the way I was I would have become a City supporter because most of my other black friends went to City. Their first games were at City and so they became City supporters. City was also in Moss Side and that's where the black community lived, still do. City was a strong team in those days, so it was a toss up whether you were a Red or Blue. It just so happened that you get integrated into one or the other. No, I didn't get any stick from my other black friends, because there were others supporting United as well as me.

RUDI KIDD

It's quite funny really, but initially I was brought up in a family from Cambridge and the first game I actually went to I was taken by Dad down to London to see games not involving United. It was an annual treat. I was taken to see Spurs playing Nottingham Forest and Spurs playing Manchester City. These were in the 1967–68 season. But even at that stage, maybe because they were the top team of the day, my loyalties were with Manchester United. I don't know why, but perhaps it was the 1966 World Cup and the influence of Bobby Charlton; the glamour of Best, Law and Charlton. But certainly when we came to move up to Manchester in 1969 Dad said, 'Guess where we're going to go. It's where you support the football team.' So we knew instantly that we were coming to Manchester. I was absolutely ecstatic.

The other thing we had seen when we were down in Cambridge had been the European Cup final and I do remember listening to those games on the radio, like the semi-final, the away match at Real Madrid and listening with my brother in my bedclothes. I think we were hiding under the sheets because we weren't supposed to be up so late listening to football, listening to the commentary of that second semi-final. So if it had been fairly mild before, by the time we left to come up to Manchester, United was our team. And then again it started off as a birthday treat. You'd get taken off to a football match. I remember, must be 1969, we went to see United play Coventry; that was my first glimpse of George Best in the flesh. We won two–nil, I think. The feeling of being among so many people was exhilarating.

ROGER HENNELL

When I started working as an apprentice I used to knock off work early and make my way by train from Liverpool up to Manchester and then get the train from the station to the football ground and watch the night matches and make my way home again. It was a long journey but well worth it and I used to do this on my own and I used to glory in it. Really, it was wonderful coming back the next day and telling all the Merseysiders how great United were. Actually I think the first time I went on my own was when I was fourteen, so that was while I was still at school, obviously. So it was quite an adventure in those days to do that sort of thing, really tremendous.

I'd get the train from Lime Street in Liverpool to, I think it was Central station, and the whole station was full of United supporters hurriedly getting on the train which went to Old Trafford station. All the red and white scarves, et cetera, full of anticipation and a really good atmosphere because in those days there was very little violence and it seemed a very, very safe place to be in, even for a Merseysider.

I remember I went to a game against Tottenham – in the mid-sixties, something like that – and the game was called off because we were all in the ground and all of a sudden the fog came down and they had to abandon, they had to postpone the game, and we were all given tickets to come back on the next Wednesday or whatever, so I stayed up in Manchester and duly came in on the next Wednesday to watch the game.

Also I went to a friendly game with Real Madrid and Di Stefano scored a couple of goals. Was Goodwin in goal in those days or was it Dave Gaskell? That was a friendly or a testimonial and Real Madrid won, but what an occasion, to see the likes of Gento and Puskas play. They were the legends of the day because they won the European Cup five years in a row. Wonderful occasions, wonderful.

KEVIN McALENY

The first football match I can remember was a televised game, a Cup final. It wasn't United but I watched it with my dad and was enthralled. We played football in the street and I was aware of Manchester United up the road; I would be about eight at the time. More or less simultaneously to that game my dad got a part-time job as an agent for Manchester United working for the Manchester United pools. Along with that came some complimentary tickets for kids. I think he came with me for the first couple of times and then after that I went on my own. When I say awareness of Manchester United, I mean a total awareness. We could actually see the ground from our house and hear it very well on night games. I lived in Old Trafford and you could stand on the front step of our house and see the lights of Old Trafford, day or night. At night time we used to see this amazing glow and hear this great wall of sound. The sound seemed to travel further then or maybe there was just more to roar about in those days with Law, Best and Charlton. So there was always this fascination with the place.

So, once these tickets came along, I started to go. Even when Dad stopped doing his work as an agent I just continued going. I would go in the youth gate at the back of the Stretford

End. It seemed incredibly cheap. Big long queues, lots of excitement, seeing people I knew and the expectation brewing. It was a little community. You got inside and it was the finest spectacle you could imagine. That's what the draw was, that was United in its heyday in lots of ways. This was 1965–66 leading up to 1968. Your memory does strange things but every game seems to me to have been exciting, lots of skilful play, very attacking, hard for other teams to weather the storm at Old Trafford. It may not have been the case away from home but at Old Trafford they were difficult to handle.

All sorts of players stand out, not always those who were in the headlines. Paddy Crerand was one of my favourites, Tony Dunne was another. Of course we all revered Charlton and in many ways he was at the height of his powers. He had a mature control over what was going on on the pitch. He had that fantastic long-range shot, drilling the ball. There was an expectation when he had the ball; players would back off him, and you'd think he's about to shoot. Then you had Law. The hairs stand out on the back of my neck when I talk about him. He was so exciting, goal-hanging. But he was lightning quick over a short space and a great opportunist. Billy Foulkes was another big hero. I remember Best coming into that side and we were all bowled over by him being so slight and almost insignificant-looking but suddenly the game would be drawn in his direction and you realised after weeks and weeks of this that he was making a massive contribution in a side that was already full of powerful characters. He could do everything, this guy, and that's what amazed us. He was riding tackles, tackling, playing on the wing, moving in, scoring lots of goals, and also a growing reputation in his social life, so he was a bit of a hero in that respect as well.

And there were the unsung heroes like Johnny Aston who in the European Cup final played the game of his life. He was one of those people I used to feel sorry for because he was barracked by the crowd a lot of the time at Old Trafford. He had a very difficult career I think, but he would come good on the big occasion. Brian Kidd was another guy who people that I know knew. Looking back on his contribution it must have been difficult coming into that side at his age. But I think he made a mark. He became a skilled front man, and a hell of a nice guy. You noticed him more as time went on. When he left, you realised just how much of a contribution he had made.

I went to most home games, but still being young I did not go to the away games until I became a more adult attender. There were never any problems. The difference then was that the whole day was taken up with the excitement. *Grandstand* would start on television and there'd be some coverage about the game, so you'd sit down and watch that and get very excited and then you'd walk very early to the ground. I'd certainly be there by 1.30–2 p.m., queue up but enjoy the build-up, all the energies of the crowd. You had to get there relatively early because of the crowd. That doesn't happen now.

I've been there with my brother-in-law whose company has some smart seats – in fact we were late – we were in the new stand but without the build-up and the queuing you didn't feel quite so involved, more hermetically sealed. You arrive by car, go up in a lift, past restaurants and you could almost have been watching on television. When you looked up at the boxes at the back people were watching it on television. It used to be rough and ready. The accommodation in the ground was poor; I can remember as a little kid being held up to see. The toilets, food and drink were very rough and ready whereas now it's very slick. It's now very obviously a business. Now they take account of their customers whereas in the past you were there simply to see a football match; anything else was a bonus.

SIMON THORP

I was a newsagent at the time, working a thirteen-hour day. Anyhow, it was the time of the Manchester United–Real Madrid semi-final, 1968, and I was determined to go, so I found cover for the shop while I knew I was going to be away. I told the wife, 'I won't be here Wednesday. I'm going to see United playing Real Madrid.' 'OK,' she said.

Anyhow, a few days later she comes storming in. 'Hey,' she says, 'you've got it all wrong. You've made a mistake. The *Manchester Evening News* has just arrived and it says here that United are playing Real Madrid in Spain.'

'That's right,' I said.

'But you said you were going,' she replied.

'I am,' I said. She went berserk. She hadn't realised. But I went.

When I was at the game, I was coming out of the stadium. There were a group of Man United fans in front of me, all wearing their red and white scarves. They were getting a lot of hassle from the Spanish fans who were spitting at them and threatening them. I said to them to be careful. I could see that it was all going to get out of control. I've seen before how the Spanish police can react, so I told them to watch it and I pulled them away before it all got out of control. Anyhow, one of the lads introduced himself to me. He was called Joe Glanville. He was very grateful for me intervening and said thanks.

The next month I was at the European Cup final at Wembley and as I'm coming out of the ground I saw the same guy sitting on a fence. I said hello and we had a bit of a chat about the game. It was amazing that I should have bumped into him again in all that crowd. But then a couple of months later I went to see United playing Blackpool and as I'm coming out of the ground, who should I see but this same bloke. So we had another chat. He came from Malta. He said he was a United supporter and ran the United Malta supporters' club. We exchanged addresses and used to write to each other every month or so. Well, one thing developed into another. He used

146

to edit a newspaper called *Echoes of Old Trafford* and he sent me a copy. They were having a competition in the newspaper, a draw, and the winner would spend a weekend in Manchester going to see the match and being put up in an hotel. Anyhow, I wrote to him and said, 'Look, I've got a big house, don't waste money on a hotel, they're welcome to stay with me.'

And so they did. And of course when the winner came he wanted to meet Matt Busby. Well, we were lucky. We had tickets for the guest lounge and who should come in but Bill Foulkes. I knew him, so I asked him if he could get Matt and ask him if he'd come and meet these supporters from Malta. So Bill says OK, and off he went and came back with Matt. It was wonderful. Since then I've been to Malta a number of times and they've all been over here. It's now got to the stage where everybody comes and stays with me. They've all been wonderful friends.

JOE DILLON

I had been to see the semi-final in Madrid. It was my first-ever trip abroad to see United. In fact it was my first-ever trip out of the country, and the first time I'd ever been on a plane. It was real adventure. I think it cost about £20, which was a lot of money in those days. The match was the icing on the cake. I was a fanatic by then and it was really an amazing experience. The stadium was filled to capacity with one hundred and twenty-five thousand. We'd won the first leg one–nil and nobody really gave us a chance. By half time Real were winning three–one and it looked curtains for United. But in the dressing room Busby told them that they were really only a goal behind. We went out and scored two goals; Foulkes, the most unlikely scorer, got the winner and United were into the final. After the game the Real supporters turned nasty. They were throwing stones at us and wanting to fight. The Bernabeu was an awesome sight. It was all concrete, concrete tiers, concrete terraces and concrete seats. You didn't sit on a proper seat, you just sat on concrete. But it was a fantastic atmosphere when the Spanish chanted, it was just an incredible, amazing scene.

The final was the answer to every United person's dreams. We were the first-ever English club to play in Europe and winning the competition was almost a mission. I'd have preferred to have won it somewhere else, say Milan or Rotterdam. I suppose winning at Wembley, which was kind of our home ground, took some of the gloss off it. But it was a fabulous night. I went down on the train. It was the most noise I've ever heard. Remember, there were about ninety-eight thousand United fans in Wembley and only a couple of thousand Benfica fans. Forty thousand came down from Manchester alone. I was eighteen at the time and it was another crucial stage in the development of a fanatic.

The homecoming was unbelievable as well. Half a million people were in the streets, crowded around Albert Square. United weren't as disliked in those days. We had the country on our side for that final. Everyone wanted us to win. Had we reached the final this year [1998] it would have been very different. I guess anyone who was not a United supporter would have wanted us to lose. We're not universally popular any more, except with United supporters. People look on us as being arrogant. But it was different in 1968.

CLIFF BUTLER

We had a training session at Old Trafford and this always sticks in my mind with Sir Matt. He was relating certain stories about the Cup final team of 1948 and certain players, great players who got caught up in the occasion. I always remember this because I tried to carry it out myself. 'Play the game, not the occasion,' he said.

We were sat down at Old Trafford and he told us, 'If it's the tickets or anything else, forget it now, that should be done. Just concentrate on the game. Play the game, not the occasion.

Just concentrate on that.' The game doesn't change, be it a League game or a semi-final of the European Cup. Sir Matt was good at that; if you believe in what you're doing you'll get the results. I don't believe you should be chopping and changing no matter who you're playing, just worry about yourself.

BRIAN KIDD

When I was a child I lived in Malta because my father was in the Navy. He was born in Manchester, in Collyhurst, but brought up a City fan. It was a split family; some supported United, but my dad supported City. In them days City were a Second Division side just before they became good in about '65, '66. United had Best, Charlton, Crerand and all the rest. Malta had a big United support base, and I probably did not even know City existed in those days. I thought Dad was a United fan and it wasn't until years later when we got to discuss football that I discovered that in fact he was a City fan. I suppose I was lucky because he could have tried to influence me more but he didn't, and I could have been going to Macclesfield next Saturday instead of Barcelona next Wednesday.

I went to boarding school in 1967. I always remember my first year at the school was when they won the European Cup. That was the big day. Some lads were allowed to go to the match; they had tickets and were let off school for the day. Unfortunately, I got in a bit of trouble and I spent the evening weeding. I was in tears. I was eleven years old and wanted to watch the match on television. We weren't normally allowed to watch TV and that was the only time that term we were allowed to watch anything because it was United versus Benfica. But while I was weeding one of my friends would nip out and tell me the score; 'Bobby Charlton's scored,' and I would then weed away very happily. Then with about ten minutes to go someone nipped out and said it was one-all,

149

they'd equalised and I thought, 'Oh, no.' By then it was getting dark and I thought, what am I going to do now? But then the housemaster came out and said, 'Go on, you can go and watch the rest of the game.' So I got in, just in time to see Georgie Best weaving through their defence to make it two–one. So I did see the best part.

For the big European game against Real Madrid in Madrid I went to bed at 9 p.m. and I think the match finished about 10 p.m. and I had this radio under my bed listening to the match. The score was three–one to Real and I was so upset, I thought that's it, we're out, and I turned my radio off and went to sleep. Of course the next day I discovered they'd drawn three–three and gone through to the European Cup final. I went to sleep unhappy but woke up a very happy lad.

The other time was when we played Estudiantes in the World Club Championship in 1968 and of course it was three in the morning played in Argentina. I set the alarm to go off at 1.30 a.m. so that I could go to the toilet and listen to this match on the radio. But they were good days at school.

Fortunately my grandparents lived in Manchester, so I got to see a couple of games. I think the first game would have been about 1969; they played Liverpool. It was the same weekend Sandie Shaw won the Eurovision Song Contest. I always remember that. I went in the scoreboard end. They said don't go in the Stretford End, there's always trouble there, so I went in other end. It never stopped fighting where I was. The Stretford End was fine of course, because there were no Liverpool fans up there. I was stood in the corner of United Road and the scoreboard end and non-stop battling. I've never been so scared in all my life. I think Liverpool won three–one which didn't help.

ROBIN MURRAY

It started really with the FA Cup in '63 and of course that time in the early sixties Matt did strengthen the side considerably.

He brought in David Herd, Noel Cantwell, Maurice Setters, Denis Law, Pat Crerand, players like that, so he did start to spend quite heavily in the transfer market and started to bring the success in, starting in 1963 with the FA Cup and the two League Championships in '65 and '67.

I always felt that United's best team was probably in '66 and that was the team that probably should have won the European Cup; but they let themselves down in the semi-final against Partizan Belgrade, having had that great victory against Benfica in the quarter-finals. So, in a way, I think *that* was the peak of the sixties side. The players that won it in '68 were just that little bit old and were probably just starting to decline. In fact that was the last trophy they won and they did go into decline. It was a wonderful period and wonderful that Bobby Charlton and Bill Foulkes were still around because they had been through it all, from the beginning to winning the European Cup. It was a very emotional night for Matt and the players. I can remember it very well.

I was in the official party going to the final and we went down by train and we all stayed at the hotel, went to the game and there was a big banquet afterwards with Joe Loss playing *Congratulations* as the team all came in after the game. I remember the tremendous crowds on the journey back in the open top bus. We were in one of the buses following on behind and it appeared that the whole of Manchester turned out for the celebrations that night. I've been involved in celebrations ever since but I don't think anything has ever matched that return to Manchester after the European Cup.

MARTIN EDWARDS

I was very, very lucky to be taken to the European Cup final which was fantastic, even thirty years on as we speak, the most remarkable event in my life. You can see everything about the club, all the things that bind you to the club come together on one incredible evening. When you remember things in your life you remember them in little bits and pieces, but not that night. I remember chunks rather than shafts.

I went down on the train. My dad got tickets for my brother and I. We went down early, we were in the ground early. It was a most fantastically good day, warm spring, summer day. My mum had made us sandwiches and as I say we were there really early, eating the sandwiches as the light was fading before the game. The ends at Wembley were standing ends. It was absolutely phenomenal. Worship, hysteria and colour, fantastic atmosphere.

The Charlton goal went in at our end. All the other goals were at the other end but it didn't matter where they went in because it was at Wembley. And because United have always been very cosmopolitan. Out of the hundred thousand there were probably about ninety-eight thousand United fans or more. Wembley had been taken over. Everyone was full of passion. You can go to Wembley and you can see passion, particularly when they had the two standing ends, but not like that, not like that.

We got a train to and from Wembley station. It was really late and I was small. I just remember these amazing feelings of contentment and happiness. I think the trains had been delayed. There were several trains going back to Piccadilly. They had the old-fashioned carriages. It was really difficult to get a seat because people were stretching out and going to sleep across the seats. The mood was amazing. It was really late. I was only eleven at the time. My school was very near where I lived, I was just there for the morning. At the break-time, some of the guys were pig sick that I should be the one going. I just went in the morning. An abiding event. It's hard to imagine with all sorts of nice things having happened to me since, how things can be much better than that.

LEON SWERLING

Manchester United was my home team; it was my dad's team. I

152

lived about a mile away. So I never had any choice in the matter. I did it the proper way. It seemed like you had an apprenticeship in those days becoming a supporter. First of all your dad took you to first-team games. I think my dad became a season ticket holder, then the following season, this is about the mid-1960s, I was allowed to go to reserve games with my friends on our own. I always had the impression that they were always large crowds. I remember standing behind the goal as a kid and they were large crowds at those games. So I did that for a little bit, then we were allowed to graduate to going to first-team games on our own with my mates. We were only ten. My dad was worried about me because I had a bedspread, a table lamp, everything was football. I played constantly, all the time. Every school I went to, I played in the first team.

I have a number of distinct memories of the European Cup final. One is of going up Wembley Way and seeing the big boards with all the rosettes on and the George Best rosettes. I would have been about ten. It could well have been on my dad's shoulders. I have a vision of looking down and seeing all the heads, the crowd as one and these islands of rosettes in the middle, these bright garish colours, those huge big ones they used to have.

I have real memories of being swallowed up by the stadium, the size of it; the other of being sat next to a vicar, plying me with sweets. We were opposite the Royal Box side, to the right, towards the tunnel. I was sitting next to a pillar. My dad had some close friends in London, we stayed there. I remember extra time; the players sat on the pitch at the end of full time and Matt Busby going round to all of them; the players looked so tired. It was quite a poignant moment. In hindsight they were really done and Busby did seem to earn his corn. I just remember him going round to all the players. I don't remember them lifting the Cup.

In the sixties footballers used to lend their names to companies, to be on their books. And Nobby Stiles for some reason was an electrician. My father had an electrician's firm in

Trafford Park and he had Nobby on the books. I don't think he ever did any job but they were close family friends, particularly my mum and Nobby's wife. So Nobby Stiles was basically my uncle, he'd hop round regularly, go out with my mum and dad. He bought me my first Subbuteo set for my birthday. I remember going to his house and he getting all his caps out. And this one particular incident, probably the most powerful thing that's ever happened to me in my life was that Manchester United were in a film, this is 1967, the film was called *Cup Fever*. I can still see the film in my head. I can still run scenes from the film. It was about a good team and a bad team. The good team lost their boots or had their boots stolen for this cup final game and Manchester United stepped in and helped them and there were scenes with the full team, the '68 team were in the film, training with these kids and of course they beat the baddies in their brand new boots.

They had the preview, the première of the film at the old ABC in Deansgate and I was taken by Nobby with Bobby Charlton in Bobby's car, a white Ford Escort. I can still see myself sat in the back of that car between the front seats with Bobby Charlton driving and Nobby sat on his left chatting away. Bobby Charlton never said a word to me, never said a word. The première must have been something like six, seven o'clock at night. My mum says I was waiting from the morning. I was sat for hours. I had this big chipboard, square piece of chipboard, and I had all my pictures, rosettes stuck on it. I remember a silver FA Cup, and I stuck that on it. I can still see myself arguing with my mum; my mum saying, 'He's not going to have time to look at that, you're just going to have to get in the car and go.' We had a big bay window in the house in Seymour Grove, sitting there waiting the whole day long.

So we end up in Deansgate. Crowds outside, hundreds and hundreds of people. The press are all there and the team are all in front of the cinema including Matt Busby, so I go over with Nobby. Matt Busby comes to me, puts his hands on my shoulder, stands behind me and we have our photograph taken by the photographers. We go into the cinema and we're sat amongst a row of Denis Law, Paddy Crerand, and me. I can just remember all the way through this film people leaning over me asking for their autographs. I was there. If I had died then and there and gone to heaven I would have been a contented boy. The greatest moment in my life.

TIM BAMFORD

The player who most excited me was Denis Law. In his first two or three seasons I think he was the most exciting, exhilarating player I have ever seen. When he got the ball the speed and the electricity of him was just extraordinary. I don't mean in terms of skill. If you start on who's the better player – Pele, Eusebio, Jairzinho – I don't think Law was in that class. He was in the class below, a good international player as opposed to a world superstar. But just in terms of sheer excitement, the way he headed the ball and the speed with which he ran past players, it was just exhilarating. I think also partly the personality, the arrogance, the speed. I think you can make the case out that Bobby Charlton and Best were superior players to Law – and both lasted longer, surprisingly – but Law was the one who had the electricity. He could make you laugh, the sheer impudence.

GRAHAM STRINGER

I always think Denis Law was the best in terms of personality and panache. George was the best in terms of sheer skill on the ball, and Charlton was the best for athleticism and sheer grace of movement.

KEN HASTINGS

I queued all night for a ticket for the European Cup final. I had a full set of tokens. I queued all night outside Old Trafford and got a ticket; there was a big queue over the canal. We went down to Piccadilly bus station with my mates and we caught the first all-night bus out of there. And then I gave my ticket away. I would never have sold it. I hated spivs and touts; I had the ordinary fan's disgust of them. I'd got my A level physics exam the next day and I desperately wanted to go to university and it was a straight choice.

On the day of the game I went to the library but I couldn't concentrate. I then came back and watched the match on telly. My dad went and he went with the person I gave the ticket to. My mother and I drank a bottle of Liebfraumilch which I suppose was quite unusual to have in the house then. I had some sleep although I was very excited, so I went into the A level physics exam with some sleep but a slight hangover. I suppose the only good thing about it was that my mates with whom I had gone all over the country to football matches, they all went down to the game. They took a different decision which I suppose meant that they were more committed than I was, and they all failed their A level physics. They got back at six o' clock in the morning; they turned up boggle-eyed and failed. Most of them have done very well since; they re-sat their A levels and went on to universities and got good jobs. I passed as well. It was a defining moment.

GRAHAM STRINGER

I didn't go the European Cup final; I watched it on television. I remember breaking my record player. The record player – it was one of these old-fashioned ones with the speaker in front of it – was positioned under the television and I pulled my chair up in front of the television and, of course, when the first goal went in, my foot shot out, and it went through the speaker of the record player.

DEREK WYNNE

I first went to Manchester United when I was eight years old; it would have been about 1968. I remember being so excited I couldn't eat my tea before I went. It was a night match. I can't remember who it was against but I went in the car with my dad. I had a United scarf which he'd bought for me which I had stuck into the window so that it was flapping outside the car. All the way up the Chester Road there were other cars with flags going up the road. I was so excited I was almost beside myself. I couldn't believe how big Old Trafford was. And the noise. The noise was tremendous; there was loads of singing. And the colour; it was totally red. It was marvellous. I don't really remember much else about that game. I remember walking back to the car with all the fans. We'd parked on Trafford Road because my dad's office was opposite the dock gates on Trafford Road and walking through the docks to get there and everybody was talking about the game and how brilliant it was. I couldn't get to sleep when I got home because it had been such a great night.

When I was quite young like that we must have gone four or five times a year. When I got older, into my early teens, and I was at secondary school I went more frequently. When I got to about the fifth year at school I used to go with my friends from school. We went as a group, on Saturdays. We'd go on the bus, the 264 from Altrincham. Get off at Old Trafford. We went in the Stretford End a couple of times but we didn't always go in there. It was a bit squashed. We used mainly to go in the south stand, standing. Standing was all right. If you were in the Stretford End and United scored you'd get thrown into barriers and if you weren't careful you'd get slightly crushed and winded but it was all right. Sometimes the guys were a bit of a pest but it wasn't really ever a problem. They'd make sure you weren't standing in front of a barrier, they were pretty good like that.

I saw some Derby matches at Maine Road and Derby matches, whether they were at Maine Road or Old Trafford, were always my favourite matches. It was so tense. And one of my brothers was a City fan which made things even worse. It was the local rivalry; you were either a Blue or a Red and come Derby day everybody was really excited, waiting for it to happen.

Apart from the fact that tickets were available for us to go and see United, Georgie Best was playing. I did see George Best playing. I saw Charlton play. It was amazing, seeing Best flying up the field. It was totally awe-inspiring, really.

JUDITH SWIFT

I vividly remember Georgie Best. He used to roll up in this superb E-type Jag. He was just so different to all the other players. I think he had it sprayed a few times because it was scratched so many times by girls. I used to hear so many stories because there was a groundsman here called Freddie Cook. He used to be George's gardener as well. He used to tell us tales, but I'm not going to tell you.

BARRY MOORHOUSE

People who now talk about footballers drinking in the modern day and age as though it didn't used to happen should have been with me on occasions, because there have always been some heavy drinkers among footballers, not just with United. But I saw a lot of it with United. It didn't seem to stop them playing pretty well. Busby, of course, was said to rule with a rod of iron but I used to know Matt very, very well. I used to go to his house in Kings Road and chat to him and Jean; Lady Jean as she later became. I still see various members of their family – the Sandys, the Sheilas – socially, lovely people. But I don't think Matt did rule with a rod of iron because I don't think Matt knew the half of what others at the club pretended he knew.

I don't think he ever knew that George Best was a heavy drinker from the age of probably seventeen, because I remember walking into a club. I wouldn't call it a nightclub because that would be too posh a term for it. I'd been working very late on a late-news bulletin which was then part of Granada's scheme of things. I used to finish work at eleven, half-past eleven, midnight on something called *Granada in the North* which ran till midnight, so I used to go to various little nightspots in Manchester near Deansgate before getting the late bus home.

I walked in one of these places one night and it was probably frequented by pimps, taxi drivers and the odd prostitute; that sort of place but it was handy, convenient, just off Deansgate. I spotted this highly recognisable slim little figure at the end of the bar with a glass of clear liquid, obviously drinking in a very solitary fashion, which later I learned is the mark of real drinkers with problems. He probably was standing at the end of the bar and I looked across and I looked across two or three times and thought, that is George Best, that is undoubtedly George Best. George Best had already become famous and he already had strings of women allegedly attached to him, but there he was by himself at half-past twelve, one o'clock in the morning. So I went over and said, 'I'm Bob Greaves, you don't know me but I think you're George Best.'

'Yes I am. Yes I am.'

'Would you like a drink?'

'Yep, I'd like one,' he said and I thought he was drinking tonic water, but in fact he was drinking large vodkas with probably tonic water in it. I bought him a large vodka and it didn't occur to me at the time, but it seemed to me later to be a signal of the problems. He might never say it was a problem but it probably was that he was into drink in a very big way. And I'm sure the club didn't know at that stage and if they did they should have done something about it, sent him to a counsellor; yes of course they should, but they probably didn't know. But people like me knew and that was when he was just sixteen or seventeen years of age.

I think I learned a lot from that when I thought about it a bit later. Sir Matt wasn't *able* to rule with a rod of iron because he didn't know what was going on. Of course nobody blabbed to tabloid papers in those days, nobody rang in and said . . . there was nowhere to ring to. There weren't the local radio stations galore, there weren't the tabloid papers with the paragraph every day with the 'If you know a good story ring us on this number free'. People just accepted it as part of life and I often wonder if George might have been helped. Who knows? I don't know the answer, but it is possible if the club had known. And if they did know they should have done something but if they didn't know, they couldn't do anything.

But it was sad because I think that was the beginning of his problems because he was living in digs at the time. I knew him very well when he ran his club just off Deansgate within a stone's throw of that place I've just been talking about. When he opened Slack Alice's I used to go there four, five, six nights a week to socialise there with him, the beauty queens, the footballers, the men about town, the girls about town. Great years, but I think George's problem might well have been nipped in the bud. Maybe I should have rung the club at that time and said, 'Do you know?' But nobody did and I didn't and there you go.

BOB GREAVES

CHAPTER SIX

The Seventies and Eighties

Decline and Fall

All good things come to an end. After the European triumph
of 1968, United's reign at the top came to an abrupt finish.
The truth was that even that European Cup winning side was
already past its peak. The years were catching up. Bill Foulkes,
Shay Brennan and Bobby Charlton were all over the age of
thirty while others were fast approaching that milestone. Denis
Law's best days were also behind him, to say nothing of his
dodgy knees, while George Best was about to nose-dive into
an alcohol-induced mist. Let's face it: Law, Best, Charlton and
Foulkes were irreplaceable.

The 1970s and 1980s were not to be good years. The
League Championship eluded them time and again. True,
they picked up the FA Cup on a few occasions, but it was
hardly compensation. The Championship was the one trophy
they really craved, the one that really mattered. Even worse,
United crashed into the Second Division in 1974, courtesy
of a memorable back-heel from their all-time favourite Denis
Law, then playing with Manchester City. Though truthfully,
United were down irrespective of Law's nifty footwork.
Thankfully, United's sojourn in the lower ranks was brief
and they stormed back as Second Division champions and
with a following every bit as big as it had ever been.

Managers came and went. After the European triumph
Busby stood down to make way for his young protégé Wilf

McGuinness, but McGuinness had been unfairly left with the impossible job of finding new players to succeed the European stars. There was the added problem of George. It was a hopeless and thankless task. McGuinness's hair turned white in the process and then dropped out. McGuinness was too young, still one of the players and with little experience. Busby was briefly persuaded back, but in June 1971, the board felt they had found the answer in Frank O'Farrell, the shrewd and genial Irishman who had guided Leicester City back into the First Division. O'Farrell lasted eighteen months, buffeted by the continuing problem of Best.

Into *his* shoes stepped Tommy Docherty; ebullient, extrovert, single-minded. Docherty promptly set about restructuring the side but not before United crashed out of the First Division. It was their lowest moment since the War. But Docherty had a masterplan and to his credit the side swept back within the year. Twelve months later they stood on the verge of a League and Cup Double only to be thwarted by Liverpool and Southampton at the last moment. A year later they were back at Wembley to beat League champions Liverpool. A new era looked set to dawn until stories leaked out into the press about Docherty and an extra-marital affair. The United board frowned upon it and Docherty was out, making way for the more respectable and dignified Dave Sexton. The days of cavalier football were over.

Sexton lasted four years but failed to win one major trophy. He had bought expensively but had not produced a side of flair. The days of Docherty were fondly remembered. Sexton's loss was to be Ron Atkinson's gain, as the board turned once more to a flamboyant character.

Memories of the period are mixed. Some recall the cavalier approach with affection; others simply remember the grinding success of Liverpool. Yet surprisingly, those days in the Second Division are recalled with a certain fondness as fans visited grounds they had never seen. They would arrive in their thousands and simply take over the small, makeshift grounds of the Second Division. It was like a crusade. But for many, the initial realisation that United had crashed out of the top division came as an appalling shock. Suddenly, City were the top dogs in Manchester.

Although many fans have exciting and fond memories of the period, there was much that was bad about spectating in the seventies and eighties. Travelling to away games was cheaper than ever and even the young now had the money to afford such travel. Led by this band of roving young thirsty for excitement, the violence which had first reared its ugly head in the sixties erupted into an even greater threat. There was fighting inside grounds, rioting in the streets, and unpleasant pitch invasions. Old Trafford did not escape either. When Denis Law scored for Manchester City to send United into the Second Division, it was accompanied by a pitch invasion: the referee had to abandon the game. While United could take over away grounds with their vast following, their fans were preceded by a fearsome reputation. It wasn't just about winning on the pitch; it was also about out-shouting and out-fighting the local fans. The arrival of United anywhere was not greeted with too much enthusiasm by local residents. Shops were boarded up, pubs closed and locals went in genuine fear. It was even worse in Europe as travelling abroad offered the added opportunity to flaunt their chauvinism.

Yet it was also to their credit that United fans packed Old Trafford every week, even in the bad times. The football may have occasionally been dire but the optimism rarely wavered. As for the players, they had long left the terraced streets of Stretford, Chorlton and Urmston and now lounged resplendent in their detached homes in Bowden and Altrincham. You only spotted them on the training ground or maybe at Old Trafford itself. Mostly you just saw them on the television.

McGuinness, O'Farrell, Docherty, Sexton, and Atkinson. They all came and went before finally Alex Ferguson was lured from north of the border. Fortunes were spent in the transfer market; some wisely, some not so. Each manager stamped his character on the side. Docherty produced a swashbuckling team, dedicated to attack, but as many have testified, a team with more than a few cloggers. O'Farrell wrestled with the worsening problem of Best; in one week, playing truant the next. Sexton bought big names and played thoughtful football. Atkinson meanwhile bred a champagne side, expensive and often intoxicated as well as intoxicating. What United needed was a man who could combine the best of all these individuals – charisma with technique.

------◆------

I didn't have the time as a manager which I felt I deserved, or certainly needed. You need time to settle in at a club like this. I think Alex Ferguson needed the time and he got it. He changed the club. People call Martin Edwards names but when you look around at this stadium, I don't care if he's become a multi-millionaire. The man is United daft. But Fergie has been very good for his former players, always been accessible. They're never too busy for us.

I was very hurt. After eighteen years. I was offered my old job with the reserve team but I couldn't do that after I'd been manager, although I still loved the club because of all the memories and players. Yes, it hurt a lot. They tried to make it nice in some ways but there was that feeling. When you're demoted it's not nice; you feel rejected and hurt. So I left and went to Greece. I was offered the job at Bolton with Nat Lofthouse but I needed to get away altogether. I felt bitterness, you do after eighteen years. I was a good pro. But I was never one for going public on it. I could see their reasons. Matt was a hard act to follow, unbeatable. I was in an impossible position. It would have been better had he stayed on and had me as a number two for a lot longer, rather than me come straight from the reserves. I was very young at thirty-one. It was a pity he didn't wait a few years. But that's life.

WILF McGUINNESS

I always got on very well with Louis Edwards. We'd be in the directors' box having a drink at half time and he'd say, 'Don't rush back, stay and have a drink.' I knew if I did, that would be it, I'd never get back. He was a rogue but a likeable one. He never pretended to be other than what he was. He was working class, he had a good war record, a sergeant-major in the tanks; he was no coward. He wanted to put his sons through everything that he had never had.

When I was a minister in the Northern Ireland office and the detectives would be with me, he would pat their guns and say, 'You won't need that today.' I was made Minister of State for Northern Ireland with Merlyn Rees as Secretary of State. It soon became apparent that whether or not I wanted protection I would have to have it. So I had full protection, like the Prime Minister, and that meant three Special Branch officers with me, two on duty, one off. They came and lived up here and went everywhere with me. Of course it was pointed out by them, rather gleefully, that I couldn't go and sit in my usual seat at Old Trafford, where I had a season ticket. Anyhow, Louis said, 'No problem, you must come and sit in the box and bring your detectives with you,' and so I went into the directors' box. All the time I was sitting there with the police with their guns.

LORD STAN ORME

I remember a Cup game at home. We were playing Plymouth Argyle and it was going to be George Best's comeback game. He'd played a few games and this, we thought, against Plymouth, this might be a special game. And, of course, he missed training the week before and the number eleven was

Mick Martin. Mick Martin was never the most inspiring player, an ordinary journeyman. We were so disheartened that Best wasn't playing and I remember my brother Gordon saying to me recently that he remembered that game and what he remembered most was that it was the day Best's career finished. He was kicked out after that. We won one–nil, Macari scored a goal with a header but it marked a special point as far as I was concerned. I was a big George Best fan but my one regret is that I didn't see him a great deal when he was playing in the sixties and it meant that I went to an awful lot of testimonial games to watch a fat, overweight George Best play because I wanted to see a bit of him. I even went to see him play for Fulham when they came to play Notts County and you were willing him back to be the player you wished you'd seen before. It's sad, he's not grown up even now.

ROGER HENNELL

It was a difficult time for many of the managers. I used to read a lot in the papers and try to get any snippets of information. We were always wondering what was going to happen because we did go through the managers at that time. Wilf McGuinness seemed to me to be a disastrous appointment. The club coped with that situation very badly. I think Wilf was appointed as the natural successor and the chosen one but in fact his personality was not suited to the pressures immediately put on him. He came up against a bunch of players who were really very famous; rich, strong-willed people who were not going to be told what to do by anybody but Sir Matt. And here comes this young guy, not much older than them. He sounds like a good guy to me but I think he felt he had to pull rank and be very assertive with them and it just didn't work. It just seemed to be a terrible time. There were all sorts of rumours about player power and Willie Morgan being cited as somebody who was very difficult. One thing about United there is never any shortage of rumours and news stories.

McGuinness went, his hair grew white and then fell out, so there were incredible pressures at the place. The team was ageing and disappearing and they were not doing very well at replacing it.

My memories of O'Farrell are of a distant kind of bloke. He was effectively a very transitional guy; you didn't seem to get much of a reading of what he was like as a person, although I did hear people say that he was a distant person, a man in his overcoat most of the time. Sexton came along and I liked the cut of his jib. He's a very good coach and I still think that. He had problems with the massiveness of the job. He seemed to me to be quite a quiet, reserved person and I think the big and loud and colourful thing that is United was a bit difficult for him to handle. In terms of what was going on on the pitch I think United began to adopt some policies of bringing youth through at the time. We seemed to be getting consistently better players. Players were also well looked-after. The team seemed to be growing again after a period when desperate measures were being taken and we were buying badly and so forth. I think Sexton can take credit for re-establishing United, although he had his critics, and although his reserve and his coming from Chelsea meant people were ready to jump on him. But he did a good job.

Then there was the Doc who was always in people's minds. But I thought of the Doc as a bit like Churchill; he was great in wartime but had difficulty in coping with the peace. I think the Doc had his limitations but during the Sexton era everyone was saying let's have the Doc back, 'cos he knows how to make exciting football. But long term I don't know that the Doc would have been able to do any more. He was a man for the crisis and coped with it. Sexton had a thoughtful and intelligent approach but without oodles of charisma. But then charisma's not everything, is it?

Big Ron I've grown to appreciate as I look back. One thing you can't deny about Ron Atkinson's teams is that they are always attacking sides. I remember a fantastic game between

United and West Brom and he was at the helm there and they won four–two or four–three [Manchester United 3, West Bromwich Albion 5, 30 December 1978]. Regis and Cunningham were playing and there was wave after wave of West Brom attacks and they had the better of us. At United I think he did all he could to make United an attacking side. He had the opposite of Sexton, in a way. He could live with the pressure, the press, the tradition of Sir Matt and so forth but the finer details of things I'm not so sure. Perhaps he wasn't so measured and intelligent in his approach to the game. He's an impressionist, whereas, say, Sexton would be a classical painter. I warmed to him towards the end. At first I didn't like the Champagne Charlie image. He made a massive leap to be United's manager but in many ways he coped with it very well and United were certainly not abysmal during his years; on the contrary. It's a hell of a job.

SIMON THORP

I just accepted defeat: 'Oh, they've lost again'; but it would never occur to me not to go the following week. You always thought they would turn the corner, get out of it. Even at the last game you felt something would happen and even when they went down, you thought they'd have a big clear out; Tommy Doc's giving a big speech, yeah that's the way to do it, we'll go for that. As it happened, that one season in the Second Division was great, going to obscure places like York, places you would never go to normally. I really enjoyed it. They'd win an awful lot of games; it was good fun, a good season, but I wouldn't fancy doing it again, mind. Just the once. If you went down in those days you were odds-on coming back but if you go down now you do have a hell of a problem getting back because there are an awful lot of good sides.

I think on their day they could play football second to none. If things were going well they played great football but

168

if things weren't going well it was a case of 'you shall not pass' and that often got in the way of it. In the days of Jim Holton, yes, he could be a real stopper but there was nothing better than seeing him ploughing forward for corners because you knew that nine times out of ten he'd get the ball. The same could be said of Gordon McQueen. When you see someone head the ball from the edge of the penalty area and it crashes in – you don't see that same kind of header much now. There are few around today with that kind of power to head the ball. It was great to see. Most teams could do the same – Norman Hunter. But yes, they did have a few stoppers is the polite way to put it.

I think they went through an era of not much happening. In some respects I felt a bit sorry for Sexton. I think when he got elbowed he'd won eight on the trot and the last game they'd won was, I think, at Leeds, away. But they weren't playing the style of football United fans wanted to see. And unfortunately he was elbowed. It's a bit of a kick in the teeth to win games like that and then get sacked. If you've lost ten on the trot, fair enough.

My personal view is that Atkinson was not one of the people. He did have good teams and they did play good football and it was good to watch. But you could never get close to him, I always thought. He was wandering around with the gold chains and drinking champagne, Armani suits, et cetera. Great for looking good, but I'm not sure it helped the fans associated with him too much. He did reasonably well. I think he often spoke a good game rather than produced one.

ROLAND COBURN

When they did get relegated there was a feeling at the club that it would not happen. We thought, we're a massive club, it can't happen. But it can. Some think the name will keep them up. It was awful at the club. People said it's a blessing in disguise, but I don't go for that. You should never get yourself in that position.

BRIAN KIDD

I can remember it, even though I was only, say, about thirteen or fourteen, as a really depressing thing to see them fall into the Second Division. It was very sad. It was a way of reflecting the bond between the fan and the club; it was a saddening thing. And you were hoping against hope that they would come back the next year.

When they went down it didn't look as though they would come straight back up. I think the summer signings were the things that helped. They'd become a clogging team as well; some of the signings seemed not to be United-style players really. They seemed to be behind the times. Players like George Graham. Holton hadn't established himself and he didn't look much of a player. It's an odd thing, but even as they were winning the European Cup, I can remember my brother and father talking about this as a team that was already in decline. When they won it, it was their last hope of winning it. That was another thing that made it very sweet.

LEON SWERLING

The season when they were struggling against relegation, 1973–74, that's when Gordon, my brother, and I started to go regularly. I don't know whether it was decided we were old enough or we suddenly decided it was important, but we used to go to virtually every home game that season. There was a feeling at first that we were going to go down and then a feeling that with a run towards the end of that season that we were going to stay up because there were youngsters coming in. Brian Greenhoff was coming in at either centre half or centre forward. I suppose he typified the fighting spirit of the team of that time. You know, there had been an awful lot of

170

old stagers that Docherty bought who weren't really up to it. He had George Graham there for a bit, he had McCalliog. You thought, these are not people we want, they're not playing in the United way and suddenly these younger players were coming through showing no fear. Jim Holton was bought, someone the fans could really identify with. There was no finesse about him but he was real heart. You felt you wanted people in the team who were going to give their all, their honest endeavour.

When we were relegated we felt desperate. There had been a feeling for a long time that we were going to go down. Then you kept feeling, depending on the results, that they will stay up. But it was especially the manner of it, with City doing it and Denis Law scoring the goal. Afterwards it was immaterial because Norwich won but that wasn't something you could explain to people at the time. It was too hurtful for that.

I think we went into the next season with hopes because towards the end of the previous season we had played pretty well, so we felt that this was a team that could get better and that was maybe what we had needed. Right from the beginning of the season Pearson had come in and Buchan was in his prime. In previous seasons he seemed to struggle because the people around him didn't know what they were doing. They just looked so organised. They were so attacking, the confidence was sky high. They started with some really good results and you just expected them to win. They started at the top of the table and that's where they stayed. They were getting as many people as they had in the First Division. There were very few games when it wasn't pretty full. I remember going to a big game against Sunderland, who were one of the potential other promotion rivals, probably November time. We got tickets in K-stand behind the goal. It was a full house, fifty-five or fifty-six thousand, absolutely heaving and that was a game which we eventually won three–two. My abiding memory was Pearson being on the edge of the corner of the box, right near where we were sitting and him banging in the third goal. It was a wonderful match. It was on *Match of the Day* and I was thinking is this Second Division stuff or is it First Division?

But you also had some odd moments. We had Leyton Orient coming and playing a game. So sometimes you'd have the big teams, and then sometimes we had a team and you said, 'Oh yes, we are in the Second Division, aren't we.' There was a bit of unpredictability about the team. They could go two–nil up and you thought 'This is easy,' then the next thing you know they would get two goals back. It would then be a see-saw game; we'd be really worried, but in the end we got the winner and won it three–two. So there were lots of those exciting games. There was very little that was drab. Willie Morgan was coming to the end and Steve Coppell had just come in and the amazing thing you noticed about Coppell was that he pushed the ball past a player and then ran, a bit like watching Michael Owen today. The guy didn't know what to do. He'd gone. It was so simple and direct when you compared it with Willie Morgan. He was very intricate and very clever but he wanted to beat a player six or seven times and he'd lost the speed, so players were waiting for him to do it whereas Coppell got going, put it down the wing, got it over and that was it. Pearson, of course, was usually on the end of it. It made for very exciting football.

Most of that season we were standing. We sat if it was all ticket or if we were going with Dad. But that season and the following couple of seasons we went and stood at the front end of United Road by the half-way line for every game. We did enjoy it. The only time I remember being worried or frightened was when we went to a testimonial at the end of one of those seasons, against Glasgow Rangers. There were only about twenty, twenty-five thousand turned up for the game but it's the only time I've seen the whole mass of the Stretford End run in the opposite direction. There were all these drunken Scots facing them after the game. You just felt, 'Gosh, I don't want to be around here. This doesn't look at all friendly.' I never had any interest in the violence from a macho point of view. I never thought, I want to go to the football and have some bother. Gordon and I always wanted to go along and watch the football, and we didn't find any hooligan element exhilarating but something we wanted to be apart from.

I always went with my brother. He'd be sixteen, I'd be fourteen. We lived in Chorlton. We might be given a lift to the game, but we'd walk back after. The police horses always passed us. It was a wonderful thing, walking back from Old Trafford, walking home together. You'd start with the huge crowds and gradually, as you get further away, people are spinning off to other places. I don't know whether more people walked to the game then; you got the feeling that they did but that's probably because we were walking. It was a forty-minute walk back to Chorlton, something like that. It was impractical to get anyone to pick us up and waiting for the bus would have taken hours.

ROGER HENNELL

By about sixteen or seventeen we'd go to away games as a group. Not to all of them, but a selection. Cash was a problem. I do wonder how people afford it today. It was all about getting to places. The season when I went to most away games was the season we went into the Second Division, 1973–74. I used to meet up with my pals and go to the game. For the away games we'd go by car which one of my mates would own. We had some adventures. Again, it was a rough and ready arrangement but we travelled far and wide. It was a very exciting period in United's history. The terrible shock of being at Old Trafford when Denis Law consigned us to the Second Division and shed a tear in so doing. We all did. I didn't invade the pitch, I was too shocked. But having gone through the pain and horror of all that we had a battling and exciting season, determined not to stay down more than one season.

173

We went to the oddest of places. Having had only First Division football, suddenly I was sat on a roof of a shed arrangement at Leyton Orient's ground because it was so full. It was, I think, the top of the loos but it was a wooden shed. I can remember leaning on it and eventually, in order to get to see over this sea of red, I found myself being pushed up on this roof. The ground was packed with Reds, cockney Reds as well, I didn't see any Orient fans. There was trouble at that game as well. I can remember Sir Matt appealing to the crowd to calm down. I suppose that's the other aspect. During that period of time the supporters were becoming more and more renowned for their troublesome ways. Going to these smaller venues and often there was a crush getting in and the hassles of just getting in seemed to spill over into a lot of trouble. So it was very exciting on the pitch but a bit scary with the fans off the pitch. Nothing ever happened to me and I didn't get close to any problem, but we were always held back and marshalled around by the police. It was a minority.

When we played and lost to Southampton in the Cup final, I was in France at the time. But my dad got me a ticket and I flew home for that. It was a dreadful game. One thing I do remember is going there. I flew to Manchester, then got the train down with my usual friends. I felt like a potential criminal the way the police marshalled you from the station to Wembley and back. It was all very much controlled because they were frightened at what the United fans might do.

I left Manchester to go to Lancaster University. I was very engaged at being at university but I would not miss coming home to see United. I often brought people home with me. And we'd come down for night games as well. I can remember coming to City the night the lights failed and both teams were ordered off by the referee because it was getting so violent on the pitch. Doyle, and I think Macari, were having a go at each other – a very uneven struggle – and there were little fracas going on all over the pitch. Tueart was playing. It got really nasty. A bunch of us had come down from Lancaster without any tickets and we paid a horrendous price for tickets in their new stand, right at the front, and we had a ringside view of what turned out to be a boxing match. It was packed with incident but incredibly exciting.

It was a whirligig of a season because of the way we played. I was older by then and more mature, that's when I began to hero worship them in many ways. They played such a buccaneering style of play. Coppell on one wing, Gordon Hill on the other or swapping wings. Gerry Daly in the middle, a lovely mobile fluid attacking musketeer type of team. It took us through that season with much success. Then we came into the First Division with a huge expectation that the same would be the case. And it was, at first. But I remember the reality setting in. We played Liverpool at Old Trafford and they had obviously watched carefully what we had been doing and noted this wide pattern of play, these waves of attack. So they just stopped us doing it. It was an awful game; it was a nil–nil draw but they had the know-how. They said, we can stop this and they did. After that it wasn't quite the same; United had to adapt their game and become a little more wily. The football died down a bit after that, it wasn't as exciting a spectacle. It was a sobering moment. We'd got away with it in the Second Division and for much of that first season back, but when the professionals got in the ring with us they knew how to handle it.

I can remember going to League Cup games on a Wednesday night and that sort of thing. Loads of people would come down which is a good testament to what was going on on the pitch. Although United were not the force they had been, they were still an attacking side, a world-famous team.

SIMON THORP

I lived in Portsmouth and when I was on holidays went to the London games quite regularly or if United played in Ipswich I went to see them there. When I left school which was about

1972, 1973, I saw an advert in the United programme for United fans who lived in Portsmouth or Southampton wanting to set up a supporters' club branch and looking for new members, so I phoned this bloke up who was organising it and he said yes, we're running coaches up to Old Trafford, and to most away matches. So I used to get up at 6 a.m. on a Saturday and go on my little motorbike down to Southampton station and park up or sometimes Mum would take me from Portsmouth to Southampton. It was the season before they went into the Second Division. I went to most of the games. It was dire but just being there was fantastic. The coach would leave Southampton at 6.45 a.m. We used to stop at Cirencester for breakfast, about forty people. And sometimes we'd go to Cheltenham to the Vauxhall Pub. It was owned by a City fan and he was quite welcoming and then we'd get to Old Trafford about 2 p.m. so that some of the lads could go into the local pubs. We'd go to the game where we'd be beat, of course, and then go home. We'd be back at about midnight. They were long days when you're getting beat.

I was at Old Trafford when they went down. It was one of those inevitable feelings. We knew we'd go down. The football was awful. It wasn't just the game against City, it depended on other results. In fact we were already down whether we beat City or not, though at the time we didn't know it. There is this misconception now that City sent us down. They didn't. I didn't run on the pitch, I can say that. I wasn't into hooliganism. The match was stopped. It was a very depressing day.

I was going to every game by that stage. It would cost me a fortune. I went to away games. If we went to somewhere like Blackpool we'd go overnight. We'd leave at midnight and travel through the night. We'd get to Blackpool at 6 a.m. – this was obviously when they were in the Second Division – we'd be home about 2.30 the next morning. All for one-and-a-half hours of football. Blackpool, Hull, Newcastle, all overnight stays. We went on a tour of Belgium on a minibus with no seats, fifteen of us. It was the pre-season tour just as we started the Second Division. Stuart Pearson had just signed. We went to Ostend from Southampton. I think we were all drunk. But there were a lot of United fans there. We won two–nil. That was my first European adventure.

I was seventeen years old. I worked in a factory in Portsmouth in those days. I went to every match bar three in the Second Division. I thought it was absolutely fantastic. It was the best days ever for supporting United when they were in the Second Division. You'd go to places like Blackpool and there'd be fifteen thousand Reds, both ends of the ground full of United fans. A lot of trouble which when you're seventeen – I didn't get involved in any trouble, mind you – but it was looked upon as representing United. I didn't fight but I was very vocal. There were days like when we went to Bristol. There were cars overturned. It was really bad, riots, really awful. I went to the Sheffield Wednesday game. It was four–four and mounted policemen fighting on the terraces. Horrendous but exciting. Every ground was taken over by United fans. We had the highest-ever attendance in the Second Division. I just loved those days. And of course we won the League. It doesn't matter which division you're in, as long as you're winning it.

They were an exciting team. There was Coppell and Hill on the wings. It was Tommy Docherty's team. Although they went down, they weren't ready for the First Division. He had to add to them. He bought Stevie Coppell from Tranmere, Gordon Hill from Millwall. They bought Stuart Pearson upfront, Jimmy Greenhoff. They swept all before them. When they went up the next year, 1975, they came third to Liverpool in the League and got to the Cup final, which was one of the worst days of my life because they played Southampton and got beat. We went on an overnight coach just to soak up the atmosphere. There were thousands of United fans outside Buckingham Palace singing. There was a policeman about six foot seven standing outside Buckingham Palace. I always remember this. We were all singing to the Queen and this policeman just swore at us and told us precisely where to go. I was horrified at a policeman swearing like this. But it worked. We said, 'Oh, sorry,' and all walked away. We'd booked on an overnight coach to go back to Manchester in order to celebrate this great Cup final win. A lot of the fans hadn't had the chance to celebrate a great Cup win – the last one had been in 1968 with the European Cup – we were going to paint London red. It was so depressing. We ended up getting a coach straight back to Manchester.

The Cup final against Arsenal. I think it was the only time I've cried twice in a minute for different reasons. When they scored we were jumping up and down hugging everyone, so happy. We cried with joy. Then one minute later Sunderland scored the winner for Arsenal and it was the worst moment of my life. We were in tears again.

In those days we used to hitch up to Manchester as well. If the coach was not running for some reason like they couldn't get enough people, we'd have to hitch up, those of us who were really dedicated. I had a motorbike and sometimes I'd ride it from Portsmouth to Manchester, which took about six hours. I'd never ever do that again. It'd been a freezing cold February day and I came up on the bike. I had to stop and warm my hands on the exhaust pipe because they were so cold.

I went to Millwall on a Monday night and I stood with the Millwall fans. I've never been so frightened in all my life. Luckily I had a southern accent. United won one–nil with a penalty by Gerry Daly. I was telling everyone it was never a penalty, never a penalty. It was the only time I've never cheered for a United goal. It was frightening. They were frightening days, fighting, wrong accent. Never wear a scarf to a match.

ROBIN MURRAY

I was a football hooligan, yes. I was about fifteen or seventeen at the time. It was in the sixties and seventies, and I was a

Man United fan; still am. We used to go into towns and take them over. That's what it was all about, taking them over, a crowd of you, all in the name of Manchester United. It was a free for all. You got a buzz out of it. A crowd of you looking for trouble and being boss. We didn't really hurt anybody but we'd give them a bit of a going over if we had to. Mostly it was smashing up trains or pubs and occasionally shops. I had a skinhead haircut. We were in the National Front, and just wanted to stir things up a bit. I didn't stay in the NF very long. But I gave it up after a while. I got older, I grew up. I'm in my forties now. I just got fed up with it. I don't really want to say any more about that part of my life. I'm not really very proud of it.

ANONYMOUS

There was racism at games twenty years ago. It was the time when there was a great deal of hooliganism and it deterred you from going. If you were in the wrong place at the wrong time you could very well be beaten up so it was not wise to tempt fate and go into a hostile environment. To a large extent that was true of going to Old Trafford because you would be in a hostile environment, standing on the terraces with just the one or two black people who went, even if you had a United scarf on. But if you were in a gang, it would be totally different. That's what we did. We did it at Maine Road and at Old Trafford.

I remember one memorable time at Maine Road in the Kippax, we took one of the younger lads who was about ten or eleven. We were fifteen, sixteen years of age and to protect him we made a cordon around him, but we got missiles coming in from the City fans, you know, 'What you black bastards doin' 'ere?' But in those days, because we were in a gang, we were not afraid of anyone. Say you went on your own, just two or three of you, it would be that much more difficult to defend yourself. But if you went with ten or fifteen, which we did do – deliberately, it was a planned thing – nobody messed with us, because we were from Moss Side. And if they wanted to fight, we weren't afraid. We did fight on the terraces on a number of occasions just to make that point known that we weren't afraid to fight. We would be fighting with our own fans, both at Maine Road and Old Trafford.

Once a certain degree of respect built up they tried to enlist us to fight opposing fans. You didn't get many black fans travelling away. Over the years I noticed that you got black fans travelling up in gangs. I would feel an empathy with black fans from opposing clubs because we knew what they went through, but there was also a north–south divide. Irrespective of colour it was always there. I remember once we went to London – a group of us in a twelve-seater van – and we didn't know our way around London. We approached this couple of black guys to ask directions and they totally ignored us. One of our lot says, 'We're black guys from Manchester, surely you can help us,' and he said, 'No, we don't help you.' It was that sort of attitude, a north–south divide.

The stronger divide? Racial without a doubt rather than north–south. We got the respect simply because we were prepared to stand up. If they thought they could take advantage physically, they would have done. It was principally because we had a couple of big guys who weren't going to back down, someone like Billy Hughes, a legend in Moss Side. He was our leading light. If Billy hit you, you stayed down. He was a City fan and if he said, 'We're meeting up on the corner of Lloyd Street, you lot be there,' we were there and we had to go to City's ground.

If a bunch of guys were being racist, we didn't keep quiet: we met it. If you're stood on the terraces somewhere you always get a few taunts. You get it once, twice, but we didn't take it a third time. We'd give them the benefit of doubt because they're trying to prove themselves. They might say it once, nothing happened. They might say it twice, but never a third time without something being done about it. There was no talk, straight in. No communication, just turn around and that's it. On the terraces you get that sway from the back, it's usually someone from the back. Once, and they'll push you forward then pull back. Then twice, and you know that the third wave is going to come. When it's mentioned you just turn round and grab the nearest one, throw him over to get to those who are at it. You know they are coming. There'll always be a few in there who don't want to fight, so you throw them out of the way so you can get to the culprit. That usually sorted the problem.

Black players for the opposing side were role models: Cyrille Regis, Brendan Batson, Clyde Best; always great to see them. You'd get the taunts from the fans but we personally didn't taunt them. We never did that, it wasn't done. And when United signed a black player, that was wonderful for us. We perceived United as a Catholic team. They had no black players until Viv Anderson, I think he was the first. We just saw them as a Catholic club. With Viv Anderson and Remi Moses it started to change. The thugs on the terraces had to look after their own players. At first it was a big step for them. The running battles they had with ethnic groups, there was some mention made of the black players but it soon died away. They were United players now, so they either accepted it or didn't come any more. It marked a watershed. Of course at City there was Dave Bennett. We were rooting for Dave Bennett because we knew him, he was a local lad, he lived at the back of where we were living in Rusholme. I went to both clubs; even now I'm concerned that City are slipping away. My son goes to Platt Lane for training, it's so difficult to get into United. But I still have connections with United, and even though I don't have a season ticket, they're still my team.

There's no racism on the terraces any more; it's all gone. There's a total sea change to what it was and quite honestly I prefer it this way. The rules now are that the stewards on the terraces, if they hear someone making racist taunts, they can eject that person, turn them over to the police. Then it's up to the police, if they have a case, to bring it to the CPS. I think that change came about because the black fans who went to see a football game had to defend themselves. Also the black players coming in, so the hooligans can't make racist taunts against black players with another team when they've got black players on their own side. Then of course, to back that up you've got the law. And the seating makes it that much better for families, that helps eradicate hooliganism although we do know that hooliganism is occurring after the game. There are still pitched battles being fought between gangs, but not black against white. But yes, there are a lot more people from the black community going to games, particularly in London. There's still a problem at Old Trafford because of the availability of tickets. Even for me, with all my contacts at the club, it is impossible to get a season ticket.

RUDI KIDD

The first game I can remember seeing was the 1963 FA Cup final. I am generally back three times a year now on our branch trips. I was born a Red; actually, my older brother introduced me to the club. He watched the Busby Babes as a kid. All my friends know how passionate I am for the club, and I would have to also say that for all our members (the MUFC Supporters Club) who regularly make the trip across the Pond to see the lads.

A couple of incidents stick in my mind. There was a trip to Burnley in the late sixties and the game at Old Trafford when Denis Law scored for City. The Burnley trip resulted in myself and a few other Reds almost being crushed as fans fell on top of each other in the United end. I remember being taken on to the pitch by the St John Ambulance staff and looking down at my feet to find I had no shoes. The resulting trip back home was one of worry as I knew my parents would probably not let me go to see another game. Thankfully, that did not last — and I didn't like the shoes anyway!

The match against Manchester City at Old Trafford generated quite a few passionate moments back in 1974, especially when the majority of United fans ran on the pitch. Now I am no hooligan, but I did run on to the pitch and my claim to notoriety is that when a book was published called *The Red Army Years: MUFC in the 70s* the picture on the front at this particular game of the lad with long hair and flares was me. I still have the flares!

PETE HOLLAND

My early memories are quite confused, really. I remember going to matches but I don't remember individual matches; I just remember the whole atmosphere thing. My first match was a night match and I have absolutely no idea of who we played but I remember going along and being absolutely enthralled by the lights and the noise and the horses and everything else. That must have been the early seventies and then I sort of went on and off as my dad felt like taking me, and then stopped going for a long time because I was at college and working Saturdays and that sort of thing. And then I started going seriously again about ten years ago and haven't missed a match since.

When United went into the Second Division there was sort of a subtle shift at school. I remember before then when we were in the First Division everyone was a United fan and everyone was going on about United being fantastic. The City fans used to sit around in a kind of a decline in the corner and then all of a sudden it was switched around; no one wanted to wear the red armband when we were playing school sports and United were the sort of denigrated side and humiliated utterly for a year. Plus the fact, of course, that it was Denis Law that did the business was particularly humiliating at the time. I don't know; you suddenly felt for a minute that you were the lesser half of Manchester which you hadn't really thought before, because I'd always assumed that United were the most fantastic thing ever and absolutely invincible. And my dad was getting ribbed by his mates and people would come round and say 'Oh, you're not still supporting United,' and he used to get really upset about it because obviously he's been going for ever, it seems like. So I don't think I really thought it would last more than a year. I thought it was just a temporary blip which, as it happens, it was. It wasn't too bad.

My mother and her father and the whole family are actually City so when I was a very little girl I was brought up with the idea that City were great but I didn't really go to matches; I wasn't really that bothered but my granddad used to sit there with his Watney's Party Four, going on about how great City were and then all of a sudden my mum married this bloke who was absolutely mad about United; he's about sixty, sixty-five now, I'd say he's been going since he was about ten. When he lists the highlights of his life, one of them's lifting the FA Cup. Obviously he knows all about the Munich disaster. He went to the first matches after the accident and wherever they are in the world, he's always absolutely rooting for them. He turns from a respectable accountant to this screaming maniac who will stand on a seat at Wembley and defends them up to the hilt, won't have a word said against them. At the start of every season he gets this big ledger book out and prepares this very complicated thing on how many points they're going to get at every stage of the season and generally speaking by the end of the season he's never far out. I think this year he was absolutely spot on with the points total so he takes it all very seriously and views it as something of a science.

MAXINE DUNHAM

I think my first game was the 1972 season but for the life of me I can't remember who we played, but I think it was Ipswich. I remember more about the day itself and having to

184

lie to me mum about where I was going because she told me I couldn't go to United as they had such a bad reputation at the time, fans-wise. So a lad down the road took me. I remember asking my dad to take me but he was always working. So I started going with this lad down the road, three or four times in the season. I went steadily on and off through school and then in the late seventies I started to go a bit more regularly with friends.

I always stood, I stood until I had no choice a couple of years ago. I stood on the Stretford End. I liked it and I would go back to it tomorrow. I really liked the banter, it was a funny place to be and even when it was going terribly wrong there would be somebody behind you with a funny remark to make. Being six foot three inches I could get in at five to three and still see. It was typical Mancunian dry wit, just one-liners. Things which when you hear out of context you wouldn't think funny, but at the time had hundreds of people laughing. There was the singing as well. I must be honest, when I first started going with my cousin, his dad told him that the only way he could go was if he went in the Stretford paddock. Well, that was full of old men, so we used to climb over the fence into the Stretford End so that we could have a sing-song. Then I let the cat out of the bag and his dad found out and it was my turn to be in trouble then for misleading him.

I was not at the City game, but my main memory is at school some time afterwards and playing football. And the games teacher who was obviously a City fan telling me that I couldn't wear a United shirt to play football in because we didn't recognise Second Division teams. He was obviously being highly sarcastic but I took it very seriously at the time, being about ten.

I was going on and off still, not going all the time then, but that's really when it first meant a lot to me. I'd always gone before but there were always people telling me that George Best was brilliant. But other than watching him on the telly or on video he was always somebody else's hero, whereas that team after relegation started to be my team and my big hero was Stuart Pearson. He was the first player I picked out as my hero and whenever I scored in the school playground it was a clenched fists salute.

I never honestly thought about who I supported. I was a United fan. It must have just come from my dad but I can't ever remember making a conscious decision. I was a United fan and it goes back to the school teacher. I remember standing there, full of resentment for his remarks, thinking how dare he talk to me like this? Who were City to talk like this? They might be in a league above us but that was it and I never gave it a moment's thought.

MATTHEW REYNOLDS

The first game I went to was at Newcastle. It was away, 1976, and I pestered my dad – I must have been eight then – to get me tickets and the only tickets he could get was at the Leazes End [where all the diehard Newcastle fans stood] which was a big wooden Kop stand. There was me wedged down the front with my silk scarf around my neck with my zip right up to the top and ten thousand Man United supporters down the other end causing absolute bedlam. And United won four–two, with two own goals from Newcastle. That was it, I wanted to go as much as possible after that. I was young and at school and couldn't get to games but I'd try and go if any were near me, up in the north-east.

My first Old Trafford game was the following season, just before the Cup final. When I started going regularly was when I came to university in Manchester. Coming to university in Manchester was definitely part of the decision. There was a certain course I wanted to do but Manchester had that golden attraction: to live just down the road from Old Trafford and go to the games. So since 1985–86 I've been going. The first time I went was against Bolton and we sat at the back of the Stretford End in the old E-stand and United got beat two–

one, I think. But I was so excited. I must have been nine. It was when the old souvenir shop was tucked away in K-stand and I bought a few things. It was just the size of the place and being there, quite breathtaking really. We came down with Dad in the car. I was looking out of the car all the time after we came off the motorway; so exciting. And all that thing about which scarf to wear. I remember getting an *Evening News* Cup final special. It was just after the semi-final.

When I was living here I started going to every home game. I got a season ticket in 1989–90 which was for standing in the Stretford End. It was mainly convenience; it meant I could go later and didn't have to queue up.

ADAM BROWN

In May 1968 I was eight years old. Manchester United had just won the European Cup and City had become League champions. It's at that kind of age when your allegiances are truly formed. You become aware of what's going on around you. My sister was a United fan but my dad was not. He wasn't really interested in football or sport at all. He was an academic but out of a strange sense of duty he had taken me to watch Altrincham a few times when I was between about six and ten. Meanwhile the greatest party in the world was going on six miles down the road! In fact I think the first big game I ever saw was probably going to see Altrincham playing Everton at Goodison Park in a Cup game. But once I'd reached the age of eight or thereabouts I decided it had to be United or City and I chose United, probably because they were the European champions. I remember playing for the school once and talking about United having won eight–one. So, I became a United supporter.

After junior school I went to Manchester Grammar School and there was much more peer-pressure in the classroom there to identify with one or the other team. You had to show your allegiance and be committed to one of the two sides. There were lots of City fans at MGS and sometimes I did go to Maine Road. The problem was that my mum wouldn't let me go to matches by myself. But I was a train-spotter and that provided me with an ideal excuse. Every Saturday, I'd tell my parents I was going train-spotting. I'd go off with my plastic bag full of my train-spotting books and with a scarf tucked in the bottom of the bag, but instead of going to Piccadilly station or wherever, I was going to Old Trafford with my mates. My dad was a transport economist and he would ask me questions about what I'd seen and so on. All the time I was lying to maintain my allegiance. I suppose it was the forbidden fruit.

I just found it so incredibly exhilarating, the noise, the chanting and singing. We used to stand in the bottom right-hand corner of the Stretford End. We'd have to get there incredibly early; the crushes were prodigious. There were really huge crushes. I'd catch a train at about 1.15 p.m. from Altrincham, the scarf hidden in my plastic bag along with all the train-spotting paraphernalia. I had to be decked out in the scarf, that was part of the ritual. I was about eleven or twelve and I was quite slight and there were always kids coming up to me and challenging me to a fight. They could spot someone who was not one of them a mile off. The first game I can remember seeing was about 1973, against Sunderland, but I can't remember much else about it. But I can remember the first goal I really saw. It was scored by Willie Morgan who was my hero at the time. He was standing on the edge of the area in a League Cup tie and scored with a magnificent shot.

I must have eventually reconciled my going to Old Trafford with my parents as soon I was going regularly. I used to go and see them in the Second Division. They had two glorious years. I went to the FA Cup finals in 1976, '77 and '79. I was going to all the home matches when they were in the Second Division and once they were back in the First Division I was going to away games as well. I used to go with a group of mates. My best mate's brother had a car and we'd all pile in and go off to Stoke, Leeds, Sheffield Wednesday. He'd tell his parents we were off down town. I remember going to Leeds once and we stopped off at a pub on the Pennines somewhere. This was before the M62 had been built and we did a spot of under-age drinking. We got to the ground late and missed the first United goal. I'd had too much to drink and was desperate to go to the toilet. I went and missed the second goal.

When I was in my final year at sixth form I had a girlfriend who was an even madder United fan. We used to go in the paddock then, it seemed more civilised, we'd evolved from the Stretford End. Then I went to university in Bristol which fortunately coincided with Bristol City's three seasons in the First Division, so I saw United every time they visited. I would also go up to London to see them. Now, being a journalist and living in Oxford, I only get to see United ten or fifteen times a season. It's astonishing how it's all changed. It wasn't fashionable in those days. When I was at university I'd play up my Manchester and my United connection. But you wouldn't do that now. You'd just keep your United allegiance quiet otherwise you have to justify it with everyone. You didn't have to do that twenty years ago.

JIM WHITE

I remember that after a lot of devious activity I got a Cup final ticket in 1976 for the match against Southampton. At first I did not know how to get hold of a ticket, so I looked in the personal columns of the *Manchester Evening News* and there I spotted an advert for tickets. So I rang this number and was promptly told to ring another number. I then rang that number and was told to call another number. Every time I rang one number I'd get passed on to another number again. This happened half a dozen times. Eventually I was told to rendezvous in Moss Side at a hairdressers. I was a bit dubious but I went. When I got there I was told to go inside, sit down and wait for George. Well, eventually I got my ticket and it wasn't a fake. I've still got the ticket. It cost £2.50, standing just behind the goal, and I think I paid £25 for it. It wasn't too lucky. Unfortunately United lost one–nil and the winning goal was scored right in front of me. Not a good memory. In 1990 I went to Wembley again to see them play Crystal Palace. United drew. I've decided not to go again; they don't seem to have any luck when I'm there.

KEN HASTINGS

The team I remember the best was in the seventies with Willie Morgan and Martin Buchan, that's when I went a lot. Tommy Docherty lived quite near us in Hale Barns at the time. You used to occasionally see United players in Altrincham. It was seeing these players like Best, much like Ryan Giggs has done in more recent times, that made us young girls want to go. I mean the way they play is very similar, the speed and the skill. Seeing Ryan Giggs fly up the wing going past three or four players, I think is what every nine- and ten-year-old aspires to when they're playing for their local school team.

I went to an all-girls' school and we played football at lunchtimes on the front lawn of the school which was quite frowned-upon. But we were all into football, particularly as it was 1974 and the World Cup, and although England weren't in it, Scotland were, and I was supporting the Dutch team. Johann Cruyff, there's another one, fabulous player to watch. So we used to play football every lunchtime. To some of the staid mistresses of the school it wasn't really on.

When I was at school, United used to start their procession if they had won the Cup from St Margaret's Church in Bowdon, which wasn't too far from where we lived. So we used to find out what time they were due to start on the coach and it was always an open top double-decker and we used to get there as early as possible in order to get a really good view. And then we'd watch the players arrive and all get on the coach. They'd stay there for about ten minutes, so that everybody could see the Cup and take their photographs, then they'd head off down the Chester Road and towards Old

Trafford. On some occasions they used to go into Albert Square with the Cup which was great as well because the whole of Albert Square would be filled with people with red and white scarves and singing. They would go and show the Cup to everybody there. That was really good. That was always just a fantastic atmosphere. It felt like the whole of Manchester was out.

I remember when United were relegated. I was just totally gutted and with having a brother who was a City fan, this made it all the worse. I remember sitting around the house weeping for ages. I was still at school. All the United fans at school were extremely depressed and all the City fans were rubbing it in. But revenge has been had recently.

The Ajax game always sticks in my memory because you didn't see a lot of foreign teams at that time. I've had a semi-interest in Ajax ever since. They always seem to produce good players. They're a bit like United in that respect; very exciting to watch.

I kept going until the upper sixth but when I went to university, although I was still here in Salford, I didn't really go. I may have gone once or twice during the whole time at university. Why did I drop off? Boys! I picked it up again later. I started by watching on the television and I only started going to Old Trafford again when my son Alex was about five. Nowadays we tend to try and see the pre-season friendlies with the international teams. We do send off for tickets but it's so popular now and with the capacity of the ground reduced because of all the seating you don't always get the tickets.

JUDITH SWIFT

I was at Old Trafford for the game where we beat St Etienne in Plymouth to go through to play Juventus. It was 1977, I think. Those were the days when the mob ruled and the Reds had rampaged after being incited in France. There were three giant TV screens of the game and about thirty thousand

191

showed up at Old Trafford that night.

I had a season ticket for years but I would often sell it and stand in the scoreboard paddock where the away fans sit now. I saw the classic West Bromwich Albion game there – we lost five–three – and it was one of the best games I've ever seen live.

DAVID MENASCHE

I came back to Manchester in 1981, '82, my dad saying you've got to go again. It was part of the structure of the family. But being away from Manchester, particularly being somewhere like Cornwall, it was the wrong time for me to move as a football fan, because that's when you start to build up your memories, particularly your teenage years. I wasn't a football follower then really. So when I came back, I came back being able to look at it one step removed to start with. I was twenty-three then. So the really vivid memories I've got are from the eighties onwards when it became emotionally involving.

I remember going with my dad to see a couple of games after we had moved to Cornwall. We went to see them playing Coventry after Tommy Docherty had taken over. They were a dirty team, full of Scotsmen kicking shit out of the opposition. My dad was like crestfallen. He was a big, big United fan.

TIM BAMFORD

My first game was Manchester United against Sunderland and I was actually a Sunderland fan at that game because I come from the north-east and I had come down to the University of Manchester. I think it was early on in the season and a few of us from the hall of residence went along. I was taken so that I could cheer on Sunderland. I stood in the Stretford End and when Sunderland scored first I just had to dig my friend in the ribs and then Man United equalised. I'm sure it ended as a draw. That was back in 1983.

After that I think I would go to a game a month and Manchester United would be playing other teams and gradually I started to cheer on Manchester United. Bryan Robson was in the team and he was from Chester-le-Street, County Durham and I came from County Durham so there was a sort of link there. He was a friend of one of my mum's friends so it was nice to cheer him on. That's how it got going and when they were in the Cup final in 1985 that was quite a big thing to be in Manchester for that. I was watching it around a telly with other friends and we were debating whether to go to Albert Square to join in the celebrations when they came back with the Cup. I used to follow football in the north-east but down here it was United I made tracks for, because City were in the Second Division.

ALISSON THORNTON

I lived in Colchester. I first became a Man United fan when I was about six or seven. Man United were in the old Division Two, and had been relegated the year before and I think I was half asleep sitting on my dad's lap at home, and everyone was round. It was a big family do and everyone was sitting around taking the mickey out of Manchester United because they had just lost to Oxford United. The room was full of Ipswich and Colchester fans. So I thought, if they're all going to have a go at Man United, then I'll stick up for them. So I thought I'd start supporting them. I've always been an awkward bugger and as everyone was supporting Colchester and Ipswich I'd do something different, whereas nowadays supporting United isn't anything different because everyone else has joined the bandwagon.

I didn't start going regularly until I was thirteen or fourteen. I'd get up at about eight o'clock in the morning to get the coach that would take about five or six hours to get up to Manchester and you wouldn't get back home until 10.30 at night. So it was a whole day out just to see an hour and a half

of football, which is pretty stupid really. And about £30 a tim
as well. I couldn't afford it too many times at that age.

When I applied to go to university I deliberately applied t
Manchester. I put a compass on Old Trafford and applied t
the five nearest universities. Manchester was first choice, the
I applied to Salford, York, Lancaster and Sheffield. I wa
already so well ingrained not to apply to Leeds or Liverpoo
because Man United fans don't go anywhere near the enem
When we'd been to visit the university with my dad we'
managed to arrange the visit, which is normally two or thre
hours looking around the university, on the night Unite
played Dundee United in the UEFA Cup. And as a bonus w
went up to see Manchester University in the afternoon, staye
on and went to the Dundee game at Old Trafford in th
evening.

I can always fit in a United game. We used to go o
holidays to Manchester. I had a brother who supporte
Everton so we'd have a week in the Lake District and find
game at Goodison and a game at Old Trafford. One
my worst memories was when we went up and saw Ma
United at home to Bolton in the mid-seventies and Unite
were winning one–nil with ten minutes to go when Fran
Worthington scored two goals. So having spent a week
holiday in the Lake District to see United lose at home was
bit disappointing.

I started university in October 1985 and then I starte
going to all the home games. It was kind of mid to en
Atkinson. The team were entertaining – Olsen on the le
wing, Strachan on the right wing, Whiteside at his prim
Remi Moses and Bryan Robson. They were hard, a hard team
but with the wingers they were entertaining. But the big thir
in those days was that they weren't good enough to get clo
to the League, so it was all about beating Liverpool. In a
those years with Atkinson, how many times did they lose
Liverpool? Just two or three times. They were the big gam
of the season. To beat Liverpool made the season. It was su

big game, to stuff Liverpool. You knew you weren't going to win the League, you had lower expectations. If you had a good Cup run and finished fifth or sixth in the League but turned Liverpool over and the big teams, it was OK. It was playing well at home to the big teams; if you could beat Liverpool, Arsenal and Spurs. But then you knew they'd end up losing at home to Coventry or Stoke or someone equally stupid and not getting anywhere near the top of the League. You weren't really too bothered but you didn't have higher expectations because United hadn't won the League for so long; you got caught up into thinking that beating Liverpool was the key thing.

United fans had turned against Atkinson because it was obvious they weren't good enough to catch Liverpool or Arsenal or whoever. It had not been as entertaining. Strachan had gone totally off form, Olsen had either been sold or was about to be sold. The attacking flair had gone and they weren't winning. United fans will always support a manager if the side is flamboyant, playing attacking football and the goals are going in. If you're not winning and the football's boring then the fans will get bored. And that's what happened with Atkinson.

JIM THORNTON

CHAPTER SEVEN

The Nineties

The Fergie Years

Alex Ferguson rolled into Old Trafford on a raw November morning in 1986. Ron Atkinson had just been sacked and Ferguson was about to become United's sixth manager in sixteen years. The rest, as they say, is history. But it deserves a little more embroidery.

Big Ron had been popular with many fans but at times his champagne style did not sit comfortably with those in the boardroom. He was just a bit too flash for them, more like an agent than a manager. Atkinson may have been a cavalier in the Docherty fashion and although he had lifted the FA Cup twice with them, at the end of the day he failed where it mattered: in the League. What United needed was a forceful personality with the wit and intelligence to mould a club as well as a team. It was certainly time to let somebody simply get on with it and give them the time and space to make their own decisions. Fortunately, with Ferguson, United were to do just that, although his early days were often tinged with gloom on the terraces.

In his first full season with the club, United finished runners-up. Anywhere else they would have been reaching for the cheque book to give the manager a pay rise, but at Old Trafford coming second barely counted, especially as fierce rivals Liverpool came first. But United had made a fine start to the season and lost only four games throughout the ampaign. Only an astonishing unbeaten run by Liverpool had robbed them of the title. In any other season United would almost certainly have been crowned champions.

From such a promising start United fell away the following year and the first groans of discontent on the terraces could be heard. With the start of the following season it grew even louder. United had lost four games before September was out and nine by the end of the year. The rumbles were now universal. But then in January came a dramatic change in fortune that was to save Ferguson's skin. In early January, with all hope of the League gone, and already out of the League Cup, United travelled to Nottingham Forest for a tough FA Cup third round game. They were hardly favourites to win; defeat would spell the end of their season and possibly the end of Ferguson. Of course those in the boardroom deny it now, but had United lost at Forest, the roars of disapproval would likely have signalled the end of Ferguson. Chairman Martin Edwards might have been left with little option although he did have the advantage of seeing what Ferguson was doing behind the scenes.

As it was, United beat Forest with a goal from substitute Mark Robins. It was to prove a turning point. Robins may not have figured much longer in Ferguson's plans but the new manager will always owe him an immense debt. United went on to lift the FA Cup and then the following season the European Cup-Winners' Cup. Then finally in 1993 came the crowning glory as United eventually clinched the League title. It had been a long wait – twenty-six years – and those at Old Trafford that night will never forget it.

Although some may prefer to forget their initial doubts over Ferguson, there is no question that he was unpopular with many fans. Even most of those interviewed in this book have admitted to chanting 'Fergie out' on more than one occasion. At least they have been honest. We shall never know just how close the board came to sacking Ferguson. The spin emanating from the board of course is that it was never even considered, but then it's easy to say that in hindsight.

Whatever, there is no doubting that Ferguson was t
combine all the qualities of Busby: determination, wisdoɪ
and ambition. Since that first League triumph United haʋ
gone on to clinch another four titles and three FA Cup
including three Doubles, and have even emulated Busby
great European triumph with a never-to-be-forgotten triump
of their own as well as a unique Treble. There is little questio
now that Ferguson stands in his rightful place alongside Ma
Busby rather than in his shadow.

What Ferguson has achieved above all else is to build
club, starting from the foundation through to a successful fir
eleven. At youth level, United have once again won the F
Youth Cup with players soon progressing through the ranl
to become United and England stars. Starting with Giggs, tɪ
conveyor belt of talent has been every bit as impressive as th.
achieved under Busby. Even the reserves have regular
finished champions of their league. Everywhere, the motiv.
tion has been about winning silverware. Giggs, Beckham, tɪ
Nevilles, Butt, Scholes, Brown and so forth soon becam
known as Fergie's Fledglings, inspiring a new generation
young followers.

For those fans it has been a golden era. Memories of 'Fergɪ
out' are now distant. All that Ferguson has achieved has beɛ
for the fans. Above all, they have been his guiding spirit. It
a compliment to all at Old Trafford that even when Unite
play a Third Division side in the likes of the League Cup thɛ
can still attract a full house at Old Trafford.

But it is a far different Old Trafford to which the fans no
flock. Watching football has changed more in the past deca⸱
than in the previous fifty years. The noisy Stretford End
gone; the swaying and crushing a thing of the past; tɪ
experience of deciding to go to a game on the spur of tɪ
moment a distant memory. Today's spectators need to ɪ
organised well in advance and have a deep pocket.

For the fans, the nineties have marked a major turniɪ

point. Two mighty new stands have been built, more are planned, with Old Trafford becoming an all-seater stadium, one of the finest in the land. There are restaurants, megastores and even the streets around Old Trafford have changed beyond all recognition as three-lane roads sweep the traffic towards the new stadium. And that experience of queuing for hours on end simply to get into the ground is also something of the past. Today's fans can arrive at 2.45 p.m. or they can come earlier, eat lunch in the restaurants that overlook the pitch, sit in executive boxes, often behind closed, soundless windows. The only queuing at Old Trafford these days is to get into the megastore. And the only time they see the stars is on the pitch or on television. If you don't have a ticket there is no hope of getting in. It's all a far cry from the thirties, forties and fifties. Even the violence that marred the seventies and eighties has all but disappeared. Women also flock towards Old Trafford as football has become a family event. Television has provided the funds and helped turn football into a middle-class spectator sport.

The United directors may have played their part in creating the new Old Trafford and the new commercial Manchester United, but at the end of the day, it could not have been half as successful without a winning team. And the applause for that winning team must largely go to one man: Alex Ferguson.

———◦•◦———

Fergie came about November 1986. The first nine months were extremely dire. He said he wanted to give the players a chance and give them seven months to see what they could do. He did inherit an old team. He had Whiteside and McGrath, Robson, Duxbury and Stapleton who were all getting on a bit. The rest of that first season was pretty poor but then you thought, in the summer he'll kick out half the players, get some new ones and get them all going.

Then his first full season was, if anything, even worse. The

performances were so uninspiring, so boring. He didn't hav
any wingers or good strikers. They could lose at home
anybody – regularly – they almost got relegated. Boring, dou
unexciting. Team selection seemed crap, signings unexcitin
no imagination. First impression was that he was a do
Scotsman producing boring football. Bring back Atkinso
After twelve months we wanted him out. First impressio
were not good. I'm sure I joined in the 'Ferguson out' chant.
wanted him to go already after a year. When they look ba
and say Edwards wouldn't have got rid of him if they had lo
that Cup game against Forest, I think that's rubbish. If Unite
had gone out of the Cup and got nowhere in the League, the
the fans would have demanded Ferguson get the chop.

If United fans jeer a player regularly, then there is no wa
he'll make a success of it, whether or not he's got the guts
keep going. It's the same with the manager. The board wor
put up with a manager if he's just being booed the who
game. Winning the FA Cup in 1990 turned it. They hadn
won it since 1985. It was the first bit of silverware for fi
years. There is a big difference now with winning things.
those days winning the FA Cup was a bit like if we were
win the European Cup now. The FA Cup was a trophy li
the Holy Grail. Now we're really blasé. If we win the FA Cu
we don't give a stuff. So Ferguson won us a trophy, so all w
forgiven.

JIM THORNTO

Getting up to 1989 I was thinking I'd had enough of this. The
was some dire football. This is Ferguson's early year
Even with Atkinson towards the latter stages, he was buyir
Sivebaek, Gibson, the worst players to ever pull a red shirt o
an absolute disgrace. It was horrible stuff and the playe
weren't committed to it. And although I have never ever se
big trouble at United, there was an element of 'Why am I comir
here?' You know, this is a shit ground, shit team, standing f

hours, because I used to go to the Stretford End, and you'd go an hour before kick-off to queue up. I did actually get to a point, it must actually have been the Hillsborough thing, when I wondered about the whole thing. The fanzines came out then. I remember reading about the fun people were having in lower-League games, particularly non-League games. I actually thought at one point of giving it up and going to Maine Road. It was a low point for football. I actually got the feeling that football was going to exist only as a small minority sport. And the ban in Europe also had an effect. No team was being tested, having to learn the lessons abroad as Liverpool did. I'm seeing it now, the edge that Liverpool had on English clubs having been at the forefront in Europe. That had gone. So, as I say, at that point I just thought I was going to give it up. But for some reason I decided to buy a season ticket and then they won the Cup.

Nobody knew Ferguson or knew of him which is a bit bizarre really, given his record with Aberdeen. But it didn't count for much down in England. He'd won the Cup but it wasn't really perceived as a big trophy. And he also didn't change much for the first couple of seasons; he kept the same players. It was only in about his third or second season that he brought in a load of new players.

I used to go with a guy who had an inside track into what was going on, saying what he was doing with the club was different. One of the first things he did was to sack his chief scout. And at the time they didn't have a youth team as Edwards had run it down. The story was that the club was going to show a loss for the first time, and that was one of the reasons why they sold Hughes. They also cut back on operational costs, youth teams, scouts. That's where City came in; they had all the local scouts. I don't know how authentic this is but by all accounts they didn't have any scouts at all, not even in Ireland. Atkinson was a bad influence on that club, a very bad influence. Atkinson's policy wasn't to go for youth players, it was to go for ready-made players; he'd have his little cabal of first-teamers and the rest were outside of this circle. What an appalling way to run a football club; you're just stoking up trouble, aren't you?

Atkinson wanted ready-made players, at the top. He had this group of about eight of them and anyone outside of that eight couldn't get in. Mark Hughes talked about it a lot: even though he got to the Cup final, he wasn't part of the circle. It was Robson, McGrath and people like that. He alienated a number of people like Wilkins, who I think was one of the finest players we've ever had at Old Trafford, marvellous player. I can never forgive Atkinson for what he did to Whiteside. I think he just drove the kid into the ground. If Whiteside had come through now he wouldn't play half the games he played. He played so many games, he went straight to the World Cup. He had nine or ten operations on his knee in the end. He played for United at sixteen. He was a brilliant player, he'd be a fabulous player now, he could be at the peak of his career now. That's the one thing I've always held against Atkinson.

But we had some great nights. I remember that ten game run. It was unbelievable. The weird thing about that was that there is no record of it because there was a television dispute at the time over coverage. We had a ten game sequence of wins. I remember Whiteside against West Ham getting a hat-trick. Absolutely tremendous stuff. And the noise just seemed incredible. It seems like the culmination of all that was the Barcelona game. Maradona, Schuster and all that. That was the noisiest game I've ever been to in my life.

I remember the Sheffield Wednesday game in 1993, the two-one win at Old Trafford, the one that went on for seven extra minutes. That was because the referee went off for five minutes. But nobody ever says that. He went off injured and there was a five minute delay. That was the moment I have come closest to mass hysteria when you actually begin to lose control. It was a sobering reflection afterwards, wondering is this some sort of personality defect that I can get carried away with something. It was essentially trivial. It is just a game but there is nothing quite like it that affects you so much. You can feel the bottom of despair, where you can step back and say, 'This is not death', and it was like that. That game really epitomised it. But it was the making of them as well. You just felt then that you couldn't leave them alone. There was a cast-iron certainty that they were going to win it this time, after the despair of the previous season.

There are defining moments of a season. The majority of times in the eighties the season was meaningless, with high points in particular games where they would turn it on. I think the nineties were defined by the losing to Leeds or the possibility of losing that first League Championship to Leeds. You can't get worse than lose the Championship race to one rival at the home of another. You can't get it any worse than that. I mean that game against Liverpool. I remember watching it. I couldn't believe it. We hit the bar about three times that day. Liverpool won two–nil. Leeds were playing Sheffield United and the ex-City player Bryan Gayle put through his own goal – twice. The goalkeeper saved the first one, so he put it in again. We had Ince and Robson patched up. I watched them stagger on the field. I thought, such courage really, you could physically see them dragging their bodies on, just trying to achieve the impossible. It was appalling.

TIM BAMFORD

Nobody could deny that they didn't have any doubts about Alex Ferguson. I think, though hindsight is a wonderful thing, that Alex Ferguson was working hard behind the scenes. He'd bought a number of players around 1989–90. He bought about five players and they had to be given a chance to fit into the side. There's no point in spending all that money and expecting them to gel straight away. And they did take time to settle. In fact we got the reward at the end of that season when we won the FA Cup, although our League position was poor. The following season we won the European Cup-Winners' Cup, then the League Cup, and into four Championships in five years. It was a slow build-up but having spent the money you have to support the manager. Obviously there were doubts because it did take Alex time. He had to learn about the English game. He probably didn't know as much about the English players as he thought he did when he arrived. I think he'd admit that. I think there was a learning curve there which he had to go through. Thank goodness we did stick with him.

MARTIN EDWARDS

Yes, I was a 'Fergie out' man. When he first came I thought well, yes, he's done well in Aberdeen. But 1987–88 the football was bad. I thought, like everyone else, it's time for a change. I went to that game against Nottingham Forest which United won one–nil. Great support. Even though they won that game we still weren't sure. It was a Cup game and a lot of people have suggested that had we not won, Ferguson would have been out. Martin Edwards has of course denied it. But you never know in football. Gates were down, there was nothing good in being a United fan in 1988, '89 around then. Then of course it just took off. Since then I've been everywhere: Barcelona, Juventus, Rotterdam, even Wrexham!

ROBIN MURRAY

The early Ferguson years were dreadful. You always think to yourself that I was not one of those people who wanted Ferguson out but if you're honest with yourself, everybody did. When he came in, United was in a right shambles and to be fair he has turned it completely around. And now from juniors to reserves are all playing and looking well. But unfortunately, when you are a fan, you can't wait. When somebody says, 'It'll take me five years to do this', you don't want to wait five years, you want to wait a couple of games because winning is important. You don't like watching your own team being humiliated. I don't always agree with some of the things he does now. I'd just let them play because they play beautiful football. If they lose, fine, hold your hands up, and say the other team is better. But all this 'We won't play him, or we won't do this.' No, just let them play. But you can't knock him for what he has achieved; it's just brilliant. I still think that when they lost the Championship by one point they should have won it. It was there for the taking and they threw it away.

ROLAND COBURN

I remember standing on the terraces and everyone around me screaming 'Fergie out' and the general opinion at the time in the Stretford End was that he wasn't going to last very long. Thank goodness they let him have a bit of a chance to see what he could do. I remember when he arrived thinking, 'Well who the hell is he?', although he'd got quite a good pedigree. I think his manner didn't go down very well. People around me used to go on, 'Bloody Scotsman, what does he know?' and so on; and I think the way in which he fell out with players and his quite dour manner, I don't think he was very popular. I remember many a Saturday afternoon if things weren't going very well by half time there'd be twenty-odd thousand people stood around me, all screaming for him to go.

I think he was trying to change things too quickly, get rid of players who were popular and the way in which he dealt with the press. People thought he was going to shake up what they knew and loved too much. As it happened he did it for the better. I think at the time people were a bit dubious about him. I remember people being quite purple in the face, screaming at him, 'He's got to go, he's got to go.' Thank goodness he didn't.

I remember seeing an interview with him on the television in which he used the phrase 'little triangular passes will get you everywhere' or something like that. It was a reference to the way in which he thought the team should be playing and you could suddenly see little triangular passes around the pitch, rather like Liverpool were doing at the time, as opposed to booting the ball up and hoping for the best. It took him to use the phrase for me to notice the change that was happening and I thought, 'Ooh, that's good,' and all of a sudden the sophistication of the kind of play seemed to come in and you began to think maybe we're on to something.

There were two important games against Sheffield Wednesday. There was one at Old Trafford which went on for about an extra ten minutes. The referee went off and it almost seemed like we were just going to carry on playing until we equalised. That was a funny one, because ten minutes before you'd been absolutely waiting for the final whistle to get you out of your misery because we weren't used to having the floor wiped with us, and then all of a sudden we got this new lease of life and by the time the final one went in it was incredible. We've had a lot of funny games with Sheffield Wednesday which really stick out in my memory. There was one just after that at Old Trafford when the heavens opened and I think we were something like four–nil up and it started hailing and snowing and storming and everything else and they thought they were going to abandon the match at one point. We've had quite a few odd ones with them but certainly that one at Old Trafford I remember very well. Sometimes you do wonder about luck in football.

Another match which particularly sticks in my mind was at Carrow Road. I think we scored three in the first fifteen minutes; Giggs, Kanchelskis and Cantona all scored in the first fifteen minutes. My dad had stayed at home – 'I'll just do the washing-up before the match starts' – and by the time he sat down to watch the match on Sky they'd scored three goals. I think it finished up three–one in the end but that was another match when we looked invincible. Kanchelskis was on top form, wingers flying up; it was just brilliant.

MAXINE DUNHAM

National Service was due to come along but I didn't wait to be called up – I went along and joined up at the age of seventeen – and I did three years, came out and went playing for the likes of the Manchester YMCA, and to be fair I wasn't a bad player. To my delight I got a knock on the door one evening and it was Joe Armstrong from Manchester United asking me if I'd come for a trial with the club. This would be about 1957, definitely before Munich, because being a bit older than some of the other boys they put me in with the elderly players such as Peter Jones, Alex Dawson and people like that. I went to the same school as Albert Scanlon so they let me train with them. I trained at the Cliff on a Tuesday evening and on a Thursday evening we came here and we were allowed to go into the first-team dressing rooms. That was one of the magic things about Manchester United, how they let you hang your clothes up where famous players – Rowley, Pearson, Mitten – had hung theirs. That was the great thing. You used to run up and down the stadium and to the cricket club and back. I never played regular, I never got a game for Manchester United and instead of waiting I left. They didn't ask me to leave; I just packed my bags and left because things were difficult at home. I worked on the milk with my dad because you had to earn a few bob. But it wasn't only United, I turned down Joe Smith at Blackpool who wrote and asked me to go for a trial, and Stan Cullis at Wolverhampton Wanderers. But in those days I had to go out and work and I ended up playing for New Mills, Glossop, Stalybridge Celtic, Accrington Stanley. So I moved around a little bit.

I've had some great times. I remember when I first joined the club we went to Notts Forest and we won one–nil. That was a crucial game. I put money on that game for us to win the Cup. I think I won £400, a lot in them days. People say it was a crucial game for Alex Ferguson but I think people have made that up. I don't think it was a crucial game for Alex Ferguson. I don't think he was near to getting anything. We're not a club like that, we've not hired and fired them, you know that as well as I do.

Alex Ferguson and Martin Edwards have been great with me and Alex has let me get into areas I could never have got into in my life. He's let me into the dressing room which is part of my job, but when we go away I go away with the team. I sit on the coach, I have a meal in the evening with Alex and Brian Kidd, the secretary and so on. We have a table of ten. We talk about football. All Alex and Kiddo are interested in is football and it's lovely to be a part of that. I know it's my job but it's part of being a supporter. Sitting in the directors' boxes was something I'd never dreamt of but it's happened to me. Eric Cantona, Ryan Giggs, meeting with people like that, that's been a great thrill for me.

When we won the Championship, the party we had here, they slung me in the bath, fully clothed. Brian McClair did it and I've got photographs to prove it. Kidd, Hughes, Robson all in the bath and I'm sitting in the bath with them, with my blazer and flannels on. That to me is a great feeling. The European Cup-Winners' Cup final in Rotterdam, I went to the party afterwards and we stayed in a little hotel and obviously the hotel didn't know if we were going to win or not. When we arrived back they had sheets from the beds and put them all criss-cross across the entrance and they had a champagne fountain which they'd done for us and everybody stayed up 'til seven the next morning, just having a good time and Mick Hucknall came there as well.

That's the good thing about Manchester United: it's never changed its attitude. It's a big club but it's also a homely club. If you lose that you're losing Manchester United, I think. And that's what's good about Alex Ferguson. He cares about people, he has good rapport with the supporters. You take Brian Kidd – if you cut his head off he'd come out Man United. He's Man United through and through. The only thing he's interested in is the club doing well. You need those type of people in the club. Martin Edwards – I don't know anybody who could beat Martin Edwards answering questions on Manchester United. He beat

Cliff Butler, the club historian, on answering questions on Manchester United, who played this and so on. When it's time to go I'll hang my hat up and look back, not with regret, but with gratitude. That's how it's been for me.

DANNY McGREGOR

What magnificent success the boss had had up in Scotland. Then he came down here. The Football League, as it was then, was a hard league. Like everything, it does take time and sometimes it takes a little luck. The boss came in and, in his defence, he was trying to build a club. And that's not having a go at any previous managers. I think that was the difference and it does take time.

I don't think there was anything specific. The players who came in had terrific characters, your Steve Bruces, Pallisters, Paul Ince, Sparky coming back. Great warrior, Sparky. It's not just a hundred per cent; there's more to Sparky than that. He was technically a very good player. People think he was just strength but he had a lot more. Robbo was in the dressing room, strong characters. Eric comes as well. Howard Wilkinson was trying to sign Denis Irwin, and then the boss asks if he's got anyone to sell and Eric's name comes up.

I don't think we had doubts. We're aware to this day that it's not easy. You can have eleven world-class players but eleven world-class players aren't necessarily going to give you a world-class team. When you're building a house you need your carriers and your bricklayers and it's the same with a football team. It's part of the jigsaw. It's formulating how you want your team to play. My belief is that you don't have a system, your players dictate the system and that's what you've got to build on. You go into the transfer market but you don't know how they're going to come off. It's always a gamble. You've got to be strong mentally and physically for the job at Manchester United.

BRIAN KIDD

I suppose I've been a more patient type. I see the best in people and hope they'll come good. I'm a bit like that with Andy Cole. They seem a nice person, so I wish they do well. I wasn't into all that anti-Fergie stuff – I just see how it pans out. I suppose I started to go regularly when they got rid of Ron Atkinson. I'd seen one flamboyant character go and then Ferguson came and seemed a bit different.

I used to go with just a group of lads from the university. I was the only girl. Now we have seats and we sit in the same seat for each match and now I'm aware of more women around me than ever before. Before, we'd stand and we'd stand in various parts of the ground and it was male-dominated. I guess I would find a safe place to stand so I didn't get crushed and all that. But now there's women around. I didn't find it a problem before, though. I knew where to stand, where I wouldn't be squashed if a goal went in. I had a bad experience at Newcastle. James and I got split up in the Gallowgate End for the whole game. After that I tended to go in the seats at the back of the Stretford End. It was safer and more family orientated. I suppose for a woman it's the lack of height because you can't see when you're stood with the rest of them. I never had any problems with sexism. I'm a bit of a tomboy and never had any abuse except that time at the Gallowgate End when we got split up. And somebody got a bit fresh. But never any trouble like that at United.

We went to the Crystal Palace Cup final and the Chelsea Cup final. We got tickets because since 1988 we've been League match ticket book holders so we collected the tokens and having the right number, we then queued. The seats were desperately poor as they always are at Wembley. My sister lived in Epsom so we got the train and the tube. That wasn't very nice. We were on the same line as the Chelsea fans. It was all right going because the Chelsea fans thought they were going to beat us. They'd beaten us twice that season and were on a high. On the way in we were in a carriage and there was a good atmosphere, quite friendly. Then they started to

210

sing the Munich song. Much to James's horror, I stood on my tiptoes and yelled in this guy's ear, 'You're sick.' And they all shut up. The whole carriage went desperately quiet. And there was me and James and a couple of United fans in the carriage cringing in the corner, thinking what did she do that for? But they kept quiet until we got to the tube stop. Then they piled out and started singing again. So I think I had a lucky escape. I just didn't think. There is something about the Munich song. It stirs up such anger in people. I don't like the hateful chants. I'd rather cheer on our team rather than sing or chant against the other team.

The game itself, however, was really good. And that was the Double. But unfortunately we had to get back to Epsom and we had to travel back with the Chelsea fans and that was horrible. James just had his red shirt on with Cantona on the back and no coat to hide it with. And he was threatened so many times. It was so nasty on the tube and when we got off the tube as we were going up the escalator, these two skinheads came in behind us and said, 'We've got a knife and we're going to get you.' I just put myself between them and James. I thought, surely they won't touch a woman, and they didn't. They just kept being nasty, threatening. When we got to the top of the escalator we legged it into the train only for them to get into the same carriage. So it was a very tense journey. We were hiding in the corner. I'll not forget that. It's a shame with Chelsea doing so well these days, because you think it would be nice to see them do well, but I remember their fans on that day. That was the last time I've been really frightened at a football match.

Back in the late eighties we went to a Derby at Maine Road. The instances I've seen trouble have been few and far between. I was still at university so it must have been 1986, 1987-ish. We got lost coming out of Maine Road and we were only trying to get back to Fallowfield so we decided we'd turn round and head back to the ground, only to see all these fighting hordes coming towards us. So we decided to stand under this tree just trying to let people pass by and a police car mounted the kerb and stopped about six inches off us and two Alsatians were flung out of the back. But we clung on to this tree and waited for it all to go away. It's days like that when you think, what am I doing here? But they are the exceptions to it all. If there is any trouble on the forecourt at Old Trafford we don't see it, although it sometimes happens.

ALISSON THORNTON

Leaving United was a wrench but the time was ready. It was an amicable agreement. I sat down and had a long chat with the boss, Alex Ferguson. He thought I was getting a bit stale with all my injuries and so forth and I had to agree with him. It was time for a change, so I moved on to Everton. But don't get me wrong, we left on the best of terms. I even had a tabloid newspaper ring me up and offer me £50,000 to dish the dirt on Alex Ferguson but I refused. I had no argument with him and the club, and Alex knows that. No way would I have taken money from a tabloid.

I think Alex had teething problems when he arrived at Old Trafford. United is a big club and, all respect to Aberdeen, but they are in a different league. It takes time to come to terms with the size of United. Some never manage it. Garry Birtles never adapted, never came to terms with it. So it took Alex Ferguson some time to find his feet. I think he always had a plan. I think he knew what he wanted. He's a thinker, but it did take time for that plan to work out. I'd left by the time it did work out but even when I was at Everton I used to have a young apprentice come and give me the United result when I was in the bath after the match.

NORMAN WHITESIDE

I've done some pretty stupid things in relationship to United,

212

such as missing the 1968 European Cup final. My dad died in 1990 and he was a season ticket holder in the United Road stand. He'd moved from the Stretford Road End to there and I handed the season ticket back. I must have been the only person to have ever done that, I think.

One of the funniest things that happened to me, odd in many ways; it made me realise I've become different. I'd watched Law, Best, Charlton in the sixties, and when we started pursuing the Olympics bid in 1989 I had to travel to Puerto Rico via New York with Bobby Charlton, who I had never met before. And I realised that I had changed and the world had changed when we met and he came up and introduced himself. 'Hello, Mr Stringer,' he said. Being called by a formal title by a superhero was quite humbling and made me realise the way I had changed quite a lot.

GRAHAM STRINGER

I was once lecturing in Finland. I'd gone to give a lecture at the anniversary of the department of a university. I was flown over there, treated as an honoured guest and so forth. Anyhow, the person I was staying with had told me to bring some clothes to wear under a ski-suit because they were going to take me cross-country skiing. So I took my United shirt to wear underneath. It just so happened that after I'd given this lecture I went back to the house and I was taken for an afternoon learning how to ski. And then they said they were going to get someone from the press to come and interview me about the lecture I had given. When they arrived and saw the United shirt, the only thing the journalists were interested in talking about was my United shirt. So – it was just after the Cantona incident – I ended up talking the whole time about what I thought about the Cantona incident and what it meant to United fans generally and how important United was as a football team. It ended up with this photograph in the paper of me in a United shirt juggling the ball on the top of my head.

I went to Barcelona, away, three or four years ago with about one hundred and twenty thousand supporters. People there told us that only Real Madrid and Manchester United could fill the Nou Camp. I have friends in Barcelona who go and watch Barcelona on a regular basis and they said that they had never seen it full before, apart from Real Madrid games.

DEREK WYNNE

I'm originally from England but have lived in Australia for about five years. My sister-in-law is a mad Red and is totally responsible for my passion. She took me to my first match, against Chelsea in 1992. It pissed with rain – this was when there was just open terracing in the visitors' end – and we all got soaked. I saw Eric Cantona score his first goal for United and after that day I was hooked. Clare, my sister-in-law, thought I'd never want to go again having been subjected to the elements. However, it all just served to heighten the experience.

Ironically, I emigrated to Oz the next year but my passion didn't wane and Clare keeps me up to date as does the Internet. I've been back a couple of times and have been lucky enough to see eight games in the last three years, which is not enough, but not bad for where I live. I'd like to go every week. Supporting a team so far away does demand its own peculiar dedication, working harder to get news and getting up at 2 a.m., 5 a.m., or whatever time to watch a match or sometimes just to hear the radio commentary if it's not televised. My favourite player that I have seen play is Eric, but of all time I'd say Duncan Edwards. I'm fascinated by him.

SALLY ORPIN

I was lodging at a house in Miles Platting. I had joined the police by this time and had moved to Manchester. I moved to

Manchester in December 1974. I joined the police solely so that I could come to Manchester. That was the only reason. I shouldn't say this really. I was coming up from Portsmouth for every match and at £3 on the coach it was too expensive. It was killing me with my £16 a week wage. I had relatives in Manchester and I had an uncle in the police force in Manchester. He just said why don't you join the police, you can see all the football you want, live with us. So I applied, went to the interviews. I had a lovely southern accent, been to boarding school. They thought I was a star. 'Love to have you,' they said.

So I moved to Manchester. I lived in a police hostel which was absolutely horrendous. I'd visited Manchester but I just didn't realise how rough some of the places were until I moved up here. I thought I'd last about six months. I'd not seen anything like it, working around Gorton and Ardwick. I was born in Haslemere which is really posh. I went to Whitworth Street police station and I was lucky; there were about three other lads who were big United fans. There were only half a dozen lads in the group. Trying to get off on a Saturday was murder. There was a pecking order and I was pretty low down. But they were usually very good. If you were to finish at 3 p.m., they'd let you go a bit earlier and put time in later. So I kept up my record. In the past twenty-four years I've missed only about half a dozen home matches through work commitments. I've done well really. The police force has done me proud.

My first European match was St Etienne. I'd been in the police about two years. I'd moved out of the police hostel and was living with a Polish family. I went to see the St Etienne game – £39, three days on the coach. It wasn't an official trip. I've never been on a United European trip on a coach since and I never will. It was awful. There was rioting in the ground, no segregation. My friend, who I went with, got forced out of the ground before the match started, but luckily we found him. We were chased all around St Etienne by the French fans. The fighting started off with the St Etienne fans throwing bread at the United fans. One thing led to another. I think we got banned. We had to play the second game in Plymouth. The next game was at Juventus. I found myself sitting next to my friend Roland. He was sat next to me on the plane. I'd known him at Old Trafford. He sat in front of me at the Stretford End. I hated him. He always wore the same shirt and he had the biggest mouth of anyone on the Stretford End. I used to wind him up. He was always moaning. 'Shuuurrup,' I'd say. And there I was having the pleasure of sitting next to him on the plane. He worked for Granada Television and we've been going together ever since, twenty-two years later.

In those days at Whitworth Street I could do Maine Road on a Saturday if I wanted to and Old Trafford the next Saturday. I'd volunteer sometimes. If City were playing on a Wednesday and United weren't playing, I'd do it. It was great, the overtime, and I love football. Occasionally I still go to see City if United are not playing. It never bothered me watching City as a policeman. I'd just get on with the job. But watching United was very hard as a policeman. Sometimes if I couldn't get time off I'd volunteer to do the football. I'd be doing crowd duty. It's so hard to remember that you're a policeman and not a fan. The worst occasion was 1984. We had a Cup run, played West Ham at Old Trafford. It was a close game. United were three–one up and they scored and made it three–two. Norman Whiteside had scored two goals. I was pacing up and down. Norman Whiteside scored with five minutes to go to make it four–two and I went berserk. My helmet went up in the air. I was so happy, I forgot I was working at the match. To this day I don't know what stopped me running on the pitch. I remember the sergeant coming up to me and telling me I was supposed to be watching the fans, not getting ready to run on the pitch. There's been a few times like that.

There was a game against Sheffield Wednesday. From my shouting it was obvious I was a United fan. The Sheffield Wednesday fans were baiting me because I was a United fan. They'd gone one–nil up, and I was very depressed, giving

216

them some verbal back, all very light-hearted of course. Then United got a penalty. You have to stand up and face the crowd. I thought, this is it. They were all swearing away at me. Frank Stapleton goes and misses the penalty. I had to stand there for the next forty minutes or so facing the Sheffield Wednesday fans. At the end of the game every Sheffield Wednesday fan went by me, giving me hell.

There was a game last year against Wimbledon and I was sat, on duty. Now when United score you're supposed to stand up and watch the crowd. But there I was, I was caught by the *Match of the Day* cameras and every time United scored, I leapt up in my uniform and cheered, before facing the crowd. When I saw *Match of the Day* that night, I thought, I hope nobody saw that.

I don't do it any more. The wages are £60–£70 for doing a football match but I'd rather go now. There's always the chance you might finish up doing traffic duty outside the ground and spend ninety minutes just waiting, trying to find out what the score is.

There's no trouble now except for a few games – Leeds, Liverpool. Leeds is really bad. At Elland Road they keep you in the ground after the final whistle so everyone knows who you are as you come out. If I go to the game at Leeds I show my police pass and get out as soon as I can, get to the car and I'm off. Leeds – evil. So when they come to Old Trafford there's revenge. But there's rarely trouble inside the ground. I think Old Trafford is one of the best-policed grounds in the country. If there are problems, it's on the concourse area. I still think that if it wasn't so well-policed there'd be trouble. Maybe it's just because they are United and they are universally hated.

In an FA Cup match against a lower division side they come and want to show you. I remember playing Swindon a couple of years ago and there was trouble. Reading in the Cup as well. They just wanted to fight. The lower division sides are the worst. Wrexham, Cardiff, they're the worst.

ROBIN MURRAY

The first European away game I went to was 1977 when I went to Juventus and that in itself was a bit of a chaotic trip. The flight was fine, but they gave you tickets outside the stadium half an hour before kick-off and it was absolute chaos. They were handing out tickets and people were saying, 'Well, I ordered two and I've only got one.' No one knew what was going on. That wasn't through the official supporters' club; that was through looking in the paper and getting a package deal which might have been a bit cheaper. In retrospect it wasn't as good. But then I went to Valencia with a package deal and actually ended up staying in a five star hotel which was only £5 more than a day trip from United. All the Valencia players were in the same hotel – Kempes and the rest – it was staggering to be sat by the pool waiting for the kick-off in the evening. You do wonder who prices all these set-ups.

Unfortunately there have been a lot of difficult moments on foreign away trips. The big problem is alcohol. I don't drink so I don't fall into this bracket; I'm lucky. If they get there early in the day, especially if it's Spain or France which is quite local, they could be there for a few days; they are out of their trolleys by the time the game starts. All it needs is one clown to say something and once it starts, bottles are thrown. The Spanish police aren't the most friendly. There have been lots of times when you're cornered. Once that starts all the locals come out. We've had all our coaches bottled and windows smashed. At the Valencia game there were twelve coaches going back and every coach had every window smashed. We all got out of the coaches and ran into this huge mob of Spanish fans. Luckily, as it turned out, another gang of Manchester United fans appeared around the corner who had obviously made their own way to the game and it all petered out. The police aren't used to that kind of away following and are not used to the way English fans behave. Some are good and are not a problem, but as I say, alcohol causes the majority of trouble.

It's quite interesting. When they went into the Champions

League you do go to the smaller ground. Montpellier before it was redone had this stand put up which was literally just lumps of metal and everybody was on it and the whole thing was swaying as we watched the game. But on the bright side it is great to go to all these countries. A two-day trip, if you can keep out of the hassles, is great. Poland, Czechoslovakia, Italy's great fun as well. Places you wouldn't normally go to on a holiday.

It costs a lot of money. Everything is relative. You are talking £200 for a day trip, but it's worth it if you've got through. But then of course, a lot of fans who can't go to every round wait until the later stages. But if they get knocked out in the early stages it means you've never had the chance to go. Some of my friends went to Russia and then Turkey. It cost them a fortune, but being there and seeing it made it all worthwhile. Great fun. Even with the hassles I still want to go. You also think that you can avoid the trouble. It's the same with any away ground in the country; you know that you will be confronted at some time, so you park on another side of the ground or walk to the ground this way; you always think you can get out of it. Up to now that's always been the case – a few close moments, but nothing too much.

It's great when you go to an away ground in Europe and you turn round and see all these fans there. I went to Rapid Vienna. I think about eight thousand Manchester United fans were there. It was bloody cold but at the end of the day we won and it was great. Even when we lost in Dortmund – we lost one–nil – there was a huge following there and the atmosphere they generated was great, it was good fun. Again there were a few minor scuffles in and around the ground. But I don't think that was so much football, more political-led clashes.

ROLAND COBURN

The first time I started going abroad was the season of the Cup-Winners' Cup and I went to Legia Warsaw. I went with

UF Tours who were one of the independent groups. We just flew out, a whole load of us, settled in the hotel and then instantly went out and had lots of beer. The thing about going away is that until the day of the match, the match has little significance. For a lot of the blokes it is a lot about territory marking – the way in which huge gangs of United fans take to the streets and claim particular areas of the town as their own and take over bars. It's almost like a showing of strength really. It's almost like invading somebody's town. I mean the usual thing is that at some point during the course of the trip there will be a town square, for example, which is completely full of United fans, where everybody congregates for the whole of the three days that you're away and everyone knows to go there. You all meet and do the drinking there and the locals just stand there, absolutely mystified, and don't get a look in.

The next significant away match that I remember abroad is when I went to watch United play Torpedo Moscow where the match was an absolutely hideous disaster, losing on penalties, but the trip was fantastic. The champagne was a dollar a bottle and vodka was two dollars a bottle. There was no food in the hotel so some people went to McDonald's and we finally found a Pizza Hut, but the main meal in the hotel was a sardine to start with followed by a sausage every day. But they were quite prepared to serve champagne any time of the day or night, so we sat having champagne for breakfast and just carried on.

It absolutely poured down the whole time we were there. I've still got my programme from that. It's got little cut-out pictures of Clayton Blackmore with Bryan Robson written underneath and things. Because I speak Russian I was reading an article in the programme which said that the Moscow fans were invited to ask the United fans to exchange souvenirs at the end of the match, which of course meant that when we were trying to get back on the coach we had all these Torpedo people trying to rip our shirts off and everything. I ended up hiding behind a tank with some boys from Eccles while a big riot went on. I've still got the video now and I sometimes look back on it and you can see all these huddled figures, absolutely soaking, wet to the skin, praying for the match to be over.

That was my first experience of heavy-handed policing abroad as well. There was a solid line of the official Red Army in front of us all the way through the match so that you could barely see over their heads. Then a guy with a big truncheon. Anyone who stepped out of line was swiped at with this big stick. And then afterwards a complete lack of protection. All the fans were trying to grab at us and all our stuff and the coaches deciding to leave us alone and having to make our own way back to the hotels. That was my first experience of chaos abroad.

There weren't many women on the trip. There was one other woman on the trip on that occasion so I obviously shared a room with her. She was quite a seasoned traveller with them as well. Generally speaking, we were just accepted by the lads and looked after in some respects if things got a bit nasty. It was a huge mixture of postal workers from Swindon and then chartered accountants from Surrey and everything you could possibly imagine in between. Some people had gone with just enough money to buy themselves some beer for the week and then some people were buying crystal to take back for their wives.

MAXINE DUNHAM

The first European away game I went to was Montpellier in 1991. I didn't go to any of the early eighties and then from '85 there wasn't any. The first game we had that season was Pecsi Munkas in Hungary. I couldn't go to that. I was in a band at the time in Manchester called Ratfink and we were due to be on tour at that time in France and I arranged a gig for the night before the game in Montpellier. I got loads of publicity out through the fanzines and got leaflets distributed. I spoke to the management of the club during the day and said, 'There won't be any problems, will there?' But of course on the night the bouncers wouldn't let any English fans in and certainly not any United fans, so it all went immediately pear-shaped, the riot police came in, closed the club down and the gig never took place.

So that was my immediate introduction to European policing; a salutary lesson. We got five hundred tickets for that game and there was about two or three thousand people there; almost everybody ended up getting in one way or another. They'd kept one corner of the ground entirely free and they just piled all the United fans into that corner. And that was the first 'Always look on the bright side' at that game. We won two–nil. That was one of the best games I ever went to. I went back to Montpellier this summer, back to the club where we played; it was great, it's been reopened.

There's something about European aways, something special; you just meet up with all these people you know who go regularly to away games and everybody arrives by a million different routes. One of the things that alienates supporters more than anything is the attempts to control that when there doesn't seem to be any cause. Yes, there's been problems with policing and also there's been problems at this end, the way tickets have been distributed, rip-off packages you get both from the club and other travel agencies who charge exorbitant fees for what is fairly basic travel packages and the kind of restrictions that are put on. Travel through Europe is very easy these days and there's this presumption that if you want to travel by yourself or with your mates, maybe have a bit of a holiday as well, go to the game and not be marshalled around, then you must be some kind of troublemaker. I think it's changed but there is still that fear. If you look at the record since the return to Europe, the problems, certainly with United fans, have been minimal. The number of arrests is just into double figures.

The worst was Porto, but then I wasn't arrested in

Galatasaray. I had travelled independently to Galatasaray; I was staying in an hotel just down the road from the one that got done. The police just went in and arrested everybody; a lot of people I knew were in that hotel. You turned up at the game and they weren't there. Having said that, going to the game was a tasty enough experience itself. We arrived two hours before kick-off thinking we had plenty of time and the stadium had been full for three hours before that. Absolute bedlam, people throwing cans. We had to go through this rat-run of a tunnel to get to the gate and the police were just extremely violent. You noticed there were a lot of empty seats when you got in there; suddenly they were all filled by police because the supporters were sitting in the nick.

The noise – I've never been in an atmosphere quite like that; phenomenal. We were in the corner of the ground in the lower bit and there was a tier above us and there were drums going all the time, and mocking cut-throats, and stuff like that, things thrown at us. The smoke when the players came on, you couldn't see over the other side of the pitch. Les Sealey came running over, there were only a couple of hundred of us, and he was yelling, 'Come on, you've got to make as much noise as possible.' Against this? Afterwards we were staying on because we had another night in the hotel and we walked out, just got to the police cordon outside the United bit and these two lads came out, one with blood running down his face, saying, 'Don't go in there.' So we jumped on an official bus taking the United party back to the airport. So we went to the airport and then got a taxi back to the hotel and on the way back in we could see them all piling out to the airport. They were stopping cars in the street and banging the heads off them. It was like a revolution was going on; it was totally out of control. It was quite frightening. The taxi driver stopped at this petrol station and we were just in the car, heads down, pretending to be tourists; there were people all over the petrol station. After that it was all right; we got a bit of 'English hooligans' but you get that everywhere. That's one of the sad things about going abroad. There is this perception that will not go away. Ninety-nine per cent of the time, people do nothing more than Irish or Scottish supporters do when they go abroad, and if the same behaviour was happening, and you were wearing a kilt of green and orange, you'd be perceived totally differently. There's a job of altering that perception that still needs to be done. I've got a really good friend who was a student over here for three months who is Portuguese and a big Porto fan so I went over with a few mates for a week. He had come over for the Old Trafford game; I'd got him a ticket and we did things like arrange games between one of the United fanzines and a group of Porto fans because I was there a few days earlier and had gone to the Porto–Sporting game. It was generally very quiet, but then a few days later numbers started to arrive. You can never quite tell how many will arrive until they turn up. But there were about twelve thousand – a phenomenal number for a European away game. There's a main square in the port and I remember coming around the corner and suddenly seeing it full of United fans; it was absolutely brilliant, flags everywhere.

By and large there was absolutely no problem in Porto the day before and the day of the game. Then we got to the stadium. It was quite hard getting to the stadium. They hadn't laid on extra buses, they hadn't prepared for that number of people. I sat on the Manchester Council working party to deal with Euro 96 and the preparations put in to deal with ten thousand Germans was considerable. The Portuguese had not prepared. We got up to the ground with plenty of time – about an hour before kick-off – and the end United were in had a concrete corridor around. There's quite a big crush and we were all being directed to this one gate; there were three or four gates around that end that had been shut off and people were getting crushed against the barriers. There was one Greater Manchester policeman there. I went to speak to him but he said, 'Well, what am I supposed to do?' I think they had completely lost control.

What I found out afterwards was that there was one tour

224

company who had got tickets down the side of the pitch, not in the United section and until then they had been told that would be fine, there'd be empty seats down there; but for some reason on the night the police decided to put everybody in one end which they had already sold all the tickets for. So they were adding two thousand to a section that didn't have space. The tickets had bar-codes on and of course the two thousand people come round to the turnstiles and the bar-codes won't read them. The police then jumped to the conclusion that those tickets must be forgeries and shut the turnstiles down and wouldn't let them in. People were coming in behind them as well.

It was just gross mismanagement and frighteningly familiar in terms of what happened at Hillsborough. What they ended up doing was that they had this gate, a big metal concertina gate that I think was for letting people out rather than in. They would just open it up, let fifty or so in, then close it. Inside there were two lines of police with batons and people were getting pushed straight into these police, so the police reacted by just hitting them as they were coming through. That tunnel went straight down on to the staircase into the stand. In the stand there were no crush barriers, just big concrete steps, and people coming straight in on to the staircase which was already full were being hit by police and running away. I took one look and thought, this is an absolute nightmare. I tried – I had my FSA card – to talk to the police. So I asked if they could get in touch with their superiors and they said no, they didn't have any radios. So the police were not even in touch with each other.

That went on for most of the first half. Some people did not get in until after half time. We were trying to get people to move around. It was already over-full. Then in the second half I saw a reporter from GMR, and he said, can I have a word? So I went out to do an interview and it was a case of, 'Well we can see fifty or so riot police coming.' So I thought, I'm going back inside. The last thing I remember saying to him was that I hope to God they don't shut this gate after the game. And of course, they did. People started leaving early, thinking let's get out of here. But the police panicked thinking people were leaving early. At least that would have spread the chaos.

Later people were trying to open the gate and the police opened up with tear gas, rubber bullets, into a space five to ten metres wide. Anyone with any knowledge of policing knows that tear gas is a dispersal weapon but if you don't have anywhere to disperse to, it's pointless. They were firing ball bearings covered in rubber which was another dispersal technique which were supposed to hit you in the legs, but people were getting hit in the shoulders. It was one thing wrong after another. I can't remember anything about the game. It was the most frightened I've been at a football match. We came back and I did a report for the FSA and with United's own report, all the Manchester United fans were exonerated by UEFA. Porto were fined for lack of organisation. I got a copy of the Portuguese police report which was the biggest tissue of lies.

ADAM BROWN

Porto wasn't too clever either. We went to Vienna last year which was fantastic and very civilised, everyone as drunk as skunks in the street but not a spot of bother. And then we got to Porto and all of a sudden it was a different kettle of fish again. The days leading up to the match were fine; no trouble, meeting lots of Porto supporters in bars and generally having good crack with them and everything seemed OK until we got to the ground.

We arrived quite late because we'd had trouble getting a coach or bus to the ground. We had to queue for ages at the gate to get in and just as we were getting to the door it was shut. The way that the ground was laid out, there was a road that got narrower and narrower and finally finished around the side of the ground and we were being funnelled into this finite space. And as we got to each of the gates they were slammed shut as they said that part of the ground was full. We found out that they were letting people in without tickets which was why the ground was getting full. We were being pushed from behind by more people trying to get into the ground and were being pushed from the front by the police who were trying to hold us back. I was watching the United stewards and one of them was getting really worried and was saying, 'You've got to stop pushing; we're going to have a real problem here.' That was when I started getting worried. And just as it seemed it couldn't get more squashed, they decided to open the gates and let people in, tickets or no tickets. We had to jump over turnstiles and get in. Obviously when we got on to the terracing area it was already crammed around the stair areas and people were trying to move out of the way to make room for us. It must have been twenty minutes into the match at this point. The people we were with got lost completely; they ended up in the Porto end. I was just very relieved that we hadn't been crushed. The point I started to get worried was when the United stewards were losing it.

Then, the state of the ground when we got in. Each of the steps of the terraces were concrete blocks higher than my knees and they were rocking. You tried to climb up and they were wobbling under your feet. To the right of us somebody fell and everybody went like dominos down the whole terrace and obviously that preoccupied us more than the match. I don't remember watching the match, I think it was pretty uneventful anyway. There was this terrible fear that if one person fell the whole lot would go. Then at the end of the match we heard what we thought were firecrackers and then people running in said it was plastic bullets. One bloke ran right down to the front of the ground and showed himself off to all the photographers and newspapers to say look what they've done. You could still hear them going off to the side and everybody was very worried. We found out later that they had been told to stay in but the message was in Portuguese and not in English. So when they opened the gates they just shot through the gates. I remember seeing Gary Neville standing on the pitch, trying to see his family who were in that area and also trying to say to the press and the first aid, 'Come on, you've got to do something'; and they were all stood around saying, 'What do you want?' So we were obviously quite terrified about going out of the ground afterwards and we got outside and it was all perfectly calm, nothing. We all got in a massive big gang and walked back to the hotel and it was fine after that.

But you start to fear for your safety in foreign football grounds. I didn't go to any this year because I've had two very bad experiences. I've had a couple of close shaves, like in Moscow when there was a bit of a riot going on. You start to wonder is it worth it? I think there is going to be a hideous disaster quite soon and I'm sure that it will involve someone like United that takes a lot of people. There's been so many close shaves and you can't apparently trust the people who are put in charge of you when you're there. The club generally don't want to know unless you've gone on an official club trip.

They were official in that United allowed us to buy tickets from them, football tickets for the match, but they weren't official in that we didn't go with United's travel club. The official travel club don't do a three-day trip. The trips they do tend to be when you fly out to see the match and come back. You tend to get put in some kind of compound or kept amused during the day like a pack of animals, then allowed to go to the match and then shunted straight on to a plane and sent home. As far as I can see, one of the points of going abroad is to soak up the culture, soak up the atmosphere, have a look at places you wouldn't normally get the chance to go to for three days. So you do get very much babysat on the club trips, very regimented and more expensive as well, more to the point; whereas on the other trips you fly out there, you've got three days and you get to do what you like, within reason.

You try to behave yourself but things just seem to happen.

When it happens at the ground, it happens whether you're on an official club trip or not. I believe Eric Cantona's dad had a load of trouble at Porto. He was being squashed and shoved around. So the executives who go with the club get treated exactly the same way when the trouble happens at the ground. But when it's trouble in the town you're obviously more at risk when you're not on a United official trip. Certainly this year I didn't have the stomach for it after last year.

But then Vienna was so great, Vienna was fantastic. We started to develop a theory that it might be hot countries, cold countries – that if you go to hotter countries you're more likely to get into trouble because that's the way it seems to go. Because in Vienna you expected the Viennese people to be the height of respectability and not stand for any messing and here's all these pissed up Salford lads spilling around on the streets and they just tolerated it quite happily, with some amusement in fact; no trouble at all. The police were OK. They put their riot gear on at one point at half time but they didn't ever show any signs of doing anything funny and you can buy beer and cakes in the ground at Vienna which is fantastic. I think sooner or later something bad is going to happen and we saw when it was England–Italy that the police were going berserk. And they don't seem to bother that the world's watching them on television; they just seem to have this remit to wade in and cause havoc, and that's how it was in Porto. At a moment's notice they seemed to be able to make bizarre decisions about shooting people who don't even know that they have to stay in the ground because the message was in Portuguese.

MAXINE DUNHAM

I would go to all away games if I could. The season we blew it to Leeds I went to every game home and away, including Europe. The strangest place was Moscow when they played Torpedo Moscow. That was a real culture shock. We left at two o'clock in the morning from Longsight and there was a problem getting to the ground straight from the airport because there had been a traffic hold up. I remember driving through the Moscow traffic thinking, I don't believe I've paid all this money and I'm not going to get there. But we did. The thing was that there were eleven hundred United fans and I remember feeling rather smug with myself, thinking this was a great credential for being a real United fan because only eleven hundred of us had made the bother to get there. I know it's pretty sad but that's what I was thinking, standing there in the rain. And when I got back I had the worst dandruff I've ever had after standing in that rain and somebody said, 'You've got Chernobyl dandruff.'

I've been to Atlético Madrid, Montpellier, Juventus, Rotterdam. Going to Juventus was a bit sterile; it was under the control of the police. I wasn't impressed by the journey. We spent too long on the coach and it was all a bit ruined. Atlético Madrid was a good trip. I always try to travel independently and we did on that trip. It was one of those strange things. We arrived at the hotel, checked in, and we were told that at such-and-such a bar there'd be a few United fans. We walked down a few side streets, found this bar and I must have known about fifty people in this bar. I'm in the middle of Madrid, never been to this place in all my life, and I'm in a local. We consumed a few that afternoon. It's the only time I've ever fallen asleep in a football ground. I woke up just as the teams were coming on to the pitch. Just in time somebody gave me a nudge. And that all went drastically wrong. We were one–nil down with about two minutes to go. We ended up losing three–nil. We were praying for a Robbo-like resurrection, like we'd had a few years before at Barcelona. But it never materialised.

One of the best trips I've been on was Feyenoord this year [1998] because we had a week in Amsterdam. I can honestly say that travel really does broaden your mind. Apart from Montpellier years ago, my only experience of France had been going to Paris. But to go to Monaco this season [1998], I couldn't believe how friendly everybody was. It was a good time, hassle-free, laughing and joking with the police which is ironic when you see what's going on now in the south of France in the World Cup.

MATTHEW REYNOLDS

I never made it to the match in Galatasaray. I was really excited about the prospects of going because it was the first European trip of the year. I remember sitting with the radio on at work to hear the draw and when I heard it was Galatasaray I thought who the hell are they, but I'll go for it anyway. Booking the trip and then as the match got closer there was all sorts of stuff in the press about, 'We will kill you', and, 'Welcome to hell', and the Turks threatening to give us a really bad time and I was very unsure about what to do, whether to go or not to go. I phoned my dad up the night before and said, 'What do you think I should do, because I'm really not sure about it,' and he said, 'Well, you know, if you don't go, you might regret it.' Well, heaven help him, he feels so bad about it now.

So I decided to go and we flew into Turkey and immediately it was obvious there was quite a lot of hostility towards us. When we managed to get on the buses to be taken to the hotel from the airport we were being bricked and stoned. There were cars racing alongside the coaches trying to cut us up but then when we got to the hotel the atmosphere was completely different, there were nice waiters, going, 'Would you like a drink, madam?' It seemed quite civilised so we sat in the hotel for a while drinking and then a group of lads came in and said there's a big gang outside, so we looked round the palm trees and sure enough, there was a big gang of very aggressive-looking blokes outside the hotel. The hotel called the police and moved them away and we thought it must be all right.

So then various small groups went out on the town with a plan to meet up later and we all ended up in a bar in the town centre. I think Ajax were playing Besiktas or whatever they're called – the other Istanbul side – and it was on the television. There were a lot of Turkish blokes having a go at us because they thought we were Ajax fans and then it was even worse when they found out we were Manchester United fans and the next thing I knew, we'd all had to retreat inside the bar. There was a big gang of Turkish people chucking stones and things. The police arrived and escorted us all back to the hotel whereupon a bloody riot ensued. The plate glass windows at the front of the hotel were smashed in, United fans lying on the ground covered in blood from the glass. There was a guy hit over the head with an iron bar and it was just absolute chaos. All the hotel windows were being broken; it was horrific, the noise and not knowing where to go and what to do, not under-standing what was going on because I didn't speak the language. It was horrific and wanting to go and hide behind something but also thinking, 'I need to know what's going on here because I don't know what's going to happen to us.'

Then the police arrived and it sort of quietened down and the hotel decided to open the bar and we all just sat there, a bit shell-shocked, thinking, 'My God, what's happened?' And a nice thing that happened was that we then started to have a big singsong in the bar which went on till some time after midnight. People started up all the old songs from the sixties and the seventies and everyone was getting mildly drunk. 'We're here for United, we're doing this for United, whatever else happens.' Then we all went to bed and three o'clock in the morning we got woken up by the police telling us they were taking us to another hotel, which turned out to be a series of jails around Istanbul. They split us up into small groups of about ten and sent us all to different police stations. The men had to take off their belts, their shoelaces, their watches, any jewellery and got locked up in really filthy, disgusting cells with people that were already there for whatever crimes and the women and the older people were allowed to just sit in the office with some big Turkish gentleman who was typing furiously all day.

We had to give statements in Turkish, signed statements in Turkish. I was asked all sorts of weird questions, like, 'Is your boss very rich, quite rich or a little bit rich?'; my mother's maiden name, that sort of stuff, sign the statement. We got paraded in front of television cameras at one point. The bizarre moment for me was when everyone was complaining that they hadn't had any food and all the passports needed photo-copying so I got sent out on to the streets of Istanbul with all the passports for the group and a load of money which had been shoved through the bars to buy kebabs with two armed guards. So, I went out with these guys with big guns to a photocopying shop, had all the passports photocopied and then had to go and buy thirty kebabs and a couple of big bottles of Coke. I got back and I was posting these kebabs through the bars of the jailhouse door. We were quite badly treated, generally. If I wanted to go to the toilet I had to have a Turkish guy go with me and watch me while I was doing whatever I was doing. They kept assuring us that we'd get to the match, which of course we never did.

It slowly dawned on me during the course of all this that in fact the Galatasaray side and the police are quite closely related because all round the jail there were posters of the Galatasaray team with garlands draped round them and pictures of the policemen in Galatasaray strips and God knows what else. We finally heard the first half of the match on a police radio and I kept hearing the word Schmeichel, Schmeichel all the time so I thought, oh dear, hearing Schmeichel's name so much, obviously the match isn't going very well. At half time they dragged us all out on to buses, sort of beating and kicking people as they went and took us to the airport. One bloke on the bus was trying to video the police and got his video camera smashed and his glasses smashed. And just as we got to the place where the plane was on the runway, the match was obviously over because all the Turkish police were just jumping up and down kissing each other and just going berserk on the tarmac.

They got us on to the plane which was overcrowded. There were people on that flight who shouldn't have been on that flight, but they were just trying to get rid of us all. There was no food, no water on the plane; there was no nothing. The cabin crew and the pilot were fantastic; they were trying to make sure everyone was OK. And it was only as we took off that we realised we'd left some people behind who were the ones who ended up in jail for six weeks over there. We got back to Manchester Airport to find all the national press waiting to see the English animals returning and I felt very bad when I came back, because obviously my mum had seen reports of hooliganism which resulted in all these hideous United fans being locked up. It was only about a week later, thanks to radio coverage and everything else, that it suddenly started to look like we weren't quite as to blame as people had thought. I certainly didn't see anyone doing anything that warranted the kind of treatment that we had. I've still got the two halves of my ticket as a souvenir of the match I never actually got to but I tried.

MAXINE DUNHAM

In a funny sort of way the Cup final between United and Everton was a very peculiar Cup final. This very sterile game was being played until Moran got sent off and that seemed to represent the sort of thing we've talked about, the United 'sod you' attitude. When they had their backs to the wall, that's when they'd play the best. So they beat the greatest team in English football at that time – who were on their way to the Treble – with ten men, because they're Manchester United. Some sort of injustice was being redressed in that win. But only from the moment Moran got sent off. I can remember my heart was beating all the way back, probably beyond

Birmingham. I wasn't capable of driving back. I had to let someone else drive.

I still think about that Nottingham Forest fixture because in a funny sort of way I still can't believe that they won it, when they won the third round away at Forest [United beat Nottingham Forest 1–0 in January 1990 and went on to win the Cup]. It didn't seem possible that they could win, but they did win and things moved on from there. I feel that even if the board was supporting Ferguson, or was purporting to support him, had they been defeated, I don't believe that they would have done.

Things seemed to turn round from that result. It seemed to create, things became more hopeful. I don't think there was much objective difference on the field. I think they came quite close to the relegation area by the end of the season. We were just about above it but there was just the vaguest sign of a turnaround. Even before Cantona as well, they seemed to be a very mechanical team, slightly more proficient than most but nothing that was marking them out. In one of Cantona's early games at Hillsborough, which is never an easy ground for United for some reason or other, I can remember switching off the radio as they went three–one down and I was quite amazed that they had actually drawn that game. I think that might have marked real green shoots rather than notional ones. I think had they lost that game they would have been out for the count for that season. It was a very important Christmas game. Also, I had got used to the idea when Atkinson was manager that it was not a good thing to turn on the radio in the eighty-fifth minute of the game to find out what was going on. It was inevitable that they would concede a goal. United were like a posh City. The frequency of their ups and downs were slightly less extreme but nonetheless they were there. Often when Atkinson was manager I can remember them being three–one ahead then scrambling three–three draws out of it. So we were very erratic; exciting, but erratic. They would take you into their own peaks and troughs.

One thing in the very recent years is that generally at Old Trafford that sort of nervous tension has disappeared. Sometimes it's labelled boredom but certainly as we speak now I think we are back to the traditional United tension mode. We've decided to make things exciting again for everybody else (*laughs*). I can remember recently talking to a City fan saying that United provide entertainment for the nation but not for their own supporters and he said, 'What on earth do you mean?' And I just quoted the fact that they went five–nil up at Stamford Bridge and then allowed three goals to go in, three good goals and provided a game of great beauty for everybody else, but drove us United fans to distraction that they should do such a thing.

The night they won the title against Blackburn Rovers to win the title for the first time since 1967, the mood that night was like the European Cup final. It was amazing, all the colours. It was the feeling of relief. The waiting was over. There was relief everywhere. The bond with the past was still there, twenty-six years on.

I can remember the idea of Wednesday night under the floodlights at Old Trafford. I remember watching the Real Madrid semi-final, sixty-three and a half thousand in the ground and you just knew it was special. Just before the game against Monaco this season [1998], a friend of mine at the office said, 'It's Wednesday night, it's a warm day, under the floodlights in the European Cup quarter-final and it can't get better than this.' I'd had this paranoid vision of a goal going in early in the game and then United chasing the game. I had to live that nightmare out. But that morning when I was feeling anxious, yes, it's Wednesday night under the floodlights, it's warm and it couldn't be anything better. That is United's natural place. Wednesday night in Europe under the floodlights. Manchester United is not really a provincial team. People may be very fiercely devoted to them but they're not a provincial team. They're not even England's representatives either; they're a very cosmopolitan team reflecting the spirit of Manchester people who are not afraid to go out into the world, go visiting places, whatever, and that's a very special thing about them. Manchester is that sort of city; it's not quite a provincial city although it shows the signs of it.

A few years ago I went to Barcelona for a Wednesday night, a warm night and I can see a close affinity between Catalonians, Barcelona and United. Luckily here we don't have the political violence. We're cosmopolitan people going out in a spirit of adventure exploring the world.

LEON SWERLING

It's hard to put into words how much that first title win meant. It was so exciting the first year they won it. We had an away game at Palace and we went to Old Trafford and watched it live on the big screens. Sitting there biting your fingers to pieces. When United scored and went one–nil up the noise was just incredible and there was all the singing. There were no players out there but there were thirty thousand people at Old Trafford watching this TV screen and singing their songs as normal: 'We're gonna win the League. We're gonna win the League!' You couldn't believe we were going to do it. You kept turning around and pinching each other, couldn't believe it was really going to happen. Winning the League that first time. Just the excitement, the adrenaline, like a pulse of electricity. Everything else was irrelevant. The month leading up to it, your job didn't matter, nothing mattered, all that mattered was winning it.

I was visiting family and the Aston Villa game had kicked off at four and I was in a friend's house and he kept saying, 'Jim, Jim shall I put the radio on, do you want to know the score?' and I said, 'No, no.' I didn't want to know. 'I'm just going to turn the telly on later tonight, it's too exciting.' I wanted to wait to get back to Manchester to celebrate properly. We got back in the car about twenty to five so I knew there was about seven minutes to go. We turned the

237

radio on and there was a voice saying, 'This is going to be one of the biggest shocks of the season.' We turned the radio off straight away. We knew Oldham were winning. Driving along the A66 in the middle of the moors between Manchester and Newcastle we turned the radio on again to listen to the last minute. Oldham were still winning, so we turned it off again. I was turning it on and off a second at a time. I knew that if I listened to it Aston Villa would equalise. It was bad luck.

Then when the final whistle went we had to stop the car, pull into a lay-by and go straight to the phone. I rang my mum. I was screaming, 'Mum, Mum, Dad, Dad, we've won the League, do you realise!' I was in the phone box for about an hour telling everybody we'd won the League. Then hurtling down the M6 to Old Trafford with a bottle of champagne and just running around the ground. Amazing. I think we were still at Old Trafford 'til about two or three in the morning singing songs, running around, pissed out of our heads with about ten or fifteen thousand others outside the ground. And it's been like that every year we've won the League. Everybody goes to Old Trafford. Less people now than then. It was just chocka.

JIM THORNTON

I was present for the League title win in 1993, the first time they had been crowned champions since 1967. It was a terrific atmosphere. There was this tremendous buzz about the place. I was in the centre of G-stand, in the thick of it all. It was also the first time that I had personally experienced the Mexican wave. It started in the stand opposite me. I saw with amusement this rapidly moving, mass-fluttering of hands and bodies. Within seconds this crescendo of noise and movement had come to my area. Like everybody else I was up in the air joining in. It happened recurrently throughout the rest of the match, each time creating an even greater instinctive sense of obedience. I thought about this later and thought, that's what it must have been like at the Nuremberg rallies, and it led me to think about why we become football fans. I think there are a number of reasons. First, it's the embodiment of the fighting instinct. Second, it's a substitute for religion, the hero worship; and third, it's cathartic. It's the sublimation of aggressive instincts. And finally it's a harmless obsession and I think everyone is entitled to have one harmless obsession. You know, Matt Busby used to say that there was no disgrace in defeat. My worry now is that United have moved away from that philosophy and I think that's sad.

KEN HASTINGS

It's hard to say what makes United so much more exciting. I don't know if it's because I'm biased because that was the first team I was ever taken to see. I have seen other teams play. I've seen Everton play, I've seen Liverpool play, I've seen City play. I think it must be something to do with the style United play. They do play very attractive football. I think the 'sod it, let's go for it' attitude is very appealing. I was devastated when Eric Cantona left. He was such an attractive player; you never knew what he was going to do next. It was just a shame he decided he wanted to be a film star instead of a footballer.

United have always had very powerful characters associated with them whether it was George Best or Matt Busby; they've always had this appeal, then there was the Munich crash. I think people had a lot of sympathy for United because they got up off their feet and got on with it.

I don't think the rivalry with Liverpool is as intense with women as it is with men. There are clubs I dislike more. There's no point in hating them. You should appreciate them for the football they play. You can take it too far. I can't imagine not being a football fan. If there's football on the telly, it has to be on. Not just United. If it's a good game I have to watch it.

JUDITH SWIFT

My father and brother were keen United supporters and when I was growing up, football on television was always something we watched as a family. My mother as well. Manchester United was always our team. My father was brought up in Manchester and the fact that United had won the European Cup, and the influence of Bobby Charlton in the World Cup squad, meant they were very much the team of the moment, the glamour team. That's how my brother latched on to it; although my father, being a Manchester man, was always interested.

I didn't go to any football games until I came to live in Manchester, by which time I'd met Roger. He was a keen supporter and I started to go along with him. The fact he was a United fan was another thing we had in common and supporting the same football team is a bond. I don't know what would have happened had he been a supporter of another team. Fortunately, that never happened and never had to be addressed.

There was an Everton game in the early eighties when a fight broke out near where we were sitting. That was the only time I have felt under physical threat myself. I think the games are well-policed and it was just that this particular fight – only a small incident – happened to be near where we were and it was quickly dealt with. We always make a point of waiting until the end of the game when most of the crowd has gone. I don't like the feeling of walking in a big crowd and being jostled. In the old United Road stand we had to walk down a slope to get out and I used to hate that when surrounded by a lot of people, because people would push and I just felt nervous about that, so we've taken to waiting. I've stood once and I found that a much less enjoyable experience. For a start, I couldn't see as well. I don't enjoy the sensation of being hemmed in by a lot of people. I don't know whether it's a particular male exhilaration in being caught up in a crowd like that.

I think with seats there are a lot more women going to United games now and the facilities are better for women – just in terms of the number of loos – in the new stand. There are a lot more women go now and certainly in the area where we sit, a much less macho atmosphere, I think. You still get swearing and shouting, but somehow swearing in that context is not offensive; it's part of the atmosphere. You get the odd yob who stands out like a sore thumb. There are some contexts where I do find swearing extremely offensive but in the context of the game it seems appropriate, somehow. I've never encountered any racism at Old Trafford. That I would find deeply offensive but it doesn't seem to be any part of any of the people who watch the game anywhere around us.

I don't feel untypical when I go. There are other women who sit fairly close to where we are, and on a regular basis, who appear to be professional women. We don't talk about anything but football when we are there. There are people you feel you know really well because you've been watching football with them for years. You don't know their names, you don't know what they do but it doesn't really matter. There are people there I've talked to for hours on end and I don't know their names. That's not what it is about. But there are certainly women who sit fairly close to us who I would say it is a strong probability that they are professional women. But I don't feel particularly unusual or odd being a professional woman there.

The other thing that has changed for us is that we have got so fed up of going by car that we now cycle there. We leave our bikes in car-park A which is directly opposite the ground and chain them to the railings there. It takes us about the same amount of time as it would to drive and park the car and of course we don't have to pay £3 or £4 to park it. There's a certain exhilaration in being able to weave through all the standing traffic on the way home. I've never worked out whether it's uphill or downhill but it feels downhill in both directions. Maybe that's something to do with the enjoyment of the experience.

TERESA HENNELL

Just after the death of Sir Matt Busby I went to see United playing at home to Everton. It was 22 January 1994. There

241

were forty-five thousand inside Old Trafford and about fourteen thousand outside. The people outside just went in order to pay their respects. The touts were there as usual selling tickets at ten times their value. Giggs scored the only goal of the game. It was a wonderful game, although when I read the press reports I felt that the press had not done justice to Everton who played so well that day and contributed towards a wonderful game of football. So, I wrote to the then Everton manager Mike Walker to express my thanks to him, the players and the club for showing such dignity on the occasion. There had been a one minute's silence which had been magnificently upheld by the Everton fans. It was the first time I had ever written to the manager of any football club. Anyhow, a few days later I received a reply from Mike Walker, thanking me for my letter and saying that my sentiments had been shared by many Manchester United fans. I thought that was interesting as clearly others must have written to him as well. I was impressed by that.

KEN HASTINGS

We usually meet at the ground about an hour before we're due to leave, load all the kit up, load all the various goodies that the players have on the coach for away games – drinks and snacks and things like that. They're on a high-carbohydrate, low-fat diet so there's all sorts of things like rice pudding, jelly, cakes. You don't really associate those sorts of things with footballers but it does give them the sort of energy that they're supposed to have. So we load all that on to the coach and we wait for the few players that usually travel from Old Trafford. And if we're travelling south most of the players we pick up en route because they tend to live in south Manchester. When the players get on the coach, the first question I am asked by most of them is, 'What time are we going to be home tomorrow?' You wouldn't really believe that but their main concern is how quickly we can do the journey.

We have lots of things on the coach to try and occupy the players' time. The video's used quite a lot. The lads tend to bring their own videos with them. I do supply some as well. A couple of the players like to play their video games, Play-Stations, and we have one of the monitors set up so that they can use that. And, of course, we've got the card players. There's a couple of card schools on the coach, the manager is an extremely good card player, so I'm told. He's very competitive. One or two sit and read. Brian McClair, who's now left us unfortunately, is quite a reader really.

There's no alcohol on the coach. It's actually against the law. We do occasionally stop for fish and chips but that's a bit of a treat because, with the diet that they're on, they're not really supposed to have it.

We will stay overnight for virtually everywhere we go to. We will generally have a police escort from the hotel and depending upon where it is, you either just follow the police motorcyclist and he stops at every red traffic light and he's really just a pilot for you, or there are some places where they want to get you to the ground and the players off and into the ground as quickly as possible. So we have the old blue lights and wrong side of the road and things like that. It can be quite exciting.

Most grounds it's fairly tight. It's quite difficult to get in. I don't think you hear cheering very often but there are always a lot of people waiting for us to arrive at football grounds. Certain places, particularly Leeds and Liverpool, are probably the worst receptions that we get. Very rarely do we get any trouble, missiles thrown that sort of thing. It does happen occasionally, but it's usually very loud booing and other verbal abuse.

Sometimes people write on the side in permanent markers or there are little dints and scratches. These things do happen, it's very unfortunate. I mean the vehicles that we're talking about cost us somewhere in the region of £250,000 to £300,000. They think they're getting back at the club but it's nothing to do with the club. At the end of the day, it's me that has to pay for the repairs to the vehicle.

Myself and the kit manager, the physio and usually the masseur go to the ground and we lay the kit out first thing in the morning before the game. It's a double-edged thing really as it means we can plan our route to the ground in the morning, make sure we know where we are going. There's nothing worse than getting lost on the way to a ground because footballers can be extremely critical and you tend to get quite a lot of ribbing anyway.

We do the reserves, A team, B team, youth team as well and we also do the under-11 upwards to under-16s so it's quite involved. I used to drive all the younger teams when I was a bit younger myself when we first did the contract but I tend to spend most of my time in the office and my little perk is to do the first team. I enjoy doing that and I will continue to do that but I let some of my other staff do the younger sides because it takes up too much of my time.

When I was first driving the coach, doing the reserves and the youth team, I got to know the younger players. I've known David Beckham since David was about fourteen. It was always known to me that David was a player who was highly regarded and would do very well from such a young age. It's very nice to see David do as well as he has done. I've seen all the young lads that are in the team at the moment – Philip and Gary Neville, Nicky Butt, Paul Scholes – seen them come up the youth team and the reserves into the first team and I know them very well and they know me very well and from that respect that's why I get a lot of ribbing off them. It happens in football. They say something to me and I'll shout something back to them and it's all part of it, it's all part of the banter. I feel sometimes I'm there as a bit of a buffer as well. Sometimes they need to let off a bit of steam and say something. I've never had anybody be nasty to me in any way, it doesn't happen. I get on very well with the players and it's all good fun.

SIMON JONES

CHAPTER EIGHT

Eleven Days in May

This book was originally published part-way through the never-to-be-forgotten 1998–99 season. As a consequence most of the events of that dramatic season are barely covered elsewhere in it. There is obviously no talk of the Treble and there is only scant mention of Sky's proposed takeover of the club, which was only made public as the final interviews were being recorded. On the field the 1998–99 season was clearly the most successful in the club's history, while off the field, the proposed takeover catapulted United, yet again, on to the front pages. It was only right therefore that we should revisit many of the people we originally interviewed in order to assess the impact of the season on their lives and their love for the club.

Just three games to win; three cup finals, and the world is yours. So easy to say but, of course, it ignores the months of hard slog, commitment and patience. In truth, we're not really talking months, more years, of work and preparation. The Treble was a dream nobody dared contemplate. But once the title had been secured, the idea took on real meaning. Of course it was possible, you only had to win the next two games, never mind that one was at Wembley against Newcastle and the next four days later in Barcelona against Bayern Munich. All you had to do was focus, one game at a time, keep on winning. The players themselves must have sensed they could do the Double; after all they had done it twice before in recent years. But no one was really concerned with the Double. It was old hat. The one that really mattered was the European Cup, the chance for Fergie and his lads to emulate the great Busby side of 1968, the side that had gone down in history alongside the Busby Babes. But there was always the worry that if they had lost at Wembley, they would probably lose in Barcelona as well.

But if that had not been enough of a worry, earlier events at Old Trafford had caused enough tremors to bring down the towering north stand. The proposed takeover by Sky television, which hit the front pages in September, caused a storm, not least among United fans, though football fans everywhere had strong opinions on this one. The board had sensationally agreed to sell the club for £623 million. But was it really theirs to sell? Many fans thought otherwise. There were others who hoped the deal might swell the coffers of Ferguson's transfer chest, with the likes of Ronaldo, Zidane and Rivaldo being tempted to Old Trafford. The more astute, of course, realised that Sky, for all their promises and talk of making United the finest side in the world, were not going to throw money at players like confetti. Their motives in taking over United were complicated, more to do with business than football. In the event, although the United board desperately wanted the takeover, the deal was rejected by the Department of Trade after a long inquiry, thanks primarily to a campaign led by the fans, who ganged together to oppose the bid. For many it was as momentous and significant an event as the Treble.

But back to football. Of course luck plays as much a part in the game as it does in any other walk of life. You need luck and, as Alex Ferguson has suggested more than once, you also need lucky players. At times it seemed that all eleven of his players were talismen as the side rode the season with more than their fair share of good fortune. But you do create your own luck, I hear you say. Of course, and as long as you battle until the final whistle or sometimes take a gamble with your selection, then there is always the possibility that luck will intervene. Fortune, they say, favours the brave.

And so it wound up to an eleven-day finale, three games and three trophies at stake. The League title was wrapped up at Old Trafford against Tottenham Hotspur, the first time United had won the title on home territory since Ferguson took charge. And even though they went a goal behind there was never any doubt that United would end up winners. It was that kind of season. The fates had decreed it; you simply had to be patient and all would come good in the end. In the FA Cup they almost stumbled at Old Trafford against the old enemy Liverpool, a goal down until the ninetieth minute. Then sensationally they scored twice in injury time, leaving the Liverpool hordes aghast. Gobsmacked they call it in Liverpool. It was an omen of things to come. Lucky? Maybe, but you could hardly argue that United were fortunate in the draw. Middlesbrough, Liverpool, Fulham, Chelsea, Arsenal and then Newcastle; it was as tough as it could be.

There were titanic struggles in Europe as well – Barcelona, Inter Milan and Juventus all posed headaches and when United fell two goals down inside fifteen minutes against Juventus it looked to be all over. But no, they battled on, pulled one back, equalised and then had the audacity to win. By then the season had taken on its own inevitability. United seemed invincible, no matter what obstacles were placed in their path. Even their goals tended to be spectacular rather than run-of-the-mill tap-ins.

Six days after lifting the title they were at Wembley to take on Newcastle in the Cup final. Nobody expected United to lose, but when Roy Keane limped off after just a handful of minutes, and with Newcastle caressing the ball across Wembley's silky turf, it seemed United's dreams of the Double, let alone the Treble, were set to collapse. But again, the reversal acted as a spur. On came Teddy Sheringham, much to the surprise of many, and with almost his first touch, struck.

247

From there on United cruised to victory. Two trophies down, one to go.

Four days later they were in Barcelona, at the Nou Camp, facing arguably their sternest test since 1968. And the opposition had not become any easier. Bayern, champions of Germany, legendary European winners of the past. United went a goal down in the sixth minute; not a disaster, after all they had pulled a deficit back before. But this time, as every minute crept by, it seemed less likely. United were wearied by their exhausting campaign and missed the decisiveness of the suspended Keane and Scholes in the midfield. Eighty-nine minutes and the Germans were already celebrating; United's dream surely over. High in the stands blue and white ribbons were being tied to the trophy, George Best had deserted his seat and gone off home, others were preparing for the exit. It was now simply a case of trying to be philosophical. Then it all happened. Eleven days. Three trophies. The stories hardly need to be recorded, they'll be remembered forever.

───●◉●───

Well I've seen some fairly astonishing seasons at Old Trafford from the fifties, through the sixties, seventies and eighties. But who would ever have thought of a Treble? Hardly anybody a few years ago, because the Treble was rarely talked about. But there, suddenly, last season, it was in the frame. I didn't think United could do a Treble because I don't believe in miracles and rainbows with crocks of gold at the foot of them.

Sonia, my wife, and I had planned a holiday in Barbados. It was only after I had booked the holiday that I realised it clashed with the FA Cup final date. But then, I had booked it long before the FA Cup final and before I knew who would be in it. So it didn't really matter. But there I was flying off, thinking, 'Oh golly, the Cup final, I don't like missing cup finals, even on the telly. But maybe they'll show it out there.' Anyway, we were staying in this wonderful hotel near St

Lawrence Gap. After a few days – this was a week before the FA Cup final – one or two people around the beach were saying, 'Will you be watching the Cup final? It'll be on in Bubba's Sports Bar on a big screen.' This was a couple of miles down the road. I thought, 'Am I that bothered really?' I thought it would be crowded with thousands of Brits in red and white shirts. I wasn't too bothered, but I was bothered about seeing the European Cup final and nobody had mentioned that.

But all journalists buy newspapers on holiday, and I eat newspapers! Every day I walked down to the little grocer's store: if there was a two-day-old copy of an English paper I would get it but I always got the – I can't remember its name – the *Barbadian Globe* or whatever it was called. The day before the FA Cup final I looked in the paper and it seemed to suggest that on Channel 15 there would be the Wembley Cup final.

We tried it on the telly which we had in our apartment, and it turned out to be some sort of strange channel and didn't always tally with what was listed so I didn't give it any more thought. Anyway, on the day, I switched Channel 15 on about half an hour before the game was due to kick off and there was a litle ten-minute programme on that seemed to coincide with what was in the listings. 'So maybe,' I thought, 'we *will* get the Cup final.' Then suddenly – Sonia had gone down to the beach – the telly went off. I thought, 'The telly has gone off, the telly is at fault!' Sod's law. I tried the light switch and they didn't come on. You always imagine, of course, that it's just your apartment. It was raging sunshine outside so there was no real way I could work out if it *was* just my apartment. Anyway, I walked out and realised the fountains had ground to a halt. It was a power cut. I popped down to reception and asked, 'Do we have a power cut?' 'Yes we do sir, it is all along this road. Two other hotels have gone down, they are working on it.' I thought, 'This is Barbados, it's a Saturday afternoon, will they get it mended? No, even at home they wouldn't.' Three minutes to kick-off time and suddenly everything came back on. I called Sonia to come in and we sat down and watched the Cup final. It wasn't a great game, but it was all right and, most importantly, we had seen it.

I hadn't given the European Cup final much thought, but people kept saying, 'Will you be going to Bubba's Sports Bar to watch it?' Then suddenly – and this is where the mystery begins – under the door of our apartment appeared a copy of a message that had been faxed from somewhere on Barbados from, allegedly, some friends of ours who mysteriously happened to be on the same island. Basically the message said 'To Sonia and Bob, see you in Bubba's Sports Bar, Wednesday noon' (or whatever the correct time was before kick-off), and was signed 'Your friends from England'. I thought, 'This is a wind-up,' because everyone had been talking about Bubba's bloody Sports Bar. 'It has to be a wind-up from somebody I've talked to!' Anyway we rang Bubba's Sports Bar and discovered that we could pre-book for twenty Barbadian dollars, which is a fiver or a tenner. We thought, yeah, we'll do that. So we booked two seats and later got a taxi to the bar. It turned out to be brand new. It was an amazing place. We walked in, paid our twenty dollars and were immediately given twenty dollars of vouchers for food and drink, so there was actually no charge.

We sat in there, wondering who was going to turn up. We had gone deliberately early and it was quite quiet. The air conditioning was so fierce we had to buy two Bubba's Sports Bar sweat shirts to go over the puny shirts and shorts we were wearing 'cos it was freezing cold. Then the place started to fill up. We had a wonderful meal. The place was full of huge screens and had loads of small screens too.

Then about an hour before kick-off, in come two friends of ours with whom we socialise in Sale. A man called Don and his partner Kath. We had no idea the note was from them. We knew they used to go to Barbados and they knew we were going, but they had done a late booking and hadn't told us. So, as you can imagine, we had a wonderful time watching this astonishing game. What can you say about the game that hasn't already been said? No, I never thought they would win it, not even draw it. It had been a great achievement to get there, but miracles and rainbows with crocks of gold at the end do not exist in my life. But, then, on this occasion they did. It was astonishing and we all went through physical exhaustion, heart attacks, mental breakdowns, you name it, everybody felt it. Sonia said she felt utterly, utterly drained and so did I.

After the game, Don and Kath and me and Sonia went outside where I suggested we re-enact the winning goal. Don was definitely Beckham. I asked Don if he had ever played football and he just smiled, so I said, 'Okay, you can take the corner, swing it in from the left.' We went down to the car park, we didn't have a ball or anything like that! 'Sonia, you be Teddy Sheringham, you flick the header across, and I'll be little Ole Gunnar,' 'cos I fancied scoring the goal and I knew I could get my leg up to the right height. Then we realised we had no role for Kath, so I said, 'Kath, you're the referee, you blow the whistle.' So she whistled and Don put the corner across but it wasn't a very good one, not up to Beckham's usual standard. Sonia's header was neat and my boot in was pretty good. But I didn't think it was perfect and there had been too much delay between Kath's whistle and the corner kick. So we re-enacted it four times before I decided it was perfect. Nobody had a camera, nobody had a video, nobody had nothing, no football, not even a tennis ball or a rolled up rag. But it was brilliant and it was as good as the game! You can't follow a Treble with anything better.

BOB GREAVES

There had been some rumours back in early 1998 that Murdoch was interested in getting a stake in United. The Premier League knocked back pay per view and were also facing a court action over restrictive practices which they thought might rule them as a cartel and would break up Sky's monopoly over live Premier League football. So, almost as an insurance policy, Murdoch wanted to buy Man United. When the story actually broke, it was a huge shock. I got a call at about half three in the morning from the BBC asking what I'd like to say. By nine, ten o'clock it was clear that the story was sound and that Sky had made an offer.

Those first couple of days consisted of frantic phone calls, trying to judge what people thought about it and beginning to think about what we could do. Andy Walsh, almost from that moment, was on the case. To say he was full-time is an understatement. I don't think he saw his kids for two weeks! It emerged then that the best option for stopping the takeover would be through the Government and the Office of Fair Trading. The first target was to get the Office of Fair Trading's decision delayed, because it gave us time to wait until the MPs got back into Parliament. They obviously hoped to rush it through before there was any political fuss. We delayed it by bombarding the OFT with faxes and letters. They had a record number of submissions, some 350 or 400, against the deal. By the end of October, the matter was finally referred to the Monopolies and Mergers Commission (MMC). A lot of people suspected that, because of New Labour's links with Sky and Murdoch they would let it go through on the nod. Certainly, we know now that Mandelson saw nothing wrong with the deal but referred it to the Monopolies Commission as a superficial exercise to show that the government was doing the right thing and jumping through the hoops. They had no expectation that the Commission would knock it back and there is a question mark about whether, if Mandelson had still been in the post, he would have rejected the Commission's report, or allowed it to go through with certain conditions attached whereas Stephen Byers accepted the whole report. In one sense once it got to the Commission the matter was beyond the control of Sky and United because, very quickly, the MMC were looking at the deal along the same lines as we were and thinking in terms of the threat of competition both in the pay TV market and in football, as well as raising the public interest argument against increasing the power of an already over-powerful club. To give United the backing of a huge multinational corporation would further exacerbate the wealth gap in football.

I went down as an individual to give a presentation to the MMC at the beginning of December, and it was clear that they were beginning to think along these lines and that was very encouraging. There was a huge groundswell of political support among Labour and Conservative MPs, because a lot of them have constituencies with small clubs so they were under pressure from their own constituents as well. Just before the deal was referred to the MMC, we had a lobby of Parliament. We had about twenty-five different clubs there, represented by hundreds of supporters. They ranged from Slough Town to Newcastle United via Leeds and some other unsuspecting allies who you would not think would jump to United's aid. There was a recognition that this was something which was going to have a much wider effect and would affect the whole finance and structure of English football.

There was also support from across Europe. When Bayern Munich came for the Champions League game at Old Trafford they brought a huge 'Stop Murdoch' banner which was about forty feet long. They gave it to us and we carted it around to Inter Milan, Barcelona and other places. That kind of support was hugely encouraging. There were some other fans who thought United would get what they deserved, but, generally, there was plenty of support. We got loads of e-mails from Liverpool and Leeds fans, who are United's biggest rivals. When you knew that that kind of support was coming in from such people, you knew this was an issue affecting everyone.

One of the key elements of IMUSA's (Independent Manchester United Supporters Association) strategy was the establishment of the shareholders group, which was called Shareholders United Against Murdoch, to try to put on pressure from within the plc. We worked out that about 25 per cent of United shares were held by individuals, most of whom would be United supporters. That's when the move started to try to create a voting block of shareholders to, firstly, stop Sky getting overall control. If it got 90 per cent plus one share, it could force the other people to sell their shares to BSkyB so that United would be a wholly owned subsidiary of BSkyB. So the first target was to get that 10 per cent. The second target was to get 25 per cent plus one share who were against which would stop Sky gaining legal control. It would then have to go to the shareholders to make any radical legal decisions. And then, obviously, the ultimate aim was to get over 50 per cent of shareholders to oppose the deal. It was a huge amount of work and although it was only 25 per cent of the club this amounted to twenty-eight thousand shareholders and it involved writing to all people. It was no easy task. There were late night sessions in O'Briens pub up in Stretford where legions of people stuffed envelopes with letters asking people to oppose the bid.

The other thing IMUSA got was some very good legal advice from a big law firm in London. They advised IMUSA on their submissions to the MMC and Office of Fair Trading. There were various other people – city lawyers and city financiers – who kept feeding information to us. Having friends in those high places was very important.

Michael Crick and one or two others even went down to see some of the city financiers and drew up documents outlining why the deal was bad for them. We had a profitable stand-alone company that was paying handsome dividends and was being, in many people's eyes, undervalued, especially given the television rights. It would become a subsidiary of a huge multinational corporation. Phillips and Drew refused to back the deal from the outset so there was some institutional disquiet as well, which showed it was a bad deal on Martin Edwards' terms. When you think Barcelona has done a television deal for five years for £250 million, it was selling United cheap.

Me and Andy Walsh did have a tip-off back in February

from someone on the inside [of the MMC] that things were going our way. To some extent, we knew that, but to hear it was encouraging. But obviously we couldn't jeopardise anything by telling anyone, so we had to sit on it for two months. But there were still plenty of counter-rumours. On the day, I honestly didn't know if the deal would go through. I think Andy was much more confident, I didn't know if I trusted the Government or not. But it was thrown out comprehensively. The MMC made a point of saying that they were raising public concerns about the distribution of wealth in football. It went further than any of us had hoped for. We were jumping about the forecourt at Old Trafford.

We've stopped this deal and it's very unlikely that we will get another attempt at a full takeover by a television company, but the danger is that they will do it by the backdoor. Sky is still the biggest shareholder in Man United; it also has 9.9 per cent of Leeds and is now taking a share in City. Combine that with Granada at Liverpool, NTL at Newcastle and rumours of Carlton at Arsenal, and you begin to realise that television companies are buying themselves a seat at the negotiating table, which raises all sorts of complex questions about the distribution of football wealth and the future of the game. We've still got some work to do.

ADAM BROWN

The other interesting thing about the season was the row, controversy, chasm of opinion, from all sides over Mr Murdoch's bid to take over United. Personally I would not have been unhappy. I'm not a Manchester United shareholder, I must stress, but I would not have been unhappy had they been allowed to move into the club because I believe United would have benefited by many millions of pounds more than Martin Edwards will ever be able to find or produce. I think it would have been a brilliant move for the finances of the club and that, as we all know, is what football is now about; it's

255

about huge amounts of money. Fergie could have gone and bought four of the world's finest, and therefore most expensive to buy and pay, footballers. And although that is maybe not ideal, it is the real world. I expect the real world would have been welcomed at Old Trafford after a year or two. But who knows? It didn't happen but I was on the side of selling. At the current time with the current rules I believe Murdoch's money would have benefited Man United plc.

BOB GREAVES

I actually felt disappointed when the Sky deal fell through. I was for it, but it threw up the dilemma of being a football fan and a socialist. When it comes to footballing matters, socialism tends to get subjugated to the greater glory. Winning the European Cup has put United on a different level now. The only way they can meet the new challenges is to compete with the wages the top stars earn. They do earn too much, but that is the name of the game. I think that is how Fergie has viewed it. To improve the squad, you have to get the Rivaldos and Edgar Davids and the only way you will get them is if you pay them the money they want. Barcelona have signed a £250 million television contract, and that's all profit, so we have to be able to compete at that level otherwise we will just go back a step. It's the laws of capitalism; the more successful you are, the more you have to invest.

TIM BAMFORD

I thought the Treble was on after they won the League. First the League, then we start thinking about the others. I think if they had lost the League they would have lost the other two, although they might have won the FA Cup. When they lost the League to Blackburn and then played the FA Cup final and lost to Everton, you just knew that would happen. It was the first League title they had won at Old Trafford under Ferguson. I thought they played brilliant last season, breathtaking football. Some of the goals were wonder goals, hardly any tap-ins, really good football. No, I didn't get the jitters when they went a goal down against Tottenham, I rarely get the jitters at Old Trafford now; I have more trust in the players now, this is something you learn.

It was a bizarre week in Barcelona, a great week, it was good fun. We were asked to be part of a video diary about the trip which was shown on Granada television, called *Red Skies Over Europe*. We were the nice middle-class element of the film. We went to Sitges. Four of us went for a week. The film was a nightmare. We flew to Bilbao, hired a car and drove down to Sitges on the coast where we stayed. It's the 'in' resort for people from Barcelona. We stayed in a bed and breakfast and had a great time. We had three or four days there. We didn't get to the game because we didn't have tickets. We had hopes that there would be some available. We went to the ground on the Wednesday and were willing to spend up to £200 but it was absolute madness, it was chaotic, so badly organised. These Spaniards, who were obviously Barcelona season ticket holders, had bought handfuls of tickets thinking they would be able to get £600 a ticket. They weren't touts. I was amazed at the restraint of the United fans. These Spaniards were going around offering tickets, wanting £600. You're joking! We were offered some by a German for £175 but by then there were so many rumours going around about forgeries. We handed the film over at threeish and then went to the stadium, but called it quits at about half six and picked up a mad taxi which drove back to Sitges at about a hundred miles an hour. We could have found ourselves stranded there. Apparently there was a screen at the stadium but it was difficult to see the screen as there were trees everywhere. There were a lot of people without tickets and then all these people with suits walking in. I don't think the stadium was full, I think everyone could have got in. The German end was apparently not full. We had a great day there, though, and went down the Ramblas which was full of United supporters the whole way, absolutely brilliant.

We got to Sitges and went to a bar. Because of the film and everything, the idea that they could lose had never entered my head. I had been wrapped up so much with the film that I hadn't thought about the game that much. It wasn't until the eighty-ninth minute and I can remember it now, sitting there looking at the television and it's the eighty-ninth minute and thinking, shit, they're going to lose. Suddenly I got depressed, thinking, 'The film is not going to get shown, we'll lose the European Cup.' And then it happened. Everyone went hysterical. Why couldn't they do it in the first five minutes rather than keep us waiting so long! It was the whole drama of it. The Spanish also had no love for the Germans so they were rooting for us. If they win it again it'll never be quite the same. Brilliant.

TIM BAMFORD

The collapse of the Sky deal was great. When it was first mooted, there were only about three days of 'What shall we do?' Then IMUSA (Independent Manchester United Supporters Association) announced a meeting at the Bridgewater Hall. Adam Brown, who I work with, was heavily involved in the organisation. They tried to get a number of places, including the Apollo, but ended up at the Bridgewater which cost them something like £5,000. I was with Adam when they booked it and they had no money. They even tried to get hold of Mick Hucknall to underwrite the costs. In the end, someone else from out of a band put the money up. There were about 800 people there and it snowballed from there. I went out leafleting at three or four home games and most others were leafleting for three or four months. I was helping write stuff to the DTI. It was all very well organised; they even had a website with details about how to protest. It was mainly Andy Walsh, Adam Brown, and Michael Crick who did the organising.

Where I sit in the south stand, the opinion was a bit mixed, but as the weeks progressed the argument got through. When it was first announced, some people thought we'd be able to buy anyone we wanted. But the point was that why should United, a company worth £600 million, need Murdoch's money? The money is already there and there is potential for more. It was clear that Murdoch needed United to push his media interests in south-east Asia. If he could get red shirts on television each week across Asia, it would help enormously. He'd also bought into a sports organisation in the States and got rid of the best players, just to help his media interests. You start making those arguments about football; Giggs being sold here, Beckham being sold there, a Malaysian player bought to up the interest in south-east Asia – it's this type of thing that could have happened. Even in the south stand, once these points had been made, people began to understand.

DEREK WYNNE

The first Arsenal game at Villa, it was all about that penalty Bergkamp missed. Had he put that away, that would have been it – no Treble. But he missed it, so we had another chance. It's sort of luck but . . . It was a good game, that first game, and so was the second, either team could have won. Giggs' goal was made for that occasion. The first game, I had gone down in the car with a bunch of mates; the second game, because a lot of them were working, I went by myself and met up with a couple of people at the game, although we had tickets in different parts of the ground. Of course, as soon as goals go in everybody is everybody's friend. It was good, but because I was not with anyone I knew, it was not as good as maybe it could have been. I can't remember that much about it to be honest. I can't remember much about the Newcastle Cup final either. When Keane went off, the Newcastle fans thought, 'That's it,' but the very opposite was true; after that they didn't do anything. So that was a bit muted, and so was the Tottenham game when we won the League. We were expected to win and it was just a case of how long will it take us. It was the same with both, a certain inevitability, another Double. A bit blasé really. In some ways you lose something with that kind of feeling. Domestic cup finals are no longer the highest priority.

There were four of us went to Barcelona in a car – Adam Brown, Annabelle, who teaches politics in Glasgow, Sean Elleman and myself. We had already arranged to hire a car at Le Havre on the Monday. We went to the Cup final on the Saturday, back in Manchester on the Sunday, and then set off for Portsmouth on the Monday afternoon. Adam organised picking up a car in Le Havre. It was cheaper to take the car to France and leave it at Le Havre and then hire another car, a big Passat turbo diesel. So that's what we did. Anyway off we went, right through France, down into the Pyrenees and found the best hotel in Berga: £15 a night.

We got up on the Wednesday morning and got into Barcelona at about eleven o'clock. The first thing we did was to stop at the supermarket and buy four crates of Cava for celebration afterwards, then drove to an underground car park and left the car there. We then walked up the Ramblas, which of course was full of United fans. The Plaza Real was also full of United fans. We had arranged to meet up with other people, as one of my work colleagues, Justin, had been working in Barcelona for a few weeks and had managed to get a ticket from a Spanish friend who had queued up for him all day to get it. So we met up with him and two or three other United fans that I work with, had some lunch and then made our way to Sagrada Família, a fantastic cathedral. There's an Irish bar nearby, so we sat outside having a drink and chatting. Eventually we made our way to the ground.

We had no problems getting in, except for a bit of a crush finding the right entrance, but we saw the United youth team walking to the ground, in their ties and blazers, surrounded by half a dozen minders – they were all singing United songs.

We got into the ground and my ticket was in the second tier behind the goal, whereas Adam and the other two were right at the back of the second tier where the third tier comes down and there were all these banners hanging down in front of them so they couldn't actually see the whole pitch. So they came down and joined me; there were four of us standing in the space of one seat. Nobody was sitting, we were all standing, singing and chanting. What was interesting was that, although we were a goal down for most of the game, we never stopped singing and chanting. It was phenomenal. When the first goal went in, it was unbelievable; half an hour extra time and we would win. But when the second goal went in it was *absolutely* unbelievable. I came home three or four days later and had all these bruises over my back and big red marks on my thigh. I knew I had fallen over and some guy had fallen on top of me, but I hadn't felt anything, bodies all over the place, jumping up and down, it was incredible.

At the start, all we had wanted to do was get in the ground. Getting a programme had been impossible. The only programmes we saw being sold were out of the back of cars. After the game we went to meet up with some fans and I spotted programmes being sold from out of the back of a van, so I got my wallet out. By the time I get to the van, I've got two thousand pesetas in one hand and my wallet in the other. I remember grabbing the two programmes and then minutes later the wallet has gone. Surprisingly it wasn't a disaster. I really didn't know what had happened to the wallet, I assumed it had been stolen and it must have been a United fan. I don't know where it went. So I phoned Jenny, my wife, on the mobile. She phoned me back five minutes later, having phoned AMEX, Barclaycard and so on and saying it was all sorted out. When she got through the woman said, 'Oh it's another one in Barcelona!' Their phones had been jammed with people losing passports, wallets, credit cards and so on. And all the calls were from wives and partners on behalf of those in Barcelona. They'd never had anything like it.

There was a guy standing next to us in the ground who kept telling us this story about how he'd got in. He'd obviously bought a forged ticket. The officials at the ground had run after him when they realised it was a forgery and had grabbed his fleece coat and as they were pulling it off, he was undoing it and running into the ground. Of course, he then realised that he had all his money, passport and so on in it. He had to go back to where it had been taken off him, so they gave him his fleece back and then threw him out. He then bought another ticket, another forgery, but he didn't care, he just wanted to get in. And the officials of course realised again that it was a forgery, but they took pity on him and just let him in. After the game, we did what everybody else did, we went to the Ramblas. The Munich fans were okay, there was no trouble. There was a statue, and a kid who must have been no more than twelve had climbed to the top of this statue, sitting on the top with his legs around the neck of this huge figure. God knows where his dad was! Everybody was just having a good time. We were paying £7 a litre for beer, but I'd drawn the short straw for the first stint of driving back so I didn't drink after midnight. But nobody seemed to mind the price.

DEREK WYNNE

I think my greatest moment last season must have been against Liverpool but that's only by historical accident really, as I got ruled out at the end of last season. The night after the Juventus semi-final, which I watched on a big screen at my brother's house with stereo sound, leather chair and everything, I had a fantastic evening out. Then I went to play football the next night in a friendly game, but unfortunately shattered my shoulder so that ruled me out of the run-in to the end of the season. My shoulder was so bad that it was in pieces and had to be put back together again. I've still got, even now, a long way to go with it. I knew that I was not going to be able to

Manchester United coach Johnny Aston explains a few points to the younger players at the Cliff. Brian Kidd, hand on head, looks to be finding it all a bit difficult. However, in years to come, his influence on the training ground would be crucial to United's success in the 1990s. (*Popperfoto*)

Denis Law, Brian Kidd and George Best celebrate a goal against Spurs in September 1967. (*Colorsport*)

United's greatest night. Bobby Charlton and Matt Busby hug each other after the side's 4–1 victory over Benfica in the European Cup final in May 1968. After Munich it was a dream fulfilled. (*PA*)

The United team parade the European Cup around Wembley. Bringing the trophy back to Old Trafford has been United's holy grail ever since. (*PA*)

When he became manager, Wilf McGuinness had trouble with his wayward star George Best. (*Popperfoto*)

Bobby Charlton in action during his 606th and final League appearance for United, against Sheffield United in April 1973. It was truly the end of the Busby Babes era. (*Colorsport*)

That Denis Law was a hero to the Old Trafford fans was never better shown than when his goal for Manchester City against United in 1974 relegated the club. United fans even consoled an obviously distraught Law as he walked off the pitch at the end of the game. (*PA*)

A year later and there was a much happier pitch invasion by the United fans. A 4–0 victory over Blackpool secured the Second Division title, and the fans knew they were back where they belonged. (*Popperfoto*)

Norman Whiteside in action during the 1983 FA Cup final against Brighton. Five days later, during the replay, he was to become the youngest ever goalscorer in a Cup final. (*Popperfoto*)

Bryan Robson signed for United in October 1981 and remained a driving force with the side until well into the 1990s. (*Colorsport*)

The support of the United fans has been one of the key factors in their success over the years. (*Colorsport*)

A hero for much of the 1990s was Eric Cantona. His arrival inspired the side to four Premiership titles in five seasons, between 1993 and 1997. (*Colorsport*)

Chairman Martin Edwards took over from his father, Louis, in 1980. Despite the huge scale of the United operation in the late 1990s, he still tried to run the club as a family concern. (*Popperfoto*)

A second Double beckons for United's Eric Cantona and Andy Cole as they beat local rivals Manchester City at Maine Road in April 1996. (*Colorsport*)

A dream fulfilled: the Champions League trophy is lifted after a dramatic climax against Bayern Munich to complete an unprecedented Treble. (*Associated Sports Photography*)

In years to come one of Alex Ferguson's greatest achievements may well be seen as the way he developed the youth side of the club. The five Fergie Fledglings in the wall here for the FA Youth Cup final of 1993 are, from left to right, Keith Gillespie, Paul Scholes, Ben Thornley, David Beckham and Gary Neville. (*Colorsport*)

help United's cause if Alex Ferguson chose me! It was a source of sincere regret for me.

Immediately after the Juve game, my brother had asked me if I was going to come to the final in Barcelona. 'No,' I said, 'I can't afford it.' I was very forthright and clear. God bless him, he took no notice and went and ordered three provisional flights, one for him, one for my nephew and one for whoever. He knew me well! I got to the office next day and the atmosphere was very feverish. I said to the secretary, 'I've got to get £500 from somewhere. I need it now.' I was getting very excited until I got terminated at about quarter to ten that evening. It then became very academic. So the real highspot for me had been the Cup game against Liverpool, when it looked like we were going out. The game was drawing to a conclusion, then it went so strange. But because it was Liverpool it made it very special and very funny.

The European Cup games were all marvellous, but the purity of the competition is now disappearing. We have to get through one group and then go into another group. Knock-out was something better, proper. Now it's the team who can keep the most free of injuries who will win, so perhaps it's lost some merit. It may not be the best team who wins, but the team who can marshal its first team through the competition.

So, I didn't go to any games because of my shoulder and had to watch them on television. A friend of mine is a City fan and his wife, very kindly, invited me around to watch the Spurs game. I was so anxious because I thought it was something he might not want, so I made my wife Janet check with her; I didn't want to irritate him too much. But it was good of them. It was a room full of City supporters. In the end they all disappeared and I was left watching it by myself, just savouring the moment. It was all a bit remote, but I tried to make the best of it. I saw the Cup final at a friend's around the corner. We go to the games together and we enjoyed the stroll against Newcastle. We marvelled that, even though we had to change the formation just after kick-off, we still cruised around

Wembley. I think I was back in hospital again on the Monday and just got discharged in time for the European Cup final. I could never have gone. I arranged for my brother to phone me back in Altrincham. I had a good rest that afternoon. I remember when *Granada Tonight* finished at the Nou Camp I didn't want them to go away, I wanted so much to be there. I had all the possible media on to make me feel that I was there.

Talking to people later, it seems their experience was very common. A sort of quiet confidence until the last three or four minutes, but then the mood fell away a bit. When the board went up with three minutes on it, it didn't seem as if there could be three minutes left. I remember my spirits were buoyed up. Other people who were there also had a similar feeling. Somehow you didn't need to be there to have a sense of what might happen. The win certainly aided my recovery. I couldn't even leap out of my chair but I was ecstatic. My brother and about sixty thousand others were trying to ring and get through.

LEON SWERLING

In the end the collapse of the Sky deal was one of the great successes of last season. The small group of people who made careful and accurate representations to the Board of Trade ought to be thanked. I think it may work out paradoxically for United because it may be that the club is undervalued and when eventually it is sold, it will enrich Martin Edwards the more. But at least we are keeping focused on the real issues. Probably that victory has been overlooked in the light of the Treble.

LEON SWERLING

I was horrified when I heard about the Sky deal. I had been to watch Lancashire at Lord's and when I got back I switched on the radio as I got off the train and it announced that

Manchester United were being bought by Sky. My first feeling was horror. I'm not a big fan of Murdoch and the idea of him getting his hands on United and the fact that Edwards was prepared to sell it was just mind-blowing. The more I read about the possible implications, the more horrified I was. I thought it was the beginning of the end. I honestly thought he'd get away with it. I was amazed and quite grateful to the Government for once. I'm sure we've not heard the end of it. It bothers me. I think we'll be more prepared next time but eventually I think the club will be sold.

MAXINE DUNHAM

Last season, 1998–99, was unusual for me because I did not do many away games due to the ticket situation. And certainly in Europe where I would have done most of them before, I only went to Milan and Barcelona. Obviously I did all the home and cup games but the ticket situation has now got ridiculous. From that point of view I was disappointed but from every other point of view it was a splendid season.

I started very confidently; I was convinced we would do well, maybe a couple of trophies, though not the Treble, two out of the three – the FA Cup was a bonus. I had the odd pang of doubt in Europe. I left booking for Milan until it was getting close to the match. I had a hideous rush of doubt, thinking I had better go to Milan because they weren't going to go any further. From the point of view of the actual match, Milan was a bit of a nightmare. We had trouble with the police again. Every time I go abroad, I think, 'Oh God I'm not going to do this again.' We went down to the ground the day before the match because I had seen on the Internet that they have a souvenir shop and I thought I'd get a few bits and pieces. So we managed to walk right into the ground, sit in the seats we were going to be sitting in. It's a fantastic ground. We then got kicked out by a caretaker, or someone we thought was a caretaker. We went down the next night for the match, got held in the car park by the police for over an hour. We were standing in this car park, by the ground, when we actually heard the Champions League music which signalled that the teams had come out. We were getting a bit distraught. They finally got us close to the ground and shoved us all up against this fence and refused to open the gate. There was a lot of confusion, the police pretending they didn't speak English and lots of pushing. We finally got through the gates and into the actual stadium. People were being pushed upstairs and when they got up there and discovered the gate was shut were all crushing back down again. I stood back and thought I'd rather miss the match than get into a worse mess. It was getting very heated and anxious. We finally got into the ground about twenty minutes into the first half, nowhere to sit or stand, just crushed together by the police. It was the same old story, the same as we have experienced in Porto, Moscow, Galatasaray. I didn't see the first goal – there were too many people and I was perched on a narrow step trying to keep my footing – but turned around to see that Lee Sharpe was standing next to me. We finally got back to the hotel and of course soon forgot about everything, the hassle and so on. I was not expecting to get through but they came up trumps again. We got no help from the United stewards at all.

We then wanted to go to Turin, but that was already booked by the time we got back from Milan, so we had to give that one a miss. I didn't go to the Cup final either. There was a struggle for tickets for the Barcelona match, I was two vouchers short of what United needed. I even tried to get people abroad to get on the Internet and we tried to get loads of people abroad to try and buy some tickets but they couldn't get on. So finally, I spoke to my dad about it and he said that although he had a ticket he couldn't get a travel package to get to Barcelona so he said, 'Do you want my ticket?' So I said, 'Yes,' and he said, 'Do you want your Cup final ticket?' It seemed like a fair swap as I couldn't do both, so I was happy to forgo one for the other.

We drove all the way from Macclesfield to Barcelona. I had been desperate to get the tickets and it wasn't until the week before that everything was confirmed. By then it was impossible to get any flights or reservations. One drunken evening I had this crazy idea of driving, so we flung a tent in the back of the car, I took a week off work and off we went. We left on the Sunday and had a leisurely drive through France, stopping off at one or two campsites on the way and meeting more and more Bayern Munich fans. I didn't see many United fans until we got to the border on the day of the match. We got up very early in the morning, drove to the border and realised that everybody there was going to the match. All sorts of deals were being struck. I remember seeing a taxi from York in front of us and the driver was having a conversation with someone in the lane waiting to go across the border and then they met up having gone across and did a ticket deal. It was all very amicable. We belted down into Barcelona and thought, 'What shall we do?' We didn't have anywhere to stay that night, so we drove to the ground, went round the corner and there were red shirts as far as the eye could see. Unbelievably, we managed to find a parking space at a monastery about ten minutes from the ground, down a quiet, posh street. So we parked, and walked to the ground, gobsmacked by the huge amount of United supporters, and there wasn't a German fan in sight. Apparently they were all on the other side of the ground. My first mission was to secure my dad a programme, and then we went and had a beer. We spent the afternoon drinking in the streets, lots of songs and good fun. My big fear was that I was going to have trouble getting into the ground, so we left for the ground at about 4.30 p.m. and got in about three hours early, having had no problems at all. The police were very, very friendly, which made a nice change. We sat down and waited and waited. There were various ridiculous ceremonies but I was already suffering from a hangover and was full of adrenaline. I was a gibbering wreck, looking around this fantastic stadium where

I'd been before when we got absolutely stuffed by Barcelona. I was just drinking it in.

My mum phoned half an hour before kick-off to make sure I'd got in as she had heard on the news that some people were having trouble. Anyhow, the time just swept by and before we knew what had happened they were playing and Bayern had scored. When they scored it didn't seem to register. They were winning, but I still thought we'd be okay which after about eighty minutes began to wane a bit. I thought, 'It's a long drive back, what are we going to do for the next few days of our holiday? After all this *is* our annual holiday.' I was watching the clock across the stadium thinking we still had a chance. I thought, 'If we go into extra time, we'll have no chance because they've already run their socks off,' and after that it all becomes a bit blurred. I remember Schmeichel running up the pitch and thinking, 'What's he doing? These Germans can counter-attack like nobody's business, we're going to get horribly caught out at the back.' I then glanced down and to my disbelief the ball was in the back of the net, which was bulging out before my eyes. Everybody went berserk, I started crying, as did the woman next to me. There were people jumping over seats. I thought, 'That's it, extra time, we've got a hope here. At least we'll come home with some pride.' Then, lo and behold, another corner, and I don't even recall the minute when the ball went in the back of the net. People were standing up in front of me, anticipating it and I didn't even see the ball go in but again I saw them all running around on the pitch. The guy next to me was still kissing the ground from the first goal when the second went in. I just stood there, probably screaming, thinking, 'They've won it!' Absolute disbelief. But I had the presence of mind to pick up my camera as the whistle went and all the German players flopped to the ground. I was over the moon but not really believing it. There's been a lot said about superstition, Sir Matt's ninetieth birthday, the ninetieth minute, but I didn't think we were lucky, we were damned good!

268

The Germans just took their foot off the pedal. Yes, I was very surprised but then, no, because we have the confidence to keep going and it was so like that game against Liverpool in the Cup earlier in the year. Then there was the whole lifting of the cup in front of us. They were clowning around for ages, everyone was jumping around, and finally we left to go back to the car. It was probably the first time I have never had a drink after a match. We got back to the car and we just sat in the car and said, 'We've got nowhere to go,' so we just sat there and gawped and gawped through the windscreen for hours. That was our big night out. I was so gobsmacked and exhausted that I was completely drained. We just sat there and it was so quiet. Dave finally fell asleep about two o'clock but I didn't, I just sat gawping through the windscreen thinking, 'Bloody hell!' I phoned my dad in the middle of the night and he was cavorting around.

The next morning we dusted down the car and drove back towards France. I regret not being back in Manchester to see the homecoming. When I hear that bit of commentary from the television it makes the hairs on the back of my neck stand up. People now ask, 'Where were you?' and I can say we were there. Anything that happens over the next few years will always be an anti-climax to that. After all the other trips abroad, being arrested, deported, shot at, this made it all worthwhile.

Much as Barcelona was fantastic, it still wasn't quite the same feeling as beating Liverpool in the last minute in that Cup game earlier in the season. That sounds horrible, but there was a certain delight in that. I didn't think we'd win that one and I did feel sorry for Liverpool after the game.

MAXINE DUNHAM

I wasn't very happy about the Sky deal. I don't agree with such huge companies taking over everything. More so Sky as it's such a monopoly taking over football with pay per view and the likes. I was not at all happy. My next door neighbour, who is a Liverpool supporter, told me he was going to get rid of Sky if they took over Manchester United. He didn't think he should subscribe to a company who were taking over his opposition. But of course, I told him that if Granada were going to have anything to do with Liverpool, I was going to get rid of my television altogether! I just thought the whole thing would not have been good for football; it might have been good for United but I don't think it was a good move and I'm glad it didn't succeed.

KEVIN McALENY

It was a wonderful season. To be over here on Merseyside and watching all that went on was amazing. I thought their consistency was incredible. It was just marvellous; you kept thinking they just couldn't keep this going. They had an incredible amount of good fortune, but they were able to use that good luck to the best of their advantage. It was such a good season, with Arsenal pushing them all the way. I remember Liverpool drawing with them towards the end of the season and the Liverpool supporters thought they had denied United the title, but there were still so many twists and turns. It goes to show that it is not over until the fat lady sings.

Then there was the European Cup final. I didn't go but I got myself ready in the front room with a few cans of beer and sat down to enjoy it. I had a terrible feeling after the Germans had gone ahead that United were just not going to do it, and I'd resigned myself to this and having to go into work the next day and face all the brickbats from the Merseyside supporters. But, incredibly, in the last minute it turned on its head. It was incredible. A tremendous season and they fully deserved what they got, they worked so hard and were so committed.

When they scored I jumped around the room. I even went into the back garden and screamed my head off. I thought, 'If there are any Liverpool supporters around, they'll hear.' I must admit that, locally, Everton fans took to it a bit more readily than Liverpool fans, but the general attitude was that they are not a bad side – in an understated sort of manner – and they did give credit, because they knew that they were looking at a great side. It was marvellous, absolutely marvellous.

KEVIN McALENY

I was a 'wait and see what happens' with the Sky deal. I didn't want to jump on the anti-Sky bandwagon. Now sometimes I think I was right when we're talking about big-name players that United probably can't afford the wages for, such as Roy Keane. I just think that if the Sky deal had gone through there would have been a bit more money. I'm still 'wait and see' but they put the prices up at Old Trafford last year by two pounds and everyone was making a fuss. You can't have it both ways; everyone was saying they didn't want the Sky deal to go through, then they make a fuss because they are putting the prices up to pay for the players. Maybe if it had gone through, we would have been able to afford the big-name players like Rivaldo. Maybe next year if we lose Roy Keane he will take a lot of money to replace – all for the sake of £40,000 a week and not £20,000.

ROBIN MURRAY

Half-way through the season, in December, we had lost to Middlesbrough, beaten three–two. That turned out to be the last game we lost but at the time a lot of people thought we weren't good enough, that maybe Arsenal or Chelsea would be the teams. We were scoring a lot of goals in Europe, but against the big sides like Barcelona and Bayern Munich we were letting goals in, beating the small sides but not the big ones. We had our doubts about whether we were really strong enough to beat the big sides. We had some very tough games in the Cup – Middlesbrough, Liverpool, Chelsea, Arsenal – compare that to

Newcastle and who they had played. I think that helped us a bit, playing the big sides; every game was a Cup final. By about March, we started to believe that they could win something, especially after the semi-final against Arsenal, one of the best games I've ever seen. I went to that game and was at one of the Arsenal ends which made it even better. Keane got sent off and they had a penalty and I thought, 'That's it.' But Schmeichel saved the penalty, and although United played the better in extra time, it took a wonder goal. It was one of those games that was going to be settled by a wonder goal. You just knew then. They got to the Cup final and it was near the end of the season and you thought, 'They're going to do it.'

I didn't go to any of the away European games. We hadn't played well against Juventus at home and had scraped a one–one draw with a last-minute goal. We've never beaten an Italian side in Italy and were two goals down after eleven minutes, I just thought, 'Oh.' I sat with three women at home watching this game. But from going two–nil down they really played well and deserved to win it. It could have been more, they hit the post twice. It was just a brilliant night.

We talk about the eleven days in May. It was like three Cup finals. I think we let ourselves down a bit by not beating Blackburn. They had to fight for everything because they were going to go down. If we had beaten them we could have been five points clear with the Tottenham game to come, but because we only drew we had to beat Tottenham and hope that Arsenal didn't beat Aston Villa. We had never won the League at Old Trafford these last five or six years. We've always won it somewhere else, an away ground, so everyone was happy to be doing it at Old Trafford. But I was really nervous, I thought it could all go wrong here. Tottenham were playing well, Walker was playing out of his skin; he kicked one ball against Yorke and it didn't go in, then they went up the other end and scored. One–nil down! And that's when I wished we'd already won it. But we did well in the second half and we won it. It was just like winning the League the first time we won it and this time it was at Old Trafford.

Then the Cup final the week after. I'd been to so many Cup finals that complacency set in. It was going to be a walkover and to be fair it was. I was a bit worried when Keane went off injured and Ferguson brought Sheringham on. I thought, 'Why Sheringham? It doesn't work playing three up front.' And he scored within two minutes. So, yes, it had been worrying up to then because Newcastle had played well. But once we scored, there was never any doubt. It was a good day, apart from the fact that one of the guys who went down with us got arrested for being drunk. We didn't know where he was so we had to wait behind for an hour and a half at the police station trying to convince the police sergeant that he was a good lad even though he had verbally abused every Newcastle fan in the police station! So, I wasn't very happy about that. But we got him out in the end.

We had some good news about getting to Barcelona. I had a friend who runs a pub near this company's offices and they said they were looking for stewards for the plane and let you go free – free flight, free hotels and tickets. I thought, 'That's brilliant, it's worth the risk.' The steward duties entailed getting the people off the plane and onto the buses, supervise them, and then make sure they got onto the buses for the match. So four of my friends – all policemen – decided it was too good an opportunity to miss and would save us a lot of money. We went to a meeting and there were maybe a hundred there all wanting to be stewards. You could tell from the organisation that something was not right. I asked a few questions. I asked, 'What about these match tickets?' and he said, 'Well, we're not actually going to get you match tickets, but you'll get into the ground by saying that you work for us.' Immediately the bells started ringing. But luckily we already had our match tickets; for £25 it was worth it, 'cos we could always get rid of them at the ground. We decided we'd go just for the day trip and not bother with a hotel 'cos a lot of the lads were married.

We got to the airport and it was chaos. There must have been six or seven hundred people there without tickets who had been promised tickets by various firms. They were all looking for the representatives who would hand over the tickets. It was nothing to do with us; we were just meant to be stewards for one group of them. We kept our mouths shut. The guy who worked for our company turned up and said to us that there were no tickets. He didn't tell the fans. He said, 'Can you tell them?' We said, 'Bollocks, no way, you do your own dirty work. We don't want to be stewards if that's what it involves.' Then, of course, we had the problem of how to get there if we were not going to be stewards. But luckily our names were on the flight list, so that was okay. At the other end there were no coaches, hotels hadn't been booked. Some people had paid £200 or £300 a ticket, not the flight ticket but the ticket for the match, which they didn't get. They had to decide whether to go out there and try and get a ticket or just lose £600. A lot went out there thinking they might get a ticket but didn't. We saw loads of them coming back who hadn't got in. It was chaos, greed, a once-in-a-lifetime chance for those fans.

We got there and it was an amazing day. It was lovely weather and there were thousands of United fans up and down the Ramblas having a singsong, everyone getting drunk except me as I don't drink. Then there was the match. We got in early to soak up the atmosphere. I'd been to Barcelona before so I knew what the stadium was like. From the outside it doesn't look much, but when you get in it's fantastic – four-tiered, five in parts, beautiful. Three quarters of the ground was United. When Munich scored about thirty people jumped up. When United scored almost the entire stadium erupted. It was unbelievable. From a neutral point of view the game was a bit disappointing. I don't think United played well at all. I've not watched it again since but we missed Keane. Beckham played well but the power in the midfield was not there; they could have scored two or three. They scored the one goal but then I don't remember many chances until Bayern Munich hit the post twice. They should have scored, they were dead unlucky. Another one was the overhead kick that hit the crossbar. Until then we hadn't had a chance. Then when Ole came on he had a few half chances. I thought, 'Well, it's been a wonderful day – we've lost, but it's been good, Bayern have been the better side, we've had a good time.' Then the ninety-first minute. My first thought was, 'He's offside,' but the flag didn't go up. And, no, he wasn't offside. From where we were stood it looked like it might be. I can't describe the feeling. If we had won that match two–one from scoring two goals in the first half we would have just been clapping at the end 'cos we had won the European Cup, but to do it this way was just – I can't describe it – it was like three moments of sheer pleasure, two goals and the final whistle, wrapped into just two minutes. I think a lot of people didn't realise we had scored again because they were still turning around and hugging each other. I didn't really see the goal because everyone was still jumping up and down. The sad thing from the German point of view was the players. They were so gutted, they couldn't get up. Seven of them were lying on the floor and the referee was picking them up. If it had been the other way round . . . I remember it happening with Arsenal in 1979 when we scored two goals to equalise and then Arsenal scored a third, that was my worst moment in football. But this was the best – heaven. When I got back home I didn't watch the match again but I turned it to the eighty-seventh minute and watched it about a hundred times. ITV was awful because the celebrations were just fantastic and ITV cut to adverts. They missed it all, especially the raising of the cup when Schmeichel made the crowd go quiet and then they lifted the trophy and every player raised their arms. It was a brilliant moment and ITV missed it.

We left the ground after about an hour, and a coach was just leaving, probably the first coach back to the airport and the five of us managed to get on. We got to the airport and our plane wasn't leaving until about five in the morning and I thought, 'What are we going to do?' But one of the lads was on an earlier plane – a big jumbo jet. It was the same company, and we just managed to sneak on. We were the first plane back to Manchester. We were back by three in the morning. We didn't sleep, although the plane was probably the quietest I've ever been on. Everyone was so overwhelmed. We had tickets for the Arena that night, so we went down to Deansgate to see the celebrations but couldn't see anything, then went to the Arena which was terrific. It really was eleven days in May, the best in my life. I've never seen anything like it. It will never be repeated like that. To win the League on the final day from being one goal down and then to win the European Cup from one goal down in the final minute. Fantastic.

ROBIN MURRAY

I think I really was one of the undecideds. Murdoch, from what I've heard about him, is pretty obnoxious and it does niggle me slightly that United are the best-supported club in the world and yet we still can't compete moneywise with the so-called European giants. That's because they organise their own television packages which they can't do in England. I think Barcelona get about £80 million a year in television money. United can't compete with that and therefore we have still not been able to get the greatest players. I thought, 'Well if the Sky takeover means that we can compete, then there has to be something good about it.' But I was equally worried that we would become a marketing tool for the Murdoch empire, with games kicking off at eleven at night just so that they could catch the Malaysian market. They didn't help themselves, either, by bringing Americans into the press conference who did not have a clue what they were talking about, all of them were on the business side. In the end, I was probably slightly relieved that it fell apart. Better the devil you know.

MATTHEW REYNOLDS

276

The League was never a foregone conclusion. I don't think there is anything much to choose between United and Arsenal. I think if I was being honest, Arsenal were hard done by, seeing United win everything, while they won nothing. There's not a great deal between the two sides. The League to me is the important one. It starts in August and finishes in May. Week in, week out. That's what you put the effort into and play for. Obviously I was thrilled they won the European Cup, but the League to me is always the most important. I was, as usual, a gibbering heap of nerves. It means as much to me now as it did when we won it the first time after all those years.

I'd wound myself up into such a state by the time of the Spurs game. Someone said to me, 'Look at it this way, you've got three games left, three Cup finals, win them all and you've won the lot.' I think as you watch United now, you tend to know when they are in trouble and when they are not. When we went that goal behind against Spurs you somehow felt that United would not throw it away. I don't know why, but their heart is big and they don't know when they are beaten. They have no concept of being beaten – that comes from the manager.

MATTHEW REYNOLDS

It was the strangest Cup final I've ever been to. People I know who are married and have children will always make an effort, take a weekend in London and go to see the Cup final. But everyone I knew was going to Barcelona. We went on the Monday. Nearly all the United fans I know went down on the Saturday and came straight back home before going off to Barcelona on the Monday or Tuesday. Someone I know went down to the Cup final on the Friday and said that London was just full of Geordies. They didn't see any United fans. It was strange but we completely outclassed Newcastle. It was almost embarrassing in the end. They even gave Jaap Stam a fitness run out – in the Cup final! When Roy Keane came off after a few minutes and a striker came on for him, I was worried, but then Sheringham scored which was great for him. He had so much stick when he first came and we didn't win anything. But he took us on to the three in the end.

MATTHEW REYNOLDS

I went to the Inter Milan and Barcelona games in Europe. I thought, 'If they go through you will not get a flight to Barcelona for love nor money.' So I went to the travel agents and booked a holiday just down the coast from Barcelona. It was £190 for a week. I told all my friends that they were booking themselves on it. I said, 'The worst would be that we have a week's holiday.' So seven of us booked it after the quarter-final. We went on the Monday after the Cup final, flying out to the coast. We spent two days in the resort and then took a train into Barcelona, staying in a back packers' hostel which we've been to before on the Tuesday and Wednesday night. The best atmosphere is usually before the game, when everybody is optimistic and you're getting on with the away fans, but this time it was obviously after the game. There was no trouble, I think just one arrest 'cos someone broke a window. We met some other friends in the centre of Barcelona and then met various people at various other places.

We went up to the stadium at about five o'clock and there was mayhem. We didn't really have much chance to get into the spirit of it because a friend of mine had to meet someone to get a ticket and we had problems because the police had put a cordon around the ground so we spent an hour trying to help him out. It got sorted out in the end. Seven of us went – two of them were girlfriends who didn't go to the game.

I've been in the stadium before so I didn't get that big a shock. It doesn't look so imposing from the outside, a bit like Highfield Road. It's dug down, sunk into the ground, a huge bowl. If you've not seen it before, it's very striking. We were right behind the corner flag where the two goals came from and there was one seat between us and the VIP seats. I was just a couple of seats away from Steve Bruce. After the way the season had gone, I don't think United played well and the goal they conceded was basic. They fell for the oldest trick in the book, leaving a big gap in the wall, a soft goal. But they never gave up and even with one minute to go you didn't really think they'd lose. There were some with head in hands around me but I just knew that once they'd got one . . . I said to the lad next to me when the second corner was conceded, I said, 'Get at them, they're flapping.' It was just like Liverpool in that Cup tie, it was identical. Some of the German players had been down the other end celebrating before the goal went in. I said, 'They're German and not used to this.' I could see the expressions on their faces. When they got that second corner, I thought, 'This is going in.' And then . . . that was that. Couldn't believe it. I thought the referee would find even more time. He was walking around picking German players up. He walked back to the centre circle, blew the whistle and that was that.

I had the strangest sensation and I still feel it now. I've heard people in Chorlton were dancing on buses and in the streets. You didn't get that there. Everybody was really happy but it was a sense of quiet jubilation, they didn't go berserk. There were a few people singing songs but ultimately it was a sense of relief. It was a brilliant feeling. I'd been getting slightly niggled in Barcelona because there seemed to be so many out-of-town United supporters, and at the end of the day there was a Granada crew trying to do interviews and there were accents from the south of England. It was really niggling me. Then all of a sudden, after the game, I seemed to know everyone around me. We went to a pub by the station and had a few drinks in complete peace and quiet. Then we wandered back towards the ground and people were sat there completely chilled out. There was a Granada crew there and they were having a drink. It was about five in the morning. That feeling still goes on. The chance of an English side doing that again is basically zero. We've seen as good as it gets. But we are in no way like we were in 1968 where a good team was coming to an end; we have a young side – the Nevilles, Giggs, Beckham. They have years ahead of them.

MATTHEW REYNOLDS

I had a great deal of faith in the general public owning United and therefore the fans not being prepared to let anything happen. I suppose that proved to be naïve in light of what did happen. You can see that there needs to be major financial influences behind any club, but I felt more easy after the Sky bid failed; just, I suppose, as when United went public and everybody could get some shares. I bought some so that I felt part of the club. Admittedly, most of the shares are owned by a few people. It's always a worry that they will do something to your club that you don't want. But United seem to have a great ability to turn anything into a profit. I do think the individuals who run the club are not as they might be, but they are good business people. I have no great love for them but I don't think I get as upset about them as some of the others do.

ROGER HENNELL

I had not even been hoping to go to the European Cup final but Teresa my wife said that Gordon had suggested that we went. I said, 'No, I think it's too much trouble.' But gradually I thought about it and eventually rang my brother up and said, 'Look I've been talked into it by Teresa and now I'm thinking about it, I'm very excited. Can you see what we can do about it?' At that point we knew we had no chance of getting tickets through the club because we did not have enough tokens, we were a couple short. But Gordon knew that the travel agents he used reckoned there would be some chance of tickets so he said he'd look into it. He rang them up and they said, 'Well we did have some but they all seem to have gone; we did have some deals but no more.' So we talked about all sorts of options such as flying there and trying to get tickets at the ground, hiring a car and so on. It turned out that the nearest place we could get a flight to was Lyon, in France. So we had come to the conclusion that we would not be able to go. Gordon rang the travel agents again and they said they'd suddenly got a block of tickets which had been promised to some people but they were messing the travel agents about and had been given until two o'clock to confirm and come up with the money. So Gordon called me and asked me if I was interested. I said of course and we immediately put ourselves down as two people who would be interested. This was a couple of days before the game. Anyhow, they phoned back at 2.30 p.m. and said, 'If you can get down here with your credit card the tickets are yours.' So I came home as high as a kite.

Come the Wednesday morning of the game, we arrived at the airport at four o'clock in the morning. We had no tickets but we knew that somehow we might be all right and we had taken the precaution of taking a lot of money with us. We arrived at the airport in good time. It soon became apparent that we were not the only ones without tickets. We didn't even actually have tickets for the plane. When it came to getting on the plane they asked if we had some proof of identity, to prove that we had been promised tickets by our operators. So we showed them the forms we had and, fine, we were allowed on the plane. When we were on the plane we were told, 'We haven't got the tickets here but they will be flown out later and you will get them.' Before we got off the plane we were given our boarding cards for coming home so that there would be no trouble.

We arrived at Barcelona at 10.30 a.m. It was a wonderful morning. We had a look around the town and went up the Cathedral and made the most of enjoying a great day in

Barcelona. We were told to meet at 6.30 p.m. at a certain tube station where the tickets would be dispensed for the game. We thought, 'Well this sounds very unlikely,' but we couldn't risk not going. So come half past six we turned up at this tube station and waited for an hour. There were a few others waiting as well. So we gave it till 7.30 p.m. then thought, 'Let's go back to the banking areas, change our money and get some more from the cash points.' It was cutting it pretty fine. We had to go back to the main area to change the money. We had English money so we changed it for Spanish money thinking that when we had been offered tickets before they wanted Spanish money. We tried to go back on the underground to where the United fans were going, but you just couldn't get on the trains, they were jam packed. The stations were jam packed as well, so we thought we'd take the alternative route and go on the line which went to the German side of the ground. We managed to do that. We came out of the station and immediately a German came up to us who spoke very good English and he asked us if we wanted tickets. It was literally as we were coming up the stairs from the station. So we negotiated to buy two tickets at £250 each. He then wanted English money and we only had pesetas, but we explained to him that we were being fair in our dealings. So he gave us the tickets at £250 each and wished us luck, telling us that he was a Borussia Dortmund fan and he didn't want Bayern Munich to win. At that point, having thought we were not going to see the game, we were running to the ground full of excitement. Then as we got to the ground there were so many ticket checks we realised the authorities were worried about forgeries. But each time we got through and got closer and we finally got through and into the ground.

We must have had two of the best seats in the house. We were in the Bayern end in the front of the first tier on the eighteen-yard line. It was a superb view. There were quite a few United fans in there but it was mostly Germans who were so sporting and friendly. One of the things that was strange was that we could not hear the United fans singing at all; we were all wondering why they weren't singing but we later realised that the noise of the stadium does not carry to the other end. We spent the game enjoying the football but frustrated that the Germans were playing the better football and we didn't seem to look as if we would score. When they scored we didn't seem to have any ideas or look as if we would score. We thought, 'How disappointing. Not only are we going to lose but we have not even played well.' But in those last few minutes you could sense something was going to happen, especially when Schmeichel went up for a corner. The place went mad and the Germans around us – we were jumping up and down – were very dejected and were taking photos of these mad English people!

But after United had won, the German fans had the grace to stay behind and cheer and clap and be very sporting in defeat. I would like to think we would be generous in defeat but in all honesty I don't think we would be. When they had all left the pitch we headed back to the coaches and thought we should try and find a coach and try to get home. Well, we found one that was just about to leave and we were off. We got back to the airport and tried to find out about our flight but it was not listed on the board. We asked and they said, 'Oh, yes, it is there, just go up the steps and you can get on it, it's going in about ten minutes.' I think they were just filling up planes and sending them off. So, because we didn't hang around celebrating, we were home by one o'clock in the morning. I heard of others taking ages to get home. We came back thinking, 'Well, it was expensive but what an experience!' It was once in a lifetime. Had we not got there we would have felt very sore but we were lucky. Our story had a happy ending.

The other memorable thing was that Teresa was working in Deansgate and the office she is in is opposite Kendall's shop so we all went down there and were able to look down on the coach coming past on the Thursday evening. That was nice because all the family were there. We felt that we were part of a gigantic party, making the most of something that had never happened before and might never happen again.

ROGER HENNELL

I tend to get a bit blasé about Cup finals after being involved with the club these past ten or eleven years. Cup finals came and went, but this one was a bit special for me in two ways. Firstly, because it was obviously part of a potential Treble and secondly, because it was going to be my last one with the team. We've lost the contract to drive the team for this season, so this was to be my last time with them. It was particularly significant from these two points of view.

The Cup final was much the same as it always has been. We go down to London on a Thursday, spend a couple of days in the Windsor area preparing for the game. We stay in Windsor in a very nice hotel on the Thames. Myself and a few members of the club staff went to Wembley on the Saturday morning and laid out all the kit and equipment, had a look at the pitch and so on. We have to report back to the manager on the state of the pitch but we never have a problem at Wembley, it's always the same. It also gives you a chance to walk out on the pitch which is quite exciting. Later in the day, in our suits, we went on the pitch again; I actually had the opportunity to join the players on the pitch and soak up the pre-match atmosphere. It was good. I've done that before, the first time I did a Cup final in 1990, but unfortunately I'd not really had the chance since then. But I was determined this time that I would go out on the pitch and the lads were all saying, 'Come on out with us.'

I then had to go off and move the coach to outside the stadium and leave it there until after the game. Then I came back in to watch the game. I went back in the tunnel for a while and watched everybody preparing and then, as the team went out, some of the players who were not playing and I walked around the track and went upstairs to our seats close to the royal box. We stayed there at half time and as the game came to a conclusion, and it was fairly obvious we were going to win, we came down and stood behind the bench until the game was over and then we were able to go on the pitch and celebrate with everybody else. We did the lap of honour, it was great. I was behind them, going right up to the crowd; there were a number of suited people on the pitch behind the team.

I then went and got the coach, and started packing it up while the players and everyone went off to see their families in the hospitality area and later we picked them up from there. We then go into London and have a celebratory night at a hotel. That's the normal thing. We had a fantastic night. Now normally, the team would travel home by train, but obviously, because of the European Cup final on the Wednesday, we stayed down in London. All the families were packed off on the train on the Sunday and we packed the coach up and went out to Burnham Beeches, where the England team normally stay. They did some training on the Monday morning and then I dropped the team off at Heathrow – at the foot of Concorde! The trip to Barcelona on Concorde was all organised by British Airways – they got a lot of PR out of it. So we actually went over to the plane near its hangar and went up to the steps of Concorde. When I left the players it was quite emotional because that was going to be my last contact with the team after eleven years. I was quite upset and so were some of the players. They were all shaking my hand and I was very touched at the way they did that. As I drove away they were all waving to me. I then drove the coach home empty.

I did go to Barcelona however. The club had provided me with some tickets, or rather the opportunity to *buy* some tickets! We decided we would go and I went with my mum, who is an avid United supporter, my wife, my brother and my sister. Unfortunately, all the club flights were full but we managed to get on a flight with somebody else and we flew out quite early on the Wednesday morning. After a lot of messing about we did get to the game. Unfortunately, we ended up in Jeroma without any transport, which is about a hundred kilometres from Barcelona. What that showed me was the durability of United supporters as there was a plane full of fans trying to get to Barcelona. We were ushered off the plane by Spanish police, flexing their muscles. We went over to a row of coaches only to discover that none of them were for us. After three or four hours it finally dawned on us that there were not going to be any coaches for us, so we hired a car. We were quite lucky because we had brought our driving licences with us. So we made our own way into Barcelona. After the game when we got back, it seemed that all one hundred or so people who had been on that plane had, by hook or by crook, somehow got to the game, and all got back to the airport for two o'clock in the morning to get the flight back home. There were some people who were expecting tickets but had to watch the game on a screen and never got into the stadium.

The rest of the day was fantastic. I've never experienced anything like it in my life. It was a sea of red in the middle of Barcelona. It was absolutely fantastic. We met up with a friend of mine and went and saw the game. We thought it was all over and then three minutes of unbelievable, amazing football – a bit of luck, but a great night. From where I was sitting I was able to get down to the front of the pitch when the lads were doing their lap of honour and a couple of them saw me and waved to me.

But I did see them the day after when they came back. We had organised the open-top bus for the club, but a police officer drives that because of security. Because they went back to the MEN Arena, they had to get back from there and they didn't want to do that in an open-top coach. So I was there with the bus and I waited inside the arena for them. I saw all the cups and held the European Cup which was fantastic. That was the end of it. We've now lost the contract – one of those things.

SIMON JONES

I was very gloomy about the Sky deal. We saw it as one more example of taking football away from the fans towards business. I already have some resentment about United becoming a business. I understand it and I know it is reality but from the point of view of simply being able to afford to go, I regret it. United was built on working class origins, as indeed were all the teams in the UK, so to move into the realm of big business and away from the ordinary person in the city is not welcome. The Sky takeover bid was doubly difficult for me 'cos I am not a fan of Rupert Murdoch and his empire. At least I am able to watch football on television with my son – to have to buy Sky in order to do that would gall me. But it was much more than this. It was the idea that the voice of the fan was not being listened to. People were up in arms about it. I also heard that the players and the manager were not keen. There was some subterfuge going on at board level, with some members of the board in favour for whatever reason but not saying much and all this added to me feeling powerless. I could not see, from the footballing or the public point of view, anything being gained by going in with Sky, and their having control. I could see how it would gain money for certain people. That's business and that's the reality but I could not see what it would give to the public. So, nothing could have made me more happy when the Government intervened. In fact it's one of the few things the Blair Government has done that I have been pleased about. Somebody had to stop it or it would have gone through on the nod. A television company having control of the games of a major football team was never logically or morally acceptable, so I was delighted people came to their senses. I am sure we have not heard the last of it. I feel that the decision not to let the deal go through was an important marker which I hope will give the message that fans are not going to sit back and let this happen and will also have demonstrated that the Government is also watching and is prepared to intervene. I can't say that the club is safe in its hands but at least others are watching – the fans and others who want what I want have been proven right in this case. Perhaps it sets a precedent. The little guys have won.

SIMON THORP

We had such fantastic success, despite the fact that they did not play all that well last season. They had some difficult times. There was a point when Schmeichel was playing badly and everyone was writing him off. There were all sorts of things that weren't gelling, but through the manager's determination they did finish strong. Their opponents also all faltered. So in some ways it was in spite of ourselves that we won.

But the achievement was historic. I had a fantastic night when the team and fans came back. A friend of mine who lives in London and is a big United fan simply could not stay in London that day because he was surrounded by Arsenal fans at work and couldn't really celebrate. He hadn't been able to go to the game either. So he phoned me on his mobile – he was on his way up and wanted to meet me. We decided to meet near the Arndale Centre in Stretford which was a bit naïve really, as it was chaotic. He got stuck about three miles behind the procession. I arrived just in time, having run across the fields to where I knew the bus would be. He phoned me to say he'd go into town. It was a great feeling, we saw the players and I was impressed with the atmosphere. That evening, myself, the guy from London and his uncle Bernard, a Greek Cypriot who runs the United fish and chip shop by the ground and has done for years, met up. Bernard's a great bloke, an inveterate United fan and he had been to Barcelona with some of his cronies. We went to the Three Legs of Man pub in Old Trafford. They had all been drinking for a couple of days and there was sheer joy in that pub that night, lots of hilarity, lots of different experiences from over in Barcelona. It seemed that every person in that pub had been to this game and they weren't on the young side, more middle-aged. I thought, 'That's a fantastic effort, to have paid out and gone over there.' But the wonderful thing was that all night Bernard was the focus of our attention because he was telling us some great stories about the journey and so on. We kept asking what he thought of the game and the goals. And right towards the end of the night, his nephew asked him, 'Well what did you think of that goal?' and he said, 'Well, I have to tell you, I didn't actually see it!' He had had a drink at lunchtime and had fallen asleep, and he had been jammed so tightly in his seat that he was propped up, so the first thing he knew about the goal was when everyone jumped up. It was a supreme irony, almost absurd in a way. But he exemplified the atmosphere because he was just so thrilled. I got a buzz from just being near them for a whole week.

SIMON THORP

CHAPTER NINE

Anyone But Liverpool

There was a time when Manchester United and Liverpool were so close that their players huddled together and cooked up a betting wheeze. That was in 1915 when a Good Friday game between the two clubs at Old Trafford eventually led to the suspension of eight players from the two sides. The result had been fixed – a 2–0 win to United – with a number of players profiting from a gamble on the scoreline of the match. The Football League unearthed the conspiracy and took prompt action.

Indeed it is difficult, if not impossible, to detect any intense rivalry between the two clubs prior to the 1960s. Clearly there was competition, although United spent long periods of the thirties flirting with the Second Division, but the rivalry never spilled into violence, abuse or anger. There were direct transfers between the two clubs – something which has not happened for the past thirty years – and even managers remained close. Prior to the War, Matt Busby had played for Liverpool and always spoke warmly of his former club. There was never any discernible antipathy between the two.

After the Second World War, Liverpool took up the immediate challenge winning the first post-war Championship, but after that it was all United as Matt Busby's new side finished runners-up four times in five seasons. Ironically, Busby might well have become a coach at Anfield had United

290

not made him the better offer of manager. Eventually, in 1952, United added the title to the FA Cup they had won in 1948. In the fifties, United reigned unchallenged as the Busby Babes captured two more titles while Liverpool were relegated and languished for the remainder of the decade in the Second Division. It was no contest.

If there had been any serious rivalry between the two clubs prior to the sixties, it went unnoticed. But all that was to change. In 1964 Liverpool, now back in the top flight, won the title, only to be eclipsed by United the following season. Meanwhile Liverpool, like United, reached the semi-finals of the European Cup and then the final of the European Cup-Winners' Cup. In 1966 it was Liverpool's turn to win the League, followed in 1967 by United and then by United winning the European Cup in 1968. Add to this cocktail of rivalry the fortunes of Everton and Manchester City and you have a six-season Merseyside–Manchester domination of the First Division. And therein were sown the seeds of a rivalry that was to become even more intense as the years progressed. Yet if you were to ask any Liverpool fan which side was their fiercest rival during that period, they will instinctively answer Leeds, while United fans would almost certainly point to City. Throughout the period Busby and Shankly remained the closest of friends, with Shankly making a weekly trek up the East Lancs just to have a chat and a cup of tea with his oldest mate. 'They were like brothers,' Mrs Shankly once told me.

Munich and the European triumph had turned United from a local club into a national side and although Liverpool would go on to dominate both Europe and the domestic football scene over the next two decades, winning a dozen titles and six European trophies, they would somehow never quite be regarded in the same aura as United. That was a bitter pill to swallow. Equally, it was a bitter pill for United that Liverpool's success should eclipse their own. United regarded themselves as a European club, yet had only one trophy to show for all their description and efforts.

But, as many observers in this chapter point out, the rivalry extends way beyond the football pitch. It is also about two cities in the north-west jockeying for pole position. Liverpool, once the great sea port, the west's window on the world, flourished until the late sixties. Coupled with the arrival of the Beatles and a host of other pop groups as well as two successful football teams, it became the most envied city in Britain. People flocked to Liverpool. Manchester enjoyed a brief flirtation with pop but it was never on a par with Liverpool. Manchester could only watch enviously from thirty-five miles down the M62. The economic rivalry wasn't new; it had always been there. The Manchester Ship Canal had been built by the entrepreneurs of Manchester simply because the Port of Liverpool was lodging excessive charges.

If the seeds of football rivalry had been sown in the sixties they were finally to begin to flourish in the seventies. While Liverpool went on to win countless Championships and two European Cups, United suffered the indignity of relegation. It got worse in the eighties. Liverpool's run of success continued unabated with more titles, more European Cups. But then the decline in shipping and shipbuilding saw Liverpool's core industries slump. A few new businesses arrived but with them came a trade union militancy that swiftly gave the city a reputation as awkward and hell-bent on self-destruction.

The city might have been down on its knees economically but at least it boasted the best football team in Europe, while at Old Trafford managers came and went in the search for the Holy Grail. The United fans didn't like it. For some, violence on the terraces and fighting between both sets of fans was as much a feature of United–Liverpool encounters as the football. These were grim years for United supporters. Liverpool reigned supreme, the most successful side in the history of British football. To defeat Liverpool was almost, but not quite, as good as winning the title. And invariably during the 1980s United did get the better of Liverpool in those struggles. If only, groaned the United fans, we could play like that every game. Somehow they couldn't.

But then with the nineties came a remarkable reversal in fortunes. Suddenly the focus was on Manchester. Alex Ferguson finally ended the search for the Holy Grail in 1993 and for the rest of the decade it was all United. And just to cock a snook at Liverpool, Manchester suddenly boasted the best music and the most envied clubs in the land. For the Cavern read the Haçienda. For the Beatles and the rest read the Stone Roses, Happy Mondays, Oasis, M People and so on. None of this went down well with many Liverpool fans whose own fortunes had plummeted with the dramatic resignation of manager Kenny Dalglish. The city of Liverpool was suffering high unemployment, social deprivation, poor housing, a continuing reputation for trade union militancy, political chaos and lawlessness. Liverpool's music scene had also slithered into decline. Whereas Liverpool was once the place to be seen, by the 1990s it was the last place on earth to visit. One United fan visiting Liverpool for the first time likens it in this chapter to bombed-out Beirut. Manchester, meanwhile, was buzzing. There were continental-style bars on the streets, a massive building programme, a busy airport, quality shops, fine restaurants, a new mega shopping centre and so forth. It's all about confidence and pride.

Liverpool was shunned by industry and national politicians alike. Even its own kind were leaving in droves. It had the fastest-declining population of any city in the United Kingdom. So a new rivalry was born. This time it was Liverpool who heightened the aggravation. Fortunately it didn't spill on to the streets or terraces too often, but it was verbal and abusive enough to be apparent to all. It was Liverpool who now regarded the annual fixtures as the most important games of the season, and the games above all others which they had to win. Victory here almost compensated for the loss of their Championship status. The one-time intense rivalry with neighbours Everton now took second place to the twice-annual confrontation with United. Surprisingly, the public of each city rarely visits the other. Mancunians might like to go out into the wide world but they rarely venture westwards down the M62. A few might go for the annual game at Anfield but even that is a rare, sometimes even dangerous, venture. Better to stay at home and listen on the radio or watch on television. Scousers like to keep themselves to themselves.

So it has continued. At least now there is a grudging respect from United fans for the Liverpool sides of the seventies and eighties, though it is clear from the interviews in this chapter that there is a fear that one day Liverpool will rise again to become the dominant force in British football. One suspects also that Liverpool fans will now admit that United, with their remarkable European Cup win and Treble, have deservedly been the team of the nineties. Indeed, it would be difficult for them to deny it. This one, as they say, will run and run although it would surely be better for all if the paranoia was put to one side by both sets of supporters.

Liverpool are a good team. They have been one of the top teams throughout the seventies and eighties. Sure, there's more to it than that. They are two cities who have struggled against each other for time immemorial. The Manchester Ship Canal was built by textile merchants because they were fed up with the charges being laid by the Port of Liverpool. So you've had a rivalry since then. Just look at the geographical distance. You build a motorway – the M6 – and it's twenty miles closer to Manchester than it is to Liverpool. You build an airport five or six miles out of Manchester and there's that piddling little airport at Speke which has not had the investment and now can't begin to rival Manchester; those kind of transport decisions have changed the nature of places.

Liverpool, a once big bustling port with heavy industry, has declined relatively whereas Manchester has grown to be the third financial centre outside London. Good transport infrastructure, so it's not surprising that the fortunes of these two cities are inextricably interlinked. So there's a rivalry in that sense and the football teams reflect that rivalry. But for me, much as I don't like admitting it, Liverpool are a good side. In some ways, because Liverpool has a less corporate atmosphere, I might feel more at home supporting a team which isn't a global team but is nevertheless a good side. But that's a kind of heresy. Let's not dwell on that too much!

DEREK WYNNE

I always had a problem against Liverpool fans. Although not being from the north-west, I think when I was about sixteen, we saw a Charity Shield game in 1983; United beat Liverpool. My dad had been divorced and he was dating somebody and we had to leave Wembley early, so all the Liverpool fans had come out because they'd lost and all the United fans are inside Wembley. As we were walking outside the ground – I was only sixteen, a skinny lad, about five foot five – some big Scouser with a skinhead comes up behind me and just boots me up the arse. Sends me about five feet up in the air. Luckily my dad and uncles are big and scared them off. So that put me off Liverpool fans. But when you get to Manchester and get involved in the Mancunian–Scouse rivalry, it was easy for me to join in.

The biggest thing for United in those days was just jealousy. Liverpool were so much better. Every year Liverpool won the League, every year Liverpool won the European Cup. United won bugger all. Liverpool would ram down the throat all the jokes about Old Trafford being a trophy-free zone. That was the problem. Liverpool won everything, United won nothing. And yet Liverpool fans were still jealous and bitter of United, because even though United were useless they still got all the publicity and attention, had the biggest crowd, the most money, the most glamour. There was no reason for Liverpool to be jealous because they were the team who won everything.

The fans still don't get on. The atmosphere is still pretty bad. I went to one game in Liverpool, saw United play Liverpool in the Milk Cup in 1983 and I think Liverpool won two–one. I went there with a bunch of southern lads from London and we parked on the edge of Stanley Park. We had this pact that we wouldn't open our gobs until we got back to the car. We'd heard these stories about being asked the time and with a cockney accent you weren't going to turn around and tell someone the time. It was so hostile. The fans just hated each other. And this year it's started again. In recent years it's quietened down but at Old Trafford this year it was just a disaster again with United fans going crazy. There was an organised fight on the forecourt after the game. The police made the mistake of letting the Liverpool fans out and half-way from the turnstiles to the concourse, the United fans just charged them. There was a line of police trying to protect them and the United fans said 'sod it' and attacked the police as well. It was the worst violence I've seen for many a year. I think nowadays, because United have the success, there's more hatred coming from the Liverpool fans. They're cheesed off with United winning everything, Cantona, and all that stuff. I think it's geography as well; two big cities, Liverpool and Manchester, just in the north-west. I know people who live in Warrington and St Helens and around there – whether it's football-related or not – Mancunians and Scousers end up having fights in pubs. It might be like a gang geography thing, Manc lads versus Liverpool lads, not totally football-related.

JIM THORNTON

I think United and Liverpool are very similar. Two big clubs from big northern cities that have both experienced decline over the past century. They've got an awful lot in common. I don't think it's just about football rivalry; it's about social rivalry and economic rivalry as well. Liverpool had Merseybeat and Manchester have also had some great music success as well. Both clubs have a history tinged with disaster and triumph – Munich and Hillsborough – and on the field they are the two biggest clubs in England without a doubt; two of the biggest clubs in the world. In Norway the United supporters' club has thirty-four thousand members in a country of four million people, Liverpool have twenty-five thousand, Arsenal have four thousand.

It's also the proximity between the two cities. Everyone knows a Scouser; you're working together. Liverpool have been despised by United for a long time, and vice versa. It always gave me great satisfaction in the eighties when Liverpool were winning everything, we always used to throw a spanner in their works. We'd go to Anfield and we'd be twelfth in the table and they'd be walking away with the title and we'd beat them one–nil. That was great for United. That gave you your buzz; it was enough for the year.

You can become bigoted towards Liverpool. It's easy to take a swipe at them. The way people talk about the Kop, the way its closure was covered made me laugh because every famous Scouser who'd moved to London was wheeled out and talked about how they would stand on the Kop and then go to the Cavern. It was so rose-tinted it was unbelievable. But I've got to know some Liverpool people and I like them quite a lot. To be honest, I'd rather spend time with them than some United fans. I think Liverpool as a city is really down on its heels but they are picking up. In terms of youth culture I'm quite envious that they have a club like Cream which Manchester hasn't. But I remember the first time I went to Liverpool and I thought, it's like Beirut, this place. I was scared, seeing ticket touts aged seven outside the Kemlyn Road stand in shell suits and I thought, this is another world. We have a dig at Liverpool and they have a dig at us. There's a healthy rivalry but deep down there's a grudging respect. That side was superb. I'd never say it at the time, but they were superb.

ANDY MITTEN

The tension with Liverpool is still there although it doesn't seem to be as bitter now. It was always there. I suppose the only satisfaction we got for many a year was beating Liverpool now and again. I remember Gordon Strachan's cigar puff when we got an equaliser against Liverpool and then there was the three–three game. We were three–nil up and then Liverpool came back. I've not been to Anfield. It's not a trip I'd make.

Apart from football it seems to be a Manchester–Liverpool thing as well. Sometimes I think Liverpool have a chip on their shoulder. Manchester seems to be a bit wealthier. I suppose Liverpool, because of the past – Derek Hatton and the council – have been shown in a bad light whereas Manchester has escaped that sort of media criticism. You get the same tensions in the north-east. Sunderland and Newcastle fans hate each other's teams passionately. I'm from Durham so it's pretty much equi-distant, so classes would be split fifty–fifty. They don't hate each other as individuals like in Liverpool and Manchester but they hate the teams passionately. Even now I have my step-brother and his family and they are Sunderland fans. You just have to mention Newcastle and there are a load of expletives back.

ALISSON THORNTON

I think in some ways United have a scally, a Liverpool attitude, in terms of the culture of Liverpool. I always think the football team didn't reflect the culture of Liverpool. It seemed from our point of view that Liverpool subjugated the individual to the team machine. The big criticism that United fans had of Liverpool is that most of the time they were incredibly boring to watch. Now I know that's an incredibly biased opinion but I think there is an element of truth in that they were clinical. I've seen United do it a couple of times and I've had to swallow my pride when they've had to do it. But you know that was always the criticism from United fans and I think that reflected the two attitudes of how their teams should perform.

As I say, I think the Liverpool ethos as a team was different from that of the city of Liverpool. I think scallies and Mancs are more or less the same people. I think Manchester is slightly more 'in your face' upfront. Manchester, for all the depression and recession, has not suffered as badly as maybe it should have done, but certainly not as badly as other towns, particularly Liverpool. So I think Manchester has always been quicker to be upbeat and has not had a depression that has pushed down that spirit.

TIM BAMFORD

The rivalry with Liverpool began with City being the real rivals; City started going into decline and Liverpool were getting great success that was, objectively, greater than United had ever obtained. We would term it now as an ABL (Anyone But Liverpool) feeling. It was a mixture of jealousy and resentment and also there was a nagging little bit of respect at the bottom, but you could clearly rationalise the whole thing as whatever Liverpool did – they could win a hundred European Cups – but they would still not be Manchester United. Because we are the greatest. I can remember reading League tables from United's position downwards. We were the top, just count down from there.

I went to Elland Road for a rare away game. Leeds won five–one against United. I was sitting in that little corner stand. I was just so cross. I knew the team were in decline, had been taken apart, but only by Leeds and they didn't count. As we were leaving a few minutes before the end I did a reckless thing that only a fifteen-year-old can do. I called out towards the Kop, 'United!' and my friend pulled me down the stairs. It was just sheer annoyance that this team could ever be better than United. They might have won the game but they could never be better than United. There's only one United.

I worked in Liverpool in the mid-1980s and was a United

fan in Liverpool, which was an odd place to find myself in the midst of Liverpool's success. And that was a strange thing. Whatever Liverpool could do on the football field, Manchester was always going to be a different and a better place to be generally and United reflected that. Hatton was King of Liverpool. The 1980s was like a last vestige. I could sense Liverpool people were clinging on to the former greatness of their football club. Although Everton were great at the time they were very sterile.

LEON SWERLING

I think it goes back to the great side of Liverpool when they were winning everything in sight. And of course at that time United were going through the doldrums before they were relegated. But however bad, and whatever the position of United, they could always come good against Liverpool. They might not beat them but they would always give them a real run for their money. I think that's what it stemmed from. You're always waiting for someone who's top to be knocked down. And Liverpool were tops. You always want to knock down the team who are top of the tree, whatever sport. I think Liverpool were always concerned because United could give them a good run for their money and all the United fans thought that they might not win anything but if they could beat Liverpool, that was just as good. Luckily there were times when we did beat them, especially in the FA Cup, finals and semi-finals. I think those roles are now reversed. At the present moment, United have done a bit better but you do know that it won't last. At the moment Liverpool have not won much but they'll get their team back together again at some point. No one keeps up there forever. I'm sure Liverpool will come good again, just as Arsenal have.

ROLAND COBURN

There used to be a rivalry with City but the team United feel most rivalry with – it borders on hate – is Liverpool, partly because they've done so well over the years and partly because now in the last few years they've been their closest rival. Actually, going over to work in Liverpool has made it more camaraderie. There are Liverpool fans in the office where I work. We have a good joke about it. They pull my leg and wind me up about it and I do the same to them. But you're certainly conscious when you go to the games that there is a lot more antagonism and you certainly feel it. If you hear the Liverpool result and they've lost, it's the biggest cheer you get all afternoon. You always feel that they are the team we have to beat. If you were ahead of them, at the end of the season you might win the League. It took a few years of us winning the title to think we might actually beat Liverpool, so many years of giving goals away in the last five minutes, of being ahead. You used to really worry about the team. It's only in the last two seasons that we've thought we know we can match people, we can be confident about this team. That's probably with the youngsters coming through and knowing that they are playing for the best team. They're not coming through with the burden of expectation that this used to be a great club and hasn't been a great club for twenty years. You get it in reverse now. None of the Liverpool players have won a Championship. They play well for two-thirds of the season, then throw it away and lose silly games. It's a mirror image of what we used to be like.

ROGER HENNELL

We don't seem to both be successful at the same time. It's either one or the other. But I think it's the geographical closeness mainly. Having said that, I don't feel the same loathing for Everton as I do for Liverpool and yet they're in the same city. It's tradition; you have to hate them because they're from Liverpool. I hate Leeds as well. There's no rational reason. I like the city of Leeds very much but I don't like Leeds as a side. It's historical. It's an eighties and nineties thing. But then everybody hates United. There's the work thing as well. If I work in Warrington and United lose, then it's hell in work. It was the same when I worked in Bolton – they're all Liverpool supporters in disguise. If United lost and Liverpool won everyone was delighted. But with Liverpool it's more than just football.

MAXINE DUNHAM

I still think the BBC have this infatuation with Liverpool: there's been nothing but fondness because of their success and I see nothing but jealousy with United's success. I've had some really good discussions about this rivalry with Liverpool. It goes back to pre-football. I tell people we built the Ship Canal so we didn't have to deal with them. A lot of people in Manchester resent the sort of image that is put on Liverpool, that Liverpudlians laugh and joke and Mancunians are this dour, grey people. I don't think either stereotypes are true. But on the football side, Liverpool became everything United were supposed to be. I think that's it. I think United fans have to hold their hands up. I think it was United jealousy, that rivalry in the eighties. We were supposed to win the European Cup in 1958 or shortly afterwards and of course it never happened and then it took ten years and then within a few seasons we were relegated. I think Liverpool became everything we were supposed to. It's still the biggest game of the season. It's the Derby whatever anybody says, Manchester United v Liverpool. And I think a lot of Liverpool fans would agree with that these days.

MATTHEW REYNOLDS

Being a United supporter and living on Merseyside has

obviously at times been rather embarrassing but, you know, you have to stand up for yourself and keep faith in the team. The mickey-taking and the abuse from these Liverpool and Everton supporters has been a bit unbearable at times, but you've always got to put on a brave face.

I've never been tempted to start supporting Liverpool, certainly not. It's one thing I would never have done. OK, I do support Tranmere, but to go and support Everton or Liverpool would have been totally out of order as far as I was concerned. I had no allegiances whatsoever to either team, although I suppose if I did have a leaning it would be towards Everton because I used to go with my brother who was an Evertonian to watch Everton playing United and I did used to stand with my brother in the Gladwys Street End with all these fanatical Evertonians. Sixty thousand people watching these games and invariably United getting beat five–nil or five–one when Alex Young was playing and Roy Vernon, that type of player. So it was quite difficult, but I always kept the faith. The years of Liverpool's domination were quite hard because obviously they were good, no doubt about it, and when you are a club the size of United it's rather difficult to take the fact that you're not winning anything and you're always living in the shadow of a team like Liverpool who, as I said, deserved every success they had.

I suppose in the sixties the likes of Bobby Charlton came along who was, and remains, my absolute hero. I tried to model myself a little bit on Bobby Charlton as a footballer. And Best and Law; they were such charismatic players that really caught the imagination. So they're the sort of reasons that I've always supported United because of the sort of pure football and the passion with which they played the game. Of course there was Nobby Stiles who had his many critics, but I think basically from the time we won the World Cup he became such a great character and such a great star within the British game; a very unlikely star, but there again he was everything that United was all about; the passion, the strength with the flair involved in that. So that's always been my reason for sticking with United. OK, there's been a few gloomy times, but there again if you support a football team, you support a football team and that's the way I look at it. You don't change your allegiances.

My dad never tried to sway me. He'd always try to let me have a good understanding of all football teams. I've always been able to appreciate the finer points of any team, of any game, and basically in that respect I am a supporter of football. To me, football comes first and the rivalry second and that's why I love football and in particular I love Manchester United. I always have and I always will do.

The rivalry is very intense; it is very unhealthy. Obviously, living on Merseyside, I see it far more and actually it's become more than football rivalry. I think it's become city rivalry now but although I don't like saying this, I think there is a certain amount of jealousy between both sets of supporters about the other teams. They don't like to see the other team get any success at all and it's rather a shame actually because both teams have got such a lot to offer. I have a friend who is a Liverpool supporter, who if Manchester United are on the television won't watch the television, won't watch the game. That saddens me rather a lot although I think these days he's coming round a little bit, but that's the sort of mentality that appears to be prevalent in this part of the world with these two cities and these two teams.

I think, unfortunately these days, there appears to be a large gap growing between the financial clout that Manchester has over Liverpool. What I am trying to say is that there's an undoubted gap between the two communities. Merseyside seems to be slipping backwards and Manchester's gaining strength and you can see that by the nature of the likes of the new big shopping centre at Old Trafford, the siting of the new War Museum. It's that type of thing. Whereas Manchester seems to be booming, Liverpool is slipping behind. And I think there's little bits of jealousy in that respect.

KEVIN McALENY

There's not so much amusing banter now. But for humour, Liverpool always used to be good. There is this hatred and rivalry between them. Both sets of fans realise that both fans do follow their club through thick and thin and everywhere. So you do have a respect for each other. When United played Liverpool in the FA Cup final we all had a game of soccer outside Wembley and there must have been a hundred and fifty a side. It was great fun, all the fans playing. One guy started kicking a ball around, then someone else joined in. This was about eight o'clock in the morning. It was fine, we played for about an hour. All it needed was one bad tackle and then it ruined it. But there was all the banter going on. Everyone was pretending they were players. Someone was Rushie, someone was Pearson. Good fun. There was only nastiness towards the end when there were far too many to work out who was who.

ROLAND COBURN

CHAPTER TEN

Reporting the Reds

'There's always something to write about with United,' says David Meek, the former *Manchester Evening News* football correspondent. Meek, who had begun his journalistic career at the *Evening News* as a political leader writer, was asked to cover United in the aftermath of the Munich air disaster. The *News*'s own football correspondent, Tom Jackson, had been killed and someone was urgently needed to take over. It was a difficult time and when Meek was asked he unselfishly accepted the challenge, initially only until the end of the season. In 1996 he retired after almost forty years of covering United. As he says, with United there was always something to write about.

For any football writer, covering a major club like United is a dream. Of course there are the games to be covered every week but there is also the usual transfer speculation, injuries, the superstar players themselves and these days, the business side of the club. Then there is Europe. United is well geared up to the world of the media. Old Trafford boasts a splendid press conference room and even a bar for the journalists who cover their games. Facilities are as good as anywhere. But it wasn't always so, as Albert Thorpe remembers. There was a time when you were lucky to get a cup of tea at half time, and to do that you had to make your way to a shack behind the stand. In those days, the job of the football reporter was far more difficult. Telephones were few and far between; there were no laptop computers, no modems, no mobile phones. You had to make do with a pencil and paper and the nearest public phone.

But there were compensations. Relations with the club were much closer. Managers, coaches and players had nothing to fear from the small coterie of mostly local reporters. They could afford to be friendly with no worries that anything said off the record or in a moment of thoughtlessness would find its way into a Monday morning headline. Nor did the players have any worries about having a drink or two, or a few jokes. There was a trust. In those days the big nationals never sent their news reporters anywhere near Old Trafford in search of a story. Busby and company knew every one of the journalists regularly covering their club. At the end of the game Busby and his successors would make a few minutes to drift over to the press box to have a chat. 'Anything you want to know?' Matt would ask. And he'd give straight answers to straight questions. That's not to say that Matt always appreciated what the press wrote. There were bound to be moments when they differed. If Matt didn't like what had been written, he'd say so the next time he saw the journalist.

The trust went both ways. In return, journalists were given favours. They could travel on the team bus, talk to the players at will, were given access to inside information and offered the occasional scoop. It helped the journalists do their job and generally made life easier for them. And nor should it ever be forgotten that Munich was a tragedy not just for the club and its followers but also for the world of journalism, which lost eight of its finest scribes.

These days the trust is no longer there. The pressures are much greater; managers and players are always their guard. A pint at lunchtime could so easily find its way on to the front pages as a drinking binge. The press have almost become the enemy. The players are now superstars on a far different planet to those in the past. Thirty years ago you could pick up the

307

phone, call a player at home and arrange to interview him in the local pub over a pint. Today, you'd be lucky if you could get his number. Most are ex-directory and forced to change their numbers every six months. Instead, you'd have to go through an agent, maybe even negotiate an interview fee, and when you got there you might find the agent present. For sure, you wouldn't get much in the way of straight answers.

Then, of course, there has been an explosion of media personnel. Not only do the local papers cover United but all the major nationals will have a football writer assigned solely to a club as large as United. On top of that there are the local television stations, the local radio stations, MUTV, Sky, and other cable companies as well as a glut of freelancers. Each year the press box seems to get fuller. You might once have been able to squeeze the press on to the back seat of the team bus but these days you would need an extra coach to accommodate them. It's all become more formalised. You begin to understand why the gap between the club and media has widened.

There's always an ethical tightrope to walk. Even in the old days there could be trouble. David Meek himself was critical of the club over the sacking of Frank O'Farrell, arguing in the *Manchester Evening News* that O'Farrell should have been given more time. The club didn't like that and told the *Evening News* so. Meek had all his press privileges taken away, making his job that much more difficult. Meek was right to be critical if that was what he believed. A local newspaper should not be the mouthpiece of any football club, no matter what favours it grants their football writers. And in the past far too many football writers have turned a blind eye to some unsavoury goings on, simply to protect their own jobs.

Being a football writer is not quite as glamorous as many imagine. Deadlines are tight, conditions awkward, saying the same thing in different words always a challenge. Writing six hundred quality words by 6 p.m., or even earlier, is not the easiest task. It requires skill, commitment and experience.

Most of us could not match the likes of David Lacey's prose if we were given a week, let alone an hour or so. At the end of the day, football clubs need the press as much as the press needs them. But at times they make strange bedfellows.

———◆———

When I joined Granada Television I had to give football reporting up for a time, but not for very long because I then started working Saturdays for the *Sunday Telegraph* for about fifteen years and then for the *Mail on Sunday* for about ten years until I stopped doing it by choice about six years ago, probably early nineties. But I'd done it for over thirty years. So I used to get to Old Trafford a great deal and learnt a great deal as journalists do – a great deal more than the average fan does – about who pulls the strings, who runs the club. Unless you're different to me, you get a bit jaundiced because you probably learn too much. The average fan is probably better off sometimes not knowing the various machinations of what goes on behind the scenes at major clubs because the more you know, the more you're inclined to fall a bit out of love with it all because you realise it became a very big money-making business.

But memories of United of course go back all those years. I saw lots of the European games; I saw Best at his best. I used to love covering for Granada, particularly the homecomings of various European triumphs, the FA Cup triumphs. I did many outside broadcasts from Manchester Town Hall. I used to go out with the players later and get drunk; at least they got more drunk and I got slightly drunk, in places like the Crossfords. I've been in there with the Stepneys and the Greenoffs and the Crerands and all the rest of them after those huge celebrations and the public function side of it at the Town Hall. Then they would go and let their hair down in a very big way.

BOB GREAVES

The function of being a football reporter has changed surprisingly little. The technical trappings have changed with the advent of new technology but the principles outside the office have changed very little. We use a keyboard now instead of a typewriter and the operation is much slicker. But the principles, such as competing for stories, remain the same. The problems for a local reporter of balancing the interests of the football club against the interests of the newspaper remain the same. One can upset one side or the other just as much now as in those days. Sir Matt Busby was exactly the same as Alex Ferguson in that sense, wanting to establish a trust with the local reporter, which was exactly the quality Alex Ferguson remarked on as I retired – do you have trust or not?

How does my week pan out? The beginning of the week, Monday, is really starting with the climax of the previous week, writing a match report of the Saturday game and at the same time starting to write stories looking ahead to the next match. My day would begin with giving my verdict on the previous match and then talking with the manager by phone, checking on injuries, transfer news, team developments and so on. Then I would start to prepare for the next day which would involve going down to the training ground and talking to the manager face to face, getting ideas into my notebook that might run for the week. Also there are features for the Saturday football paper to be developed. That would then set the pattern for the rest of the week. If we were away I might travel on a Friday, or if they were away mid-week I might be staying over somewhere.

Access has become more formal; it's harder to get individual access because of the growing media interest, particularly in the last few years. Clubs have reacted by organising the access. By that I mean that in the old days I would travel on the team bus to away matches – the *Evening Chronicle* reporter and the *Evening News* reporter always travelled with the team everywhere, stayed in the same hotel. We didn't actually eat with them but we'd be on an adjoining table. But that's no longer possible. Now there are two local radio stations, clubcall, a much bigger club programme, MUTV, a club magazine, the website, plus you have national newspapers assigning specialists to write about them. We've now arrived at a dozen people. Well, you can't put a dozen people on the team bus. It would be far too intrusive, so now we have more formal press conferences with one or maybe two players coming with the manager to talk to the media. It makes it harder to get stuff on your own or to make contact with players on an informal basis. There's a tendency for the manager to control things, particularly with the younger players. He'll tell them not to give interviews unless a newspaper has contacted him first for permission. That makes it harder.

At Old Trafford we have a super press conference room whereas before, Matt Busby would give a press conference in that he might or might not wander over and give us a few thoughts or the pressmen would seek out the players themselves. Because there weren't as many of us it wasn't a problem. But it's still the same ethical dilemmas. If you wrote something that was upsetting for Matt Busby, something he didn't like, he would waylay you. I always remember down at Old Trafford, by the dressing rooms, there was also the match official's room. If Matt wanted a few words he would take you into the referee's room and have a go at you. Alex Ferguson is a different personality. He won't pull you to one side; he's much more upfront. If a reporter has upset him, the first time he sets his eyes on him he'll give a stream of invective. He can blister paint at ten yards. But it's the same principle. It's all part of the dilemma of walking this tightrope. If you go completely making the manager happy, the editor won't be happy because you might be patently whitewashing a situation and ignoring issues that should be tackled. The editor will respond and tell you you're being too soft, we want a bit of bite in your criticism, you've got to give your opinion, don't dodge the issues.

My spectacular fall from grace as far as the club were

concerned was when they were sacking Frank O'Farrell. I thought it unfair. They'd already sacked Wilf McGuinness after eighteen months. The knives were out and there was talk of sacking Frank after eighteen months. There were basic problems of an ageing team to be sorted out. I wrote a piece saying be fair to Frank and that even if they go down there's no point in sacking the manager. You have to give him time. If you want to allocate blame, well certainly the manager has to take some share but there's also the players, the supporters, and the directors who failed to plan properly for the successor to Busby. Well, the directors didn't like that and the secretary wrote to the editor to say that David Meek was no longer welcome to travel to away games with the club; I was being kicked off the bus. I was never invited back on. That was a parting of the ways. But I realised that it was probably better not to be too close, because if you had to be critical people didn't feel you were stabbing them in the back. I don't think many teams, certainly not the big teams, take the local press around with them now.

I've also fallen from grace a number of times the other way when I've covered something up for the club or been told something in confidence and haven't betrayed that confidence and maybe a story has appeared in another newspaper and the editor has said hey, we should have had that first. The fateful admission in those circumstances is to say, well I did know about it but the manager asked me not to use it yet because it might alert other clubs to this particular player. Then the editor wipes the floor with you and tells you not to sit on stories. It's walking on a knife's edge. It's not the same dilemma for a national reporter; they're more distant and if they upset the club, that's just too bad, it doesn't matter. But for a local reporter, if you upset the club, you are risking cutting off the source of your information.

A local paper sells papers on the back of the success of the club. If United and City won, the Pink sold a lot of copies. If

City lost and United won we wouldn't sell as many. But if Manchester United lost the sales plummeted, so their fortunes are intertwined.

DAVID MEEK

I started to do things for the club in the mid-seventies. I became the club statistician, recording the goalscorers and line-ups for the various teams. One thing led to another. I worked in Trafford Park as an overhead crane driver. I was made redundant so I started doing more part-time work for the club. My first job was to set up the club museum. Then I became editor of the programme and started taking photographs. Most of that has gone now and I'm just editor of the programme and club statistician. It's been an amazing experience.

I can remember travelling with the club to Moscow when they played Moscow Torpedo. I went out sightseeing with the players around Moscow. We walked around Red Square. It was just an incredible moment, to be in this famous place with so famous a football team. Lenin's mausoleum was open and we filed in, past the waiting queue. Then they took us to see some of the others who were buried in the walls of the Kremlin – Yuri Gagarin and Stalin. I've now travelled extensively with the team but I always remember that moment. I've been to Israel, South Africa, the Caribbean, Europe; I've been all over with them. The stuff of dreams.

Denis Law was my real hero. He's the only idol I've ever had. I was devoted to the club, not to individual players. But he was so easy to associate with. He was a bit of a villain, a rogue. He'd occasionally go upfield and kick someone but you could forgive him. He'd acknowledge the crowd as well, playing to the audience. He was an entertainer. George Best was the favourite with the girls, Bobby Charlton was the favourite of the dads but Denis Law was the favourite of the boys.

CLIFF BUTLER

We had world-class players – Best, Law and so on. But the media has changed. We used to have the journalists with us when we travelled abroad. We'd come home the following day so after the game we'd sit there and have a beer with the journalists. Nice and informal. Never get that now. We're far more cautious, something you may say half-joking gets in the papers. It's sad really. There were some smashing reporters – Frank McGhee, Desmond Hackett, Alan Thompson, Ron Crowther; all good reporters.

Society's changed. You've got to be more protective of the players. Life's changed from the fifties and sixties. The demands on players now is horrendous. The demands, not just games, everybody wants a piece of them. Even though you had world-class players playing for the club then, Bestie was the only pop star really. The pop stars and film stars only wanted to be around George. He integrated football into all that. He started it all. There was only George who got the modelling contracts. He elevated it to that level. The profile of players now is far higher.

BRIAN KIDD

I was always a part-time football reporter, a Saturdays man. Basically my first games were for the *Daily Mail* but in those days, in the fifties, all that you were expected to do was report the game and make sure you didn't miss a big story. You weren't expected to harass and chase players for quotes a great deal, even for the Monday morning papers. You probably needed to get a quote from the manager, or if somebody scored four goals you'd try to find him and get a line out of him, but there was no great insistence.

Then when I started working for the *Sunday Telegraph*, that frankly was a doddle because again this was in the days before there was insistence on after-the-match quotes, made-up stories, exaggerated stories. In those days you simply did a match report. No sports editor was chasing me to say why didn't you get so-and-so to say so-and-so. All he wanted for the Sunday papers was a match report.

It then developed, of course, into the Monday morning papers deciding that they didn't want mere match reports, they wanted something totally different. You could mention the match but they didn't want a rundown of every goal or every incident. They wanted quotes and so the competition among journalists over a few years became quite marked. The competition became fierce and ever fiercer so you found yourself watching the game, making notes; but you then spent an hour, an hour and a half in the bowels of the building standing in those draughty concrete corridors under the main stand at Old Trafford, trying to grab this player, that player, the opposing captain, the referee, the managers, trying to stir quotes up over was it a penalty or wasn't it, what do you mean you don't know, haven't you got a view, yes you've got a view, fine. It just became much more of a chore and much more hard work. What had been very pleasurable became a strain and then of course, although I never worked for the major tabloids, having seen them in operation sometimes I knew I didn't want to work for the major tabloids because they were working in little covies, two or three, swapping quotes. Somebody had got a quote from somebody so they'd swap with their mate but they wouldn't give it their other mates and it all became a bit tawdry. I had no regrets a few years back, giving it up, and I don't miss sitting in frozen press boxes with numb fingers round a telephone to London for hour on hour on end, it always seemed.

Then again the competition between the newspapers became so intense that when I first started reporting for the *Mail on Sunday*, they would settle for in most cases one match report, say Manchester United v Everton, and so at the end of the game you would ring in at a designated time your three hundred and fifty or five hundred words on that game. Then, depending on who they were playing, say Everton, then they'd want Irish connections, Scottish connections; they'd want a

315

running report – say four hundred words at half-past three after the game had been playing for thirty minutes, plus one hundred words at half time, plus a hundred and fifty at five past four, plus one paragraph to wrap up the rest of the game on the dot as the whistle blew at twenty to five, plus an intro to round that particular version off for the Irish and the Scottish editions. Then they would want a five-hundred-word precis at twenty to six when you'd been down to the bowels and got the manager and the players. And of course they weren't paying any extra money, so for x pounds, one week you found yourself doing twice the work. It just became hard work. What should have been a pleasure plus a bit of hard work became hard work with no pleasure at all and so I had no regrets at giving it up. And I now fill my Saturday afternoons by listening to Radio Five Live, by going to the shops and I think, would anybody in their right mind sit in a seat in their garden in November, December, January and February for the better part of two hours in three degrees of frost with no gloves on and a pen and a piece of paper, a notebook and a telephone at a table at the side of you, watching a game on television or watching the squirrels run about? The answer's no, there was no pleasure in it. When I was younger there was pleasure. When I got older, 'pas de pleasure', as the French might say.

BOB GREAVES

My whole family supported United, and it wasn't a question of if I became a Red, but when. The dedication that this now takes, travelling around the world and England, baffles every family member, but from as young an age as I can remember, I've been passionate, almost obsessional about United.

My first actual Old Trafford match came when I was almost six, in 1976, and for the next few years it was a mix of watching games and anxiously annoying all my mates as I waited for that next greatly anticipated trip. The Theatre of Dreams means as much to a young supporter as it does older ones, and that excitement of going to matches is perhaps at its brightest in your formative years. You eagerly soak up all that comes your way, from getting into the grounds as early as possible to eating up all the statistics, programmes and information that comes your way. I even fondly remember the Old Trafford Wagon Wheel.

So from this came a treasured League match ticket book in J-stand, along with the inevitable teenage introduction to alcohol and its effect in influencing time arrival at games, to a subsequent move to my cultural home in K-stand. By the start of 1987, a lengthy period of following United had led to many acquaintances and friendships, so that each match day became a social gathering of a large group of people. This, remember, was the time of the fans' fight-back against poor conditions which had seen a handful of unofficial and poorly produced magazines at other grounds. The simple question at that time was why hadn't the biggest club in the country got one – what was called a fanzine.

Our supporters' association decided to start up its own newsletter and by a system of no bugger wanting the hassle, I was elected editor. The great thing about this fanzine period was that not only was there an initial euphoria in doing something that nobody else had done before at football, you were sailing with the wind all the time, not knowing what to expect. A lot of it was hit and miss and perhaps by being such a young age a lot of the material did sail close to the wind, but that was – at the time – the allure of fanzines. They weren't wanting to be the slickly produced fans' voice that they are now. There is something I miss in finishing an unproofed piece on the Friday and selling it the next day after I've helped the printer staple dodgy pages together the night before.

The fanzine quickly moved from selling in pubs to outside the ground. The first real time was against Liverpool in that memorable match of New Year's Day of 1989 when we saw Fergie's Fledglings hammer John Barnes and co. three–one to give us at least something to smile about during a dreadful period. That was a ground-breaking issue for us; the content strong, strong enough indeed to elicit response from a number of people at the club. The message was perhaps OTT but exactly what United fans were feeling; that we had had enough of continual failure and so many false dawns. The sentiment expressed, however, was realised by some at the club as genuine but from then on, United fanzines were to be known as ones that would live on the cutting edge by refusing to toe the party line.

When things are going badly it is up to the fanzines to express feelings and try and level a general unhappiness. That year again proved to be a poor one on the pitch but a number of other United fanzines arrived – most notably *Red Issue* – and what we had started helped others. Two regular *Red News* contributors left to form *Red Issue* after a difference of opinion on where we would go after that New Year's Day issue and from then on we all continued to make a United fanzine identity. Where the importance lay in those days was to poke fun – by cruel and constructive criticism. And also point out areas where we thought our problems lay. As we suddenly became more successful, fanzines had to evolve and also keep up with the times. That is why I believe they are now sleek in style and take up larger issues, such as the fans' treatment in Galatasaray. Being the voice of the fans is as important now as it was ten years ago but there was a certain buzz about those early 'What's going to happen next?' days.

Contributors at first came from a small pool from our travelling group but as the years passed, so anonymous people began to contribute and become regulars. At last Alex Ferguson was seeing his and our dream bear fruit and, when trophies came that we never thought possible during the mid eighties, it was as if the weight of years of toil were being lifted. Perhaps now when we argue about finishing second we really are being greedy, because when we lost the League in 1992, I left Upton Park, Old Trafford and Anfield during that dreadful week thinking we could never win the Championship. That we did just twelve months later is dream-like and an achievement that should never be forgotten.

With those early Cup final and European Cup-Winners' Cup final wins there came a realisation that the pitfalls of fanzine life, having to sell at every match, was making me miss a vital part of my United life and culture. The fanzine was in a very healthy position, but although at the time it seemed that stopping it was permanent, I always kept the P. O. Box address going. That seemed to signal that *Red News* would come back some day after that last issue of 1990.

The sabbatical started at the Palace Cup final and continued until early 1993, with a period of European travel to places like Montpellier and Rotterdam that I'll never forget. I missed some aspects of the paper but definitely not the selling! And I truly believe that taking time out was vital for the way that *Red News* now appears. Although I didn't miss a game during that period, when *Red News* came back (just as Eric arrived) it was much the better.

From then on it was a case of watching success after success and reaching heights I never dared think possible. My favourite times have been compiling Championship specials but my dream is to produce that European Cup issue! Despite dreaming of the days when we came up with the name *Red News* as we basically only had those letters left on the Letraset, we have made the inevitable move to gloss and some colour pages. People want different things from a fanzine but their importance is still vital at Old Trafford as the Murdoch takeover has shown.

United fanzines must never lose their humour nor their value. We are fanzines, a voice for the fans but neither too important nor too unimportant to realise that United fans will make their own judgements. We have our own views as contributors but that doesn't mean we shouldn't represent the standpoint of the many diverse groups at the club.

Although the club distance themselves from *Red News*, the

relationship isn't a bad one. Interviews we really want are Fergie and Eric (we'll never give up hope) and the only person who has signalled total disapproval is Our Martin Edwards. But if he didn't feel like that we wouldn't be doing our job right! So as I sell in the exact same spot outside Old Trafford as eleven years ago, our team of contributors are given their deadlines and I spend a manic week getting everything ready and then usually either cock it up on the last night or see a major story (like the Murdoch takeover news) happen as the issue is at the printer. But don't overvalue your importance . . .

I really do consider editing the fanzine as an honour and a privilege. The good things far outweigh the bad and as technology continues to see changes in the way that fanzines are created, their importance in creating an unofficial and uncensored voice for ordinary United fans who have supported the club all their lives will never diminish. Our statement is 'to keep the red flag flying high'. *Red News*, as do all the other fanzines, gives at least some opportunity for normal Reds to have their own culture.

BARNEY CHILTON

Ever since I've been of a conscious age I've supported Manchester United. And I suppose that can only come from one place: your parents and particularly your father. My father was a United fan; I'm not quite sure the reasons for him being a United fan but I would take a guess that it's the fact my father's uncle Charlie Mitten was a United player. He played in the 1948 Cup final; older generations have a fond memory of him. He was one of the first players to go abroad. He had a very interesting career. But ever since I've been six or seven I've supported Manchester United.

When I was about eight or nine I can remember saying to my dad, please can you take me to a game? My dad was a footballer himself. He was playing for various teams so going to football matches was something I've done all my life. When

I got to about ten or eleven my father cut back on his playing and I started pushing for him to take me to the games. Now he was never a religious match-going man, my father. He said he much preferred to play than watch but he took me a few times. When I was about twelve or thirteen I was given a little responsibility and I was allowed to start going to games by myself with my friends. I've got nothing but happy memories, despite the football being dross – this was about 1987–88. The camaraderie among the fans and the independence was superb. You know, you try your first swig of beer and pretend you like it. Well, it was a bit like that but I started going to all the key games quite quickly. Then when I was fifteen I started the fanzine *United We Stand*. I remember being quite an angry young kid; I would be writing to clubs complaining that I had been charged £4 to stand on the open bridge end at Nottingham Forest when I only earned £2 a week from my paper round.

For whatever reason, I started the fanzine. I would say it was 1989 and fanzines, in my opinion, were not getting the respect they deserved. Decisions were being made on behalf of football fans with football fans not consulted. I didn't think that was right. That's what prompted the initial wave of fanzines all around the country. I've always had a sort of entrepreneurial spirit, even before the fanzine. I used to sell hot dogs to my friends at school and smuggle cans of Coke into the classroom and sell them. So this idea of producing a fanzine was really exciting. So I set about it on my mum's typewriter. I remember my friends saying it'll never work. But I was so determined to prove them wrong. We had all the first issue photocopied. The first issue we sold forty-eight copies but we ended up selling three hundred of the next issue. I remember going into my art class with a £20 note in my pocket from the sales that previous Saturday and showing it to everyone. The fanzine continued to develop quite rapidly. By issue eight we were selling three thousand copies. People assume that we are just pocketing that money. That's not the case: we have high overheads and production costs. We are a fully legitimate business now, selling twelve thousand copies per issue. All my friends were selling it; we were collating it on the kitchen table and selling it outside the house. It was really exciting and they would get commission and that would pay for them to go into the game. It also meant that I could afford to watch United away.

When they went into Europe I didn't go to see the games in 1990 because I was only sixteen and my mum wouldn't let me, but by 1991 I was going to the European away games and writing about them. I got to seventeen and was doing my A levels and I thought, I quite like this journalism, and I decided to do a degree in journalism at Preston. It was difficult to get in but I believe I got in because of the fanzine. I carried on watching United quite fanatically, never missing games. I remember organising a trip to Amsterdam for all my university friends. It was a football-free weekend and it was about £80 – go to Amsterdam on the Friday, come back on the Monday by coach. Then at the last minute, United rescheduled their game against Queens Park Rangers, so I ended up leaving Manchester at 3.30 on the Friday afternoon, travelling on the overnight ferry and getting into Amsterdam at nine on the Saturday morning, flying from Amsterdam to Heathrow to watch United play QPR, and then flying straight back to Amsterdam to meet my friends on the Saturday night. I got searched by customs at Heathrow. 'Where've you come from?' they asked. I was quite suspect having come from Amsterdam, young English lad as well. 'When did you arrive there?' 'This morning,' I replied. So they thought, right, we better question you, so they pulled me to one side. 'Why have you only been in Amsterdam for fifty minutes?' 'I want to watch Manchester United.' They pulled me into the investigating room and I had to show my match tickets. In the end they just said, 'I think you're crazy; I wouldn't do it myself, off you go.'

The fanzine continued to grow and that tied in with a very successful period. I was organising coaches to games, and all my friends were going. It was great football. You're visiting places for the first time in your life and you're visiting European cities and there's all the cultural side. I was still doing the fanzine at university; that's one reason why I decided to study journalism in Preston rather than London. I used to spend my weekends in Manchester doing the fanzine. I was surrounded by a bunch of budding journalists anyhow and a couple of them were United fans and they were only too keen to help out.

In the summer of 1994, with a year left at university, I was approached by the official United magazine and asked to write for them and I've been doing that ever since. Last year we were getting offers to buy the fanzine out. I was not entirely comfortable with that because we'd put a lot of work into it and I wasn't sure that a fanzine should be about that, so in the summer of 1997 we decided to go for it ourselves with a company called Zone who had expertise in areas we didn't – advertising, distribution, photography. So the fanzine went national last year. It's been a lot of hard work but at the end of last season we did a survey and sixty per cent of our readers said they preferred the new format.

We have a pool of about ten to twelve regular writers. I think my greatest achievement has been in getting that pool of writers together so that it doesn't focus on me alone. We have a team. Possibly our best writer is anonymous and he's written for us for eight years. All I know is that he is from north Manchester. He's an idol of mine. I've never met him; I once put an appeal in the fanzine and said please send us your address, we love you. And he wrote to us and said that due to reasons of national security I cannot reveal my identity, so that was that. Every month we get handwritten reams of quality writing, grammatically perfect, from him. I've got kids from council estates in north Manchester to Jim White of the *Guardian*, from Oxbridge graduate Joyce Woolridge to others. It's quality-led now. We plan it and are quite strict on the deadlines as we have to book things in. It's published monthly during the football season, ten a year. We've got subscribers in thirty-four countries throughout the world.

There's a healthy fanzine scene at United. *Red Issue* deserves a mention; we have a good relation with them. They get criticised for being vitriolic, but they've got their niche – each to their own. It still gives me pride when I get the latest copy. When I stop getting that buzz, I'll quit and move on to something else.

ANDY MITTEN

I loved being a journalist. If you were freelance it was very, very hard work. I used to envy the staff men who just had one piece to write. To do just one piece for Sunday morning – that was bliss. I would have to do all the little regional and local papers. I also had to do runners. The phone would ring every fifteen minutes or so and you'd have to put over the latest play and while you were talking, something would happen and you'd miss it. That's when you had to rely on your mates. I used to sit in front of Eric Thornton and now and again I'd get a dig in the back and he'd say, 'Was that Johnson?' and I'd say, 'No it was Jones,' and he'd say 'OK, thanks.' We all had to rely on each other. It was hard work doing a runner. When I later came to doing just one piece for the Sunday morning, it was easy.

I did a lot for the *News of the World*. They wanted the teams only at half time and five to six hundred words at five o'clock. Now, sometimes the game didn't finish until ten to five. I'd jot certain first paragraphs down and then change them. The biggest nightmare was a goalless draw. So, you'd start with some corny phrase like 'defences were on top' but it could be a struggle finding five hundred words. But then I would fill up with quotes after the match. Matt Busby was very good and the players. I also did it for the Scottish and Irish papers. The Irish papers would want to know about Tony Dunne and the Scottish papers about any Scottish lads; they didn't bother about anybody else.

I'd do four reports before half time and four after. A paper would book calls at say 3.10, 3.25 and half time and then another three or four in the second half. I'd rent a phone and it would be on the bench in front of me. The phone would ring at 3.10 and I'd tell them what had happened and then hang up. It was hard work but I liked it.

At half time we used to go down the stairs to the end corner of the ground and there was a hut, a wooden hut, not even the size of this room and there would be a lady in there who would give us a drink, some tea and biscuits. Later we got a magnificent press room with waiters. Matt Busby would come in after an hour because he would have been with the other directors, and Louis Edwards would come as well. They used to say, 'What do you want to know?' Today they don't want to know. Wasn't like that then. It was so good. All the journalists who came for the opposing side will tell you it was the best place to go because of the way they were treated. They got the stories, the drink, the access, they could talk to the players.

After the night matches we never got home. I've been there until midnight. It would get to half-past ten and Busby would come out after seeing the directors and the bar had been closed and he'd say, 'Open up, let's have another drink before you go home.' And it would be midnight before you got away. That was Manchester United. In a small way it helped them come famous because the press were always treated well. The press lads said the only club to come anywhere near that was Arsenal where you were also treated well.

Busby always used to call me 'son'. That stuck in my mind. Like the players said, he was a gentleman to everybody. Never known him, even when the result had gone the wrong way, to be irritated or to give you an answer you didn't want. His voice settled you down. Happy days. I'd go back tomorrow.

ALBERT THORPE

I grew up in a football household. I went to a rugby-playing school and I was very much into rugby from a playing point of view, but I was never very far away from soccer because my father was the correspondent covering York City for the local paper which was the *Yorkshire Evening Press*. When I wasn't playing rugby I went to see York City and became one of their fans. That's where I got the romance of soccer and the romance of newspapers from.

When I went into journalism I did not set out to be a football writer; I set out just to be a journalist, which I did in York with the *Yorkshire Post* and then in Australia. I joined the *Manchester Evening News* in 1956 as their leader writer and political writer. Then came the Munich air crash in February 1958. The editor knew my soccer background. Our man who'd covered United – Tom Jackson – for twenty-eight years was one of the journalists killed in the air crash, and the editor asked if I would help out in the emergency and start covering Manchester United. Of course, from a newspaper point of view it was a big, big, story. I agreed. It was supposed to be a temporary post. But they started on a bit of a gallop and a Cup run which took them to Wembley, so the editor said stay with it until they get to Wembley. And then at the end of the season he said, 'What do you want to do?' I was in a dilemma, but by that time I was bitten by the football bug.

I found Manchester United a very difficult club to walk away from, although I knew that once I accepted a job covering Manchester United, that would probably be it, career-wise. However, I went for it and thought I'd do it for a couple of years; but, as I say, they are a difficult club to walk away from. There's always something new and different happening; they are such innovators, and have been throughout the forty years I've been associated with them. There's never a dull moment, there's always something newsworthy happening, so I stayed with it until my retirement in 1995. So that was where the romance came from.

I went as a spectator to see some of the first European games. I saw that outstanding dramatic game against Bilbao when they fought back from five–three down. I remember standing on the terraces of Maine Road and the overwhelming passion that was coming from the crowd for this team of Busby Babes. I didn't know a lot about them at the time because I was a newcomer to Manchester, but I couldn't be anything but affected by the excitement and the passion that was coming from the terraces in response to the drama and passion on the field. It was also the first floodlit game I had ever seen.

DAVID MEEK

CHAPTER ELEVEN

Manchester United plc

In 1991 the Manchester United board took a gigantic step by opting to become a public limited company. They were not the first football club to take that initiative – Tottenham Hotspur had beaten them to it by eight years – and they would certainly not be the last. The decision to float United on the stock exchange was greeted with general approval. The club had already been subject to a couple of takeover bids. The first from Robert Maxwell barely got off the ground but a second bid by the businessman Michael Knighton came within a whisker of succeeding. In hindsight, had his £30 million offer succeeded it would have been the bargain of all seasons. In the end, Knighton's audacious antics (which included a pre-match, ball-juggling exhibition in front of the Stretford End) failed ignominiously as he ran short of cash. A few bankers must now surely look back and cringe at their failure to lend Knighton a few more pounds.

United's search for new financial partners had been spurred by the need for investment money. The Hillsborough disaster of April 1989 looked set to bring an end to terracing at football grounds and in order to tear down the Stretford End and construct a new stand, United needed around £10 million. Other improvements also had to be made, adding up to a fortune United simply did not have. Knighton's takeover bid offered a solution but once it had failed United were left in the lurch with little alternative, as chairman Martin Edwards says in this chapter, but to float on the stock exchange if they were to raise the capital for their building programme. The Knighton bid had also left its bruises, with Martin Edwards a little more determined to keep the business in-house. A flotation was the obvious scenario and for the fans it seemed that such a scheme would protect United from outsiders.

Six years later United were recording profits of over £29 million, with a merchandising arm that included a couple of megastores at Old Trafford and an outlet in Malaysia, providing a total turnover of £80 million per year. There were also restaurants, a museum, conference facilities and Manchester United Television. You could even get married at Old Trafford. United had become a multi-million-pound business.

But with it came inevitable changes. The Stretford End, where generations had been introduced to the club and its heritage, had been torn down and in its place a new stand had been constructed. Old Trafford, to the dismay of many, had now become an all-seater stadium. Prices had also risen, often beyond the reach of many traditional supporters, while the success of the club had meant full-house notices going up with every game. Getting hold of tickets for the occasional supporter had become almost impossible. The tradition of queuing up outside the ground at two on a Saturday afternoon, swaying and singing in the crush of the Stretford End, was gone. By the mid 1990s Old Trafford had become virtually season ticket only and even the building of a swanky new stand that upped the crowd limit to 55,000 seemed to make little difference. The only other way to get tickets was through a membership scheme that already boasted 140,000 members vying for a few token tickets. Those who missed out were the less well-off, kids and teenagers. A whole generation of young people were forced to become armchair supporters of the club. United seemed to be catering for a new class of clientele. Executive boxes, dining areas, restaurants were attracting money. A new elite, not just at United, was being attracted to the game.

It didn't all go down well with many of those traditional supporters who felt the game was being whipped away from them. Football, once the prerogative of the working classes, was quickly becoming a middle-class spectator sport. But then society too was changing. Increased leisure time, competition, demands for more comfort at sporting venues, television and so forth had all increased the pressure on football to update itself. There was no going back, although many might have yearned for those old days with the passion, the atmosphere and the informality of going to a game.

Football had also become a business. More and more clubs had hired top-class executives to run their clubs. There was money to be made and clubs would have been foolish to ignore the opportunities. The more money, the more attractive the stadium and the more power clubs could wield on the transfer market. Much of the change was due to television and the £400 million deal which Sky Television had agreed with the Premiership. Money was suddenly pouring into the game, making it an even more attractive business. Live television also upped the price for sponsorship deals and delivered European football on terrestrial television at peak viewing hours. The days of hooliganism, dangerous terracing, and appalling toilet facilities were a thing of the past.

Then in September 1998 the inevitable happened. Despite the view that floating on the stock exchange would keep the Maxwells and Knightons at bay, it had always made United liable to a takeover bid. Like any other profitable business, United was suddenly susceptible to predators. The predator in this case turned out to be another newspaper magnate, Rupert Murdoch and his News International company, owner of Sky Television, the *Sun* newspaper, and a host of other newspaper and publishing interests around the world. United negotiated and upped the sale price to £450 million. It was a massive deal but it had its critics. Murdoch was not liked, regarded by some as a Citizen Kane with an empire already too fearsome and encroaching. His tie-up with Sky satellite and digitial television seemed a little too close for comfort. But on the positive side, Murdoch possessed an open treasure chest that promised an untold fortune to sign the finest players in the world. There was talk of Ronaldo, Roberto Carlos, you name them and they were coming to United. Money would be no object.

In the end the deal fell through, but it was a close thing and it was only the painstaking efforts of fans which stopped the takeover. The board were clearly in favour but the supporters nevertheless succeeded in referring the bid to the Monopolies Commission, and they in turn rejected it as not in the best interests of football. Fortunately the Government chose to back that view.

But of course even if the deal had gone through, the extra cash would not have guaranteed success. Football is littered with managers who have thrown fortunes at the transfer market without ever winning any silverware. Football is about much more than that. It's about signing the right player, and as Brian Kidd testifies, it's about signing players with the right character as well as the right skills. Eleven £20 million players do not necessarily make a team.

The spirit of the club in many ways has not changed much because, at the end of the day, the core business is ninety minutes of a match and that has changed very little. You may argue that the technicalities have changed, the players are fitter and so on (that's arguable), but basically the ninety minutes has changed little. But the trappings have changed enormously. When I started in 1958, Matt Busby, once he had recovered from his injuries, ran the club totally. He had a board of directors – Harold Hardman was the chairman – and the directors had the ultimate authority, but Sir Matt pulled the strings. If he wanted something he would put it to the board knowing full well that the board would back him. So Sir Matt made all the big decisions that affected Manchester United in those early days. He made decisions about which players to sign and he made political decisions such as wanting to play in European competition. It was Sir Matt who did it all.

Now that contrasts with the Sky bid. Alex Ferguson knew nothing about it until the news broke publicly. The club has got so big and developed in so many other areas that it would no longer physically be possible for the manager to control everything. He's got enough just looking after the playing side. There are now all these other departments – media, catering, merchandising, sponsorship – they all need their separate departments. I think the growth of Manchester United has been as spectacular as anybody's. The other little story which illustrates that is that when Ken Merritt started as a boy, Les Olive was the secretary and Les carried with him on match days keys for every door in the stadium. Ken Merritt says that if he was to do the same now he would need a wheelbarrow. He certainly wouldn't get them all in his pocket.

A lot of people of course feel disillusioned that Manchester United have developed into such a sophisticated outfit. They feel alienated that the grass roots of the game have been taken away from them and, to a certain extent, they have. But I think there are two points to be made. First, the game has had to become more sophisticated because people's requirements were becoming more demanding. I don't think people would now accept standing on weedy, dangerous terraces. There is a demand for more sophisticated facilities for watching and the game had to come out of that era, prompted by the tragedies at Hillsborough and Bradford. It was just getting too dangerous. In the end the Government stepped in and insisted on higher standards. So it was inevitable that the game would be taken a little further from the grass roots because if you have all-seater stadiums you need to charge a little more in order to maintain your revenue.

The other factor is that in the seventies hooliganism was on the march and football, in order to preserve itself, had to take the game a little away from the grass roots because the grass roots were killing it. Sometimes when people get worked up from the radical point of view, about all the corporate hospitality and so on, about how they've stolen the game from us, it has to be pointed out that to a certain extent they contributed to that by their reckless behaviour – admittedly of a small section of the club's following. But we are not talking about one or two supporters of a club like Manchester United's following; the hooligan element ran into some hundreds. Inevitably, for self-preservation football had to aim for a slightly different market. So you saw a drift to the middle-class market. It's very sad because football came from the working classes, but the two elements, hooliganism and dangerous grounds, contributed to a move away from the old-fashioned background.

People criticise Manchester United for being money mad, and Martin Edwards in particular catches it; but really, although he's made a lot of money out of it personally, if you are going down a road of improvement you've got to say that Martin Edwards has emerged as the outstanding leader in the game of football. In his thirty years as a director and nearly twenty years as chairman, he has led Manchester United to the forefront in the commercial world. Manchester United is as competitive off the field as it is on it and he has made sure that Manchester United have been first. And really, instead of condemning him, the fans should be congratulating him. If ever they are in any doubt about that, what would they have as their alternative? Would they have a bumbling type of chairman who turns his face against commercial developments? Because if Manchester United had a chairman like that they would be just another club. And in Manchester you've just got to look across the city to see that it is not easy being a chairman. While the manager has the key front-line role, unless he's operating against the background of a provision of money – and money not just for players but for the development of the ground as well – you fall behind and end up like Manchester City, playing in the Second Division. Supporters who boo Martin Edwards should ask themselves would they rather have had Francis Lee, Peter Swales and other chairmen who have not presided over a successful operation?

DAVID MEEK

The first attempt at an independent supporters' association was when the Stretford End was going to be demolished; it was called Hostage – Holders of Season Tickets Against Gross Exploitation. It was partly to do with the way the Stretford End was being rebuilt, the perceived lack of ambition because people felt it ought to be bigger and, with hindsight, it should have. It was at Lancashire Cricket Club. It was against the first high increases in prices. For one reason and another that fizzled out. It was the season of our first real stab at the Championship for years and that highlights the problems with supporters' associations. The football can easily take over. If things are successful then the issues seem less critical. They also tried to get meetings with the club rather than building a campaign with organisation. It was the wrong tactic and it never got off the ground.

With IMUSA (Independent Manchester United Supporters Association) which began in 1994, many of those lessons had been learnt. With IMUSA we wanted as wide a breadth of support as possible. There has been more contact, a more co-operative attitude from the club. The club's attitude has always been that the club has x number of supporters, x number of branches, why should we listen to one rather than the others? The answer of course is that you should listen to them all. The others are branches which essentially organise tickets and travel for different areas. We are totally different.

IMUSA has always had a number of issues which it wants addressed, such as how the fans are treated inside and outside the stadium, how tickets are distributed, the price of tickets and so on. These are quite different to the branch secretary who wants to maximise the number of tickets for his branch and deal with travel arrangements.

It came to a head last season with the question of standing up. We have a growing concern about the atmosphere at Old Trafford and a growing sense of wanting the same kind of atmosphere they had on the Stretford End and they can't get that now. That's partly the way the club rebuilt the stadium which has meant that people have been split up. When you had the various stands and terraces, you had areas for the different constituents. The clubs should recognise that there are people who want to sit down and watch the match and equally there are people who want to stand up and shout and scream. I think the attitude should be that we try and accommodate all those views. What came to a head this season was that the club decided very forcibly that they would make everybody sit down, when certainly certain sections of K-stand didn't want to. United have also employed a security firm. They went in very aggressively on the first game of the season and started throwing people out for standing up. It just went on and came to a head with the game against Everton on Boxing Day when fights broke out between the security and supporters. One young female supporter was dragged out with a broken arm; people had their heads banged against walls, and they created a problem far worse than the initial problem. They created a public order problem. The only solution will be when they create areas where people feel comfortable to express themselves in the way that they want to.

There is a problem if twenty people want to stand up and there are others who have sat in their seats for the past thirty years and they can't see and have to get up. Yes, there's a problem, but the answer is not to suppress everybody but to

335

accommodate it. This is where IMUSA came in with the idea of standing areas with support from the club which now seems to have been withdrawn. The other is to create singing areas so there's a bit more flexibility about people being able to stand, because we all know that when we go to away games everyone stands up for the whole game and no one does anything about it, so what's so different, why are we treated differently at Old Trafford than we are at other clubs? After that Everton game we did have some useful dialogue with the club which really helped to diffuse the problem. Hopefully that has shown to the club that it's much better to talk and to be in consultation with the supporters' association than not.

ADAM BROWN

Obviously when it was possible to stand that's what I did, sometimes in the paddock but near as damn it in the Stretford End, close to the corner flags. For a while I used to sit. If you got there early enough, around 12.30 to 1 p.m., you could sit – this was in the seventies and eighties – behind the Stretford End. There were a few kind of benches, if you got there early enough.

The crowd was different. Now young kids can't get into United. Without a parent, the idea of turning up two hours beforehand, standing in a queue and getting into the boys' end is impossible now. If anything, that will have an impact on football support generally, that difficulty of actually being able to get into the game. Also, that fanzine *When Saturday Comes*; now it's When Friday Comes, Sunday, Monday, whenever Sky decide they want to put a game on. The Sunday papers were the beginning of the week, then you'd be reading about the Saturday results or a mid-week game, then you'd be looking to Saturday. If I think of the week, the high point is Saturday afternoon. Now, I'm guessing that that is something to do with football and Saturday afternoon. That will always be the same with me but whether that's true for eight-, nine-year-old kids now is, I guess, not the case, with matches taking place at so many different times. There is now no regular way you can support your football team. Until fairly recently, if you wanted to watch United you just got there early enough; now you can't do that.

If anything, the clientele has just got older. The people who were lucky enough to get their season tickets seven or eight years ago, they are the people who are supporting United, because having produced this Championship team, nobody will have got rid of a season ticket. So, in a way, that success might mean that you have a generation of football supporters who won't be there any more, because they just can't get tickets. You have to book your ticket in advance and games take place at different times. If in ten or fifteen years' time United are not doing so well, then the crowds may suffer and decline.

I don't think it's changed in terms of social make-up. All the people I sit with have middle-class jobs, but they were basically working-class kids. In the sixties they did reasonably well because a lot of people did well in the sixties. Social mobility in Britain was such that the expansion of the service economy and the decline of heavy industry meant that there were not enough people in the middle classes to take all those jobs. So what that meant was that kids like me, from working-class backgrounds, who were football supporters, were able to get into those kind of occupations. So I don't see that big a difference in the crowds; maybe only in corporate hospitality. The crowd is just reflecting changes in society. The difficulty is in linking that with kids. The only way kids can get to see games is if they go with their parents. If there is a middle-class shift then it is taking place there. You see parents and kids with superstore bags, they've maybe managed to get tickets for one game and come with parents, they're wearing baseball caps, football shirts. Now my feeling is, how many of those kids will go for a period of ten years without actually going to the ground and then still end up as season ticket holders?

When I was growing up, football was the only game in town.

What was once working-class entertainment has become an increasing part of the glitterati form of cultural expression. You've got an increasing creation of markets around anything that you can sell. I think with a lot of the corporate side, it's the attachment to something which is seen to be successful that is important rather than the football. I know this Liverpool supporter who got a new job over here and the first thing he had to do was organise a corporate box for United. He was a season ticket holder at Liverpool and he was expected to take clients to the game at Old Trafford every week and entertain them. I don't know whether he's still got the job!

DEREK WYNNE

I'll tell you how I joined the club. I ended up being the managing director of a cleaning company where the chairman was David Evans. I'd worked my way from the bread, being a bread man, and ended up being national accounts manager for Rank Hovis McDougall. I thought I'd done well, being a lad from St Wilfred's with no O or A levels. Now Martin Edwards then was a non-executive director of the cleaning company. So he used to come to the meetings. He must have liked me a little bit because he invited me to a dinner in London and offered me the job of commercial manager. He knew what money I was on and he offered me £500 a year more if I'd become the commercial manager at Manchester United. For me to come here, being a Red, was a tremendous feeling. That was 1985 and the club was then doing £5 million a year. And now it's doing just over £80 million. Not all down to me, but I've played my part.

There's less aggro in football now. I think families are getting involved, especially women. I think if you have fifty women and fifty men you have a better chance that you're not going to have any more fighting. I think women need to get involved in football. Seats as well. It baffles me. When we had seating and standing, the last thing to sell was the standing. If you had thirty thousand seats and ten thousand standing, the thirty thousand seats would go before the ten thousand standing. The last to go was always the standing. I think people want to sit down. We have a wonderful stadium here and if everybody sits down, everyone can see. Yet people stand up. When we score a goal, everyone jumps up, brilliant.

DANNY McGREGOR

I think the importance of the Stretford End has only really come through with the loss of it. It was the heart of the atmosphere at Old Trafford and you used to have this rivalry between one side and the other. You'd have one side singing 'right side, right side, give us a song' if one side was being a bit quieter than the other side. It was one of those legendary things. I remember when I first started going I bought a badge which had 'I am a Stretford Ender' on it, and I wore my badge. When you became part of it, and you were in there all the time, it was a great place to go. We used to go to the same place and you'd see the same faces but you still had that freedom.

I always loved standing, which is why I think you should still be able to stand at football matches. It gives you that freedom to move around. There's a better atmosphere, more camaraderie, more interaction between people when there's standing on that type of terraces. One of the best sights I remember was the game against Arsenal. It was one of those niggly games and Whiteside came on and chopped Rocastle down in about two minutes. I was right at the back and to see all the arms going up chanting 'Norman, Norman, Norman'; thousands of hands. You don't get sights like that any more. It really was the core of support at Old Trafford and a real mix of people. It wasn't just blokes between eighteen and twenty-five; I think it was much more mixed than that in terms of age range. It was obviously mostly male but there was something more democratic about watching like that. And it was very cheap.

My first season ticket was £76. It was more working class. What has happened now is that the ladder has been pulled up and some people have dropped off the bottom because they can't afford to go. £350 before the next season is an economic barrier. That is one of the most important changes that has happened in football in the last few years. When you think that it was £3 to go in, almost anybody could turn up and go in, especially 1988–89 when attendances were down.

I've lived in Hulme since the eighties but even then travelling to Old Trafford on the buses, they'd be packed with kids. But you don't get that now. That's the other element that has been lost. Class is one thing but age is another. Young teenage lads going on their own. There used to be queues and queues of kids lining up, going in by themselves. It's that period when kids have stopped going with their mums and dads any more, they want to go with their mates and now it's not possible because it's too expensive. The Stretford End embodies that democratic ethos of football that has gone. You had the popular cheap end at Old Trafford and what did they do, they knock it down, and put fifteen hundred club-class seats in the middle, a family stand at one side and reduce the number of normal price seats to about five thousand down at the front. You dispersed everybody from what they considered their part of the ground to the rest of the ground and that's had a devastating effect on Old Trafford.

Man United plc is the epitome of what's happened to football in the last ten years. I think in many ways it's overrated. I think Manchester United have just been more successful at it than anyone else and they get criticised for that success and it has coincided with success on the pitch. The problem with plcs is that the priority and the legal obligation is to maximise profits for shareholders, not to make sure that you have a successful football club that looks after its community, which Manchester United doesn't (by that I mean the community of supporters). A variety of things have been done, many unnecessary, which have alienated the supporters from the club. You get this phrase all the time that they support the team and not the club. I think that removal has taken football from the people who are its life-blood. Without supporters you have nothing.

One of the first times 'Ferguson's red and white army' was sung was in the semi-final against Middlesbrough, a League Cup semi-final that went into extra time. It went on for the whole of the second half and for the whole of extra time. I remember that as the last great atmosphere on the Stretford End, because the Stretford End started it and at the end of extra time the whole stadium was doing it. I think that was the last really great atmosphere at Old Trafford.

ADAM BROWN

I started on a match day through a friend of my father who worked at the Development Association, which is the fund-raising side of Manchester United. He asked me if I wanted a Saturday job. I said yeah, that would be nice. It was totally different. So I came and from there on stayed. I worked for the Development Association for about nine years on a match day, and then the boss at the time wanted somebody full-time. He asked me and I said no; I had a good job at ICI. And later he asked me again, so I thought go on then, we'll go for it. I took the job on and it wasn't too long before I was made manager. I ran that for ten years and part of my job then was to take the Football Pink to the chairman Martin Edwards, around about 7 p.m. when they arrived on our doorstep from the newsagents. One particular time the chairman stops me and he says, 'You know we're having this membership scheme, well we want you to run it.' Over that particular weekend he gave me a lot to think about. So we had to start from scratch. We decided to have more than just a membership card and that's why it's been so successful. It's an interesting job because you're dealing with all parts of the club. It's not always a bed of roses but it is rewarding.

I have three main tasks for the club. They are split like this. I am the membership secretary which means that I administer all the membership scheme, supporters who wish to become members of the club which gives them benefits such as being able to order match tickets. The main job, and sometimes the busiest one, is organising the travel for the club; that's both domestically and in Europe. That's at its busiest when we're well into the Champions League and progressing. The third task I have is that we are the headquarters of our branches and a lot of my time and the time of our staff is taken up helping the supporters' branches in any way that we can. We have seven full-time staff. That's backed up by casual staff which can be as many as twenty. It could be a lot more once the new junior scheme gets going. We've just ordered two hundred thousand packs, that's to start with, so this office could be inundated.

In 1986, the Government, headed by Margaret Thatcher, and following the Heysel disaster, made certain suggestions and recommendations to the Football League that First Division teams should implement safety measures. One such measure was to introduce membership schemes and one thought was that all clubs should introduce membership schemes. But such was the opposition to this that we thought we would lose all the passing trade, people who just wanted to see a game once in a while. So the bottom line was that we decided that just 50 per cent of our ground would be designated members only.

The Manchester United membership scheme was implemented in the 1987–88 season and our first target was to achieve forty thousand members including our season ticket holders. There were twenty thousand of them so we were looking to get another twenty thousand to join this brand new scheme. We wanted them to pay money and in return we would give them a package of benefits, discounts at the souvenir shop et cetera, as well as being able to purchase a ticket in the members' area. It was so successful that the scheme has developed and we have enhanced it in many ways. We hardly get complaints at all, except for getting tickets; but it has developed in such a way that we've now gone from the forty thousand in 1988, ten years on, to a hundred and forty thousand. And quite honestly, if you are not a member of the club, you cannot get a ticket for a game. I'd like to see a scheme where anybody could get a ticket but I'm not sure those days will ever return.

We invite existing members to renew their membership and we give them a specific time. For the 1998–99 season we have given people until 30 June to renew. We then open the books to people who wish to join for the first time. Once we deem that we have enough members for the season, we close our books and no further applications are taken. Last season we closed the scheme at the end of August. So anyone who is not a member wanting to see a game has little or no chance. If you are a member, we have certain procedures. If you are a season ticket holder you have a ticket for every game. If you are an individual member, you have to apply five weeks before a game to the ticket office but quite often we are over-subscribed, so all applications go into a ballot. If you come out of the ballot you are lucky. There's a lot of negative work there because we have to write back to people saying you're either successful or unsuccessful. What we'd really like is having a stadium with enough seats. I've supported the club for many years and worked here for many and I thought when we increased capacity it would be sufficient to meet the demand but I've been totally wrong. I think we need a seventy thousand seater stadium. Whether we'd fill the stadium every match is another question, but we certainly would for the big games. I think the club are looking to increase capacity again because the demand is there.

We're aware of the problem for young kids. Surveys tell us

there are four million Manchester United supporters in the UK, and in the rest of the world, I'm not sure, but maybe ten million; even that could be a conservative figure, so we've introduced a scheme to capture that support. We need to offer a service to those junior supporters for the future to make them continue to be part of the club and we are soon to introduce a new junior membership scheme which is a non-ticket related package which I think will be a winner. But no, they won't be able to get a ticket; they'd still have to join the main membership scheme.

We have one hundred and seventy-four clubs in the UK. They all operate differently. They mainly provide a travel service to games, organise a coach. Their orders for match tickets come through this office. We administer that and pass them all through to the ticket office. They don't get everything they want. They also organise social gatherings. Last year I had a meeting of all the branch secretaries and committee members – basically it's a thank you. As a matter of courtesy I had to write to all the branches and the response was fantastic. They came from Mauritius, they came from all over the world, just for this particular two- to three-hour get-together, no game or anything. About three hundred came. Alex Ferguson met them, they went round the museum. It's just a thank you because all the work they do is voluntary.

Away European games are a big job. When English clubs were allowed back into Europe, somebody at the club had to organise travel. It turned out to be Barry Moorhouse. I had no experience, but you dive in and get on with it. In 1991 when we got to the final of the European Cup-Winners' Cup, that was the biggest test anyone could have, especially knowing how many tickets we had. We had three weeks to administer the sale of the travel packages. In three weeks we organised thirteen thousand travel packages, took them all to Rotterdam and got them all back safely. It was estimated that there were twenty thousand-plus United supporters at that game.

It's members only, so in that respect, the people travelling with you are identified. There's a lot of risk. It's not only the away games; it's all games. If you misbehave we can take action, but – touch wood – we've not had to do that. Our supporters enjoy a good time and act in a good manner. In all the time I've organised the travel I've had very few problems. There have been occasions when Manchester United have been in the headlines, but that was not an official situation. In the early days of being back in Europe the only tickets that were available were for those who travelled with the club. But we've shown a little flexibility over the last few years and allowed people to make their own travel arrangements, providing we know how they travel. We organise coaches for all away games but because of ticket restrictions these days you're looking at ten, maybe a dozen coaches at the most. If it was Wembley and the FA Cup we'd get fifty coaches leaving here. On average we receive three thousand tickets for an away game and again, you have to be a season ticket holder. There's a pecking order – executive boxes, season tickets, membership scheme – but they are all balloted depending on the demand.

People sometimes think that after the game we all go home. People don't see behind the scenes. One of the important parts of our jobs is to organise presentations, such as player of the year awards, for our branches. That is a really nice part of our job, because we're bringing our supporters close to their heroes. The players are fantastic. After every game – we have a running chart like this – see Andy Cole, they love him right through this list – the branches will attend the game and then meet a particular player. That player will accept his award, sign autographs, et cetera and every one goes home happy.

BARRY MOORHOUSE

In the fanzine we've always been quite cynical of the commercial motives of Manchester United and it's been a constant theme through the seventy-five issues to date. I remember when they went plc in 1991 people didn't know what to expect. There was a stink a year later when the season ticket prices went up by 40 per cent. People now don't know what to expect. They can't demonstrate because they don't know what they are demonstrating against. They are worried and they are concerned for the club because they care about the club, but football fans are notoriously apathetic. Until they get a letter landing on the mat saying their season ticket has gone up by 50 per cent; only that will kick-start them into protesting. But United plc are a well-run company and we have been very successful. Our admission prices are not unreasonable.

But there are problems. Kids in Manchester can't get to see games now. The bus from Urmston which used to be full of kids going to the game on a Saturday is now empty and that is of concern. The culture of watching United live is now alien to fourteen-, fifteen-year-olds. I think that is so sad. They can't get tickets and even if they could, they couldn't afford them. I've spoken to the chairman about this and he said to me, 'Stop the tape recorder,' and he said, 'What do you want me to do? The ground's full, what can we do?' I said, 'Be as accommodating to the younger ones as you are to executive-type supporters; make some concessions.' He said, 'We're going to put the ground capacity up.' But it's sad that my fifteen-year-old cousin will go around in a Man United shirt and watch them on telly and he thinks he's a huge United fan. Going to the match is not something he does. That's really sad.

The argument on the kits is something which crops up every year. When United announce a new kit my phone doesn't stop all day. It's usually some clueless journalist ringing up, saying you must be outraged. I'm not. Nobody has ever forced me to go out and buy a United kit. I'm not a parent and I can't be an authority but when I was growing up I couldn't have a United kit, my parents could not afford it. I had one that lasted me four years. You can't have everything you ask for and it's the same with football kits.

I feel the club is more distant to the supporters now. I wish they would have a dialogue with organisations such as the Independent Supporters' Association rather than viewing them as some militant body. The Independent Supporters' Association have some decent people, long-standing United supporters from all walks of life. It wouldn't do the club any harm to engage in a dialogue with them, just to listen to them. But a lot of times the club are quite distant and aloof, even patronising to the fans. There are certain areas which are getting better. The membership scheme is well run, the ticket office has got its act together; these are things which the match-going fan does notice. But ultimately it's all about what happens on the pitch. It's difficult to criticise the club when they have been so successful. But we still do it every month in the fanzine.

I do think your Manchester match-going fan is a dying breed. The club have become so big your relationship with them is not like a normal fan's relationship with a club. I've found myself going to watch my brother playing for Flixton and getting a buzz which United don't give me. I can go with my friends, have a pie and pint. You can't do that at United any more. Your friends can't get tickets, you can't sit together any more and the atmosphere is not what it was. The atmosphere has really declined.

ANDY MITTEN

The Maxwell and Knighton approaches were two very distinct things really. The Robert Maxwell thing never really got off the ground and I don't think we ever got close to selling to Maxwell. The Knighton thing was totally different. It was in 1989 and we knew that we had to rebuild the Stretford End. We knew that it was going to cost in the order of £10 million and the club, at the time, did not have that sort of money in the kitty to do it. We were not a public company, so we couldn't go to shareholders and ask them to raise that sort of money. We, the club, would have had to go heavily into debt to do it.

The attraction of the Michael Knighton offer was the fact that he was going to build the Stretford End as a condition of buying the club and I felt at the time, how could I refuse that? If the supporters had known that I turned down that sort of offer where someone was prepared to build the Stretford End then I didn't think it would have been right and proper. So they certainly wouldn't have been very pleased. So there were reasons for that. Now obviously, that deal didn't take place which necessitated the flotation two years later, which did raise the money to build the Stretford End. So really, the position we were in at the time dictated that I either sell the club to a company or an individual who could develop the stadium, or alternatively we went for a flotation, which we did.

No, I don't have nightmares about that. I think the way things have gone – had we had a magic ball and been able to look into the future at the time, then obviously a sale would not have been considered. But you just have to judge things as and when, and at the time it seemed a sensible solution. The fact that it didn't work was lucky because clearly the game has changed considerably in the last few years. It has gone from strength to strength and so has United.

We have now well over five hundred employees here. If you go back to the 1950s, basically all that you had were coaches, players and a limited amount of secretarial/executives. So there were very few people working for the club, probably less than a hundred. So we have grown considerably. We have added other arms to the club. In the 1950s you didn't have catering, all you had was somebody selling pies on a match day and you had an outside caterer. Now we have a catering business of over £6 million. We have a separate catering company which employs over a hundred people with a managing director and a structure. It's the same with the merchandising. In the 1950s we didn't have a shop and then through the sixties, seventies and even into the eighties, Matt Busby owned the shop; so now we have a merchandising division that has retail, wholesale and mail order, a contract with VCI to sell videos and publications and we have a licensing business where we license other people to use our crest. So that in itself employs well over a hundred people. All these things weren't around in the 1950s.

We are now a major business. We are one of the largest three hundred and fifty companies in the country. So all that brings a different responsibility to the job. I think people working in the club still consider it has a good family atmosphere within it. That's not apparent, I don't think, to outsiders but hopefully we haven't lost all that.

I think you've still got your hard-core supporters there who have supported United for a number of years and would be there through thick and thin, no matter how successful or unsuccessful the club was. But I think what's happened today is that because of the huge media coverage of the top clubs and particularly the successful ones, it has attracted new supporters. It has almost become a cult thing to follow a successful side and now with all the videos and publications it's easy to pick up supporters who don't necessarily come to matches but support the club. We have a tremendous following. I think there was a Harris poll which showed that we have three and a half million fans in the UK. Now if you then think about the tremendous coverage that Premier League soccer gets throughout the world and you add the supporters which we get who support United we are into the millions. So we have a huge supporter base not only in the UK but abroad as well.

We still do encourage juniors. I think we have the largest family stand in the country – four thousand people in our family stand – and we do give half price to our juniors. So we do encourage them to come. They are the lifeblood of the future. But clearly when you have only got a stadium that holds fifty-five thousand people and you pre-sell forty thousand, and then you have to give three thousand to the visitors, you have only got twelve thousand tickets to sell per match. And with the huge membership and waiting list that we have, it isn't easy to get into Old Trafford unless they buy a season ticket at the beginning of the season. But it is a problem and is something we are looking to redress, such as by expanding the stadium.

This whole complex has changed. We have bought a lot of land around the ground. Also over the years we've increased the number of executives who come. Some of the hard-core supporters don't like that – they see it as a diminution of their space – but in any successful football club you have to have a balance, the right mix, because it is the executives who subsidise the rest of the supporters. But I think we have probably got the balance right. I think we have something like six thousand executive seats and that includes boxes, window tables and executive seats in a total of fifty-five thousand so I don't think that's overdone, but it's a question of keeping that balance; but they are the ones who bring in the bulk of the income. They're the ones who raise the bulk of money to expand the stadium, buy the players and so on. So I think it is a question of the balance. Now some people argue that some of the atmosphere has been taken away because of the corporate or executive members, but without them you do not get the same income. Again it's balance and this is what we are always trying to achieve.

As we've grown and got bigger then my role has become more diversified. When I first took the role in 1980, we hadn't got a shirt sponsor, we had a few match sponsors and so on. We didn't have the merchandising division, we did some internal catering but only on a small basis. Now when you think of all the other deals – the television deals, we're just starting our own TV channel – you think of the other things that have grown, so we've expanded. The job has obviously got much bigger. My job is no different to the chief executive of a major company. Basically I have a responsibility for everything that goes on and I have to spread my time and efforts into what needs to be done at a particular time. I have a number of people reporting to me from the various divisions, not ignoring the football side as well where you have a close relationship with the manager on the buying and selling of football players and the general running of the football side. In the 1950s that was all you had. In the fifties and sixties we did not have a chief executive; we just had a secretary and basically the secretary and manager ran the club. Now as we have expanded over the years, so has the structure of the management team expanded. Again, in those days, you wouldn't have had a financial director. As soon as we floated on the stock market, one of the requirements was a finance director. I now have a deputy chief executive who helps me out and even at senior management level we have two other managing directors – managing director catering, managing director merchandising – we've also taken on a new man to look after all the properties. We have a huge amount of acreage here which needs looking after. We've got financial controllers and each division needs to have its own accountant and separate accounts. The whole structure and the middle management has grown considerably. It is a structured business. If you then look at the board, at one time all you had was a football club board; now we have a plc board on top of the football board with an independent non-executive chairman and non-executive directors. You have three subsidiary boards underneath, all with their own structures, managing directors and own board of directors. It is a totally different set-up to the fifties. It is now big business.

In the future there may be even further diversification. Clearly and foremost we are a football club. Our name is built on our reputation on the field, so the first thing we have to do is make sure the team is successful. So we have to support the manager in terms of players and everything else within reason. Also we have plans to expand the stadium. We are selling out at fifty-five thousand. We need to be in excess of that and then, if we are still generating cash, which we should, we have to decide the best use of our money going forward and obviously that's only a decision the plc board can make.

MARTIN EDWARDS

It never entered my head that the ground that I first came to after the War could ever become like what we see here, even public companies, or anything like that. Obviously once the team got back after the War they were successful and were attracting big attendances, so slowly the finances improved because I think during the War we were actually in debt. It's only years later that it was commercialised, only in the last ten or twelve years. The stadium has been transformed. I think you have to give a lot of credit to the chairman Martin Edwards with the appointments that have been made. It all starts there with the success on the playing field; you have to have that, and fortunately we have. The people appointed have done a great job.

LES OLIVE

If you look at the introduction of the Safety of Sports Grounds Act introduced after the tragedy at Hillsborough, there has become a legal requirement by the clubs to provide first aid cover for their patrons. So St John has an involvement on that. We provide one member of St John per thousand people attending, so for the likes of United we are providing fifty members at least for the match. We provide people in excess of that because we ourselves are on a learning curve. So we probably provide almost sixty people. We provide one of our ambulances as well which is a fully equipped ambulance. There is a legal requirement for the statutory ambulance service to provide ambulance cover, but over and above the statutory ambulance, we provide an ambulance at United. Our reasoning behind that is that our ambulance is there in case another Hillsborough occurs so that they have a para-medic team to deal with casualties on the ground. For the actual transfer of patients from the ground to hospital they would have to call an emergency in, so we provide an ambulance to short-circuit the system and provide a better service for the casualty.

We have a senior person in overall charge who liaises with the statutory services, the fire, police and ambulance, but we have a match commander who is in overall charge. The ground is divided up into various sections and teams are allocated. In the past it was an ad hoc arrangement, when we just turned up and allocated spots ourselves. It now forms part of the major plan for the stadium. Our members, in consultation with the emergency services, are allocated spots and they cover those spots. They are not there to watch the game. Probably in the past they were there to watch the match. They used to say join St John Ambulance and you can watch the football free, but no longer could we even entertain or consider that. For United in particular, it is a seven-hour duty. We would also cover outside to start off with and as the match grows they would move inside.

St John Ambulance is a voluntary, charitable organisation. Our members are not employed; they are volunteers. If you get United, City and another team playing and an event at the Nynex Arena it's a huge call on our membership. We have nine hundred to a thousand adult members in the Greater Manchester area. Some are employed, some unemployed. There is a greater than ever call on our facilities. But we've never had any problems in getting people for United; we get plenty of volunteers for Old Trafford.

There is a nationally agreed rate from the Football League and the Premiership which is done by our headquarters. The clubs pay a rate per thousand spectators to the organisation.

We still get violence, even though they are all-seater stadiums. I don't think they form the major part of casualties we deal with, however. If you look at the age of our casualties, you will see that that is changing. There are not as many young people attending and heart conditions, faints are becoming more common. We do get the odd person falling, and the odd bit of violence. But most of the violence occurs outside the ground.

But of course we no longer have bodies passed over the heads as they were in the days of terracing. That makes our job easier in some ways. With seating there are also less people attending, more room and people can be dealt with easier. The system with people allocated to different areas helps, so instead of having to chase across the ground to get to someone, our people being allocated to certain sections all the time means that they can quickly deal with a problem. We've become more sophisticated. We now have a multitude of equipment, to deal for instance with heart attacks. The training given to our members has improved enormously over the years.

We have no involvement with players any more. If a player broke his leg the team doctor would have the responsibility of looking after that person. We are quite able and competent to put the casualty on to the stretcher and carry them off and we would probably do that under the supervision of the club doctor or club medical team. We are again competent and capable of taking them to hospital but it could be that they will call the statutory ambulance in to do that. We take crowd casualties to hospital, to help the statutory ambulance service rather than call out an ambulance and take it offstream. But with players you are looking at a lot of money and clubs want to make sure that they have control of the situation.

IAN MOSS

I think United are still a family club, look after families, but it's now too big a game. There's too much emphasis on winning. Everything's got to be towards the winning. We always wanted to win but not at any cost. We've had some great players at Old Trafford since the seventies. They've changed the game, they've changed the way football is played. The amount of money spent on the peripheries of football – the photos, the wallpaper – it's really not necessary. But I should think the revenue generated by it is greatly appreciated by Mr Edwards and his board, if not to buy new players, then to pay the twice-yearly dividend.

They still think at United that it's an honour to play for the club. Most players now would not agree with that. They realise their playing career is quite short and they have to make sufficient money whilst they are playing. Their allegiance to United is temporary until they move to another club, except for certain ones that are born perhaps within Manchester who have been fans in their youth. They, I think, appreciate more than most playing for United.

GEORGE REYNOLDS

I do have some reservations about Sky's coverage of the game, but if you support a team like United it's fantastic. There's superb coverage. For people in Northern Ireland it has been wonderful. Because of the cost and hassle of coming to Old Trafford, it's the kind of thing they can only do once in a while, so television has been a godsend. I think football should be on terrestrial television but the companies blew it.

EAMON HOLMES

The atmosphere at Old Trafford is not what it was. Seating has something to do with that I'm sure, but as I said before, teenagers, kids between the ages of ten and twenty who used to go to games *en masse* don't go any more. And they used to make the most noise. Today if you look at the English football supporters you don't get any eighteen-/nineteen-year-olds arrested, these guys are all in their late twenties. They can't get tickets; it's so difficult to get tickets and develop football support. Away games are the best because there you know you have three to four thousand supporters who will do anything to watch United play. I have friends who will spend half of their disposable income on watching United, if not more. Going to Old Trafford is a bit like, OK we're here so entertain us; whereas going to away games is about you supporting your team. That's the difference, not so much the fans being different other than the ten-/twenty-year-olds. I don't buy the idea that there is a groundswell of middle classes going to football matches who never went before. I think most of the people who go to football matches have what would be defined as middle-class occupations but went to football matches when they were kids. This London literati may go to the odd game, but they are not the people who go on a regular basis.

I think there can also be a complacency. If you are playing a lesser team, people turn up wondering how many goals we are going to score and when a team like Leicester come and go away with a win or a draw, there's a feeling that things haven't gone to plan. People are turning up expecting United to walk away with these games. The complacency means that you don't have to play your part. You can visibly see teams lifted, or not, according to the way the crowd responds. The crowd will always be important to football. I can anticipate if things carry on like this with television deals, there will be a time when you buy your season ticket and then get a reduction on the basis of how many times you've gone. Television needs the crowd. Without the atmosphere, who wants to watch? You can watch Italian football on a television on a Sunday afternoon and you know unless you can relate to the atmosphere it can be a pretty boring game. The atmosphere is everything. When they played Juventus last year the atmosphere was electric; they went a goal down then came back to produce a storming win. The atmosphere was incredibly important at that game.

DEREK WYNNE

The danger is that it is an ageing support. It's only the middle-class income people who can afford to go and the young with little income can no longer afford it. At £20 a match you don't get the opportunity to go. We've always made a point that when we have a spare ticket, when one of us can't go, to take a young lad or somebody who's never had a chance to go and the joy on their face and that is almost as exciting as the game itself. You come back and the lad is – well it might have been a drab nil–nil draw, but he comes back absolutely full of beans. We went to see a game at Stockport County against Middlesbrough. We couldn't believe how easy it was to get in, how cheap it was, and there were kids running around, going back behind the stands. It was so enjoyable I could see us taking our children to this. The standard of football was not so high, but it wasn't bad.

ROGER HENNELL

When I went to the game on Saturday I noticed that an awful lot of people in front of me and around me didn't have scarves, shirts, et cetera but there were actually quite a lot of well-dressed people or well-turned-out, I'm not saying wealthy people, but well-dressed. Somebody else who had watched it on TV remarked to me at work how very few red shirts there were. You know when you see Newcastle, it's all black and white shirts, but United? I wonder whether there's actually a slight turning away from it now.

TIM BAMFORD

I'd heard rumours about a possible takeover, though not about Sky, but I hadn't mentioned it to my ten-year-old son who's an avid United fan and very emotionally involved with them. Then on the Sunday morning when it was announced that Sky had made a bid for United, I had a terrible sinking feeling. I felt terribly depressed. Liam, my son, is in the habit of getting up very early and watching the repeat of *Match of the Day* on television. I thought, I hope he's not gone down because I'd like to break this news to him rather than let him get it from the television news. But in fact he had heard and he was lying on the settee in a state of morose inactivity. He just felt the same as me.

I could talk all day about my views of Sky, someone being in control of our team who knows nothing and cares nothing about football. I find that hard to take. But the idea of this negative figure taking over our team – I'm horrified by it, to be honest with you. I know this is a slightly naïve response, but it's an emotional response and to me that sums up the whole thing. Liam's response as a young ten-year-old is no different because we're both emotionally hooked into this team. I know that to survive in the modern era you have to make money and United are pretty good at doing that, but I wish the balance would tip back a little the other way so that, for example, teams would care about who took them over, who owned the shares.

The problem is that most of the shares are in the hands of corporate bodies. The ideal thing for me would be if all the shares of Manchester United were held by all the supporters of Manchester United. It's not beyond the wit of man to organise it like that. It has now become a rather corporate business getting into the ground. We helped my son a couple of years ago to join the club's junior membership scheme but because I'm not a member and because I've not got a season ticket, it became a nonsense. It's a shame.

We went to Stockport, to see England under-21s playing. Great game, we really enjoyed it. It just reminded me of being at Old Trafford all those years ago. No problem getting in; a bit of a queue, but there was that expectation. It was a night game, but inside it was like the lower stands, an open atmosphere. Although Liam and I will never stop being United fans I've resolved to take him to Stockport to see some live games; I want him to see football. He can also see it close-up there, you get a good view. Nowadays, I only go to Old Trafford if I'm invited, because my brother-in-law has corporate seats. Also, for me and my son and daughter it's a lot of money. You buy your programme as well and a drink. It's pricey. But I do miss going. I wish they had gone and built a national stadium. City in the new stadium here seems ridiculous. United could have made a bigger one and filled it every week.

SIMON THORP

I know that some of the players have commented on this as well, that the atmosphere at Old Trafford is not very good at all and it does get over to the players on the pitch; if somebody misses a pass, the crowd, you know, all of a sudden start booing. You can hear it and the players can hear it on the pitch. People don't think that they hear it on the pitch and it does affect them. What they need is the supporters to get behind them. Sometimes you get some idiots at away games who really probably have had too much to drink and are a bit loud. But generally they do tend to get behind the team. I know a lot of people who prefer to go to away games rather than home games because the supporters do get behind the team a lot more. Anybody who went to Blackburn towards the end of last season and heard the level of support that was provided for the team that day will appreciate what it is like at an away game.

SIMON JONES

I think the club has changed. I know it takes a lot of money to run it but I'm not so sure that they are being a bit far away from the fans. They do have an amazing following and a hard-core following and they have to keep an eye on this. They have to look after them. They say you can't have a ticket, it's going to some season ticket holder who perhaps goes to two away games a year – the Cup final – whereas some fan who's been going all year can't get a ticket. I just think it's wrong.

But having said that, when you have so many members and so many season ticket holders, how do you distribute the tickets evenly? It's always going to be a problem. Everyone still thinks that when they were redeveloping Old Trafford they should have done it a bit more. Fifty-five thousand is great but it's still not big enough by any means.

ROLAND COBURN

The club has changed. We had all this tension in the early eighties when there was a feeling Robson was about to be sold to Italy because the club needed the money. Week after week the only chant you could hear around the ground was 'Robson must stay' and this seemed to be maintained for the whole ninety minutes and there were petitions going around. But this was the time when Martin Edwards was really a hated man. It was felt that Martin Edwards owned the club and was not prepared to put up sufficient money to buy the players we need. When Atkinson bought some players, it was not actually the players he wanted. He wanted to buy Terry Butcher, Gary Lineker, Mark Lawrenson, and the argument was that he had already bought enough players and you couldn't go on buying. But if we had signed those players, a striker instead of some of the ones we did buy, we might not have had so many barren years. The thing that has changed now with the share issue is that it has grown and is a much bigger commercial venture. It's money making money. I have to say when the chance came to buy shares I bought my fifty shares. I wouldn't get rid of them for any money. It's a chance to be identified with them. If somebody else took over the club I'd be very worried. Michael Knighton came close to it and Maxwell. You look back and think how awful that would have been. The safeguard now is that a lot of the shares are owned by real fans.

ROGER HENNELL

When I compare United with what we had in the seventies and eighties I think it's better. I didn't want to sit down when seats were first introduced. I always stood; the atmosphere was brilliant. When they brought seats in I bought a season ticket to sit in K-stand. I thought I wouldn't get in. Now I wouldn't stand, maybe it's because I'm forty-two years old. I go to places in the FA Cup where you stand and I think, what am I doing here? The one thing that has admittedly gone is the atmosphere. It's not just at United. It's the same at Liverpool. The singing is sporadic, long periods of silence. You can hear the players shout sometimes. It's not the football, United have played entertaining football.

People were up in arms about Sky. It didn't affect me. I go to all the home games but it is very hard to get an away ticket. If I can't get a ticket and it's not on the television it's horrendous. I hate listening to football matches on the radio. I'd pay £5 or £6 to watch it on the television. Those people down south who can't get to any games, wanting to watch, good luck to them. What I do disagree with is playing games on a Monday night just for television. I don't think there's any need for that. You can have local Derbies on a Monday, not games like against Crystal Palace or Southampton, or early morning kick-offs. They don't think about the fans. United having to go to Southampton on a Monday night is horrendous for United fans.

ROBIN MURRAY

I never bought shares when the club went public. I thought it was a sell-out at the time. But I wish now that I had bought some shares as that would allow me to go to the shareholders' meeting. When I woke up that morning and heard that United were being taken over I felt as if I had been punched in the stomach. I couldn't believe that there were those who were going around saying, 'It's great, now we'll be able to buy Ronaldo.' That's absolute nonsense. It's never going to happen.

I am totally opposed to the Murdoch takeover. Not least because he is the proprietor of the newspaper who assaulted the memories of those who died at Hillsborough. I think that Martin Edwards does care for the club and it is a fact that prices at Old Trafford are far lower than the vast majority of Premiership clubs. But we have to realise that Murdoch does not want United because he has some emotional attachment to it. He wants it for one reason and only one reason: its commercial potential. When you realise that, you have the answer. It is a tool for his strategy. Murdoch has taken over other great cultural institutions, such as *The Times*, and has not given the least consideration for their tradition. He doesn't seem to care about emotional investment; he only cares about the commercial aspect, like the number of newspapers he sells and if that means dumbing down, then so be it. The same will happen at Old Trafford. I think Murdoch is especially brutal.

It's bad for football all round, especially for the smaller clubs who will feel the cold wind when there is pay per view on television all the time. Murdoch is positioning himself in the market. We don't know which way the market is going to go, but he's determined it'll go in his direction. Who's to say that one day he might make a commercial decision to move the club south, build a new stadium to take a hundred thousand people, and just move the club out of Manchester? People tell me that won't happen, but then who would have predicted some of the things which have happened at *The Times*?

If Rupert Murdoch took over United, would I still continue to support them? The answer is yes. We all have our reasons for supporting United or whatever club. But I couldn't throw away all the emotional involvement I have in United. And in a way that's the problem. Supporting a football club is not about market forces. You don't go around changing your allegiances because ticket prices are too high or someone is taking your club over. With football supporters you have a captive audience. And Murdoch knows it.

JIM WHITE

I suppose the automatic thing that people will say is that it's all done for money now, whereas at one time it was done for money *and* for football and I suppose there's got to be an element of that. It does affect all football clubs, obviously. I would think that the trend away from the man in the street and the terraces and the fact that we, like all the other clubs, had to move to all of the stadium being sitting, rather than any element of standing, somehow lost a little bit of atmosphere as far as I'm concerned.

I was quite happy as a youngster with the good old days. When someone felt unwell, the bodies came across the top of you and you helped the body along down to the front to get attention from the St John Ambulance and the megaphones were there, telling you, 'Will you please move forwards and let them all in at the back.' Well, all of that has now gone, clearly, and I suppose it's the thought that the club is moving totally towards money-making selling of seats, whether they be in executive areas or executive boxes, that appears to have reduced at least the ordinary man's opportunity to go to Old Trafford. I suppose I've been caught up in that to some degree because I was fortunate enough to get the opportunity of having two executive seats, which my two football-crazy daughters almost insisted I did. I pay heavily for the privilege of my seats but I have to say it's made it much easier to attend games in comparative comfort than when I was a young lad, pre-Munich, standing on the terraces with the best of them. The atmosphere is obviously affected. But there's still some magic about Manchester United which makes me pay the subscription and go and watch the games.

MICHAEL DUNHAM

A phrase that often comes up now in *Red Issue* and other fanzines is 'love the team, hate the club' and I think that would probably sum up the way in which my feelings are going. I used to feel part of a club that was Manchester United, almost a family type of thing, and I used to think that they were acting in my best interest and they were always going to do the right thing in terms of football, the enjoyment of the fan. Now I'm not so convinced about that. There are things you hear, like people in their eighties who've been moved out of the seat they've been sat in for sixty years to make way for executive boxes; and players not being bought because the plc won't put up the money; and you see in the old paddock security people wading in and pulling people out because they've actually dared to stand up. I really think it's a kind of 'us and them' situation now.

I feel much less a part of the club than I ever did. The team, I love them, they can't do any wrong as far as I'm concerned but the club, I don't feel a part of it any more and I don't know what they can do. I'm lucky because I do earn enough money and have the means to be able to keep going, but I know so many people who've just fallen by the wayside because they can't afford to get in and they're just so disillusioned by what goes on. The last game of the season, my boyfriend stood up at one point and went 'United' and all the stewards turned round and looked at him as though he smelt nasty. People bang on the seats with enthusiasm and they instantly send a load of security guards to stand round them because they're daring to bang on the seats. There's the feeling that you go to spend your money and then just sit down and shut up, not do anything, not show any reaction. I think the words on the signs outside the ground – 'In moments of extreme excitement, you may be permitted to clap your hands for a few minutes' – it's just ridiculous, all the passion's going to go. We get people sat around us, they're so bored they're on their mobile phones, instead of stamping their feet and clapping their hands and getting behind the team; they're talking on the phone and they've not been to United before so they're eating their United popcorn and looking at the flags – it's bizarre. Having been in the days when if someone scored a goal or something was going on on the pitch, you could be transported thirty yards down the Stretford End by the surge of excitement, there's going to be people who've never known that and it's just such a strange atmosphere now. I sit on the middle tier of the new stand and you are so far away, you can barely discern who they are by the way they run. I don't like the ground very much any more.

The people who support the club have changed. I know I have changed in the way I approach it now. When I used to stand on the Stretford End I used to get there at twelve o'clock. You got yourself some chips and you stood in a snaking queue with a police horse in each fold of the snake. And you have a good laugh and a chat and you didn't mind standing there in the pouring rain, even it was for hours. You paid your £4 to get in and you'd still be two hours before the match kicked off. But you thought, this is great. But now I have lunch and a beer beforehand and I cruise up in the car, put it in the car-park, stroll in, sit down and then expect the entertainment to be brought on.

I think the game has become more middle class. You can't nip into the ground any more. It can't be impulsive any more, it has to be pre-planned. You can't think, 'Oh the sun's shining, I'd like to go to the match.' And then there's all the supporters who come from elsewhere. What the hell are they doing here? Can't they find a team of their own nearer where they live? People coming from Surrey every week. You see all these big cars bulging with people just come up the M1. I've got mixed feelings about it. I don't see why anybody who wants to shouldn't support United, but on the other hand, I know so many people from around here who can't get in. And you see all these coachloads coming from other places, hospitality trips and so on and you think, what the hell are you doing here? Middle class is probably the wrong way to describe them.

They're people who think that because it's Saturday you go to a football match, whereas I think about it all the time. It's fashionable. I like the fact that there are more girls going, and I like the fact that more families can go but it does seem to be the wrong type of family. It's different somehow. It's like a theme park. You go to the superstore, buy into your Manchester United experience, you pay your money, go around the museum and get this sanitised view of what's gone on and that's it. It's polite clapping, it's not passion. It'll never be the same again. I'm so pleased I had some time on the Stretford End.

MAXINE DUNHAM

CHAPTER TWELVE

Glory, Glory, Man United

There is an aura about Manchester United. They are the nation's club; the richest, most successful of the 1990s. Yet the aura goes back even further. It is not easy to explain, but in this chapter various fans do attempt a clarification. Ultimately, there is the sense that it is overwhelmingly connected to the Munich air disaster. Prior to the Second World War, United were little different from any number of other clubs. They had won the Cup once, the League twice but had also spent some years in the Second Division and had almost plummeted into the Third Division North. They were reckoned to be something of a music-hall joke, known as the yo-yo team as they bounced up and down, season after season.

If any team could claim to be the nation's favourite in those inter-war years it had to be Arsenal whose domination of English football was complete. Three titles in a row, five in all, two FA Cup wins, four final appearances. United never came into the reckoning. But the image of United certainly changed after the War as new manager Matt Busby took over the helm and guided them to a title win in 1952 to add to their 1948 Cup triumph. And then, of course, there were the Busby Babes.

Undoubtedly the Babes captured the imagination. There had been plenty of youngsters in football before (Dixie Dean was only eighteen when he was leading the line for Everton back in 1925) but the Busby Babes were different. It wasn't just one player; it was a glut of players. It was also about a theory that captured the minds of the nation's youth. Men, now aged fifty or sixty, vouch in this chapter for their impact on the game. The Babes also coincided with the romantic notion of European football. They might not have been the first team to challenge the might of Europe – Wolves were doing that in 1954 when they played a series of famous floodlit matches against Honved, Moscow Dynamo and Barcelona – but United were the first to do it in formal competition, reaching the semi-finals at the first attempt, only to be thwarted by the great Real Madrid.

But then came the Munich disaster and almost an entire team were wiped out. The nation wept, though nowhere more so than in Manchester where there was a genuine feeling of personal bereavement. In that one moment, Manchester United Football Club changed. Everybody wanted them to win. They were carried to an FA Cup final on a tidal wave of emotion and when they lifted the European Cup ten years later it was with the wholehearted support of the nation. How times have changed. Matt Busby, unlike almost any manager since, was a popular figure wherever he went. There may have been many who disliked United, but they would never say a word against Sir Matt.

Somehow, United were always one step ahead of the pack and they have continued to be so. In more recent years they have built the finest stadium in England, they have floated on the stock exchange and in 1998 they looked set to join forces with Rupert Murdoch's Sky Television. It might not be to everybody's taste but at least it might ensure that United remain in pole position.

United's flirtation with money and the media has not endeared them to everyone. You could divide the footballing world today between those who love United and those who hate them. There seems to be little space for negotiation in between.

This chapter also tries to explain not just the passion which many have for United, but their love for football as well, accompanied as it is by highs and lows of emotion, superstition, and drama. There are those who wear the same pair of red socks to every game, or go through the same superstitious ritual prior to each game, including one person who has to buy an iced bun. And there are those who travel huge distances, week in week out, in support of their favourites as well as some who even moved to Manchester simply to be near the team they loved. Football dictates their entire existence.

At the end of the day, though, supporting United is probably no different from supporting any other club. Talk to fans of Arsenal, Liverpool or even Torquay and they will tell you the same superstitions and passions. Supporting a football team is nothing to do with logic. It's a love affair that begins at a tender age and goes on forever, passed on usually from father to son; a childhood emotion which rarely loses its intensity, never really grows up and leads to all sorts of foolishness and irrational behaviour. Long may it continue. It's a good job the rest of our lives are governed a little more by logic.

I don't know what the magic of Manchester United is. I guess it's many things. I think it was there even before the War with the likes of Billy Meredith, the great Welsh winger. And then there were all those other things – the bomb that fell on Old Trafford during the War, that magical youth team, the Busby Babes, Munich, the European Cup win, and then everything that's happened in the last few years: Ferguson, Cantona, Beckham, Giggs and all those other youngsters. The thing about Manchester United is that it's an on-going story, there's always something happening. You never know what's going to happen next but it will always make headlines.

SIR BOBBY CHARLTON

I wasn't really a United fan when I was a youngster living in Belfast. My dad was, and most of his family were, but I wasn't at all. I was just interested in playing football. But United were the first club to come in for me and make me an offer. I know that other clubs were interested – Ipswich, Arsenal, Liverpool and Nottingham Forest – but they didn't make any offers. It was United who invited me over.

I came over for four days and was really impressed by the way they looked after me. I had to go to the United States with the school and United were very accommodating, allowing me to cut short my visit. They looked after me, and then took me to the airport so that I could go to America. I didn't think about the size of the club at all. I was twelve at the time and I just fell in love with it. And it all worked out perfectly. I used to come during the holidays. Then at fifteen, I would fly over on a Friday night, play for the juniors on the Saturday morning, watch the big game at Old Trafford in the afternoon, then fly back to Belfast. I'd have got a million air miles today! I used to come over on the plane with my skinhead haircut, Doc Martens and my football boots in a plastic bag over my shoulder. The plane would be full of businessmen; I don't know what they thought of me looking like that. 'Who's he?' they must have thought.

Then at sixteen I became a full-time professional. Again, the club really looked after me, although I had been coming so often that I knew the place inside out. The club put me up in digs in Chorlton-cum-Hardy in Ellesmere Road. We all lived in Chorlton at the time – Paul McGrath, Kevin Moran, loads of us. I was there for a while.

I made my debut in 1982 on 24 April at Brighton and Hove Albion. Mike Duxbury was injured and I came on for the last twelve minutes. I was only sixteen and I was earning £16 a week. We won that game, Ray Wilkins scoring a rare goal, and I got an £800 match bonus. It was fantastic. We won all the next four games and I finished up with £3,200, and I was still only earning £16 a week. That was just amazing for me, a sixteen-year-old. Then that summer I went to the World Cup finals with Northern Ireland and suddenly, from nothing, I was swept into the limelight.

It's difficult to put your finger on what makes United such a huge club. It's lots of things. There's the support, which is enormous. And there's Munich, the many Championships they've won, and of course the players. Players like Best, Charlton, Law, Cantona; great players who have become icons. The support is worldwide, it's phenomenal. I was in Australia recently and I toured all the club branches. There are so many of them. The support is just fantastic. There must be a lot of brainwashing going on in a lot of homes. Without the fans the club would be nothing. But the club have got to keep a happy medium, they mustn't leave the fans behind. They've got it just about right at the moment. They've got the corporate side, and the family side, and then the ordinary fan.

NORMAN WHITESIDE

One of the things I was thinking about with this interview was that when I went to university I couldn't get back at weekends as much as I wanted to, although I went to the first Derby. I was sat in Sheffield where I was at university. It was twelve o'clock and, I thought, I'm not going to miss this Derby. I've never missed one yet, so I persuaded a mate to drive me over and we parked illegally at five to three and bought a ticket off a dreadful tout. But the real story I was going to tell was that at university, which can be a hermetically-sealed environment, I thought I'd lost my enthusiasm for football a bit. I still played and watched it and I looked at the results. United were going through a bad patch but they had beaten Liverpool four–one away and I think Charlton scored a couple. I had the greatest Saturday night out with my mates and I realised that my mood would always be affected, and it still is, whether United have won or lost. However successful or otherwise I have been in life, my mood drops if United don't

371

win. I wish I could tell myself it's only a game, but it doesn't work. It's in the blood. If they win I feel better.

GRAHAM STRINGER

It was my first senior game and I can remember it quite vividly. It was Boxing Day, 1958. I remember the build-up particularly because my sister told me so much. She was eight years older than me and had already been with my dad to Old Trafford. She told me about the journey, about getting a bus into the city from the east side and then taking a train. She said it was incredible on the train, going over that huge viaduct just outside Central station and looking down on the canals. She'd told me all about this journey and how exciting it was. I was only nine at the time. But the build-up of excitement was terrific. And she was right, it was an incredible journey.

When we got there we stood in the Stretford End paddock, in the corner. You seemed as though you were miles away from the pitch. I was peering over people's shoulders. The atmosphere was fantastic. It just got a grip of me. I think I was always a fan of the crowd, more so than the team. It was that atmosphere which converted me: the noise, the steam from the crowd from the cigarettes, and the steam from outside. It was the days of steam trains and just outside the ground the trains would be getting ready to take the crowds back into central Manchester. They'd be hissing and getting up steam, in time for the final whistle. I don't recall much about the game itself but I was hooked by the atmosphere. It gets into your blood. I was already a Red but that atmosphere really got to me. My dad was a United supporter although he went to both United and City, something which doesn't happen these days. He was at the biggest-ever League attendance at Old Trafford, United versus Arsenal, and at Maine Road when City played Stoke [84,569, March 1934, FA Cup sixth round]. That was the biggest-ever attendance outside Wembley. If you came from a major conurbation, a city like Manchester, then you just got embroiled in football.

CLIFF BUTLER

I was a very keen footballer as a lad. I played for my school and got picked for Salford Boys. I was always on the fringes as a sub, or occasionally I would get a game at right-back. I didn't like that because I always thought of myself as a Glenn Hoddle-style creative midfielder. We used to train at the Cliff on a Thursday. One week one of the lads forgot his trainers and the coach said, 'Borrow these, they're Lou Macari's.' I don't know if they were Lou's, but the next week we all forgot our trainers! The scouts used to come down but I was pulling my face because they had put me at right-back. They wanted me to lump it up the field, but I wouldn't have any of it. I had great ambitions to be a footballer, but instead of knuckling down, I was a bit of a moody so-and-so and I blew it.

CHRISTOPHER ECCLESTON

I certainly think fans can influence a game. You certainly sense it when the crowd are with you. It gives you a sense of well-being. It gives you the confidence. When you're winning games you've got that confidence. If you're having a bad time and you stick with it, the nice part is when you win the crowd over if you're having a bad time. It can certainly help the team. Sometimes the crowd is up for it like a player. A crowd can get spoilt, you know. If you get complacent and lose your enthusiasm, you will get problems. I was there with the European Cup win and reaching the semi-finals playing AC Milan the following year. Five years later, we were relegated. People say it can't happen but it can happen, I tell people it can happen. I've said publicly, you mustn't get complacent. This is my eighth year with the first team and in seven years prior we've never been out of the top two. But you look back at the great Liverpool and they were not out of the top two in nineteen years. I've got a lot of admiration for Liverpool and what they did over that period of time. Manchester United is not about profits, it's about profits and silverware. It goes hand in hand and always will. That is the demand that comes with its heritage.

Fans look on you being a local lad and always give you a chance because you're local. You're one of them. You've come off the streets of Manchester and got a chance to play for the team you supported as a kid. They look at you and know it's something hundreds of thousands would like to do. I always had a decent relationship with the fans. Even today, I'm only a fan working for the club. It's as simple as that.

BRIAN KIDD

My son Jim has got a whisky glass of Matt's because Matt used to go to charity do's and I went to one at that pub called the Manchester Regiment just under the Hulme flyover and Jim went with me, aged about fifteen. At the end of the evening I introduced him to Sir Matt, which sort of knocked him cold. Sir Matt left a little whisky glass with the remains of a smell of whisky in it and Jim's still got it in Canada, never washed it, with the smell of the whisky still in it. We said to Jack Thomas, the landlord, when Sir Matt went, 'That whisky glass there, what're you going to do with it? He said, 'Wash it, put it on the shelf.' And we said, 'Can we take it?' and Jim's still got it.

BOB GREAVES

The fans come from all parts of the world. I'm quite surprised really. We've got branches in New Zealand, Scandinavia – that's the biggest with thirty thousand-plus members – Japan, Hong Kong, America, Malaysia; it goes on. But what surprises me really is that some people would travel from, say, South

Africa just for one game at Old Trafford. Can you imagine the cost? They arrive on the Friday, watch the game on the Saturday and go home on the Sunday. Now that's tremendous support. We even have people who come over from Malaysia simply to purchase official souvenirs. They come one day, make the purchase and go back the next day. Support for United is phenomenal. The Scandinavian branch has four full-time employees. They've got a mini souvenir shop, they translate the official Manchester United magazine to re-sell to their own members.

BARRY MOORHOUSE

My first United game was against Ipswich Town. I was nine years old, 1982. We got beat two–one. We still had an outside chance of winning the League. There was a pal in my class and it was his ninth birthday, so we all stood on the scoreboard terrace at the back and I just remember this swirling mass of bodies around me. I vividly remember the first ten or so times I went to Old Trafford. You just walk in and it hits you. The sight of a stadium. I don't get it now because I've been so many times.

ANDY MITTEN

I was born in Northern Ireland in 1959 and one of my first recollections of football was of England winning the World Cup. My other recollection is of Celtic winning the European Cup the following year. And of course a year later United won it as well. Like many of my mates at school I was a George Best fan. He was the local boy who had made good. Life in the province at the time was horrendous and this guy had world stardom by simply wearing a red shirt. That was a great inspiration to many people. United became something of a cult following for us.

The first time I ever saw United in the flesh as it were, was on 17 March 1973 when they had a two—one win over Newcastle. I remember we had tickets for the Stretford End and being a bit timid I said to my father, 'Oh no, we can't go in there.' It was quite scary at the time. So my dad changed the tickets and even worse, we ended up in the Newcastle end.

I just love going to games. I'm very boisterous and vociferous and really enjoy the banter. But that doesn't make me want to punch the guy next to me. I don't want some sanitised version of the game which I fear is the way it's heading. I like the passion and the noise. At the end of the day it's a game and that means wind-up, banter. As long as it's not done in a malicious way, you do it with a smile on your face. I would never claim to be a football expert. I'm just a very keen fan with all the flaws a fan has.

EAMON HOLMES

I think it's the sort of greatness of the club, the atmosphere, their history; you get sort of sucked into all that and I suppose the Sir Matt Busby character. That established the character of the club. It seemed a nice club. When I came into it the hooligan days were well gone so there wasn't that nastiness that the United fans had the reputation for. Even though they were going through lean spells there were always great players to watch, like Bryan Robson and then Mark Hughes when he came back from Barcelona.

ALISSON THORNTON

I've always been interested in football. I was captain of the school team, Stamford High, and I was in another team called Hillgate Ashton who were in the Sunday League. As well as playing I used to spend most of my Saturdays travelling across Manchester to Old Trafford where I would stand at the old scoreboard end. I don't remember the first game I ever saw but one match does stand out from the mid-seventies. United were playing Sheffield United. It was the first home game of the season and we beat Sheffield five–one. There were fifty-odd thousand there. It was absolutely jam-packed. It was a great game. I was in the Stretford paddock for that one with my stepdad. I suppose I was about ten or eleven.

I also appeared on the pitch once at Old Trafford. It was about five years ago and I was playing in a charity game for the Primetimers XI, which was a team made up of radio and television personalities. We were playing a side of politicians made up from all the different parties. They were known as the Westminster Wobblers and also had a few guest players. We were rubbish; we had a terrible side. I was marking Bobby Charlton. Now I know how good he was.

SEAN WILSON

I think there are a number of things. I am a Manchester lad so I've only ever known supporting United. I've never had to say, 'I like United because of . . .' United are my local side, the ground's five miles from my house. If I was born in Stoke I'd probably have supported Stoke City. I only truly realise it when I watch the team abroad, especially on pre-season tours. You'll go to somewhere on the other side of the world, such as Bangkok or Kuala Lumpur, Hong Kong, and the reaction is phenomenal. I've travelled quite a lot but it still opens my eyes. You can get in a taxi anywhere in Thailand and the Thai taxi driver will know who United are playing at the weekend. I always remember a letter in a City fanzine a few years ago when a City fan went to Benidorm one summer and at no time when his passport was checked did a customs official say Law, Best or Charlton. They take the piss out of us, us thinking everybody in the world goes around saying Nobby Stiles. But I've seen it for myself. There's a huge worldwide appeal. It's quite unnerving. I was in a bar this summer in Norway and I got chatting to this lad. He knew I did the fanzine, and he says, can you tell us did we receive a fee for Kevin Pilkington?

I thought, he's our reserve goalkeeper! and I thought of him lying awake in his bedroom in suburban Oslo. Why does that trouble him? These people are walking encyclopedias of United.

I've noticed in the last few years it's difficult being a United fan. A lot of times I've been introduced, 'This is Andy, he does the United fanzine but he's all right. Most United fans are wankers but he's OK.' And they say, 'God, you come from Manchester as well.'

We've got huge support in this city and always have had. I come from Urmston where the majority of people are Red. But you meet so many bigoted people who hate United. I wouldn't go around wearing the colours of United any more or getting involved in a casual conversation, say on the train, about United, because people look down on you. Everybody in the country has an opinion about United. We are hated. Why?

I sat in the Birmingham City end at St Andrews pre-season this year, and everyone around me was singing 'Stand up if you hate Man U'. Well, I don't, so I didn't, and the bloke next to me started to suss me out. So he says to me, 'When do the Vale tickets go on sale?' in a Brummie accent. So I said, 'I don't know mate, I'm a Man United fan.' Ten minutes later he was saying to me, 'I don't hate Man United, I think what Ferguson has done is brilliant, the stadium is magnificent and I hope you do well in Europe. I just hate the fact that you've got fans all over the country.' I can understand that. If I lived in Hereford and I was a Hereford United fan and I watched them home and away and I got back to my pub in Hereford and there's a smart-arsed Man United fan in his shirt and he doesn't know where Manchester is, he only watches United on television, and he was giving me abuse, I'd hate Manchester United as well. I can understand it. But I just ask people to give credit where it is due. Our only crime is supporting our own football team.

To my knowledge Liverpool didn't suffer like this in the eighties. The trouble is, there is an arrogance about United, epitomised by somebody like Cantona. There's also a siege mentality which has built up. United fans can be quite paranoid at times. They think all football fans hate them, which they do, and this breeds a siege mentality. It's evident throughout the club; the manager uses it as a motivational tool.

ANDY MITTEN

When I retired from the House of Commons someone said to me, 'Where are you going to live?' I said, 'What do you mean, where am I going to live?' 'Well, are you going to go abroad or are you going to go to Southport, Eastbourne?' I said you must be bloody mad. Here I am three miles from the theatre of my dreams, Old Trafford at one end of the road, Lancashire at the other. When I think back and all the players I've seen play for United from Jack Rowley, Carey, Delaney to Crerand, Charlton and Cantona. Extraordinary. You couldn't have wished for better. We've seen the cream. Nothing to equal it.

Roy Hattersley summed it up for me one day. He put it into words that epitomise it for me. Sheffield Wednesday were playing Tottenham Hotspur. We were in the House and there was no Whip. Roy said to me, 'Look, I'm going to Tottenham to see Sheffield Wednesday, would you like to come? The BBC have put a car on for me because I'm doing a broadcast later. A car there and bring you back, no vote.' Well, I'm always game for a football match, so I said right. Well, we get in the car and like any football ground as we got nearer there was a crowd, we slowed down. Roy turned to me and says, 'This is when it gets me, as we get near the ground; I want to get out and run, I want to get in, in the ground. That's what it's all about.' And it's true. It's magic. I think I've been very lucky to see what I've seen. There's an excitement, a tingle that's difficult to explain, but it's there.

LORD STAN ORME

My earliest memories of the games I went to would be in the early eighties. The football was not particularly brilliant, the team were not very good at the time, but it was the theatre aspect of it. I remember thinking, the first evening game I went to, coming up the steps into the ground and it was dark and the lights were on and the pitch was a very bright green under the floodlights and there were the colours of the supporters. It was the only time in my life when I wished I could paint. It was just so theatrical, so live that I felt a desire to capture it somehow. A very compelling experience; the lights, the colour, the theatre of the whole event. I very much got caught up in it. I can get very involved in games when I'm watching. I carry a lot less of it with me at other times. Roger remembers games in detail, who scored in what minute, whereas I have an overall impression and while I'm actually watching it I get very caught up in it.

TERESA HENNELL

I lived in Gainsborough until I was eighteen. Football was one of my great loves. I would always be out in the street kicking a ball around, scuffing my shoes, even breaking windows. Albert Hall, who had played for Tottenham Hotspur, lived in our road, so that was another strong link with the game. He was a rent collector. I would go and see Gainsborough Trinity play and even going to their ground was a similar experience in many ways as going to Old Trafford would be years later – the noise, the rivalry, the urgency of getting to the ground. It was just the same feelings even though Gainsborough were a small club.

I then went off to war and in 1944 was posted to Manchester. I did not actually come to live in Manchester until some years later, in 1959. I watched United for the next twenty years until I was exiled to Yorkshire. I then took up watching Leeds United but I finally decided that my heart was not with them. I had a season ticket to Elland Road but I gave it up. I was so disgusted with their fans and their shabby attitude towards the team. They were always complaining, always getting on the backs of the players. Fortunately I came back to the north-west in 1986 and started going to Old Trafford again.

In my first attempts to see decent football I went to Maine Road. I stood on the top of that steep terrace. I scrambled up the bank and by the time I had found anywhere to stand, three goals had already been scored. Every time there was some movement towards us the crowd concertinaed one way, then another. It wasn't a comfortable way to watch a football match. But I was fortunate in that I had a neighbour who was closely associated with Barnsley Football Club. He obviously had good connections as he was able to get me two season tickets for United. That meant that I had a seat. I got to know people who were sitting by me pretty well but the odd thing is that you never learn anything about them. You only talk about football, and all you know of them is their football leanings and knowledge. You don't know anything about their personal lives.

KEN HASTINGS

My son is now ten months old but when he was ten days old he was put in his pram and wheeled around Old Trafford and had his photo taken under the Munich clock. He was two months old when I registered him as a junior member. Alisson's sister bought him the red shirt and shorts and he's already had his photo taken in them. He hasn't actually been to a game yet, but for the Cantona match coming up [in 1998], I thought I might try and sneak him in.

One of my friends at work, who's also a United fan, has a daughter and we have regular chats about what length we would go to make sure that our children are United supporters. Unless he doesn't like football he'll be so indoctrinated that he won't have much choice about supporting United.

He'll just be brought up knowing that if wants to get on with his dad he'll support Man United. If he supported another team he knows he'd never get to see them play. I'd never ever take him to another ground. If he didn't want to come to United then he doesn't go to see anyone else. But everyone says if he's a son of mine there'll be no problem. I've got two season tickets so when he's four or five he'll be coming with me.

JIM THORNTON

My devotion to United goes back over thirty years. I was four years old when we moved to Cheadle in Cheshire. We were only there a couple of years, but that's when I became a United fan. I remember a programme on television called *United* and that must have had some influence on me. I'm always grateful for moving to the north because of supporting the right team.

Law, Best, Charlton and Kidd. Brian Kidd was one of the most exciting young players of the late sixties, especially his performance in the European Cup final. The players I liked through the seventies were ones like Stuart Pearson, Willie Morgan, Gordon Hill, Steve Coppell and the Greenhoff brothers. Not enough people remember Willie Morgan who was brilliant, and you always remember Gordon Hill's free kick against Derby County in the 1976 FA Cup semi-final. Goals like that will always bring back really great memories.

I try to get to the games in London but being a chef means that the busiest day is Saturday. London games are handy because I can get there in the afternoon and be back for work. Like any young boy, I wanted to be a footballer but I didn't have the ability; then I wanted to be a policeman. I started cooking out of necessity when my mother went back to work and I absolutely loved it. I've cooked with Alex Ferguson and with Bryan Robson. Bryan was, and still is, my ultimate United hero. And as for Alex, there is no better manager. When people come for interviews to work in my kitchen, they are always dead nervous. The first question they expect me to ask is,

'Where have you cooked before?' Instead I usually ask, 'Which team do you support?' And if the answer is United, then it's a case of 'When can you start?' That's how mad I am about United.

GARY RHODES

One of the odd things was that it was into the sixties when I realised how special United were because of course when I started supporting them, they weren't winning very much. I thought that the Wolves and the Spurs were the really successful sides at that time. It was only really when I read about the forties and fifties – and then they created what was a wonderful side in the sixties – that I realised they were bigger and more special than other clubs. I think having watched them over such a long period of time they clearly got a lot of sympathy and support after Munich, locally, nationally and internationally. They attracted people nationally because they were so fashionable. Best was a phenomenon, supported by Law and Charlton. I think that's all explicable.

I think what is less explicable is the growth of United in the seventies. If you went to Old Trafford in the seventies you would see coachloads. There had always been supporters from other parts of the country but the crowds went up the whole of Warwick Road, and the roads adjacent to Old Trafford had all got coaches from more and more remote parts of the UK and beyond. Why United didn't decline in terms of support I don't really know. They've been loved and respected by everybody in the fifties born out of tragedy, to now when they are loathed by more supporters and loved by the multitudes of United supporters. And I don't think you can just explain it in terms of United. They've got all those supporters, a lot of people live around here, they've played wonderful football but why they should have the impact they have, I don't know. They're bigger than other clubs, they've not won as much as Liverpool over the last thirty years, so I don't know.

I think you have to look at society generally. This is a bit intellectual, but basically I think our society does not like success so much and United are successful. They're brash, they're bigger. No, that's not quite true; they're not brash, they're bigger in themselves as a club even when they have not been winning things. Liverpool have always had a bit of a chip on their shoulders about United even when they were winning the Championship five times out of six seasons and winning the European Cup four times. They always felt they had to do better. There's something in the national character that doesn't like success and I think that is very different to the way we were thirty or forty years ago. It's not something particularly pleasant about the British character. I suspect that if you transplanted soccer to the USA you would have a very different reaction. So I think it's cultural. Why the size and support has continued to grow in what was one of the worst periods in the club's history is curious.

When I think of those coachloads, Reds from Plymouth and Southampton who used to come week after week, even when they were in the Second Division. They were getting good crowds and when they got back into the First and were challenging for the Championship under Docherty there was tremendous support which Liverpool never managed to get over two or three generations of success, not the same wide support. I still get a thrill, but that's probably indoctrination at an early age.

GRAHAM STRINGER

Duncan Edwards obviously stands out. I think he would have been captain of England for many years. He was very self-effacing. Cantona, obviously. A great man, great intellect, great ego. You accepted him as he was or you didn't and he couldn't give a toss either way. He was the last piece that Ferguson needed. I think that he turned the fortunes of Manchester United around in the nineties. Of course, lots of the Busby Babes – Eddie Colman, and David Pegg. Johnny Berry was wonderful on the wing and Ray Wood, a wonderful goalkeeper who is not as appreciated as he should be, and, of course, poor old Dennis Viollet who is ill in Florida. I think United could do more for those heroes who have fallen on hard times.

GEORGE REYNOLDS

My love of United stems back to my father. He's got pictures all over his wall and when they're on television he goes mad. My husband Vicente is also a mad keen United fan, and has been since the age of seven. Not long after I first met him I decided to give him a real surprise by taking him to his first game at Old Trafford. I got some tickets and arranged everything. On the day of the match I blindfolded him and took him in a taxi. I told the taxi-driver not to mention where we were going. When we arrived he could hear all this noise and told me later he thought that he was at the fair. When he saw that it was Old Trafford he was ecstatic. I'm really into it as well now. I try to copy all the words of the songs, even though I don't really know what I'm singing.

I remember we were in Mexico in 1992 when we lost out on the title. The news came through that Leeds were catching up and when we heard that they had won it was such a let-down. The worst training camp I ever had.

DIANE MODAHL

United are well marketed. The Theatre of Dreams, that's just a marketing ploy. To a lot of people they are the club the nation hates. They have a certain magic, I suppose. Why? Because it's so difficult to see them live, and because they've always been associated with big-money transfers. But Munich made United the nation's team. A lot of old United fans, however, will tell you that United's best side was the 1948-49 team, the pre-Busby Babes; but in addition to Munich they have always gone in for flair players – Law, Best, Cantona and

385

so forth, the more showmanship version of football. It's probably a characteristic called style. Compared to Arsenal, although they've played pretty well this season [1997–98], they do have that tag 'boring boring Arsenal', but nevertheless that's a tag they have been saddled with. Leeds were seen as efficient, hard, the Don Revie team – not flair. Whereas United's best teams have always had a lot of flair and have played with enjoyment. Even today United fans would sooner see a United team going forward and attacking than a United team that is, let's say, efficient. So, in that sense, they have been a bit special.

Ferguson has produced two teams that are not only efficient, in terms of their defence – the best in the Premiership over the last few seasons in goals conceded – but also with flair players like Cantona, Beckham. He's produced a side that is a delight to watch, a combination of flair and enthusiasm. You look at United, and for all that has happened in English football in terms of European players, just count up the number of English players in the team. There are others but out of that large squad the majority are English and many of them local. I think the local input is also important and certainly the supporters I sit with, who all come from Manchester, appreciate that. I still also think the vast majority of support at Old Trafford is local, if you define local as a ten-mile radius.

That's another thing about being a United player: you become a United player, an honour is bestowed upon you, it's an honorary thing. There is this feeling among the fans that the players are incredibly lucky to be United players and if they don't want to be United players, I don't care how good they are, then forget it. So there is this feeling that whoever they buy, they have found their rightful place, they have been elected, they have managed to make their way to the place they ought to be. You could even say that about Cantona. He's retired, he's not gone anywhere else after United. Prior to United he'd been a problem wherever he had been. He comes to United and he realised it couldn't get any better. It's being admitted to the inner court, taking your rightful place among the United greats. Whether some of the players of the seventies fit into that category is another matter.

DEREK WYNNE

I can remember United bringing the cups home. I still think it's sad that they don't allow this now. I saw the French coming down the Champs Elysées touching the buses, incredible. Now we can't go in Albert Square, it's not allowed. I can remember them coming down Deansgate turning into Quay Street. I'm a member of the YMCA and the YM was on the corner and I'd go on the first floor. I'd open the window and you were level with the bus, you had a great view. I saw everyone come home from there, European and all, from that view. Then you'd go to Albert Square and it was a mass of happy people. Where do they go now? They're taking things from the fans. There's no focal point any more. There should be something where the fans can worship.

DANNY McGREGOR

I still think the United style should be all attacking. I don't mind if the other team score four as long as we score five. The problem now is that winning is so important to every club and you know that if a side goes one up early on, they will just block it up. United's defence has never been that good to be able to do that so they have to keep attacking. There are times when they have been two–nil down and you know they will come back because they know no other way than to go forward and forward. I think that's good to see; great shame they don't have two wingers at the moment as they have in the past. But if any team comes with two wingers they'll do well because you can't mark everybody.

ROLAND COBURN

Being a supporter carries a responsibility. You feel that they are your team and you feel that you have to do your bit not to let them down. Considering the attitude the club have to their fans, it's surprising the attitude that comes back. They are good in some ways but you feel they are keen to get your money. It's a commercial attitude but you felt very responsible. They were your club and you were doing your bit by going along to support them. Even after twenty years of not winning anything, it gets worse, you feel even more of a responsibility.

I've got a number of football tops, not the newer kits. Gordon, my brother, got me a 1960s United red shirt once as a birthday present and I usually wear that for the game though occasionally – he got me a blue European Cup final shirt as well – so that it'll be one of those two. And there's an Eric Cantona black shirt with profound sayings on the front from Philosophy Football, so I'll probably wear that underneath with the other two on top. Yes, it's a football garb that I go out in, but I don't say that I must wear that particular shirt because we won in it. But yes, I do dress up for the game to a certain degree. It's the wearing of the colours and feeling that you're part of it. Funny really, but when I went as a fifteen- or sixteen-year-old I don't think I wore anything special.

ROGER HENNELL

They're different. They've got a world-wide fan base. Local Mancunians criticise the southern and foreign fans who come over every week, but without them we'd be just another football club. What do we want? Do we want to be one of the best football teams in the world supported by millions of fans, or what? I remember 1989 playing Wimbledon, the football was bad, there was only twenty-three thousand there. Where were these Mancunians then? Maybe they're jumping on the bandwagon a bit. I've still got a lot of southern-based friends and they came when the football was bad. In 1974 we had three coachloads coming and the football was bad.

I'm football mad. I own shares in United. My telephone number is based on United, and my car number-plate is United-based. I'm quite sad really. I love football and I love United. I'm lucky that people in my life realise that.

Players? Legends like George Best, Denis Law and Bobby Charlton I never saw at their best in the sixties. I was always on the periphery. It was in the papers and on television. I saw Best and Charlton late in their careers. Mine are more modern. Heroes have to be Bryan Robson and of course Cantona, always the number seven shirt. Eric is probably my favourite player. The rest of the world hated him which made him more of a legend at United. The incident at Selhurst Park made him a king. Four Championships and a couple of them were down to him.

ROBIN MURRAY

I've got lots of superstitions. For the last two years on match day I always wear what I've got on now: these brown suede shoes, red socks and I always wear the red shirt. But if they lose a game, you can't wear the red shirt again until they've won again, so I have to put another T-shirt on. Another really sad one is that I always have to go to my local bakers on a Saturday morning and buy an iced finger and if they haven't got one, I have to hunt around until I find one. You have to have an iced finger on a Saturday morning. If I don't eat one it means United will lose in the afternoon. But the main thing is the clothes; it has to be the right socks and shoes.

JIM THORNTON

United have always been part of me. For a long time, with them being a big club and not having the success that was assumed should go with a big club. And eventually it's come about, the success. You're sort of bonded together against all odds and there was such great attendances when they have been playing appallingly; like in the eighties when they almost got relegated again, they were still getting thirty thousand at Old Trafford. That doesn't seem great, but considering the way they were playing at the time ... And especially now United have done so well, the resentment is unparalleled. It's another case of 'everybody hates us and we don't care'. I'll defend them even stronger. I won't admit to anybody other than United fans that there's a problem. We'll keep it in house. I don't think I socialise with any City fans. Everybody I know is a United fan. It's backs against the wall. I never imagined being successful would be like this.

Stuart Pearson was my first hero. And then – I always struggle with this – but it's between Bryan Robson and Eric Cantona. I always admired Robson's leadership because he wasn't just leader of the team, he was leader of the club. His whole outlook was what I epitomise United to be. Cantona just because they used to talk about players being the new George Best. Now they talk about players being the new Eric Cantona. That says it all really.

MATTHEW REYNOLDS

I'd always been keen on sports, all sports; the chances were it would have come down to United or City but there was never any choice for me because my father used to take me. I was taken when I was seven. I have all the old programmes, some from the early fifties. My father used to bring the programmes home on a Saturday night and I used to read through them about the team even though I was not necessarily going to the matches, so it was ingrained in me from an early age. So it's difficult to know what would have happened had my father not been a supporter.

MARTIN EDWARDS

My very first football game was City and Grimsby. I was in

the main stand with my dad taking me. It was a very exciting thing. I was amazed to see twenty-five thousand opposite me standing up. But United had always been talked about in the house and then ultimately one day I was taken to see United and Nottingham Forest, in their Championship-winning year. They were their closest rivals. We had seats in the old stand behind the players' tunnel. You noticed that it was a very special place. The abiding thing is that going to United is always an occasion and even when they were a failing team I still carried that sense of occasion with me. It's only very, very recently, probably in recent weeks, that it seems to be moving away from that feeling. I saw a quote from David Conn's book where he described United as soulless and you can certainly see that sort of idea coming into being. It is very corporate, commercial; but you know, the sense of occasion still over-whelms everything.

I think it's partly collective and I think it's partly individual, fifty thousand souls bound together in common worship which is a very special feeling. I don't tend to participate in anything that's very mass in any way but that thing is a very special feeling. But also it's a sort of affinity. Whatever the commercial thing, you tend to feel close to the players. You pin your hopes and aspirations on them. And when they are struggling it reflects life and when they're doing well it reflects your hopes. A bit like going to school, because you've got this common thing. You're all bound together by one common thing. The Cantona thing became like that because it was all focused on one man.

I think that the mischievous side of United is more in the way the club is run rather than in the players. They seem to be the masters of disinformation. Liverpool seem to win by collectivism while United are a talented bunch of individuals. But there's also a strong bond as well. The Red Flag song is an amazing potent mixture of collectivism, politics, pride, senti-mentality, everything all at once. It's a key United song, that one.

It was always a big family thing and this is another part of the bond with the club, because my father would go. It was my father, my brother and I and after my father died my nephew had already been primed. So we've already moved down a generation, so we're into the second generation of support there even though we may not be that old. The bond is tight, it's an hereditary bond. It was a family thing. And my brother-in-law sat a couple of rows behind with his friends. It was, I suppose, a thing for the male side of the family, both sporting and social.

LEON SWERLING

My mother's sister, my auntie obviously, lived in Northenden and I used to spend an awful lot of time visiting them during summer holidays and obviously I got to know a lot of the people, one of them a fanatical Manchester United supporter; in fact, I went a few times to the game with him. And during that time I was playing football at school and I ended playing for Birkenhead Schoolboys. Unbeknown to me someone put my name forward to Manchester United and I had a trial. So this meant travelling up to Manchester, staying at my auntie's and travelling from Northenden off to the Cliff which involved two or three bus rides and when I arrived there we were taken into the dressing room, names read out, given a shirt and off we went and played a full-scale trial match. Unfortunately nothing came of it, but what an experience to have a trial for your team; a wonderful, wonderful feeling for that to happen.

I was quite upset but it had to be tempered with the fact that I had had a trial for the team of my heart; so in one way obviously disappointment, but in another, elation that I had had that opportunity. Maybe I wasn't good enough, but there again, I had the opportunity and I'm very grateful for that.

KEVIN McALENY

I saw George Best on telly and I think he was doing one of those football skills programmes and I asked my older brother who he played for and he said Man United. This was about the age of four or five and that was it. Also my grandad supported United and watched them in the late forties. That had an influence as well. I remember my gran knitting me a red and white scarf which was the first scarf I ever had. So that was where it first started. And obviously that is someone who was brought up in Durham as well, so somewhat removed. The accusation you get is 'out-of-town glory supporter' but you have to remember that at that period United were pretty poor and within a couple of years they were in the Second Division. It wasn't instant glory by any means.

Durham is a bit of a funny place. It's not Newcastle and it's not Sunderland, so it is somewhat removed from that. However, Man United supporters were few and far between and you did get a bit of stick for it. But it's not something that I ever felt. I don't ever remember thinking I had any choice. I was a Man United supporter and that was it. The club chooses you.

ADAM BROWN

I somehow feel it is the ability to confound one. Obviously the consistency of good play is important. But going back to 1968; City were delighted to win the League but then the confounding United won the European Cup and stole all the glory. They have that ability to raise their game, to achieve success. And of course we are spoilt by the quality and the success of the side is taken for granted. I hope we don't fall into the trap too often but it has become expected to have a Wembley visit and see games that can affect the outcome of the League title. Certainly in the nineties we have become very used to that.

MICHAEL DUNHAM

They can take you up there and put you down there within minutes. In the European Cup-Winners' Cup final in Rotterdam, they were two–nil up, then Barcelona score and it ends up with Clayton Blackmore clearing the ball off the line which would have made it two–two. It's that, yet they come through.

Obviously there's the history. I think the history does play a large part in it – every club has its history and every supporter at that club would say that that history is important to them, but I think there's various factors at United which have made it something a bit special of which Munich is one and the Busby–Charlton–Law era is another. But it's a tradition of football as well – the club's got to win but they've got to win well and if you think of the 1994 Double team, two wide wingers flying down the flanks. There was something special about that and that's the way you want it. That goes back to when I first started watching the team which was the Docherty period when you had that four–two–four and Docherty on *Match of the Day* saying the thing about us is that we can concede three goals and still win four–three; attacking, exciting football.

ADAM BROWN

I threw my old red socks away at the end of last season when they didn't win the Championship. I'd had a pair of red socks – only through the nineties – but they seemed to work through the nineties. If I wore them United won; if I didn't, they lost. Now they're threadbare and gone in the bin. So United's demise last season was entirely down to the socks losing their magic. They've paid the price and have been binned.

GRAHAM STRINGER

INTERVIEWEES

Tim Bamford
A forty-three-year-old research officer with the Shopworkers Union, USDAW. Plays a mean five-a-side game every Friday night at Manchester City's training ground but is still waiting to be spotted by a United scout. Unable to find a European Cup final ticket even in Barcelona and forced to watch the match in a bar.

Warren Bradley
Winger who joined the club from Bishop Auckland immediately after the Munich disaster. Continued working as a teacher, putting in a day's work before playing in the first team in an evening. Later became a head teacher. Played 66 games for United, scoring 21 goals. Won England honours at amateur and professional level. Lives in Urmston.

Shay Brennan
Swept to stardom following the Munich disaster when he made his debut in the first match after the air crash, against Sheffield Wednesday. Scored twice and again in the FA Cup semi-final but did not play in the final. Won European Cup honours as well as League honours in the sixties. Left United in 1970 to become player-manager at Waterford. Aged sixty-two.

Adam Brown
Member of the Football Supporters' Association and the Football Task Force. He is also research officer at the Institute for Popular Culture at Manchester Metropolitan University. Helped lead the campaign to stop the Sky takeover of United. Aged thirty-two.

Cliff Butler
A lifelong United fan, forty-nine-year-old Cliff Butler began as the club's statistician and then photographer. Now editor of the programme *United Review*.

Laurence Cassidy
Lifelong United fan, now aged seventy-six, who played for the club 1947–52. Played mainly in the reserves, making four appearances in the first team. Later became a teacher and then headmaster at St Patrick's school in Collyhurst and was responsible for feeding a number of players towards Old Trafford, including Brian Kidd.

Sir Bobby Charlton
United legend. The most caps, the most appearances and the most goals for United. Joined the club in January 1953, making his debut in October 1956. Survived the Munich air disaster and went on to make a total of 752 appearances, scoring 247 goals before retiring in 1973. Capped 106 times by England. Now a director of the club.

Barney Chilton
Twenty-eight-year-old editor of the fanzine *Red News*. Saw his first United game at the age of five.

Roland Coburn
Film editor at Granada Television who works on *World In Action*. Lifelong United fan who has travelled the length and breadth of Europe in support of United. Aged forty-six.

Alf Davies
Member of the St John Ambulance Brigade since 1935. First saw United in 1928 and regularly watched them when they were in the Second Division before the War. Now aged eighty-three.

Joe Dillon
Retired shopkeeper who started supporting United before the War. Saw his first game in 1937. A devoted follower of the Busby Babes side of the 1950s. Died shortly before publication of this book.

Maxine Dunham
Daughter of Michael Dunham, Maxine has travelled extensively following United around Europe with more than a few adventures. Was imprisoned in Turkey when she went to see United play Galatasaray and never got to see the game. Thirty-five-year-old graphic designer.

Michael Dunham
Sixty-four-year-old accountant and a United supporter since the War. Vivid memories of the day United played Blackpool in the 1948 FA Cup final. Still a season ticket holder. Father of Maxine Dunham.

Alan Durrans
Born in Manchester and started supporting United in the fifties. Once had a trial with the club. Now lives in Chorlton.

Christopher Eccleston
Salford-born actor. Starred in the films *Shallow Grave, Jude the Obscure* and *Elizabeth I* as well as the highly regarded BBC production *Our Friends in the North*.

Martin Edwards
Son of Louis Edwards, the former United chairman. Martin

Edwards became chairman of the club in 1980. In September 1998 he agreed to the takeover of United by BSkyB Television and to sell his personal stake in the club, valued at £80 million, subject to the deal being approved by the MMC.

Bob Greaves
United fan Bob Greaves was a journalist with the *Daily Mail* at the time of the Munich disaster. He subsequently became a presenter with Granada Television. Will recite the entire 1948 FA Cup final team to anyone who will listen.

Ken Hastings
Retired Government education inspector, now living in Cambridge and no longer able to attend Old Trafford regularly. Nevertheless his support remains undiminished. Although he was born in Gainsborough, his father had become a United supporter after regularly watching them play Gainsborough Trinity at the turn of the century. Aged seventy-three.

Roger Hennell
Quantity surveyor and husband of Teresa Hennell. Season ticket holder who works on Merseyside – and has survived. Born in Cambridge and became a United fan, but later came to live in Manchester. Aged forty-two.

Teresa Hennell
Forty-year-old solicitor and wife of Roger Hennell. Season ticket holder who now cycles to Old Trafford from their home in Didsbury.

Pete Holland
Born in West Gorton but emigrated to the United States in 1977, a few years after he had invaded the pitch, flares and all, following Denis Law's famous goal that plunged United into the Second Division. Manages to watch live coverage every week. Now the forty-three-year-old operations director for a

British offshore data-capture company.

Eamon Holmes
Presenter of GMTV. Born in Belfast and inevitably a fan of George Best as a young lad. Later worked in Manchester where he was able to follow his favourites.

Hugh Jones
Founder of Jones Executive Coaches and former first-team coach driver. Now retired, aged sixty-three.

Simon Jones
Used to be the first-team coach driver until the summer of 1999. He was the butt of much mickey-taking by the players. Also managing director of Jones Executive Coaches. Thirty-two-year-old son of Hugh Jones.

Brian Kidd
Former assistant manager at Old Trafford. Left United in 1998 to become manager of Blackburn Rovers but was sacked in November 1999. Had a long and distinguished career with United, winning Championship and European Cup honours. Scored 70 goals in 255 appearances for United. Also played with Arsenal, Manchester City, Everton and Bolton. Lives in Middleton, a short distance from where he was born in Collyhurst.

Rudi Kidd
Forty-four-year-old black solicitor who over the years came face to face with racism on the terraces and decided there was only one way to combat it. Now a lawyer representing media clients.

Denis Law
Joined Manchester United for a record fee from Torino in July 1962. Previously played with Huddersfield Town and

Manchester City. Returned to City in July 1973 and scored the goal at Old Trafford that sent United into the Second Division. Regarded by many as the player who epitomises the style of United more than any other.

Kevin McAleny
Born on Merseyside but became a fan of the Busby Babes when he was young and has remained a United fan all his life, although he also supports his local side Tranmere Rovers. Once had a trial with United. Aged fifty-two.

Pat McDonald
Was seventeen years old at the time of the Munich disaster. The tragedy was to mark a turning point in his life as he quit his routine job to join the Navy. Years later, he became a computer consultant but United, he says, still remain central to his life.

Danny McGregor
Born in Moss Side and supported the club as a young boy after the War, watching his first game in 1947. Now the club's commercial manager, he has overseen a growth in turnover from £5 million in 1985 to a current £80 million a year. Aged sixty-four.

Wilf McGuinness
Busby Babe, born in Manchester, who missed the trip to Munich through injury. He was also forced to retire early through injury. At the age of thirty-one he was appointed successor to Matt Busby but was sacked after eighteen months. Later managed in Greece. Also had spells at York City, Hull City and Bury before retiring in 1991. Now a highly entertaining after-dinner speaker. Played 85 games for United, scoring two goals. Now aged sixty-two.

David Meek

Born in York, David Meek moved to Manchester to become a political leader writer with the *Manchester Evening News* but was given the task of covering United when the *News*'s football correspondent was killed in the Munich air disaster. He retired in May 1995 after thirty-five years of service with the paper. Aged sixty-nine.

David Menasche

Owns a small temporary staffing agency in San Jose, close to San Francisco. Still supports United from afar, usually via the Internet, but makes the occasional trip to Old Trafford.

Andy Mitten

Began the fanzine *United We Stand* when he was a fifteen-year-old schoolboy. Nine years later the fanzine sells 12,000 copies per issue. Now a full-time journalist. Aged twenty-five.

Diane Modahl

Olympic athlete who was finally exonerated following a 'positive' drugs test in 1994. After many years of fighting the charge she won a bronze medal in the 1998 Commonwealth Games to add to her gold from the 1990 Games.

Barry Moorhouse

Club membership secretary who has seen membership increase from 40,000 to 140,000 in ten years. Aged forty-nine.

Johnny Morris

Born in north Manchester, joined United aged fifteen, shortly before the War. Served in the Army during the War, returning to Old Trafford for the 1946–47 season. A lightly built inside forward, he was a Cup winner the following season but left following a disagreement with Matt Busby in early 1949, joining Derby County for a record fee of £24,500. Capped three times by England. A total of 92 appearances for United with 35 goals. Now aged seventy-six and still a keen golfer.

Ian Moss
Former policeman and now county manager of the St John Ambulance Brigade. Aged sixty.

Robin Murray
Although born in Portsmouth, forty-three-year-old Robin Murray became a United supporter at school. He travelled regularly to Old Trafford by motorbike and coach before eventually joining the Greater Manchester Police, a decision not wholly unconnected with his support of United.

Les Olive
Appointed assistant secretary of Manchester United in 1942 and took over as secretary immediately after the Munich disaster when Walter Crickmer was killed. Retired in 1988 and is now a director of the club. Played twice for the first team during the early fifties as a goalkeeper and probably knows more about United than any other living person. Aged seventy-one.

Stan Orme
Now Lord Orme. Was Labour MP for Salford West 1964–83 and for Salford East 1983–97. Held various Government posts including Minister of State for Northern Ireland 1974–76 and Minister for Social Security. He was a Cabinet Minister between 1977 and 1979. He was created a life peer in 1997 and is still a regular at both Old Traffords. Aged seventy-six.

Sally Orpin
Member of the Manchester United Supporters' Club in Victoria, Australia. Has lived in Australia for five years. Now aged thirty-two.

George Reynolds
Fifty-four-year-old shopkeeper in Chorlton who has rarely
watched United since the Munich disaster, a tragedy which
still greatly upsets him.

Matthew Reynolds
Assistant manager of Chorlton Healthfoods. Much travelled
around Europe in support of United. Aged thirty-three, son
of George Reynolds.

Gary Rhodes
Television chef who became a United fan after his family
moved to Cheadle. Now based in London.

Graham Stringer
Lifelong United fan. Former leader of Manchester City
Council 1984–96, and has been Labour MP for Manchester
Blackley since 1997. Spearheaded Manchester's bid for the
Olympic Games and the Commonwealth Games. Once
skived off school to go and watch United play. Now aged
forty-nine.

Wilf Sudlow
Seventy-seven-year-old former deputy head of St Ambrose
School in Manchester. Began keeping a United scrap book in
the fifties which today is a fascinating collection of photos and
information covering forty years of United's history. Lives in
Didsbury.

Leon Swerling
Forty-two-year-old solicitor and lifelong United supporter
with vivid memories of the 1968 European Cup final. Season
ticket holder, living in Altrincham. A broken shoulder sus-
tained while playing five-a-side football put an end to his
dreams of seeing United in another European Cup final.

Judith Swift
Mother of two who began supporting United as a schoolgirl
in the late 1960s but whose football is now mainly confined to
watching her son from the touchline at Chorlton Park School.

Alisson Thornton
Born in the north-east but converted to United while at
university in Manchester. Now a thirty-four-year-old accountant, married to Jim Thornton and mother of a young son
destined to be a United supporter.

Jim Thornton
An accountant living in Bolton. Born in Colchester but began
supporting United at an early age. Came to university in
Manchester solely in order to watch United. Married to
Alisson Thornton. Aged thirty-two.

Simon Thorp
Forty-five-year-old Chorlton-based writer who remembers the
Second Division days with affection and a few far-flung places
where he watched them. Saddened at the commercialisation
of United and deeply shocked by the news that Martin
Edwards was prepared to sell United to Sky.

Albert Thorpe
Now aged eighty-six, Albert Thorpe was for many years a
journalist covering Manchester United. First watched United
in the early 1920s. Lives in Sale.

Jim White
Journalist and broadcaster who regularly writes on football
for the *Guardian*. Born and bred in Manchester he secretly
visited Old Trafford while telling his parents he was going
train-spotting. Was strongly opposed to the Murdoch takeover
of United.

Norman Whiteside

United legend who joined the club in 1978 as an associate schoolboy. Made his debut in 1982 as a sixteen-year-old and became the youngest World Cup finalist when he played for Northern Ireland in Spain. Also the youngest ever scorer in a Cup final when he scored against Brighton in 1982. Played 254 games for United either in the midfield or upfront, scoring 67 goals. Transferred to Everton in August 1989 but retired two years later due to injury. Now a podiatrist, working mainly with lower league football clubs.

Sean Wilson

Coronation Street's Martin Platt. Has even played on the pitch at Old Trafford in a charity game, given the job of marking Bobby Charlton.

Paul Windridge

Brought up in a rugby household but was finally forced to confess his allegiance to football and United. Is the creative director in a graphic design business which he runs with his partner.

Derek Wynne

Although born in Staffordshire, fifty-one-year-old Derek Wynne became a United fan at an early age. Once a full-time professional player with Port Vale, he then became an academic and is now director of the Institute for Popular Culture at Manchester Metropolitan University.